HALL OF NAME

HALL OF NAME

Baseball's Most Magnificent Monikers
from 'The Only Nolan' to 'Van Lingle Mungo' and More

by D.B. Firstman

Foreword by Jayson Stark

Hall of Name:
Baseball's Most Magnificent Monikers
from 'The Only Nolan' to 'Van Lingle Mungo' and More

published by DB Books
71-40 112th Street, Apt. 510, Forest Hills NY 11375

ISBN 978-1-7341674-0-5
Electronic version of this work: 978-1-7341674-1-2

published 2020 by DB Books
Cover design by Tim Godden
Printed by ingramspark

For dad,
who gave me my love of baseball,

and for mom,
who gave me everything else,
including a love of words
and a slightly warped sense of humor.

CONTENTS

NO FOCUS GROUP CONVENED

FOREWORD

Back when I was in college, my buddies and I once had a brilliant idea. We decided to invent the coolest names ever for a fictitious basketball team. Our point guard was the great Flaxton Emmitt, fastest dude in America, fluent dribbler, shot 98% from the line. Our power forward was the smooth Washington Lane, named after a street I once drove along on my way to school. We had a big man named Maxwell House. Boy, could he fill it up. And, well, you get the idea.

I mention this because that, I'm pretty sure, was the first time it occurred to me that the coolest people in sports never seemed to have names like, oh, Doug Jones. You might think there's no scientific evidence to back this up. But tell it to Old Hoss Radbourn – or, if you don't have a time machine handy, possibly Mookie Betts.

So since my formative years, apparently, I've had this incredible thing about names. You wouldn't think there would actually be any other sane people in the world who share it. But then along came D.B. Firstman, to write a whole book about names – and quite an amazing, entertaining book at that. So thank you, D.B., not just for this brilliant book, but for helping me to understand that this is totally normal – not to mention tremendous fun.

I have to admit, though, that I had other hints before this that it wasn't just me and D.B. who loved awesome names. Back in the 1980s, when I was covering baseball for the *Philadelphia Inquirer*, I was at a game in San Diego when the Padres sent a pitcher with the fascinating name of Juan Tyrone Eichelberger to the mound. I'm not sure if any player in history has ever had a more confusing name than that. I'll let you ponder everything about it. All I know is, Juan Tyrone Eichelberger had one of the weirdest deliveries I've ever personally witnessed. I'm pretty sure the very first warmup pitch I saw him throw, from this strange, crouching non-windup set, hit the screen on the fly. And I thought, "I need to keep track of this guy." So I never got tired of typing that name, Juan Tyrone Eichelberger. And he was helpful enough to win my box-score-line-of-the-week award many times, with gems like this: 1⅓-2-5-2-6-0. So after I'd worked him into way too many goofy references, somebody even wrote a letter to the editor of the Inquirer to thank them for allowing me to write about this actual person, Juan Tyrone Eichelberger. My mother then cut out the letter – and framed it! If that isn't proof that great names make everything better, what is?

In this book, D.B. writes about the legendary Coco Crisp, because, well, of course they did. His real name, if you want to get all technical, is Covelli Loyce Crisp, but that's what books like this are for – to reveal that sort of blockbuster information. He'll always be Coco to those of us who care. And here's why I care: Not just because Coco Crisp was a tremendous guy and fantastic interview, but because once, if I recall this right, he got hit by a pitch, and the pitcher who drilled him was (seriously) a gentleman named Pascual Coco. So it turned out that Coco Crisp wasn't too delighted to get drilled – even by a fellow Coco. He then made that known with some menacing strides toward the mound. The conversation got heated. And they both got thrown out of the game. I only remember that because it made for one of my favorite goofy notes ever: "Two Hot Cocos to Go!"

As these tales prove, I've been writing about important Name Game news for a long time. And I guess other folks caught onto this, because now, when something monumental happens – like Cliff Lee pitching against Dillon Gee, for instance – people seek me out on Twitter. They need to know stuff, you see. Is Lee versus Gee the fewest letters ever in the last names of two starting pitchers? OK, how about the fewest by two pitchers whose names also happen to rhyme? Stuff like that. I need to know this stuff, too, of course. I'll confess to that.

But I can't always hunt down these important tidbits myself, unless they're rattling around in my head like loose screws. So to unearth these answers, my cagy strategy has always been just to throw these questions out there to the Twitterverse – where other people, who also need to know this stuff and, more importantly, who can also program a computer better than I can, can provide all of us with the answer. This is social media at its finest, don't you think? Random, baseball-loving strangers, all banding together for a common purpose – like answering this critical Lee-versus-Gee mystery? What did we used to do back in the olden days, by which I mean like 2008? Did we write letters to each other? Search for random AOL Instant Messenger screennames? Doesn't matter, because now we have Twitter.

And, that, as it turned out, is how I first crossed paths with D.B. Every time one of those critical questions involved a Name Game theme – Martinezes homering off other Martinezes, one M. Gonzales (Marco) outpitching another M. Gonzales (Miguel), yada-yada-yada – it seemed as though it was always D.B. furnishing the Last Time That Happened answer. Then again, it seemed that way because it was. So after a while, I realized there was no more need to involve the rest of Twitter Nation. I just appointed D.B. as the official Name Game Guru of my Useless Information column, and the rest is history.

D.B. has been answering my ridiculous name questions – and unearthing thousands of fun and astounding baseball nuggets in the process – for years now. So I think, in some goofy way, that means I helped inspire this book. If I played any role in that inspiration, it's one of my proudest achievements, because this is the baseball book that most needed to be written. Anyone can tell us why, say, the Nationals won the World Series. Only D.B. Firstman can tell us why there's such a person as Boof Bonser – and even why he changed his legal name to Boof!

So I'm looking forward to this book becoming a runaway best seller. And if it does, the only people happier than I'll be will be Juan Tyrone Eichelberger, Coco Crisp and their good friends, Flaxton Emmitt and Washington Lane.

Jayson Stark

"What's in a name?"
     —William Shakespeare, Romeo and Juliet

INTRODUCTION

*"Firstman? What kind of name is that? Firstman ... like 'first man on the moon?' ... That's crazy!
Do you have a brother named 'Adam'?"*
— A typical line of "questioning" during my formative years in the early 1970s

Anthroponomastics (or anthroponymy): the study of the names of human beings.

The name bestowed upon us at birth is the first attempt at our unique identifier. Before we really start to show distinguishing characteristics, abilities and character traits, our given name sets us apart from the newborn in the adjacent crib in the hospital nursery. A boy might inherit his given name from their father or their grandfather, or their great-grandfather. Some kids might get a given or middle name from a relative's first, middle or last name and thus perpetuate a family name.

The sources for given names are as varied as the names themselves. Popular culture can drive naming trends. The name Madison was rarely if ever used for girls before the 1984 movie Splash (for you young ones, in the movie Daryl Hannah plays a mermaid who is unable to say her real name in human language, so she selects Madison from a street sign in Manhattan). Madison became a top ten girls name in the 2000s.

Popularity of specific names change from generation to generation. My mother's name was Beatrice, a not-totally-uncommon name for someone born in 1927, as she was. That name has fallen out of fashion.

Surnames often speak to the place from whence we (and our ancestors) came. For example, my mother's parents were Slutskys (no snickering please). Slutsky has Jewish (eastern Ashkenazic) and Belorussian origins as the habitational name for someone from Slutsk, a city in Belarus. Surnames can also reflect occupations (baker, farmer) or lineage ("Mc" or "Mac" generally denotes "son of" in Scottish or Irish names).

I've always been inquisitive and a lover of words. I love to anagram, make spoonerisms, puns and the like. When I come upon an "unusual" name, I am drawn to it, perhaps out of affinity and curiosity, with a dash of kinship thrown in. Baseball, given its ever-widening reach beyond the United States, has provided many such names. These names, be they given, middle and/or surname, can be alliterative, or rhyming, or naughty-sounding, or just plain throw your hands up and say, "I don't know what their parents were thinking."

Sometimes a player becomes memorable, or adds to his cachet, through his name. Mickey Mantle would still be a legendary player given his 536 homers, light-tower power and career .298 average for the dynastic Yankees of the 1950s and 1960s. But, the alliteration and pronunciation of his name ... "Mic-key Man-tle" ... is pleasing to the ear and memorable on its own. Similarly, Mickey Morandini (born Michael Morandini) was a pretty decent second baseman for the Phillies in the early 1990s. Part (most?) of his popularity stemmed from the way Phillies play-by-play man (the late) Harry Kalas enunciated each syllable of Morandini's name.

I wanted to pay homage to some of the great "names" in the history of this great game. I originally put a few of these appreciations on my baseball blog back in the early 2010s, but then I got the idea to put them and many new ones in a book, which you are holding now.

Before I go any further, I want to address a concern some of you might have ... that I'm being culturally insensitive in highlighting names that in their own respective cultures would be quite ordinary or otherwise commonplace. I wrestled with this a lot before I decided to forge ahead because, in almost all cases, I am celebrating the name of the player.

That being said, there are a few names that are included here primarily for the giggles they produce for most U.S.-born, English-speaking readers. I dare you to read the names Johnny Dickshot and Jack Glasscock and not chortle.

Now, you may thumb through this book and say, "hey D.B. ... how come you didn't include so-and-so?" There are a couple of reasons for this:

1. The person does indeed have a memorable name, but so much has already been written about him already that I would be very hard-pressed to add anything new to the conversation. Mickey Mantle is a prime example of this. Its indisputably a great name even if he hit .150 in a career that lasted only six games. But there are multitudes of books on "The Mick" (I for one recommend *The Last Boy: Mickey Mantle and the End of America's Childhood* by Jane Leavy). I wanted to give some time and ink to some of those on the lower rungs of the "baseball fame" ladder.

2. I was saving that person for a possible sequel.

The names I'm profiling here are divided into four groups (admittedly a few of these players could qualify for more than one category):

- Baseball Poets and Men of (Few Different) Letters: Players with rhyming names and/or alliterative names.
- Dirty Names Done Dirt Cheap: Players with scatological or otherwise naughty names.
- Sounds Good to Me: Players with mellifluous/melodious names.
- No Focus Group Convened: Players whose names don't fall into one of the prior three categories, or ones that might involve us questioning the intentions of the player's parents.

Each player profile has the following:

- general demographic information (name they played under, their full name at birth, date of birth/death, years active in the majors, positions played, etc.)
- etymology/definition of each part of their given name
- baseball biography (generally, how they made it to the majors, what they did while they were there)
- best day (a recap of a great day in their major league career)
- the wonder of his name (why his name is memorable to me/us)
- not to be confused with (names that sound and/or look like the player's name)

- fun anagrams (anagrams of their given names, just because I can)
- ephemera (factoids, tidbits, trivia about the player, details regarding their parents, their family and their life after baseball)

This book wouldn't be possible without the Society for American Baseball Research. SABR is an organization (at www.sabr.org) that has been around since 1971, bringing together baseball fans from around the world to pursue studies and analysis of the national pastime. I'd specifically like to thank those members who did the pain-staking research needed to produce detailed biographies of hundreds of players, managers, owners and other assorted personnel.

You see, some of the players I have profiled in this book have little if any biographical information printed on them in the mainstream media. There are niche publishers that are willing to produce books on specific baseball folk, but in many cases, no player-specific books exist for players of limited "importance." That's where SABR members come through. Within the SABR website, there are on-line biographies of many of the "lesser" subjects (at www.sabr.org/bioproject). A glance at any particular biography's endnotes reveals just how much digging went into each bio. In several cases, I have distilled the most important aspects of those biographies for use in this book, primarily in the "Baseball Bio" and "Ephemera" sections.

If you have a suggestion about a name to include in a future edition of this book (crossing fingers as I type), drop me a line at greatnamesbaseballbook@gmail.com.

D.B. Firstman[1]
Spring 2020

---

[1] "D.B. Firstman" anagrams to "Mr. finds bat," or "Ran fit BDSM."

GLOSSARY

Stats that are shown as .000-0-00 refer to batting average/home runs/RBIs, in that order. So, .300-30-100 would mean a .300 batting average with 30 homers and 100 RBIs.

The first **American Association** ran from 1882 to 1891 and is considered a major league. It was founded as a cheaper alternative to the National League, charging 25 cents admission usually instead of the 50 cents common in the NL. Additionally, Sunday baseball was allowed, and beer was served in the stands, both a contrast with the tighter-laced NL. The AA placed teams in Cincinnati, Ohio (deserted by the NL due to its love of Sunday ball and beer) and other huge non-NL cities including New York and Philadelphia.

Batting average on balls in play (**BABIP**) is a measure of the percentage of batted balls that safely fall in for a hit not including home runs. The formula for BABIP is (H-HR)/(AB-K-HR+SF), where H is hits, HR is home runs, AB is at-bats, K is strikeouts, and SF is sacrifice flies. There are many factors that affect BABIP, including batted ball types, ballparks, team defense, foot speed, and randomness (luck). As with any stat, sample size is also an important consideration here. A typical league average BABIP is right around .300.

Cognate (adjective) (of a word) having the same linguistic derivation as another; from the same original word or root (e.g., English is, German ist, Latin est, from Indo-European esti).

A **cup of coffee** is a short stretch spent in the Major Leagues, supposedly named that because the player has only long enough to drink a cup of coffee before he's back in the minors. Players may get a cup of coffee for several reasons: 1) As a major league tryout for a relatively unknown player. 2) As a short-term replacement for a player on the disabled (injured) list. 3) To acclimate a prospect to the majors.

The **diminutive** form of a word, as compared to the original form, has been modified to convey a slighter degree of the root meaning, to convey the smallness of the object or quality named, or to convey a sense of intimacy or endearment. In many languages, such forms can be translated as "little" and diminutives can also be formed as multi-word constructions such as "Tiny Tim." Diminutives are often employed as nicknames and pet names, when speaking to small children, and when expressing extreme tenderness and intimacy to an adult.

A **double diminutive** (example in Italian: *casa – casetta – casettina*) is a diminutive form with two diminutive suffixes rather than one.

A **double unique** is a guy with not only a first name never seen in baseball, but also a last name that hasn't shown up either. There have been roughly 19,000 individuals to have played major league baseball since 1871, and through 2018 roughly 425 of them have "double unique" names.

Hypocoristic means relating to a nickname, usually indicating intimacy with the person named.

LOOGY (Left-handed One Out Guy) is a typical modern situation-dependent role for a left-handed relief pitcher, who comes in to face just one left-handed batter or two. There are ROOGYs too, but those aren't as plentiful on major league rosters.

Metonym(ic) (noun) a figure of speech consisting of the use of the name of one thing for that of another of which it is an attribute or with which it is associated (such as "crown" in "lands belonging to the crown").

Metronym(ic) (noun) a name derived from the name of a mother or female ancestor; (adjective) denoting or relating to a name derived from the name of a mother or female ancestor.

The **National Agreement** is a pact which governed relations between rival major leagues, allowing them to respect one another's player contracts and providing for a championship series between the two leagues' champion teams. The first National Agreement was signed between the National League and the American Association in 1883. The Agreement ushered in an area of peaceful cooperation between the rival circuits and allowed for staging the first championship series between the champions of the two leagues, the 1884 "World's Series." A second National Agreement was signed in 1903, ending a two-year war between the National League and the upstart American League.

The **National Commission** was a three-person committee which oversaw organized baseball from 1903 to 1920. The membership consisted of a chairperson, the American League president, and the National League president. The Commission was created by the National Agreement of 1903, which gave it the power to enact and enforce fines and suspensions. The Commission was plagued with problems as many of its members were often club presidents while they held their post on the body. This often-raised suspicions of conflicts of interest and that self-interest influenced some of its decisions. The Commission was replaced in 1920 by the Commissioner of Baseball.

OPS+ refers to on-base percentage plus slugging percentage, relative to the league average. League average OPS+ is set at 100, so a player with an OPS+ of 126, for example, is 26 percent better than league average.

Patronym(ic) (noun) a name derived from the name of a father or ancestor, typically by the addition of a prefix or suffix, e.g., Johnson, O'Brien, Ivanovich. (adjective) denoting or relating to a name derived from the name of a father or male ancestor.

Reserve Clause was part of a player's contract that stated the rights to players were retained by the team upon the contract's expiration. Players under these contracts were not free to enter into another contract with another team. Once signed to a contract, players could, at the team's whim, be reassigned, traded, sold, or released. The only negotiating leverage of most players was to hold out at contract time and to refuse to play unless their conditions were met. Players were bound to negotiate a new contract to play another year for the same team or to ask to be released or traded. They had no freedom to change teams unless they were given an unconditional release. In the days of the reserve clause, that was the only way a player could be a free agent. The clause was abolished in baseball in 1975 and replaced for the most part by free agency.

Slash stats refers to batting average/on-base percentage/slugging percentage, in that order. So, .300/.400/.500 would mean a .300 batting average with a .400 on-base percentage and a .500 slugging percentage.

The **Three-I League**, formally known as the Illinois-Indiana-Iowa League, ran from 1901-1961 with several interruptions (periods of WWI, the Great Depression and WWII). A class B league throughout its lifespan, no other league at that level survived for as long.

The **Union Association** was a short-lived professional baseball league in the mid-1880s. It was created by Henry Lucas, who had visions of raiding the National League and American Association for frustrated veterans chained to their teams by the reserve clause.

WPA stands for Win Probability Added, which quantifies the percentage change in a team's chances of winning from one event to the next. It does so by measuring the importance of a given plate appearance in the context of the game. For instance: a homer in a one-run game is worth more than a homer in a blowout.

Baseball Poets
and Men of (Few Different) Letters

BOOF BONSER
Mom's Mysterious Nickname for Him

BIRTH NAME: John Paul Bonser
PRONUNCIATION OF DIFFICULT PARTS: BAHN-zur
NICKNAME: Boof, which he eventually officially took as his first name. Bonser has stated that his mother Eileen gave him the nickname when he was a baby. He doesn't know why and never asked. But apparently his mother (herself nicknamed "Ollie") nicknamed all the kids: His two brothers were "Junior" and "Walty" and his sister was "Wiener." Bonser legally changed his name to Boof in 2001.
HEIGHT/WEIGHT: 6'4" 245 lbs.
BORN: Oct. 14, 1981, in St. Petersburg, Florida
POSITION: Pitcher
YEARS ACTIVE IN THE MAJORS: 2006-2008, 2010
NAME ETYMOLOGY/DEFINITIONS: The name "John" is the English form of "Iohannes", the Latin form of the Greek name "Ioannes", itself derived from the Hebrew *Yochanan* meaning "YAHWEH is gracious," from the roots *yo* referring to the Hebrew God and *chanan* meaning "to be gracious." "Paul" has English, French, German, and Dutch roots, from the Latin *paulus* meaning "small." Merriam-Webster defines "boof" as "the sound made by a dog: bark." According to the Oxford English Dictionary, a "boof" is "a blow that makes a sound like a rapid, brief movement of air." Other sources relate it to sex, drugs and/or kayaking. "Bonser" is of English origin, as a nickname from Old French *bon sire* meaning "good sir," given either to a fine gentleman (perhaps ironically) or to someone who made frequent use of this expression as a term of address.

Boof Bonser attended Gibbs H.S., where in his senior year he went 7-3, 1.88 and hit .523 with 11 home runs. He was named the Pinellas County H.S. Player of the Year and played in the Florida State All-Star game.

Bonser was selected out of high school by the Giants in the first round (21st overall) of the 2000 amateur draft. He made his professional baseball debut at age 18 for the Salem-Keizer Volcanoes. In 2001, he had a breakout season for the Hagerstown Suns, leading the South Atlantic League in wins (16), and finishing second in strikeouts (178), which earned him South Atlantic League Most Valuable Pitcher and Post-Season All-Star honors. He reached the AAA level, with the Fresno Grizzlies, at the end of the 2003 season.

In November 2003 Bonser was traded to the Twins organization (see Ephemera), who assigned him to the AA New Britain Rock Cats for 2004, and the AAA Rochester Red Wings for 2005. By this point, his status as an elite prospect had faded, but after a fast start at Rochester in 2006 he was promoted to the majors.

Bonser made his major league debut in May 2006, as the starting pitcher for the Twins against the Brewers: In six innings, he allowed one run and struck out eight.

That year, he made 18 starts with an earned run average of 4.22. (He would never again have a major-league season with an ERA under 5.00.) In a postseason start, he pitched six innings, allowing two runs, to pick up a no-decision as the Twins lost to the A's.

Bonser began the 2007 season as the number two pitcher in the Twins rotation, behind Johan Santana. He finished the season with an 8-12 record with an earned run average of 5.10 and had 136 strikeouts in 173 innings pitched.

He had struggled with stamina and pitching late into ball games, so the Twins encouraged him to lose weight, which he accomplished by a healthier diet, combined with more intense exercise, losing thirty pounds by the start of the 2008 regular season.

Bonser's weight loss did not, however, help his starting pitching performances and at the end of May he was demoted to the bullpen. He ended the season with a 5.73 ERA in 47 games. In 2009 he had surgery to repair tears in his labrum and rotator cuff, missed the entire season, and was traded in December to the Red Sox. Bonser started 2010 on the DL and was not activated until early June. He made two appearances for the Red Sox, who then designated him for assignment. He finished the year with the A's and then bounced around the minors for three more seasons, enduring a Tommy John surgery, before officially retiring in 2015.

BEST DAY (BY WPA OR OTHER MEASURE): On May 18, 2007, Bonser tossed seven innings of one-run, three-hit ball with 11 strikeouts and only one walk, in an 8-1 win over Milwaukee.

THE WONDER OF HIS NAME: He gets points for alliteration, and his mom gets points for the mysterious nickname which he took for his own name. Of course, a word that can involve sex, drugs and rock 'n' roll, and, umm, kayaking is cool.

NOT TO BE CONFUSED WITH: John Bonham (legendary Led Zeppelin drummer), Powers Boothe (gravelly-voiced character actor known for playing tough guys).

FUN ANAGRAMS: "Boof Paul Bonser" anagrams to "A superb fool nob."

EPHEMERA: 1) Bonser will forever be Twins trivia as part of one of the best, if not the best, trades in the team's history: He came over to the Twins along with Joe Nathan and Francisco Liriano in exchange for A. J. Pierzynski. 2) Bonser was named the AL Rookie of the Month for September 2006. 3) He was inducted into the Hagerstown Suns Hall of Fame in 2016. 4) In 2019, Bonser listed himself as a Pipefitter at General Dynamics Electric Boat company in Connecticut.

CALLIX CRABBE
"Flower" power

BIRTH NAME: Callix Sadeaq Crabbe
PRONUNCIATION OF DIFFICULT PARTS: KAY-licks Sa-deke Crab
NICKNAME: None

HEIGHT/WEIGHT: 5'7" 185 lbs.

BORN: Feb. 14, 1983, in St. Thomas, U.S. Virgin Islands

POSITIONS: Pinch Hitter, Second Baseman, Shortstop

YEARS ACTIVE IN THE MAJORS: 2008

NAME ETYMOLOGY/DEFINITIONS: According to Crabbe, "My mom named me Calyx, which is the sepal of a flower ... but she let my brother choose the spelling." "Sadeaq" is most likely a variant of "Sadiq," which is of Arabic origin and means "friend" or "companion," or it is a variant of "Siddiq" meaning "righteous" or "upright." "Crabbe" is English and Scottish and is a variant spelling of "Crabb." "Crabb" is derived from Old English *crabba* (crab, the crustacean). It can also be a nickname for someone with a peculiar gait.

Callix Crabbe settled in Georgia in his teens and was drafted from State College of Florida, Manatee-Sarasota by the Brewers in the 12th round of the 2002 MLB draft.

His professional debut was with the Rookie-level Ogden Raptors, hitting .328/.407/.472 with 22 steals in 31 tries and 55 runs in 67 games. He tied for second in the Pioneer League in steals and was sixth in batting average. He also led the league's second basemen with 21 errors.

In 2003, with the A-level Beloit Snappers, Callix batted .260/.356/.346, scoring 79 runs and stealing 25 in 34 tries.

In 2004, with the High Desert Mavericks, he hit 291/.367/.419 with 89 runs, 34 steals (caught 11 times). That year he tied for second in the California League in triples (with 11); led Cal League second basemen in putouts (241), assists (356) and errors (21); and made the league's All-Star Team.

In 2005, with the AA Huntsville Stars, Crabbe struggled, hitting .243/.354/.310 with 18 steals in 24 attempts. The following year he returned to Huntsville, improving to .267/.368/.345. He tied for second in the Southern League (SL) with 71 walks, trailing only Joey Votto. He was 4th in the SL in stolen bases (with 32 in 45 tries). He led SL second basemen in assists (352) and tied Eric Patterson for the most putouts (237).

In 2007, for the AAA Nashville Sounds, Crabbe hit .287/.377/.435 with nine triples and 84 runs. He stole 17 bases but was thrown out 14 times.

Following the 2007 season, he was selected in the Rule 5 Draft by the Padres. Crabbe appeared in 21 games as a bench player for San Diego in April and early May: In 34 at-bats, he hit .176, scoring four runs with two RBI. The Padres then returned him to the Brewers, who assigned to AAA Nashville. He became a free agent after the 2008 season and signed a minor league contract with the Mariners.

In 2009, in 75 games with the AAA Tacoma Rainiers, Crabbe hit only .210, and then did hardly better in AA, batting .212 with the West Tenn Diamond Jaxx. The Mariners did not retain him after the season, and he moved to the Toronto Blue Jays organization in 2010.

The Blue Jays sent him to the AA New Hampshire Fisher Cats; he played 81 games there in 2010, mainly at second base, hitting .225/.310/.330. He also got into ten games for the AAA Las Vegas 51s, but hit only .200. He did steal 20 bases between the two stops.

In 2011, he was back at New Hampshire, and had his best season at the plate in three years, putting up a batting average of .259 in 69 games, with an OBP of .348. He was still released at the end of that season, and that ended his career.

BEST DAY (BY WPA OR OTHER MEASURE): On Apr. 20, 2008, Crabbe collected the only extra-base hit in his career, off no slouch (Randy Johnson). He also reached base on an error and a hit-by-pitch, scored a run and drove in another, helping his Padres to a 9-4 win over the Diamondbacks.

THE WONDER OF HIS NAME: First you have the alliteration, then you add in the "double uniqueness" of his name, then throw in the story of his brother giving him the unique spelling of his first name. A winner!

NOT TO BE CONFUSED WITH: Buster Crabbe (American two-time Olympic swimmer and movie actor. He won the 1932 Olympic gold medal for 400-meter freestyle swimming event), Neelix (a character in the television series *Star Trek: Voyager*), Mr. Eugene H Krabs (owner and founder of the "Krusty Krab" restaurant on the hit cartoon *SpongeBob SquarePants*).

FUN ANAGRAMS: "Callix Sadeaq Crabbe" anagrams to "Bad Iraq cabals excel."

EPHEMERA: 1) As of January 2019, Crabbe is one of only 14 players in MLB history born in the U.S. Virgin Islands. 2) When he made his big-league debut, it marked the first time a player from the Virgin Islands had appeared in the majors since Aug. 6, 2005, when Midre Cummings played his last game with the Orioles. 3) After his playing career ended, Crabbe went into coaching, including as head varsity baseball coach for IMG Academy. 4) Crabbe also ran his own baseball instructional program called Crabbe-ology Sports Development. 5) In December of 2018, he became the assistant hitting coach of the Texas Rangers. 5) Due to a printing error, Carlos Guevara appeared on one of Crabbe's baseball cards.

COCO CRISP
Nicknamed after a cereal

BIRTH NAME: Covelli Loyce Crisp
PRONUNCIATION OF DIFFICULT PARTS: None
NICKNAME: Coco (Given the nickname by his sister who teased him that he looked like one of the characters on the Cocoa Krispies cereal box). When he started playing AA baseball, the team had all the players fill out a questionnaire to get to know one another. Covelli listed "Coco" as his nickname on the form and his teammates thought the name was funny so they had it put on the scoreboard during the game. He was

traded to another team after a week and a half, but the nickname stuck, and he has been Coco Crisp ever since.

HEIGHT/WEIGHT: 5'10" 185 lbs.

BORN: Nov. 1, 1979, in Los Angeles, California

POSITIONS: Centerfielder

YEARS ACTIVE IN THE MAJORS: 2002-2016

NAME ETYMOLOGY/DEFINITIONS: Crisp's father is of Puerto Rican and Italian descent and his mother is African American. "Covelli" is more often a surname with Italian origins, as the patronymic or plural form of "Covello." "Covello" is a diminutive of "Iacovo," with loss of the first syllable. "Iacovo" is one of many old Italian forms of "Jacob," now preserved only in surnames. "Loyce" has German-American origins, meaning "renowned warrior." "Crisp" has English origins as the nickname for a man with curly hair, from Middle English *crisp*, Old English *crisp, cryps* (Latin *crispus*), reinforced in Middle English by an Old French word also from Latin crispus. It is the Americanized spelling of the German cognate Krisp, from Middle High German *krisp, krispel* meaning "curly-haired man." It can also be the Americanized form of German Krisp, from a short form of the medieval personal name Krispin.

The St. Louis Cardinals selected Crisp in the seventh round of the 1999 amateur draft. He started slowly in the Cards system but made his mark in 2001 playing at Single-A Potomac, batting .306/.368/.423 with 11 homers and 39 stolen bases in 139 games. He was named the Cardinals 2001 Minor League Player of the Year. He opened the 2002 season with the New Haven Ravens, then the AA Eastern League affiliate of the Cardinals. With the Cardinals in need of a starting pitcher for the late stretches of the 2002 pennant race, Crisp was traded to the Cleveland Indians on Aug. 7, 2002, to complete an earlier trade for 39-year-old Chuck Finley.

He would make his major league debut with the Indians eight days later. For the Tribe that year he posted a .260/.314/.386 line in 32 games. He split 2003 between AAA (where he posted a robust .945 OPS) and the major league club (where he had a more pedestrian .655 OPS but with excellent defense). Over the next few seasons, Crisp established a reputation as an excellent fielder and speedy baserunner. In 2005, he moved to left field following the emergence of another young outfielder, Grady Sizemore. In what would be his final two seasons with the Indians, Crisp showcased his offensive talent by batting .297 and .300, with OPS+ of 110 in 2004 and 117 in 2005, and a combined 31 total home runs and 35 steals.

After Johnny Damon signed with the New York Yankees in January 2006, the Red Sox sought Crisp to fill Damon's role as both leadoff hitter and center fielder. About four weeks after the Damon signing, the Red Sox sent prospect third baseman Andy Marte, pitcher Guillermo Mota, catcher Kelly Shoppach, a player to be named later (minor leaguer Randy Newsom), and cash considerations to the Indians for Crisp, catcher Josh Bard and pitcher David Riske.

Crisp had a somewhat rough first season in Boston. After a productive start to the year, he fractured his left index finger and missed games from Apr. 9 to May 27. Then Red Sox manager Terry Francona moved him from the leadoff spot to the bottom of the lineup, letting Kevin Youkilis' .400+ OBP spark the offense. In 105 games, Crisp had a .264 batting average (but only a .317 OBP) with eight home runs and 36 RBIs in 413 at-bats.

During the 2007 season Crisp struggled offensively due to lingering effects of off-season surgery to his left index finger. Though he was underwhelming at the plate (83 OPS+), he made numerous impressive catches in the outfield and made seven assists and only one error in over 1,200 innings. Although he was the team's starting center fielder throughout the regular season, he was benched mid-series during the ALCS for rookie Jacoby Ellsbury. He had had only five hits in 31 at-bats in the playoffs to that point. He remained benched for the 2007 World Series, only appearing late in games for defensive substitutions.

The 2008 season saw a slight improvement in his offense (94 OPS+), but he appeared in only 118 games due to injury, ineffectiveness and a suspension for his participation in an on-field brawl. His last great hurrah for the Red Sox came in Game 5 of the ALCS, when he struck the game-tying hit in the bottom of the eighth inning to cap Boston's seven-run comeback. On Nov. 19, 2008, Crisp was traded to the Kansas City Royals for relief pitcher Ramón Ramírez.

During his lone season with the Royals, Crisp's started off hot, hitting well over .300, before his batting average fell to a career-low .228 due to shoulder injuries. On June 23, 2009, Royals manager Trey Hillman announced that Crisp would undergo season-ending surgeries to repair a labrum tear in each shoulder.

After the 2009 season, Crisp signed a one-year contract with the Oakland Athletics worth $5 million. Crisp began the 2010 season on the 15-day DL with a fractured left pinkie finger but went on to put together his first above-average season at the plate since 2005, hitting .279/.342/.438 for a 112 OPS+. Crisp was the primary centerfielder for the A's for the next four years, from 2011-2014, with 2013 his best year at the plate at .261/.335/.444.

In 2015, Crisp, now 35 years old, appeared in only 44 games, playing only left field, and batted a puny .175, with the lowest on-base percentage (.252) and slugging percentage (.222) of his career. He got more playing time in 2016, mostly in left field, but on Aug. 31 the A's traded Crisp with cash considerations to the Indians for minor leaguer Colt Hynes. Before he agreed to waive his no-trade clause, Chris Antonetti, the Indians' general manager, spoke with Crisp to tell him that he would not receive enough playing time in Cleveland for his option to vest.

Crisp became a free agent following the 2016 season after he failed to meet the contractual incentives that would have caused his vesting option for 2017 to trigger. His big-league career came to an end at the age of 36, with totals of 1,586 games played, 130 homers, 309 stolen bases (caught 79 times), and a slash line of .265/.327/.402 for a 96 OPS+. He batted .279 with three homers in 43 playoff games.

BEST DAY (BY WPA OR OTHER MEASURE): On Aug. 24, 2011, while playing for the Oakland A's, Crisp had his second 4-for-4 day in the majors, at the expense of the Yankees in New York. Batting second in the lineup, Crisp launched a long solo homer against starter CC Sabathia to left in the first inning. In the top of the third, with the score still 1-0, Crisp drew a two-out walk. With the score tied at 1-1 in the top of the sixth he singled off Sabathia. In the top of the eighth, with the score tied 2-2 and David Robertson pitching, Crisp poked an RBI single between second and short to give the A's the lead. The Yankees tied it again in their half of the inning and the game went to extras. Rafael Soriano took the mound for the Yankees in the top of the tenth, and after a groundout, two singles and a strikeout, Crisp then hit another home run, this time to deep right field. The A's would hold on to win, 6-4. Crisp went 4-for-4 with two homers, a walk, two runs scored and five RBI (tying a career-high).

THE WONDER OF HIS NAME: Alliteration always makes us happy. The short, staccato sound of his name is pleasing too. His given name is cool, and his nickname and the story behind it add points. How many guys have names that could be taken for breakfast cereals?

NOT TO BE CONFUSED WITH: Quentin Crisp (born Denis Charles Pratt) an English writer, raconteur and actor), or "Coco" Chanel (French fashion designer and businesswoman). Quisp (a sugar-sweetened breakfast cereal from the Quaker Oats Company, was introduced in 1965 and continued as a mass-market grocery item until the late 1970s; it returned to supermarkets during 2012.

FUN ANAGRAMS: "Covelli Loyce Crisp" anagrams to "Spicily cool, clever" or "Cleric loves policy."

EPHEMERA: 1) He is the son of Loyce Crisp, a fast food restaurant owner and former amateur boxer, and Pamela Crisp, a former champion sprinter. 2) He is a graduate of Major League Baseball's Reviving Baseball in Inner Cities (RBI) program. 3) In 2007, Crisp was almost run over by the Seattle Mariners' mascot, the Mariner Moose. The Moose, driving a lap around the warning track on an ATV, nearly collided with Crisp as he was leaving the dugout in the middle of the fifth inning; Crisp had to jump out of the way to avoid being hit. Red Sox pitching coach John Farrell was incensed by the mascot's actions and voiced his displeasure to both the mascot and Seattle's head groundskeeper; Mariners general manager Bill Bavasi subsequently sent an apology. 4) His maternal grandfather is Milton "Nick" Newton, the inventor of track and field starting blocks considered by many to be the best in the world. 5) Following his playing career, Crisp became the baseball coach at Shadow Hills H.S. in Indio, California. 6) He has a unique tattoo/piercing combination on his neck. The design seems to resemble a bullseye with a piercing in the middle. 7) In 2019, he joined the radio broadcast team of the Oakland Athletics. 8) He officially changed his name from "Covelli" to "Coco" in March 2013, and proceeded to have the best season of his career that year. 9) He is married and has three sons and a daughter. He and his family live in Rancho Mirage, California.

FERRIS FAIN
Temperamental on-base machine
and smooth-fielding first baseman

BIRTH NAME: Ferris Roy Fain
PRONUNCIATION OF DIFFICULT PARTS: None
NICKNAME: Burrhead (He had short, kinky black hair. The nickname had an unmistakable ring of racism, yet players and managers alike commonly used it throughout Fain's career), Cocky (He was thought to have a lazy eye, but also because of his confidence in himself).
HEIGHT/WEIGHT: 5'11" 180 lbs.
BORN: Mar. 29, 1921, in San Antonio, Texas
DIED: Oct. 18, 2001, in Georgetown, California
POSITION: First Baseman
YEARS ACTIVE IN THE MAJORS: 1947-1955
NAME ETYMOLOGY/DEFINITIONS: "Ferris" is both a given name and a family name. It is related to the name "Fergus" in Ireland, and the name "Ferrers "in England. In Ireland, the Ferris family of County Kerry derives its surname from the patronymic *Ó Fearghusa*. "Roy" is an English, Scottish, and French name of Norman origin. Originating from the Normans, the descendants of Norse Vikings from Denmark, Norway and Iceland who later migrated to Normandy. The derivation is from the word *roy*, meaning "king." "Fain" has French origins, as a habitational name from any of various places in France, deriving their names mostly from Old French *fain* meaning "swamp," but Latin *fanum* meaning "temple" is also a source in some cases. It also has English origins, as a variant spelling of "Fayne."

Ferris Fain joined the San Francisco Seals of the Pacific Coast League (PCL) during his senior year of high school, when Seals manager Lefty O'Doul offered to pay $200 a month "under the table." (Fain's amateur status made him ineligible to join the team). After high school graduation in 1939, Fain signed an above-board deal with the Seals. He was noticed for his aggressive and exceptional defensive play at first base. Fain enjoyed a terrific season with a sub-.500 Seals team in 1941, batting .310 and leading the PCL with 122 runs scored. Seals beat reporter Jim McGee described him as the "backbone of the club" who played first base with "catlike grace" and "uncanny judgment." After a mysterious plunge to .216 in 1942, he went off to fight in the War and wouldn't return for three years.

He regained his pre-1942 form upon his return in 1946, getting named to the midseason PCL all-star team. Fain, playing in 180 games for the Seals that season (!), showed great discipline at the plate (a trademark of his career), collecting 129 bases on balls, while batting .301 and led the league in both runs (117) and runs batted in (112). Oh, and he also clubbed 11 home runs for the PCL champions.

Fain was selected by the sad sack Philadelphia Athletics after the season in the Rule 5 draft. They hadn't had a winning season since 1933. Fain broke in with the Athletics as a 26-year-old rookie in 1947 and established a reputation as a daring first baseman with a great sense of the strike zone.

In Fain's major league debut (which also marked the first big-league regular-season game he ever attended), at Yankee Stadium, he beat out a bunt single off Randy Gumpert, his lone hit in four at-bats. Fain made a seamless transition to the big leagues, relying on his patience at the plate and his ability to make contact with the ball.

Fain's aggressive, exuberant style of play was credited with energizing the A's, and manager Connie Mack lauded his "sheer spirit" on the field. Fain finished the season with a .291 batting average and boasted the league's second-best on-base percentage thanks to 95 walks, while the A's finished with a winning record. *The Sporting News* named him first baseman on its All-Rookie team.

Fain annually ranked among the league leaders in walks and on-base percentage in each of his first seven seasons. However, chronic and ultimately career-ending knee pain began in his first season with the A's. In spring training, he had suffered from strained ligaments in his right knee, and by September doctors detected calcium deposits. After his rookie season, he underwent knee surgery to remove bone chips; however, he reinjured the same knee while pitching (!) in a semipro game in Oakland and required a second surgery several months later.

Battling a tender knee, a broken middle finger on his throwing hand, and an eye infection, Fain managed to bat .281, draw at least 100 walks for the first of five times in his career, and drive in a career-high 88 runs in his second year. Despite limited power (seven home runs in each of his first two seasons), on most days Fain batted cleanup. The A's enjoyed their best season (84-70) since 1932. As patient as Fain was at the plate, he was equally aggressive playing first base. He was blessed with exceptional range and a powerful arm and was known to charge to the first- and third-base sides of home plate on bunts and initiate a double play by throwing out the advancing runner at second base.

While Fain's batting average slipped to .263 in 1949, his defensive play helped the A's become the first team in big-league history to complete more than 200 double plays in one season (217). Fain, second baseman Pete Suder, shortstop Eddie Joost, and third baseman Hank Majeski were hailed as one of the "greatest infields in the history of the Athletics."

Fain's desire to succeed was matched by his explosive temperament on and off the field. He took defeat as a personal insult, prompting sportswriter Edgar Williams to dub him the "Angry Champion." In his rookie year he was involved in a highly publicized brawl with Red Sox infielder Eddie Pellagrini, which resulted in a suspension. According to teammate Eddie Joost, Fain "had a lifestyle of his own and would do exactly what he wanted to do. Occasionally he'd overdrink and wouldn't be attentive on the field."

In 1950 Fain was named to his first of five consecutive All-Star teams in an otherwise disappointing year for the A's. He hit .282 with a career-best 10 round-trippers. He also walked 133 times. The A's as a team, however, fell to last place with a dismal 52-102 record. The season also marked the end of Connie Mack's illustrious run of 50 years piloting the team.

In 1951, Fain got off to a hot start and was named to his second All-Star team. On July 15 he kicked the first-base bag in frustration after failing to beat out a ground ball, broke a bone in his left foot, and wound up missing five weeks. He returned on Aug. 21 and batted .364 over the rest of the season to capture his first batting title with a .344 mark. For the season he walked 80 times and had a .451 OBP, but the A's still finished in sixth place (70-84). *The Sporting News* named Fain the Outstanding Player of the Year.

In 1952 he became the highest-paid A's player since Jimmie Foxx. Slowed by leg pain, he was batting only .245 at the end of May. However, beginning in mid-June he compiled a career-long 24-game hitting streak (37-for-99) to catapult him into the lead for the AL batting title. Despite Fain's heroics, Philadelphia ended the season in fourth place. Fain played through several nagging injuries to his knees and hands to win his second consecutive batting title (.327). Among his career-high 176 hits, he paced the league with 43 doubles. He placed sixth in the MVP voting for the second straight year.

In January 1953, Fain was sent to the Chicago White Sox in exchange for slugging first baseman Eddie Robinson and two other starting players. The A's claimed they coveted the real home-run threat Robinson provided, but Fain's behavior probably played a role in making the deal.

Fain became the highest-paid player in White Sox history in 1953 when he inked a contract for a reported $35,000. But he never got on track with the White Sox. He suffered a bruised right knee and then strained ligaments in his left knee during the first two months of the season. He broke the ring finger on his left hand in a barroom brawl after a game against the Washington Senators on Aug. 2: He missed 22 games and was also charged with assault. Fain struggled in his return and finished with a .256 batting average in a forgettable season with the third-place White Sox.

Despite the down year, he was installed in the cleanup position for the 1954 season and he seemed headed toward what might have been the most productive season of his career. He played in 65 of the team's first 70 games, batted .302, and was among the league's leaders with 51 runs batted in (in just 235 at-bats). Then on June 27 he collided with catcher Sammy White of the Red Sox, injuring his already fragile right knee and abruptly ending his promising season. A month later he underwent his third knee surgery.

In December 1954, the White Sox shipped him along with two throw-ins to the Tigers. Fain saw little action in spring training with the Tigers and was still moving "rather gingerly" with a pronounced limp. He clashed with manager Bucky Harris, who held him out of the Opening Day lineup. Father Time had caught up to Fain that season, as he batted a mere .264 and was a liability in the field. He was released on July 6. He got a second chance about a week later when he signed with the

Indians, for whom Fain filled in at first base and batted .254 as they finished second to the Yankees.

The Indians released Fain at the end of the season, and, unable to catch on with another major-league team, he signed as a player-coach with the Sacramento Solons of the PCL. He batted just .252 for the Solons and was released at the conclusion of the 1956 season, bringing his active playing career to an end. In his nine-year big-league career, Fain hit .290, with 1,139 hits, and an eye-popping .424 on-base percentage that ranked 12th-highest in history at the time of his retirement. He walked 904 times against only 261 strikeouts in his career. As impressive as the accomplishments of the five-time All-Star were on the field, he may be best remembered for his pugnacious behavior off the field. "If I had behaved more," Fain admitted, "I probably would have realized my dream of becoming a manager."

BEST DAY (BY WPA OR OTHER MEASURE): Fain had two 5-for-5 games in his career, but I would submit that his best day, the one that showed his offensive skill set the best, occurred on a day he went a mere 2-for-2 (with three walks). In the second game of a double-header on May 27, 1951 at Yankee Stadium, Fain batted second in the order against Yankees starting pitcher Fred Sanford. Early in his career, Sanford had borderline decent control, walking about 3.5 batters per nine innings. But as he came into his early 30s, the walks ballooned. In 1950 he walked 6.3 per nine innings, and Fain was ready for him on that day in May. In the top of the first with one out, Fain drew a walk against Sanford but was left stranded. In the top of the third with a man on first and the Athletics now trailing 1-0, Fain drew another walk. Philadelphia would eventually plate a run that inning (scored by Joost) to tie the game. With one out in the fifth, Fain homered off Sanford to put Philadelphia ahead 2-1. In the top of the seventh, with his team now trailing 3-2, Fain drew another walk from Sanford (Sanford walked seven in 6⅓ innings that day). Fain would soon thereafter come around to score the go-ahead run. In the top of the eighth, Philadelphia was nursing a 5-4 lead with one out and runners on first and second, when Fain singled to left off Joe Ostrowski, scoring an insurance run in what would end up a 7-4 win for Philadelphia. Over the course of his career, Fain had 17 games in which he reached base at least five times.

THE WONDER OF HIS NAME: You must love the alliteration and the "double uniqueness," along with the coolness factor of "Ferris."

NOT TO BE CONFUSED WITH: Ferris Bueller (protagonist of the 1986 film *Ferris Bueller's Day Off*), Ferris Foreman (a lawyer, politician, and American soldier during the Mexican–American War, as well as a colonel commanding a volunteer regiment and the District of Southern California during the American Civil War).

FUN ANAGRAMS: "Ferris Roy Fain" becomes "No fiery friars."

EPHEMERA: 1) Ferris's father Oscar was a construction worker and part-time boxer whose greatest claim to fame came as a jockey riding a horse named Duval to a second-place finish in the 1912 Kentucky Derby. 2) He had a "very abusive" childhood, mainly at the hands of the father, who died when he was still a child. His mother did domestic work for the family to survive. He grew up in Oakland, California, where he graduated from Roosevelt H.S. as student body president. 3) Fain missed three seasons (1943-1945) when he served in the Army Air Force. Assigned to the 495th Squadron at McClellan Airfield, near Sacramento, Fain played for one of the strongest service teams on the Pacific Coast. He rose to the rank of sergeant and was later stationed at Hickam Air Base in Hawaii. His base team included Joe DiMaggio, Red Ruffing, and Joe Gordon. "I believe that playing service ball made the difference in me going to the major leagues. That's because I got a chance to play against and with all these guys," said Fain. 4) In retirement, Fain settled down in El Dorado County, California. He worked in construction, built houses and in 1985 was arrested for growing marijuana. He pleaded guilty, served four months under house arrest, and received five years probation. He claimed he needed money and so grew the plants out of necessity. His name surfaced again in 1988 when agents raided his home and discovered a large-scale operation with more than 400 plants, processed pot, and ledgers detailing purchases and sales. Fain was arrested again, and this time spent 18 months in a state prison. He told Sacramento Bee sports editor Bill Conlin: "I grew 'em because, damn it, I was good at growing things, just like I was good at hitting a baseball."

ED HEAD
A natural lefty, an accident forced him into pitching right-handed

BIRTH NAME: Edward Marvin Head
PRONUNCIATION OF DIFFICULT PARTS: None
NICKNAME: None, though in 1945 he said that friends called him "Cajun" and "Swampy"
HEIGHT/WEIGHT: 6'1" 175 lbs.
BORN: Jan. 25, 1918, in Selma, Louisiana
DIED: Jan. 31, 1980, in Bastrop, Louisiana
POSITION: Pitcher
YEARS ACTIVE IN THE MAJORS: 1940, 1942-1944, 1946
NAME ETYMOLOGY/DEFINITIONS: "Edward" is derived from the Anglo-Saxon form "Éadweard," composed of the elements *ead* meaning "wealth, fortune; prosperous" and *weard* meaning "guardian, protector." It has been one of the most successful of the Old English given names. "Marvin" is derived from the Welsh name "Mervyn," which is itself derived from the traditional Welsh name "Merfyn," which is made up of *mer* meaning "marrow" and *myn* meaning "eminent." "Head" has English origins, from Middle English heved meaning "head," applied as a nickname for someone with some peculiarity or disproportion of the head, or a topographic name for someone who lived on a hill or at the head of a stream or valley. This surname has long been established in Ireland.

As a 17-year-old, Head's left arm, the one he pitched with for a semipro team, was mangled in a horrific team bus accident. From the scene of the accident, he was taken to a local hospital, where a doctor told him he would have to amputate the arm. Head argued against amputation and pleaded to have his uncle, Dr. L.E. Larche, who had the only fluoroscope in the area, come look at the injury. Dr. Larche determined that he could save the arm, which he did following many hours of surgery. Head's lifetime goal had always been to be a major-league pitcher, but with his left arm nearly useless, that would be impossible. Head realized there was only one way he could reach his goal, by throwing right-handed. Amazingly, Head worked and practiced until he succeeded.

"It was tough at first, but not as bad as it might have been for some kids," he remembered. "I had fooled around a lot throwing right-handed even though I was a natural left-hander. It took me about three years though, before I could throw with any real speed."

Head eventually regained full use of his left arm, but pursued pitching as a righty. He graduated from Ouachita Parish H.S. and began his professional career in 1939 with the Class-D Evangeline League Abbeville (Louisiana) A's, a Philadelphia Athletics farm team. (Making the majors after starting in Class-D ball was practically unheard of, but three pitchers in the Evangeline League in 1939 not only reached the major leagues but became stars: Virgil Trucks, Hal Newhouser and Howard Pollet.) Head went 19-8 for Abbeville and after the season the Brooklyn Dodgers bought his contract.

The Dodgers sent Head to the Elmira (New York) Pioneers of the Class-A Eastern League for the 1940 season. Through late July, he had justified the jump of three levels in the minor-league chain with a 12-7 record, 116 strikeouts, and a 2.56 earned-run average. With the big-league club in contention in July, they called up Head and the Pioneers' sensational young outfielder Pete Reiser, who was batting .378 at the time of the recall.

Head had pitched in an exhibition game for Elmira against the Dodgers a few weeks earlier. He had impressed Dodgers coach Charlie Dressen, who was managing the team for that game, by allowing only one hit and striking out five in three innings.

Dressen said that in addition to Head's outstanding fastball, he pitched with authority and never showed a trace of nervousness in facing the big leaguers. Dixie Walker and other Dodgers players raved about the composure the youngster had shown.

Head made his major-league debut with a scoreless inning against St. Louis in the first game of a July 27 doubleheader at Ebbets Field. Three days later, on July 30, he made his first start, at home against Pittsburgh. The Pirates scored four first inning runs on their way to an 8-2 victory. Dodgers manager Leo Durocher pulled Head after two innings, during which he allowed three hits and walked four.

After a day off, the Dodgers and Pirates played another doubleheader on Aug. 1. After Brooklyn won the first game, Durocher started Head again in the nightcap in what might have been a ploy to get Pirates manager Frankie Frisch to start a left-handed-hitting lineup. After Head began the game by walking Lloyd Waner on four pitches, Durocher replaced him with left-hander Lee Grissom. (In other words, Durocher used Head as the "opener.") Head's first big-league win also came against the Pirates, a complete-game 8-2 victory on Sep. 13.

The Dodgers invited him to spring training in 1941, and his strong work there appeared to have earned him a place on the club. While Durocher agreed Head was ready for the big leagues, he wanted him to get more seasoning and sent him to International League's Montreal Royals. The 23-year-old Head won his first seven games for the Royals, on his way to an 18-8 season.

At spring training in 1942, the Dodgers worked on Head's curveball while also attempting to improve his control. (He had walked 92 batters in 209 innings at Montreal.) He made the big league club, and his control improved once the season started. In his first five starts of the season, through May 16, he was 5-0, with an ERA of 2.74 and 28 strikeouts with only 17 walks. Head then lost his next four decisions and did not win his sixth game until June 29. Overall, Head finished with a 10-6 record in 36 games (15 starts). It was a frustrating season for the Dodgers, who led the league by ten games in early August and finished with 104 victories but wound up second to St. Louis.

In 1943, the Dodgers had a new president, Branch Rickey. Head's excellent spring, along with the loss of a few other candidates to the war, had earned him the honor of pitching the regular season opener, which he won, 5-2. He allowed just six hits, four of which were by the Giants' manager, future Hall of Famer Mel Ott.

The highlight of Head's 1943 season came in May when he pitched back-to-back shutouts against Chicago and Cincinnati. In his next start, he shut out Pittsburgh through six innings, and had compiled a streak of 26⅔ consecutive scoreless innings. Head's third consecutive win was also his third consecutive complete game. He tailed off after that, failing to pitch a complete game after May 29. He regained his old form in late August with consecutive complete-game wins against the Pirates (6-1) and the Phillies (8-0). After the win over Pittsburgh, Durocher informed Rickey that Head had made use of a change of pace to complement his fastball. He used it again in the shutout of the Phillies. Head had been instructed to use a change of pace all season but had stubbornly resisted. Over the course of the season, Durocher was using Head more in relief: his 47 appearances, second most on the club, included only 18 starts. Yet both his 9-10 record and ratio of strikeouts (83) to walks (66) were disappointments.

Because he (incorrectly) expected to be drafted before the 1944 season began, Head never reported to Bear Mountain for spring training. He finally joined the team four days before the season opener, and he did not make his first appearance until May 29. His first start was on June 2, when he held the Chicago Cubs to one run in six innings but was not involved in the decision. As in past seasons, he started off well and then faded. He pitched five straight complete games, winning four, before he slumped like the rest of the Dodgers. From June 28 through July 16, the Dodgers lost a franchise record 16 consecutive games. Three of those losses were charged to Head in games he started. On July 13, during the All-Star break, Head finally received orders from his draft board in Monroe, Louisiana, to report for Army induction immediately.

Sixteen months later, Head received his official discharge from the Army. He reported to spring training in 1946, but he had been gone for two years and his arm was still a little sore from absorbing the recoil from a 57-millimeter antitank gun while at Fort Hood. Nonetheless, he opened the season with Brooklyn and made his postwar debut on Apr. 23, starting against the Boston Braves at Ebbets Field, and, lo and behold, he hurled a no-hitter (see "Best Day" for more details). However, a few weeks after the no-hitter he reinjured his arm, ending his major league career.

Head spent all of spring training with the Dodgers in 1947 but was unable to stick with the club. On Opening Day, he was sent to the Fort Worth Cats of the AA Texas League. He split the season between Fort Worth, where he lost all three of his decisions, and the St. Paul Saints of the AAA American Association, where he won three and lost three. Head spent his final three active seasons in baseball as the general manager and field manager of the Monroe (Louisiana) Sports. Monroe was a member of the Cotton States League in 1954 and 1955, winning the pennant in 1955. In 1956, the Sports moved to the Evangeline League, where Head had started his career in 1939.

BEST DAY (BY WPA OR OTHER MEASURE): He made his postwar debut on Apr. 23, 1946 starting against the Boston Braves at Ebbets Field. The game, played on a Tuesday afternoon, drew a near-capacity crowd of 26,787. Head no-hit the Braves, 5-0, in the first no-hitter in Brooklyn since Cincinnati's Johnny Vander Meer's second consecutive no-hitter in 1938. Mixing fastballs, curveballs, sliders, and changeups, Head struck out only two, but he kept the opposing batters off stride all day. He faced only two batters over the minimum, as the Braves had only four baserunners, three via walks, and a fifth-inning error by shortstop Pee Wee Reese, while Brooklyn's defense turned two double plays. There were two close calls, one in the seventh inning and one in the eighth. Tommy Holmes led off the Boston seventh with a long drive to right-center field, but center fielder Carl Furillo ran it down. In the eighth Whitey Wietelmann slashed a line drive between Reese and third baseman Reiser that Reiser was able to grab with his glove hand. Chuck Workman, batting for Boston pitcher Mort Cooper, led off the ninth with a walk. However, as the following batter (Connie Ryan) struck out, catcher Ferrell Anderson threw to first baseman Ed Stevens to double up Workman. Johnny Hopp made the final out on a groundball to second baseman Billy Herman.

THE WONDER OF HIS NAME: Rhyming names are cool. Short, snappy rhyming names are really cool. One wonders if they had the phrase "going to hit the head" back in his day, and if so, did he on occasion misunderstand and reflexively flinch?

NOT TO BE CONFUSED WITH: Edith Head (20th-century American costume designer who won a record eight Academy Awards for Best Costume Design), Deadhead (Name given to a fan of the Grateful Dead), Bedhead (The condition of having unkempt hair, generally as a result of having just woken up from sleep).

FUN ANAGRAMS: "Edward Marvin Head" becomes "Evaded inward harm."

EPHEMERA: 1) Head described his nationality as Scotch-Irish-French and Indian. 2) Ed's father, Marvin Redwine Head, was a timber cutter, and his mother Ida Maude Rawls Head was a homemaker. Ed was their first son, followed by Jack and Roy Lee, who died at age 16 in 1944. 3) Head married Johnnie Mae Womack on July 2, 1940. The day before the 1946 no-hitter, Johnnie Mae gave birth to a baby boy they named Rickey. 4) Head had an unusual superstition. He would not begin to warm up before a game until coach John Corriden handed him the ball. And if he was going for, let's say, his fourth victory, Corriden would have to slap the ball four times with his right palm, and say: "There it is for you." 5) After baseball, Head lived in Bastrop, Louisiana, and worked as a preventive maintenance coordinator for the International Paper Company.

HANSON HORSEY
One game in the majors, then a mentor to future umpires

BIRTH NAME: Hanson Horsey
PRONUNCIATION OF DIFFICULT PARTS: None
NICKNAME: Hans
HEIGHT/WEIGHT: 5'11" 165 lbs.
BORN: Nov. 26, 1889, in Galena, Maryland
DIED: Dec. 1, 1949, in Millington, Maryland
POSITION: Pitcher
YEARS ACTIVE IN THE MAJORS: 1912
NAME ETYMOLOGY/DEFINITIONS: "Hanson" has English (chiefly Midlands and northern England, especially Yorkshire) origins as a patronymic from "Hann" or the byname "Hand." It also has Irish origins as the shortened Anglicized form of Gaelic "Ó hAmhsaigh," or as a variant of "McKittrick." Further origins consist of a respelling of Scandinavian "Hansen" or "Hansson." "Horsey" has English origins as the habitational name from places in Norfolk, Somerset, and Sussex, so named from Old English *hors* meaning "horse" (perhaps a byname) and *eg* meaning "island," "low-lying land."

Hanson Horsey attended southern Maryland's prestigious Charlotte Hall Military Academy. He played baseball there and by age 15 in 1905 was pitching in the summers for town teams in Galena and Millington on the Eastern Shore. In 1907, the *Chestertown Transcript* tabbed Horsey "the best college pitcher in the state."

Buck Herzog, a Baltimore native who spent 13 seasons in the majors, debuted with the 1908 New York Giants; that same season he saw Horsey pitch on the Eastern Shore and "strongly" recommended him as someone who "should make good." That was enough to earn Horsey a roster spot for 1910 with the Reading (Pennsylvania) Pretzels, an unaffiliated club in the Class-B Tri-State League. He managed only a 7-15 (.318) record in 31 appearances for the Pretzels.

In 1911, both he and the team improved. Horsey (22-10 in 33 games) helped pace the Pretzels to the 1911 Tri-State League pennant. He was selected by the Cincinnati Reds in the major-league Rule 5 draft and they signed him for 1912. Former major-league pitcher, then umpire, and ultimately Hall of Famer Hank O'Day was the club's new manager.

The *Cincinnati Enquirer* noted "This kid [Horsey] is the smallest of the recruit pitchers [but] has a fine fast ball to go with his curve and looks better and more promising every day." A month later, Horsey was still drawing raves. But the Reds already had a workhorse starting rotation, so O'Day didn't need to be in a hurry to use rookie pitchers.

On Apr. 27, at Pittsburgh, the Reds were down 11-0 after four innings. O'Day summoned Horsey for the fifth to make his major league debut, which did not go well for him. He retired the first batter, Alex McCarthy, on a foul pop to first baseman Dick Hoblitzell before pinch-hitter Mike Simon singled to center. Horsey got Howie Camnitz, the Pittsburgh pitcher, on a fly to right for the second out but then the order turned over – Bobby Byrne doubled and both runners scored on a single by Max Carey. Tommy Leach finally ended the inning with a popup to second base. Horsey gave up two more runs in the Pittsburgh sixth: The damage in that inning was largely inflicted by Honus Wagner, who singled, stole second base, was bunted to third, then scored on a double steal with McCarthy, who had reached on a walk. The Pirates again scored twice in their seventh, and then the roof really collapsed for Horsey in the eighth, when 12 Pirates came to the plate and six scored. O'Day let Horsey absorb it all, but the rookie at least had the satisfaction of picking Wagner off third base for the second out in the 8th.

Horsey's less-than-stellar outing obviously dulled the hopes O'Day had for him in spring training. He kept Horsey with the club, but off the mound in competition, until May 21, when he was, according to the *Enquirer*, "released to the Altoona club of the Tri-State League." He would spend the rest of the season pitching for Altoona, Reading, and after a trade, Allentown. Horsey turned in a composite 12-9 record in 26 games for those three teams after his demotion from Cincinnati.

He opened the 1913 season still in the Tri-State League with Allentown but was soon on the move again to yet another Tri-State League club, the Trenton Tigers. Horsey remained with Trenton for 1914, this time playing some right field and third base in addition to pitching. He finished the 1914 season 9-7 in 20 games pitched; his time as a position player was less successful – a .115 average in 61 at-bats. Horsey would spend the next four years bouncing between Class-B and Class-D league teams, with varying levels of success. After that it was back home to the Maryland Eastern Shore and local semipro baseball. He managed a town team in Centreville in 1921, until club financial difficulties ended that venture.

By 1925 he had found a new focus in baseball – umpiring – and stuck with it to become a baseball lifer. He got his start as an arbiter with the original six-team Eastern Shore League (Class D), which folded after the 1927 season. He then did some college umpiring and worked in the Mid-Atlantic League and the New York-Pennsylvania League after it began play in 1933, but when the Eastern Shore League (ESL) regrouped as an eight-team circuit in 1937, Horsey returned and by 1940 was the league's chief umpire.

He became a protégé of American League umpire Bill McGowan (who was inducted into the Baseball Hall of Fame after umpiring in the American League for 30 years) and an instructor with McGowan's winter umpire school in Florida. Three future major-league umpires – Jim Boyer, Jim Honochick, and Frank Dascoli – did their early work under Horsey's tutelage in the Eastern Shore League.

Ed Nichols, a veteran sportswriter, saluted Horsey as "a thoroughly honest and excellent umpire who knew every rule in the book and how to apply it. He had plenty of color and none of it yellow." Horsey retired from umpiring after the 1948 Eastern Shore League season, telling Nichols: "Probably Bill McGowan would give me a job in some league, but I'm tired of it all, the daily grind gets to a fellow."

BEST DAY (BY WPA OR OTHER MEASURE): His major league career lasted one game, in which he was tagged for 14 hits and 12 runs in four innings. Given his successes in the minors, the one game in the majors wasn't his "best day" as a professional ballplayer, but it will have to do. He made it into the major league baseball register and only ~18,000 people can say that.

THE WONDER OF HIS NAME: You've got alliteration. You've got what might be considered a child's name for an equine. His surname gives an entirely new meaning to "Horsey rides."

NOT TO BE CONFUSED WITH: Henry Horsey (American judge who served on the Delaware Supreme Court from 1978-1994), Tommy Dorsey (American jazz trombonist, composer, conductor and bandleader of the big band era), Leo Gorcey (American stage and movie actor who became famous for portraying the leader of the group of young hooligans known variously as the Dead End Kids, The East Side Kids, and as an adult, The Bowery Boys).

FUN ANAGRAMS: "Hanson Horsey" turns into "He's a horny son."

EPHEMERA: 1) Hanson Horsey was the third of four sons of Thomas Hopewell Horsey and Mary Elizabeth "Mollie" Raisin Horsey. His brothers were Unit Raisin Horsey (named after Mollie's father), Thomas Hopewell Horsey, and Palmer Keene Horsey. 2) During the 1912 season (during which he played his single big league game), Hanson got engaged to Marian Lockerman of Millington, Maryland. Over their 36-year marriage they had one child, Hanson Horsey Jr.

JOSH JUDY
From that baseball powerhouse Indiana Tech

BIRTH NAME: Josh Steven Judy
PRONUNCIATION OF DIFFICULT PARTS: None
NICKNAME: None
HEIGHT/WEIGHT: 6'4" 210 lbs.
BORN: Feb. 9, 1986, in Morgantown, West Virginia
POSITION: Pitcher
YEARS ACTIVE IN THE MAJORS: 2011
NAME ETYMOLOGY/DEFINITIONS: "Josh" is a truncated variant of "Joshua," which means "God is salvation" in Hebrew; it is borne in the Bible by the Israelite leader who took command of the Children of Israel after the death of Moses and led them, after many battles, to take possession of the Promised Land. It is derived from the Hebrew "Yehoshua." The name was a common alternative form of the name "Yēšūă" which corresponds to the Greek "Iesous," from which, through the Latin "Iesus," comes the English spelling Jesus. "Steven" (and its more common variant) "Stephen" are derived from Greek Stéphanos, a first name from the Greek word *stéphanos*, meaning "wreath, crown" and by extension "reward, honor, renown, fame," from the verb *stéphein*, "to encircle, to wreathe." As a surname, "Judy" may be an Americanized spelling of the French surname "Judet," a pet form of "Jude."

J osh Judy played his high school baseball for University H.S. in Morgantown, leading them to the West Virginia state baseball tournament for the first time in over 40 years. He also helped lead the Morgantown Post 2 American Legion team to the Mid-Atlantic Regional. He played collegiate baseball at Indiana Tech, where he was coached by former Reds farmhand Randy Stegall. After an All-American season, Judy was selected in the 34th round (1034th pick overall) of the 2007 Major League Baseball Draft.

He made the standard "level per year" progression through the minors, strictly as a reliever. During his first three years in the minors, he held batters to less than a hit per inning, less than a home run per nine innings, and a K/9 rate that zoomed from 7.5 to 11.7. There was some conjecture as to whether Judy would break camp with the big club to start 2010. The thought was that Judy would be one of the first non-rostered relievers – if not the first – to be called up during the season. Unfortunately for him, an injury at the end of spring training – he pulled a muscle in his arm and strained the UCL in his right elbow – shelved him for the first month and a half of the season. The injury set Judy back and opportunity knocked for other non-rostered relievers.

"It was my last outing of spring training," Judy recalled about the injury. "I got through the first inning no problem and got two outs in the second inning but the last guy I threw a slider and I just felt something tighten up and a pull feeling. I ended up finishing the inning and then got shutdown from there. It was probably bound to happen eventually as it was only a matter of time. I had been on a high up to that point and that kind of slowed everything down."

After the 2010 season split between AA Akron and AAA Columbus, Judy was added to the Indians' 40-man roster to protect him from the Rule 5 draft. Before the 2011 season started, there were still high hopes for Judy as the potential "next big thing" in the Tribe bullpen. He was a pretty talented and projectable relief pitcher armed with two plus pitches, a fastball that sat 91-93 and touched 96, and a wicked slider. He had all the makings of a big-league bullpen arm, potentially in the backend because of his aggressiveness and bulldog mentality.

On May 21, 2011, Judy was called up from AAA Columbus. He made his Major League debut a day later in the Indians' 12-4 home victory over the Reds. He pitched a scoreless ninth inning, allowing two hits and striking out one batter. Four days later, after seeing action in only that one game, Judy was sent back to Columbus. Judy was recalled on July 1 and made his second appearance against the Reds two days later. He gave up his first run, a home run to Édgar Rentería, in two innings. One more appearance two days later, then it was back to the minors until the September call-ups. September saw him get fairly regular work, as he made nine appearances during the month. But he was hit early and often during his outings. In those nine appearances covering ten innings, he yielded ten runs on 14 hits, walking three, hitting four batters and allowing three more homers. Altogether, in 12 games with the Indians, he posted a 1.571 WHIP and a 7.07 ERA. Judy was designated for assignment on Dec. 16 and was claimed off waivers by the Reds a week later.

In 2012 with the Reds' AAA Louisville Bats club, he was 2-2 with a 6.99 ERA in 40 games, allowing 68 hits in 56⅔ innings. He was released on Nov. 5, 2012. After beginning 2013 with the York Revolution of the Atlantic League of Professional Baseball, Judy signed a minor league contract with the Los Angeles Angels of Anaheim, splitting the rest of the season between the AA Arkansas Travelers and the AAA Salt Lake Bees.

Judy signed a minor league contract with the Los Angeles Dodgers for 2014 and was assigned to the AAA Albuquerque Isotopes. In 23 games, he was 2-2 with a 5.79 ERA. While with the Isotopes, he fractured his elbow while delivering a pitch. After spending 2015 with the York Revolution and playing in the Mexican Winter League, Judy signed with the Tigres de Quintana Roo of the Mexican Baseball League for the 2016 season. He appeared in 50 games, finishing with a record of 3-4 with a 1.20 ERA.

Judy signed a AAA contract with the Seattle Mariners in January 2017 but was released that March. Three weeks later, Judy signed with the Sultanes de Monterrey of the Mexican Baseball League, but they released him in early May. He cycled through a few more signings and releases in Mexican leagues, before once again signing with the York Revolution for the 2019 season.

BEST DAY (BY WPA OR OTHER MEASURE): His big-league career lasted all of 12 games totaling 14 innings, all in relief, primarily in mop-ups/blowouts, with a 7.07

ERA. In his 12 appearances, there were only one "clean" (no baserunners) one. So, let's pump that one up a bit. On Sep. 11, 2011 against the White Sox, he threw 11 pitches in relief of the boringly named Joe Smith, who himself had relieved Ubaldo Jiminez, who had 11 losses coming into the game. Sadly, Judy did not get to face Omar Vizquel, who wore number 11 for the White Sox that day. Also, the game started at … 1:12 (drat, missed it by a minute). Judy entered the game in the bottom of the eighth with the Indians leading 7-2. He retired the difficult-to-spell A.J. Pierzynski on a flyball to deep center, then got Dayan Viciedo on a similar flyball, and ended the inning by inducing a pop fly to short from Alex Rios.

THE WONDER OF HIS NAME: You must love the short, snappy name and the alliteration. Bonus points for being a name made up of two first names, and those two typically assigned to different genders no less.

NOT TO BE CONFUSED WITH: Josh Booty (Former third baseman for the Marlins), Punch and Judy hitter (A hitter with very little power. The first use of the term is attributed to Dodgers manager Walter Alston who, when asked about a home run by Willie McCovey, said: "When he belts a home run, he does it with such authority it seems like an act of God. You can't cry about it. He's not a Punch and Judy belter."), Judyville (A small unincorporated community in Liberty Township, Warren County, Indiana, founded by John Finley Judy).

FUN ANAGRAMS: Josh Steven Judy turns into "He just vends joy." or "Joy! Jesus! Then V.D."

EPHEMERA: 1) Only three baseball players have ever been drafted from the school, and Judy is the only one to make it to the majors. 2) In 2011, *Baseball America* considered Judy's slider the best in the Indians organization.

JAIR JURRJENS
Curaçao's first pitcher to make the Majors

BIRTH NAME: Jair Françoise Jurrjens
PRONUNCIATION OF DIFFICULT PARTS: jah-YEER JER-gehnz
NICKNAME: None
HEIGHT/WEIGHT: 6'1" 200 lbs.
BORN: Jan. 29, 1986, in Santa Maria (Willemstad), Curaçao
POSITION: Pitcher
YEARS ACTIVE IN THE MAJORS: 2007-2014
NAME ETYMOLOGY/DEFINITIONS: Jurrjens was named "Jair" after the Biblical judge Jair by his mother Esther. In the Biblical Book of Judges, Yair (meaning "he enlightens") was a man from Gilead of the Tribe of Manasseh, east of the River Jordan, who judged Israel for 22 years. "Françoise" is the female version of "François," originally an ethnic name meaning "Frenchman." The meaning of "Jurrjens" is a mystery wrapped in an enigma encased in a conundrum, but the surname appears to be most popular

in the Netherlands. (The Kingdom of the Netherlands currently consists of four constituent countries: the Netherlands, Aruba, Curaçao, and Saint Maarten.)

Jair Jurrjens was signed as an undrafted free agent by the Tigers in 2003. In seven games during his 2003 campaign with the Gulf Coast League Tigers, Jurrjens posted a 2–1 record with 20 strikeouts and just three walks in 28 innings. After a subpar 2004 campaign in Oneonta, Jurrjens broke out in the 2005 season with the West Michigan Whitecaps, the Tigers' single-A affiliate. In 26 games (all starts), Jurrjens went 12–6 with 108 strikeouts and 36 walks in 142 innings. He was a mid-season Midwest League All Star with West Michigan.

Jurrjens joined fellow Curaçao native Andruw Jones on the Netherlands national baseball team for the 2006 World Baseball Classic. Jurrjens pitched one inning against Puerto Rico in the WBC, giving up three runs and earning himself a loss.

He continued to improve during the 2006 season, starting off 5–0 with a 2.08 ERA for the Lakeland Tigers, resulting in him being named to the Florida State League mid-season All Star team. Jurrjens was then promoted to the Erie SeaWolves, the Tigers' AA affiliate. In 12 games with the SeaWolves, Jurrjens went 4–3 with a 3.36 ERA, with 53 strikeouts in 67 innings.

Jurrjens made his major league debut on Aug. 15, 2007, starting for the Tigers against the Indians. In that game, he gave up four earned runs in seven innings, taking the loss. He recorded his first major league win in his next start, also against the Indians, allowing only one run on one hit in 6⅔ innings pitched. In October 2007, Jurrjens and outfielder Gorkys Hernandez were traded to the Braves for shortstop Édgar Rentería. *Baseball America* rated Jurrjens as the Braves' 3rd-best prospect entering the 2008 season.

Jurrjens pitched well for the Braves during the first half of the 2008 season, compiling a 9–4 record with a 3.00 ERA. He was named National League Rookie of the Month of June. But Jurrjens appeared to tire during the second half of the season, going 4–6 with a 4.66 ERA after the All-Star break. Overall, Jurrjens finished his rookie season with a record of 13–10 and a 3.68 ERA in 188 innings. He finished third in voting for the 2008 NL Rookie of the Year award, behind Geovany Soto and Joey Votto.

Jurrjens again pitched very well in the first half of 2009, going just 7–7 but posting an excellent 2.91 ERA in 19 starts. Unlike 2008, there was no drop-off in the second half for Jurrjens, as he went 7–3 with a 2.24 ERA in 15 starts. He was named Pitcher of the Month in September. Overall in 2009, Jurrjens went 14–10 while finishing third in the National League with a 2.60 ERA in 215 innings and tying for the league lead with 34 games started.

Jurrjens went 7–6 with a 4.64 ERA in 2010, a season in which he dealt with some health problems. He underwent arthroscopic surgery for a torn meniscus in his right knee in October, having missed September and Atlanta's appearance in the National League Division Series with pain in his knee.

Jurrjens began the 2011 season on the disabled list but got off to a strong start after he was activated. He was named Pitcher of the Month in May. Jurrjens led the National League in wins and ERA at the All-Star break and was chosen to play in his first All-Star Game. He pitched 1⅔ scoreless innings in the NL's 5–1 win.

Following the All-Star break, Jurrjens went 0–1 with a 6.26 ERA in four starts. On Aug. 6, the Braves placed him on the 15-day DL due to pain in his surgically repaired right knee. He returned briefly but did not play for the Braves in September.

Jurrjens got off to a poor start in the 2012 season, while suffering from a strained groin, with an 0–2 record and a 9.37 ERA in his first four starts. On Apr. 23, he was optioned to the Braves' AAA affiliate in Gwinnett, his first demotion in five seasons with the Braves. On June 22, Jurrjens was called back to the majors by the Braves, but for the season, he posted a 6.89 ERA, and he was not tendered a contract for the next season by the Braves, thereby becoming a free agent.

The next year saw the beginning of Jurrjen's multiple years of "transaction porn." First, he agreed to a minor-league deal with the Orioles. Jurrjen's contract was purchased from the AAA Norfolk Tides on May 18. He made his first start with the Orioles on that day, pitching five innings and picking up a no-decision. He was optioned back to Norfolk twice more over the next six weeks, before finally being designated for assignment by the Orioles on July 12. Jurrjens opted for free agency instead of playing in AAA and became a free agent on July 18. Six days later, Jurrjens was signed to a minor league deal bringing him back to Detroit. Jurrjens was quickly optioned to the AAA Toledo Mud Hens. More transactions ensued: on May 20, 2014, Jurrjens signed a minor league deal with the Reds. On July 2, Jurrjens was traded to the Rockies. Jurrjens made his 2014 season debut on July 4, pitching 4⅔ innings and allowing eight runs on 12 hits. After the start, Jurrjens was taken to the hospital to be checked out after experiencing breathing difficulties during his start. He said "It was super scary. Every time I needed to take a deep breath, I couldn't do it." (The altitude at Coors Field may have played a role.) Jurrjens was designated for assignment on July 21 and was re-signed to a minor league contract.

Jurrjens began 2015 with the Rockies AAA affiliate, the Albuquerque Isotopes, but was released in August after posting a 2-5 record and a 6.88 ERA in 17 games. For 2016 he signed with the Uni-President 7-Eleven Lions of the Chinese Professional Baseball League. He was on the disabled list twice, once with a groin injury, and was 6-7 with a 5.38 ERA. He was released in August.

Jurrjens played for Team Netherlands in the 2017 World Baseball Classic. In March 2017, he signed a minor league contract with the Dodgers, appearing in 11 games (10 starts) for the AAA Oklahoma City Dodgers, going 4–3 with a 4.64 ERA. In June, he was suspended 80 games for testing positive for exogenous testosterone.

Jurrjens signed with the Tigres Del Licey in the Dominican Winter League for the 2017-18 season. During 2018, Jurrjens played for the Long Island Ducks of the independent Atlantic League of Professional Baseball. He became a free agent following the 2018 season. And … exhale.

BEST DAY (BY WPA OR OTHER MEASURE): On July 1, 2011, while pitching for the Braves as they hosted the Orioles at Turner Field, Jurrjens had the game of his life. He faced two batters over the minimum in a complete-game 4-0 shutout. The only blemishes were a leadoff walk of Mark Reynolds in the top of the sixth and a one-out single by Adam Jones in the seventh. He struck out eight.

THE WONDER OF HIS NAME: It's a double unique, with alliteration! It's also subject to mispronunciation if you don't know any better, especially the "Jair" part. There is also the coolness factor of the Francoise middle name.

NOT TO BE CONFUSED WITH: Jergens (Brand of various skin care products), jerkin (A man's short close-fitting jacket, made usually of light-coloured leather, and often without sleeves, worn over the doublet in the 16th and 17th centuries), Kenji Johjima (Japanese former professional baseball player. He was a catcher for four years with the Seattle Mariners in the American League, then returned to Japan and played for the Hanshin Tigers).

FUN ANAGRAMS: "Jair Francoise Jurrjens" turns into "Jar-Jar confers injuries."

EPHEMERA: 1) Jurrjens became the seventh man born in Curaçao to make the majors when he made his debut in August of 2007. He was the first Curaçao-born pitcher to make the big leagues. 2) In 2002, Jurrjens' Curaçao Senior League team won the Senior League World Series in Bangor, Maine. 3) Jurrjens was asked prior to a game in 2008 about how he felt facing his fellow countryman Andruw Jones that day. Jurrjens said, "It's going to be fun to face him," then said "It's going to be even more fun to strike him out." Jurrjens then went on to strike Jones out all three times he faced him. 4) Jurrjens speaks English, Spanish, Dutch and Papiamentu. 5) Jair's wife Kaylin was a 2018 participant on *WAGS Atlanta*, a reality TV series that chronicles the professional and personal lives of "Wives And Girlfriends of Sportspersons."

GREG LEGG
Lifelong Phillie

BIRTH NAME: Gregory Lynn Legg
PRONUNCIATION OF DIFFICULT PARTS: None
NICKNAME: None explicitly listed, though he himself answers to "Legger" and uses Legger as part of his email address
HEIGHT/WEIGHT: 5'7" 165 lbs.
BORN: Apr. 21, 1960, in San Jose, California
POSITIONS: Pinch Hitter, Second Baseman, Shortstop
YEARS ACTIVE IN THE MAJORS: 1986-1987
NAME ETYMOLOGY/DEFINITIONS: "Gregory" derives from the Latin name "Gregorius," which came from the late Greek name "Grēgorios" meaning "watchful, alert" (derived from Greek *grēgorein* meaning "to watch"). Through folk etymology, the name also became associated with Latin *grex* (stem greg–) meaning "flock" or "herd."

This association with a shepherd who diligently guides his flock contributed to the name's popularity among monks and popes. "Lynn" is of uncertain origin: possibly an altered short form of "Linda," or a derivative of the French name "Line," which originated as a short form of various girls' names ending in this syllable, for example "Caroline." "Legg" has English (chiefly West Country) origins, as the metonymic nickname for someone with some malformation or peculiarity of the leg, or just with particularly long legs, from Middle English legg (Old Norse *leggr*).

Greg Legg graduated from Duncan H.S. in Oklahoma and attended Southeastern Oklahoma State University, playing four seasons for the Savages. (The NCAA deemed the team's nickname to be inappropriately referencing Native Americans, so in 2006 they changed it to "Savage Storm," which, given the propensity for dangerous weather in Oklahoma, may not have been the best choice either.) In all four years, the team competed in the NAIA Baseball World Series. Legg was a two-time All-American and was named to the all-district team three times.

After college, Legg was drafted by the Phillies in the 22nd round of the 1982 draft and assigned to the Peninsula Pilots, the Phillies' A-level affiliate in the Carolina League, where he played alongside future Philadelphia Baseball "Wall of Fame" members Darren Daulton and Juan Samuel. For the Pilots he hit .343; he didn't hit for power (and never really would), but did walk more than he struck out.

Legg, Daulton, and Samuel were all promoted together to the Eastern League's Reading Phillies in 1983. Legg posted a .317 average for the season, the second-best mark among the team's regular batters. In the field, he appeared in at least one game at all four infield positions, with most coming at shortstop and third base.

The Phillies shifted Legg primarily to second base for the 1984 season; he appeared in 57 games at the position for Reading before a promotion to the Portland Beavers. In the first half of the season for Reading, Legg batted only .241 in 224 at-bats. After moving to the Beavers, Legg also hit .241, this time in 141 at-bats.

Playing for Portland in 1985, Legg increased his power, hitting a career-high seven home runs (albeit in 470 plate appearances across 115 games). He added seven triples and eleven doubles to his total for a tally of 25 extra-base hits, which added up to a mediocre .393 slugging percentage.

In 1986, Legg began the season in Philadelphia with the Phillies, appearing in three April games. He made his major league debut against the Mets, entering in the seventh inning of an Apr. 18 contest as a defensive replacement for second baseman Luis Aguayo. He notched his first two major league at-bats against the Mets on Apr. 20, while striking out once. His first hit came on Apr. 27, a pinch-hit against the Pittsburgh Pirates in a 13–5 Phillies loss, after which he was sent back down to Portland.

Appearing exclusively at second base, Legg logged 120 games for Portland, committing only four errors and compiling a .994 fielding percentage. As a hitter, he batted .323, the best mark on the team among the regular players, and led the Beavers with 66 RBIs. He returned to the big leagues as a September call-up, appearing in eight games after Sep. 1.

Legg spent most of the 1987 season in AAA with the Maine Guides, for whom he batted .241 (seems to be a popular number for him). In the big leagues for the Phillies, he appeared in one game each at second base, third base, and shortstop, scoring one run in two at-bats over the three games. He would never make it back to the majors after that, leaving him with a career .409 batting average (9-for-22).

Legg would continue to play in the Phillies minor league system, with varying degrees of achievement, through 1994. After retiring from playing, Legg stayed with the franchise, moving to the Clearwater Phillies as their hitting coach for 1994 and 1995; the team finished with the Florida State League's best record in his second year. In 1996, he was the hitting coach for the Scranton/Wilkes-Barre Red Barons that season, when the team posted a 70–72 record. In 1997, Legg was given his first managing position, leading the Batavia Clippers to the New York–Penn League finals, where they lost to the Pittsfield Mets. He's been a manager or coach in the Phillies system ever since.

BEST DAY (BY WPA OR OTHER MEASURE): His big-league resume consists of 14 games and 22 plate appearances ... so the pickings are mighty slim. Legg only started three games in his career. He went 2-4 in one of them, 2-3 in another and 3-5 in the one that we're exploring here. (Maybe he should have started more often?) Legg's best day came towards the end of the 1986 season, with the Phillies playing out the string way behind the buzzsaw Mets in the NL East. The Phils were hosting the last place Pirates on Sep. 16, with the Buccos sending Mike Bielecki to the mound against Philly's Marvin Freeman. In the first inning with a runner on third and no out, Legg singled to center, scoring Milt Thompson, who had walked, stolen second and gotten to third on a wild pitch. The Phils carried that 1-0 lead to the bottom of the second, and with Thompson on first and Steve Jeltz on second with one out, Legg lofted a flyball to right field, deep enough to allow Jeltz to get to third, but Philly couldn't bring the runners in. The squads traded three-run outbursts in the third inning, and Legg led off the fourth against reliever Bob Walk by doubling to right. After a Von Hayes walk and a Mike Schmidt groundout that moved both runners up, Glenn Wilson tripled them home to give Philly a 6-3 lead. Walk was still in for Pittsburgh in the fifth when Legg hit another long fly ball that ended up advancing two runners (Jeltz and Thompson again). The Pirates closed to within 6-5 in the top of the sixth, but Philly then put up another three-spot in their half. With the score still 9-5 in the bottom of the seventh, Legg singled to center with one out, but was then erased on a double play. That ended his day at the plate, and Philadelphia would end up winning by a score of 9-5. Legg's ledger: five at-bats, two singles, a double, a run scored and another driven in. The RBI and double would each be the only ones in his career. The three hits were a career high for Legg, and one-third of his career total. In the field that day he made two assists and four putouts at second.

THE WONDER OF HIS NAME: A short sweet name with a rhyme, and a last name that could be the alternate spelling for a body part to boot!

NOT TO BE CONFUSED WITH: Pegleg (Prosthesis, or artificial limb, fitted to the remaining stump of a human leg. Its use dates to antiquity), Keg Leg (A social 5km fun run/walk to local breweries and distilleries finishing with a fun after party with great food and beer in Victoria, British Columbia). L'eggs (Brand of pantyhose introduced in 1969 by Hanes. The hosiery placed its product in white plastic oversized chicken-egg-shaped containers).

FUN ANAGRAMS: "Gregory Lynn Legg" anagrams to "Rely groggy Glenn."

EPHEMERA: 1) He is married to the former Norine Laboranti with three children (Jenna, Tory, Cooper). 2) In February 2010, Legg established the Northeast Pennsylvania Diamond Scholarship Award, a $1,000 award presented annually to a high school baseball player from Luzerne or Lackawanna Counties in Pennsylvania. 3) Perhaps the best-known baseball player to come from Southeastern Oklahoma State University is 17-year major leaguer Brett Butler. 4) In 1996, Legg was inducted into the Southeastern Oklahoma State University Athletic Hall of Fame.

ORVAL OVERALL
Brilliant for a short period of time

BIRTH NAME: Orval Overall
PRONUNCIATION OF DIFFICULT PARTS: None
NICKNAME: Big Groundhog, given his huge frame compared to others of that era, and because of his Feb. 2 birthday. He was an agriculture student in California when he received the nickname.
HEIGHT/WEIGHT: 6'2" 214 lbs.
BORN: Feb. 2, 1881, in Farmersville, California
DIED: July 14, 1947, in Fresno, California
POSITION: Pitcher
YEARS ACTIVE IN THE MAJORS: 1905-1910, 1913
NAME ETYMOLOGY/DEFINITIONS: The name "Orval" is of Old English derivation, meaning "spear-strong." "Overall" is also of Old English derivation. As an adjective it means taking everything into account, and as a noun it refers to a garment consisting of trousers with a front flap over the chest held up by straps over the shoulders, made

of sturdy material and worn especially as casual or working clothes. In other words, the garment "covers all."

Orval Overall was born just outside of Visalia, California. After pitching and playing first base at Visalia H.S., the 19-year-old Overall enrolled at the University of California in the fall of 1900. Overall was a star in both football and baseball at Cal. On the gridiron he played guard, fullback, and punter, serving as varsity captain as a senior. In baseball, Orval performed most of the mound work as a freshman, pitching well but suffering from occasional mental lapses.

Perhaps an early indicator of the arm troubles that would plague him in later years, he missed time from pitching due to a sore arm in both his sophomore and junior seasons. During those times Overall played left field, first base, and sometimes even catcher, though he inevitably returned to pitching as the seasons wore on and his arm rounded into shape. In his junior year he entertained an offer to play baseball for a living with the San Francisco Seals of the PCL, but decided to continue his education instead.

To his father's great disappointment, Overall finally did leave Cal to go professional in early 1904, signing with Tacoma of the PCL for a salary of $300 a month, more than many veteran players earned at the time. Orval helped Tacoma win the 1904 pennant by registering a 32-25 record during the long PCL season. Cincinnati scout Fred Hutchinson wanted the former collegian and outbid the Cubs for Overall's services.

As a rotation regular for the Reds in 1905, Overall compiled an 18-23 ledger with a 2.86 ERA, pitching 318 innings and ranking fifth in the National League with 42 appearances. He returned to Cincinnati in 1906 but got off to a poor start, going 4-5 with a 4.26 ERA, and on June 2 the Reds traded him to the Cubs for pitcher Bob Wicker, a 50-game winner over the prior three seasons.

Meanwhile in Chicago, Cubs manager Frank Chance knew that the young pitcher's problem was that Cincinnati manager Ned Hanlon had been overworking him. Pitching less frequently in Chicago, Orval responded by going 12-3 with a 1.88 ERA for the remainder of the 1906 season.

His breakout season was 1907, when he tied Christy Mathewson for the NL lead in shutouts (8) and finished second in wins (23), third in winning percentage (.767) and fewest hits per game (6.74). Overall's performance led the Cubs to the World Series against the Detroit Tigers, and he received the start in Game 1 against Wild Bill Donovan. Though he ended up with a no-decision in what turned out to be a 3-3 tie, Orval came back in Game 4 three days later and beat Donovan, 6-1, putting the Cubs up three games to none on their way to a sweep.

During the 1908 season, his record fell to 15-11, as he was hampered by arm trouble for much of the regular season, but he did lead the NL in strikeouts per game (6.68) and finished fifth in fewest hits per game (6.60). In the 1908 World Series Overall once again matched up against the Tigers and Donovan, going the distance in Games

Two and Five and winning by scores of 6-1 and 2-0. One of the keys to his success in the 1907-08 Series was holding Ty Cobb to a .125 average.

In 1909 Overall put together his finest season, going 20-11 while leading the National League with career bests in shutouts (9), strikeouts (205), and opponents' batting average (.198). He also finished third in ERA (1.42) and fewest hits per game (6.44). Despite Overall's banner season, the Cubs failed to reach the World Series for the first time since he joined the team in 1906.

They returned to the Fall Classic in 1910, but by that time Orval had a sore arm, having gone 12-6 with a 2.68 ERA in just 144⅔ innings during the regular season. He didn't pitch competitively in 1911 or 1912, but his arm had healed enough to attempt a comeback in 1913. Returning to the Cubs, Overall went 4-5 with a 3.31 ERA, giving up more than a hit an inning for the first time in his career. After a short stint with San Francisco in the PCL, he retired from professional baseball at age 32. He compiled a lifetime 108-71 record and 2.23 ERA, the eighth-best ERA in major-league history.

BEST DAY (BY WPA OR OTHER MEASURE): On Oct. 14, 1908, in game five of the World Series, Overall pitched a complete-game three-hit shutout, striking out ten Detroit Tigers to help the Cubs clinch the Series. His ten Ks are still the most by a Cubs starting pitcher in a World Series game.

THE WONDER OF HIS NAME: There are 11 letters in his name (no middle name), yet there are only six unique letters. This however is not the fewest unique letters to appear in an 11-letter ballplayer's name in history. That record is five, set by folks including Pee Wee Reese and Josh Johnson. Orval Overall is another great alliterative ballplayer name, and the less-common spelling of Orville, along with having a piece of clothing as your last name, equals a winner. (Eat your heart out Brandon Belt.)

NOT TO BE CONFUSED WITH: Orville Redenbacher (American businessman and popcorn purveyor), Deborah Norville (*Inside Edition* anchor), Park Overall (actress).

FUN ANAGRAMS: "Orval Overall" nets "Roll over lava."

EPHEMERA: 1) In the first inning of that 1908 Series-clincher, he became the first pitcher to strike out four hitters in one inning in a playoff game, a feat not duplicated until 2013 by Aníbal Sánchez of the Tigers. 2) Immediately after retiring from baseball, Overall took a job with the Maier Brewery Company, but the following year his father became ill and he took control of the family's citrus farm. 3) In 1918 he ran for Congress but failed to gain election. 4) After his father died in 1921, Orval sold off the estate's numerous holdings, making him a wealthy man. He became an appraiser and a director of the First National Bank of Visalia, which later merged into the Security-First National Bank of Los Angeles. Overall continued to hold prominent positions, eventually rising to vice-president of the bank and manager of the Fresno branch. 5) In 1936 he was elected a director of the California State Automobile Association. 6) Overall's father was at one time a hotelkeeper. One wonders if his dad asked departing guests if they liked their "Overall experience."

RON RIGHTNOWAR
"Scab" during the 1994-1995 players strike

BIRTH NAME: Ronald Gene Rightnowar
PRONUNCIATION OF DIFFICULT PARTS: None
NICKNAME: None
HEIGHT/WEIGHT: 6'3" 190 lbs.
BORN: Sep. 5, 1964, in Toledo, Ohio
POSITION: Pitcher
YEARS ACTIVE IN THE MAJORS: 1995
NAME ETYMOLOGY/DEFINITIONS: "Ronald" is derived from the Old Norse "Rögnvaldr." In some cases, "Ronald" is an Anglicised form of the Gaelic "Raghnall," a name likewise derived from "Rögnvaldr." The latter name is composed of the Old Norse elements *regin* meaning "advice," "decision" and *valdr* meaning "ruler." Ronald was originally used in England and Scotland, where Scandinavian influences were once substantial, although now the name is common throughout the English-speaking world. "Gene" is a common shortened form of "Eugene," which comes from the Greek *eugenēs* meaning "noble," literally "well-born," from *eu* meaning "well" and *genos*, referring to "race, stock, kin." "Rightnowar" is a bit of a mystery, although the ballplayer listed his ancestry as a mixture of German, Irish, English and American Indian.

Ron Rightnowar graduated from Whitmer H.S. in Toledo, and then played baseball at Eastern Michigan University. After college, Rightnowar was signed by the Tigers as an amateur free agent in September of 1986. In 1987, Rightnowar spent the entire season pitching for the Fayetteville Generals in the Single-A South Atlantic League, going 7-7 in 39 appearances, mostly in relief, striking out 65, walking 37, saving six games and posting a 4.96 ERA.

In 1988, Rightnowar was promoted to the Lakeland Flying Tigers in the High-A Florida State League, where he went 2-0 in 17 games with a 1.46 ERA, 32 strikeouts and just 11 walks in 49⅓ innings pitched. In 1989, Rightnowar advanced to AA ball, pitching for the London Tigers and going 2-8 with a 5.00 ERA in 36 appearances. Rightnowar saved five games that season.

The following year, Rightnowar divided his time between three Detroit Tigers minor-league teams: London (2-2, 3.25 ERA, 33 strikeouts, nine walks) the Class-A Niagara Falls Rapids (one appearance), and the AAA Toledo Mud Hens (4-5, 4.74 ERA, 28 strikeouts, ten walks with 38 innings pitched in 28 games). In 1991, Rightnowar split the season between London (2-1, 3.91 ERA) and Toledo (1-1, 3.94 ERA). The following year, Rightnowar played solely for his hometown Mud Hens and continued his role as a middle reliever, posting a 3-2 record but a high 6.16 ERA. He pitched 57 innings in 34 games, picking up three saves, striking out 33 and walking 18. In 1993, Rightnowar began the season with Toledo again, going 2-2 with a 3.55 ERA in 58⅓ innings pitched. On Aug. 28, 1993, the Detroit Tigers traded Rightnowar to the Milwaukee Brewers for a player to be named later.

In 1994, with the Brewers' AAA New Orleans Zephyrs, Rightnowar's pitching improved dramatically. He went 8-2 with a 2.25 ERA in 51 games, pitching 88 innings, striking out 79, walking just 21 and saving 11 games. Rightnowar did not receive a September call-up because major-league baseball players went on strike on Aug. 12, 1994.

As the 1995 baseball season neared, Rightnowar was asked by the Brewers' coaches if he would be interested in being a replacement player in the 1995 season. "The major-league coaching staff made it clear that I needed to pitch," Rightnowar told the *Ottawa Citizen* later in 1995. "They said they needed to see me and see what I could offer the club." While Rightnowar did pitch in some spring-training games (which was enough for the major-league baseball players union to classify Rightnowar and all such players as strike-breakers or "scabs"), he was sent down to New Orleans once the strike ended, and started the 1995 season pitching for New Orleans.

After pitcher Cal Eldred went on the disabled list for the rest of the season, the Brewers promoted Rightnowar to the major leagues on May 19, 1995. He was to be the first replacement player to join the Brewers' big-league club that season. Before he even threw a pitch, Rightnowar was given a frosty reception from the major-leaguers. "My first day, everyone was kind of cold toward me," Rightnowar told the *Ottawa Citizen* in 1995. "I understood. I respect their right to be angry. But then I called the leaders on the club and asked to speak to the team. I wanted to tell them my side of the story."

Rightnowar allowed that there was some bitterness for him in what should have been a happy moment. "It really stunk, to be honest with you," Rightnowar told the Toledo Blade in 2005. "From the time I was 8 or 9 years old, I had dreamed of what the day would be like if, and when, I ever made it to the big leagues. I figured it would be a real special day in my life, just like the day I got married. But I felt awful. They were all giving me the cold shoulder."

Ultimately, Rightnowar explained his reasons for crossing the picket lines. "For about 20 minutes, they fired questions and took shots at me," he told the Blade. "I told them they could call me 'scab' or whatever. But I told them I hoped they respected my decision. This was my one shot and I knew it." Rightnowar, who at 30 was in his ninth season in the minors when promoted, met with the players so both sides could express their feelings. Bob Scanlan, a Brewers starting pitcher, said many of the players were upset that the club did not call up a player who had declined to be a replacement. Manager Phil Garner explained that Rightnowar was the most effective reliever in the organization when the Brewers made the move. Scanlan said he thought the players' meeting helped ease some of the tension created by the move.

"It gave him a chance to give his side of the story and why he made the decision he did and gave the other players a chance to express themselves and say why they were disappointed in what he did," Scanlan said. "I don't know that I would say it cleared the air, but it gave everyone an opportunity to say what they had to say."

At the time, Scanlan said he believed that many players didn't want replacement players to be accepted as union members. As for acceptance as teammates, he said: "There will be some guys who will never accept a replacement player. Others will grudgingly accept his presence on the team, give him respect as a teammate but probably not seek to spend time with him off the field. And there may be other guys who may totally accept him like any other player. It's each individual's decision."

On May 20, 1995, Rightnowar made his major league debut, working 2⅓ innings of scoreless relief against the Texas Rangers. He stayed with the Brewers until Aug. 5, when he was sent back down to New Orleans, and then rejoined the Brewers on Sep. 6. Rightnowar ended his Brewers season and, it turned out, his major-league career, with a 2-1 record, a 5.40 ERA, 22 strikeouts, 18 walks, and one save in 36⅔ innings pitched in 34 games. In October, Rightnowar was granted free agency. No major-league teams showed an interest, so he retired.

BEST DAY (BY WPA OR OTHER MEASURE): On May 22, 1995, with the Brewers visiting the Indians, Rightnowar won his first big-league game, pitching two innings of relief and giving up one earned run. He entered the game in the fourth inning, as starter Angel Miranda was in the midst of leaking oil and seeing a 7-1 lead start to slip away. Rightnowar came in with no out and runners on the corners with the score now 7-3. He got Tony Pena to strike out, yielded an RBI groundout to Kenny Lofton, then induced an inning-ending groundout from Omar Vizquel. In the bottom of the fifth, still protecting a 7-4 lead, he gave up a single to Carlos Baerga before getting Albert Belle to rap into a 3-6-1 double play and then struck out Eddie Murray. In the sixth, he gave up a leadoff double to Manny Ramirez, hit Dave Winfield with a pitch, and walked Jim Thome to load the bases. He was relieved by Scott Karl, who got out of the inning with only one run crossing the plate. As Miranda hadn't pitched the minimum five innings to qualify for the win, the official scorer credited it to Rightnowar. "That first major-league victory – man, what a great feeling!" Rightnowar told reporters after the game. "This is really special."

THE WONDER OF HIS NAME: Maybe we should save the talk about Rightnowar for later? I'll at least make note of his name's alliteration and "time stamp" qualities. What do we want? Rightnowar! When do we want him? Er ... right now-ar.

NOT TO BE CONFUSED WITH: *Right Now* (Rock song written by the group Van Halen from their album *For Unlawful Carnal Knowledge*), Oracle RightNow (Customer relationship management software service for enterprise organizations originally developed by RightNow Technologies, which was acquired by Oracle in 2011).

FUN ANAGRAMS: "Ronald Gene Rightnowar" becomes "Oh dear ... tenor wrangling."

EPHEMERA: 1) In 1997, Rightnowar was hired as admissions director at Toledo Christian Schools and later became its "spiritual life director." He also has co-owned a sports training center, coached a nine-team travel baseball league and been head varsity baseball coach at Genoa H.S. in Ohio. 2) Currently, he is a "mortgage originator" at Genoa Banking Company. 2) In 2014 he was inducted into the Fellowship of

Christian Athletes Hall of Fame. He had formerly been the Northeast Ohio Director for the organization.

SIBBY SISTI
You had to check your scorecard to see what position he was playing that day

BIRTH NAME: Sebastian Daniel Sisti
PRONUNCIATION OF DIFFICULT PARTS: None
NICKNAME: Sibby
HEIGHT/WEIGHT: 5'11" 175 lbs.
BORN: July 26, 1920, in Buffalo, New York
DIED: Apr. 24, 2006, in Cheektowaga, New York
POSITIONS: Second Baseman, Third Baseman, Shortstop, Outfielder
YEARS ACTIVE IN THE MAJORS: 1939-1942, 1946-1954
NAME ETYMOLOGY/DEFINITIONS: "Sebastian" comes from the Latin name "Sebastianus" meaning "from Sebastia," which was the ancient Greek name of the city now known as Sivas, located in the central portion of what is now Turkey. The name of the city is derived from the Greek word *sebastos* meaning "venerable," and *sebastos* itself comes from *sebas* meaning "awe, reverence, dread," in turn from the verb *sebomai* meaning "feel awe, scruple, be ashamed." Sebastos was the Greek translation of the title Augustus, which was used for Roman emperors. "Sebastian" grew in popularity as a name because it was the name of Saint Sebastian, a third-century Christian martyr. "Daniel" is a given name and a surname of Hebrew origin. It means, "God is my judge," and derives from two early biblical figures, primary among them Daniel from the Book of Daniel. "Sisti" is a name of mostly central and northern Italian origin, as a plural form of "Sisto." The name "Sisto" has roots all the way back to the Latin *sixtus* or *sextus*, meaning "sixth" or "sixth-born." The name "Sibby" originated from the Greek language and is sometimes used as a name for a female or girl, but in most cases (as it is here) it's a shortened form/nickname for "Sebastian."

At the beginning of Sibby's senior year at Buffalo's Canisius H.S., his father went along with Boston Bees'[2] Buffalo-area scout Jack Onslow – a former big-leaguer himself who would later manage in the majors – to meet Bees

---

[2] The National League Boston-based franchise was known as the Braves from 1912-1935. They became the Bees from 1936-1940, then went back to the Braves from 1941-1952, prior to moving to Milwaukee.

officials. The Bees had taken a liking to Sisti. Sibby didn't know about the meeting until he got a call from his dad informing him that he had been signed to a contract with the Bees' Class A Eastern League club in Hartford, Connecticut. The speedy right-handed batter hit .293 for Hartford in 1938, playing a sure-handed third base for manager Eddie Onslow (brother of the scout who signed him). He was invited to spring training next year, but when the Bees broke camp, Sisti went back to Hartford, this time to play second.

One day in June of 1939, Boston shortstop Eddie Miller and outfielder Al Simmons ran into each other going after a Texas Leaguer. Miller broke his ankle, and this on top of other injuries forced the club to call for reinforcements. Sisti was batting .312 at Hartford, and on July 21, 1939, 18-year-old "Sebbi" (as some newspapers then called him) suddenly found himself up with the Bees as the youngest player in the majors. That same afternoon at Braves Field, he made his first trip to the plate in the ninth inning of a tight game against the Cubs. Boston trailed 3-1; a reported crowd of just 2,797 was on hand to witness the moment. At the suggestion of manager Casey Stengel, he attempted to beat out a bunt and was unsuccessful.

The Bees were a seventh-place club that wasn't drawing well, so there was little pressure on Sibby to excel right away. Casey had patience and liked Sisti, getting him into 63 games that season. Although Sisti batted just .228 with one homer and 11 RBIs in 215 at-bats, the youngster showed his versatility by playing at second, short, and third. Quick and steady defensively, he clearly made an impression; when the 1940 season began, Sisti was Boston's starting third baseman

Sibby held down the job at third the next two seasons, hitting a more respectable .251 and .259 although he still showed little power and made an alarming 44 errors in 1941 alone (41 of them at third; the most by a National League third baseman in 32 years). The Braves continued to plod along near the cellar.

The arrival of rookie Nanny Fernandez to play third base prompted Sisti's shift to second in 1942, and even though his average plummeted to .211, he got into 129 games. It seemed nothing could keep Sisti down with Stengel around, but WWII did the trick – and Sibby lost the 1943-1945 seasons while serving with the Coast Guard. Stengel was fired during this same period, making the task of winning back a spot on the Braves that much harder for Sibby after the war.

Sisti recalled, "Billy Southworth was now managing the club, and he told me to work out at third, so I did. I lasted until Opening Day, when he told me he was sending me down to Indianapolis to learn how to play shortstop. I told him I was signed as a shortstop, and I sure knew how to play shortstop. But it didn't do any good; they still sent me down."

Back in the minors. Sisti earned *The Sporting News* Minor League Player of the Year Award after leading AAA in batting (.343), hits (203), and triples (14), while scoring 99 runs and knocking in 86.

Sisti headed back up to the majors in 1947, signing a contract with the Braves for what newspapers reported as "a nice raise in pay," and then earning a role as starting shortstop on an improving team. Unfortunately, in mid-July Sibby ran to field a grounder, lunged for it, landed on his left shoulder, suffered three ruptured ligaments, and was sidelined for more than a month. To repair the damage, muscle was grafted from his left leg to strengthen his shoulder, a procedure which required 24 stitches on his leg and 20 on his shoulder. Sisti wound up playing just 56 games in 1947, batting .281.

In 1948 Sibby once again fought for a spot in the regular lineup. The club had called up Alvin Dark from minor-league Milwaukee to play short, and Sisti battled hard with the much-heralded rookie before Southworth declared Sibby the starter just a day before the Apr. 20 opener at Philadelphia.

Eventually, Dark outplayed Sisti at shortstop. Dark wound up batting .322 and being named Rookie of the Year, and Sisti was back on the bench – but not for long. Second baseman Eddie Stanky broke his ankle on July 8, and manager Southworth turned to Bob Sturgeon then Connie Ryan and finally Sisti (in early August) to replace Stanky.

Sisti kept the job the rest of year with steady play in the field and at the plate (hitting near .300 down the stretch). Still, when Stanky returned in late September, Sibby was sent to the bench for the World Series against Cleveland.

In the ninth inning of the Game 6, with the Indians up three to two in games, Sisti, an adept bunter, was called upon by Southworth to pinch-hit and move the potential tying run from first base to second in a 4-3 game. His bunt attempt resulted in a double play instead, as catcher Jim Hegan caught his pop-up and threw to first to double off Connie Ryan. One out later, the Indians were champions.

That winter, he was honored at a Boston baseball writers' dinner with a plaque and a pair of cleats for "filling the shoes" of Stanky during the summer just past, and drew shouts of "No, no!" when he tried to take the blame at the podium for his team's Series defeat. "It was the best thing that ever happened to me in Boston," Sibby later said of the outpouring of gratitude.

In 1949, with Stanky back at second and Dark entrenched at short, Sisti resumed his role as "Super Sub" – capable of filling in at any infield or outfield spot. Southworth liked to platoon, and that summer Sibby saw almost equal time in the outfield, second base, and shortstop as well as one game at third base. It was more of the same the next three years; no one position to call his own, but plenty of action at a variety of spots. All told, his career of 1,016 games included 359 at second base, 290 at third, 209 at short, 74 in the outfield, and two games at first. He was never again a full-time starter after 1948, but he did get into 114 contests in 1951, batting a solid .279.

In 1951 and 1952 he helped develop his young roommate Johnny Logan into one of the National League's best shortstops. But as Logan progressed, Sisti and the team slumped. Sibby's average fell off to .212 in 1952, and the Braves finished seventh with a woeful 64-89 record. Just 281,278 fans showed up at Braves Field, a far cry from the 1,455,439 who had packed the stands to watch the NL champs just four years before.

Still, Sisti was shocked like almost everybody else on the club by what transpired the next March. The team had spent spring training in Bradenton, Florida, as usual, and there was hope that Boston would be a much-improved club with promising youngsters like Logan, third baseman Eddie Mathews, and catcher Del Crandall. In mid-March, news broke that the Boston Braves were going to be moved to Milwaukee. It was only two weeks before Opening Day, and Sisti said the concept of going to Milwaukee was "as green as apple pie to me." (In other words, he didn't care for it.) He had been in Boston nearly 13 years, and he may as well have just stayed there. He had only 23 at-bats during the team's first season in Wisconsin, and appeared in nine games as a defensive replacement (with no at-bats) in 1954 before being released and then re-signed as a coach at age 35.

Sisti was asked to manage in the minors for the Braves, and later spent a decade at the helm of farm clubs in Québec, Corpus Christi, Austin, and Sacramento. For several of these campaigns he was a player-manager. Sibby became an infield-outfield instructor with Phillies minor leaguers for a couple of seasons, coached with the expansion Seattle Pilots in 1969, then shortly thereafter quit the game and returned home to get a "real job" as a truck driver.

BEST DAY (BY WPA OR OTHER MEASURE): On July 31, 1948 the first-place Braves went into the bottom of the ninth trailing 6-3 against the Cardinals, one of three teams on their tail in the standings. It was 6-4 with the bases loaded when Sisti came up as a pinch-hitter with one out. Sisti rocked a pitch to deepest right-center at Braves Field. As UPI described the action, "The 31,841 fans stood and cheered at the top of their voices for more than a solid minute as three Tribal base runners flashed around the bases and Sisti, utility infielder, slid madly into third ... by winning, the Braves maintained a 5½-game lead over the now second-place Giants, a 6½-game bulge over the third-place Dodgers, and eight games over the fourth-rung Redbirds."

THE WONDER OF HIS NAME: Alliterative names are always fun, and the rhythm in the utterance of "Sibby Sisti" is pleasing to the ear.

NOT TO BE CONFUSED WITH: Chris Christie (Former governor of New Jersey), Dave Giusti (One of only 14 pitchers with 100 or more wins and 100+ saves in a career), Scooter Libby (Dick Cheney's Chief of Staff).

FUN ANAGRAMS: "Sebastian Daniel Sisti" turns into "It is sensible as in data."

EPHEMERA: 1) Sisti had his initial big-league tryout for the Boston Red Sox at age 15 in 1935. He donned a Red Sox uniform and took hitting and fielding practice under the eye of Sox manager Joe Cronin. 2) He had a small role in the 1984 film *The Natural*, portraying the Pittsburgh manager. He was also a consultant on the film, ensuring that it captured the feel of 1930s baseball. 3) He was one of the first four players inducted in the Boston Braves Hall of Fame, alongside Hall of Fame pitcher Warren Spahn and All-Stars Johnny Sain and Tommy Holmes. 4) Sisti is the only "Sebastian" to ever suit up in the majors. 5) In 2001, he was selected for the Greater Buffalo Sports Hall of Fame.

SCIPIO SPINKS
Named for a warrior, but his own body let him down

BIRTH NAME: Scipio Ronald Spinks
PRONUNCIATION OF DIFFICULT PARTS: Sip-ee-oh or Skip-ee-oh
NICKNAME: None
HEIGHT/WEIGHT: 6'1" 183 lbs.
BORN: July 12, 1947, in Chicago, Illinois
POSITION: Pitcher
YEARS ACTIVE IN THE MAJORS: 1969-1973
NAME ETYMOLOGY/DEFINITIONS: "Scipio" is Latin, meaning "staff" or "a walking stick." Scipio Spinks is named after the great Roman general Scipio Africanus the Elder, who defeated Hannibal during the Second Punic War. "Ronald" is derived from the Old Norse "Rögnvaldr." In some cases, "Ronald" is an Anglicised form of the Gaelic "Raghnall," a name likewise derived from "Rögnvaldr." The latter name is composed of the Old Norse elements *regin* (meaning "advice," "decision") and *valdr* ("ruler"). "Ronald" was originally used in England and Scotland, where Scandinavian influences were once substantial, although now the name is common throughout the English-speaking world. "Spinks" is of Middle English origin. It derives from the medieval word *spink* meaning a chaffinch, which is a small bird. As such it was originally given as a nickname to one who was thought to have borne a fancied resemblance to the colorful if noisy bird, or more likely as a metronymic to a professional singer, one with an attractive singing voice.

In 1966, Spinks signed with the Houston Astros. Only several weeks after he turned pro, he set a Northern League (short season A-ball) record by striking out 20 batters in a game. He obviously had a live arm but control was a problem. From 1966 through 1971 in the minors, he averaged 5.9 walks for each nine innings pitched. He also struck out 9.7 men and allowed just 7.1 hits.

In 1969 he played for AAA Oklahoma City and his record was poor on the surface: 7-11, 5.48. An emblematic game came on May 8: He let in his first run on a walk, a bad pickoff throw, and two wild pitches; the second came on two walks and a passed ball. Nonetheless, the Astros called him up when rosters expanded, and he made his big-league debut on Sep. 16, 1969, at San Diego Stadium. After a shaky start – a walk, a single, and a passed ball – Spinks struck out the last four batters he faced in his two innings.

Returning to Oklahoma City in 1970, Spinks went 9-12, but his ERA improved to 3.30 and he struck out 153 while walking 77 in 158 innings. He also pitched five games for the Astros in May.

At Oklahoma City in 1971, he went 9-6 and he struck out 173 in 133 innings. Although the control issue flared up again, Houston called him up for five more games in September.

On Apr. 15, 1972 – Opening Day – the Astros traded Spinks and lefty pitcher Lance Clemons to the Cardinals for pitcher Jerry Reuss. Initially, Spinks made the deal look good for the Cardinals. While he was just 5-4 in his first 15 starts, he suffered two tough losses to the Dodgers. On June 3, he lost a 1-0 duel at Dodger Stadium to Don Sutton. Ten days later in St. Louis, he lost 2-1 to Tommy John as Manny Mota stole home in the sixth inning. Scipio pitched six complete games, including impressive back-to-back outings on the road against the Mets – with a career-high 13 K's – and the Phillies in late June. At the end of June, the rookie trailed only Steve Carlton and Tom Seaver for the National League lead in strikeouts.

On Independence Day, however, his fortunes changed. In the top of the third inning at Riverfront Stadium in Cincinnati, Spinks singled. One out later, Luis Meléndez doubled, and the pitcher ran through a stop sign. He scored, but in the play at the plate, he tore ligaments in his right knee upon impact with Johnny Bench's shin guards. Scipio missed the rest of the season.

Spinks reported to spring training 1973 in good health and typical form as a jokester. For example, he played with autograph seekers in camp by wearing number 20 as a Lou Brock impostor. At the start of the regular season, he lost four of his first five starts, and was effective only in a no-decision against the Dodgers (also marked by his only big-league homer, off Al Downing).

After missing most of May with a sore arm, he got his last major-league win, over Cincinnati, on May 29. He took only two more turns after that, which turned out to be his last appearances in the majors. After going on the disabled list with a bum shoulder, the Cardinals recalled him in September, with an eye toward giving him limited action, but he never got out of the bullpen.

In 1974, the Cardinals traded the Chicagoan back home, receiving veteran outfielder Jim Hickman from the Cubs. He was sent down to their AAA affiliate. He spent 1974 and 1975 in the minors, bothered off and on by a sore arm. That was the end of his career as a baseball player.

After that, Spinks became a scout and a pitching coach in the Padres and Astros organizations. He currently is a pro scout for the Diamondbacks.

BEST DAY (BY WPA OR OTHER MEASURE): In the first game of a double-header at Shea Stadium on June 25, 1972, Spinks pitched a complete-game six-hitter, striking out a career-high 13 (while also walking six). The Cardinals won the game 7-1.

THE WONDER OF HIS NAME: Of course, he gets points for alliteration, and then you also give him massive props for being named after a somewhat obscure historical figure.

NOT TO BE CONFUSED WITH: *Sussudio* (Song by Phil Collins that reached No. 1 on the Billboard charts), *Serpico* (1973 film directed by Sidney Lumet and starring Al Pacino, about Frank Serpico, who went undercover to expose corruption in the police force.), C-3PO (Humanoid robot character from the *Star Wars* franchise).

FUN ANAGRAMS: "Scipio Ronald Spinks" anagrams to "Prick in old passions."

EPHEMERA: 1) His father shared the unusual given name, which is a long-running tradition in the Spinks family. "Every firstborn son on my father's side has been named Scipio," Spinks said. 2) In that Aug. 26, 1966, Northern League game in which Spinks struck out 20 batters, the opposing pitcher was future Reds star Gary Nolan. Nolan himself fanned 17. (Neither was around to get a decision, though). A total of 41 men struck out. 3) Late in the 1969 season, *Sports Illustrated* wrote, "Spinks ... also established himself as a blithe spirit by stealing the feathery headdress from the Brave mascot, Chief Noc-A-Homa." 4) During Spring Training in 1973, Scipio's closest "teammate" was a large stuffed gorilla. He had bought the toy in a Houston hotel gift shop early in the 1972 season and dubbed it Mighty Joe Young. Clad in a Cardinals batboy uniform, Joe roomed with Spinks on the road and lived in his clubhouse locker at home. The pitcher had great fun investing his companion with human traits. Joe also proved popular for radio and TV show appearances, community meetings, and hospital visits. Ultimately the other Cardinals grew fond of the ape, but not before Joe suffered assorted indignities at their hands – Bob Gibson pulled off his nose, while the team hung him from the rafters in Pittsburgh. They also stuffed him in the clubhouse dryer before Scipio's career day versus the Mets. 5) In 1980, Spinks was the pitching coach at Jackson State University in Mississippi. Among his pupils were two future major leaguers: Marvin Freeman and Dennis "Oil Can" Boyd. 6) One of his favorite tales from the road was about how he beat a speeding ticket thanks to his radar gun. The traffic cop was using a JUGS gun, but Scipio's model showed both the JUGS and SRA (typically lower reading) systems – with a gap between the two readings. He convinced the officer: "See, I wasn't going 65. I was only going 60." "Oh, OK. Have a nice day." 7) Former Reds pitcher Wayne Simpson is his cousin.

UGUETH URBINA
From the pen to the penitentiary

BIRTH NAME: Ugueth Urtain Urbina
PRONUNCIATION OF DIFFICULT PARTS: Ooo-GETT Ooor-bee-NAH
NICKNAME: Oogie
HEIGHT/WEIGHT: 6'2" 185 lbs.
BORN: Feb. 15, 1974, in Caracas, Venezuela
POSITION: Pitcher
YEARS ACTIVE IN THE MAJORS: 1995-2005
NAME ETYMOLOGY/DEFINITIONS: "Urbina" is a habitational name from Urbina in Araba province, Basque Country, or a topographic name probably for someone who lived near a confluence, from Basque *ur* meaning "water" and *bi* meaning "two." "Urtain" is a village in the Basque section of Spain. As for "Ugueth" that is still a mystery, as no reference sources list that name.

Ugueth Urbina made his major league debut as a 21-year-old in 1995, appearing in seven games for the Expos, and went 2–2 with a 6.17 ERA. In 1996 he established himself on Montreal's pitching staff, getting into 33 games, including 17 starts and a what would be a career-high 114 innings, posting a 10–5 record with a 3.71 ERA. Urbina's pitches included a moving fastball and a slider that enabled him to hold left-handed hitters in check. He also threw a changeup which tailed away from right-handers and a splitter that broke sharply.

His career as a closer began in 1997, when he collected 27 saves with a 3.78 ERA and a 5-8 record in 63 relief appearances. Urbina improved in 1998, going 6-3 with 34 saves and a 1.30 ERA in 64 games. In 1999 he topped the National League with 41 saves, while notching a 6-6 record and a 3.69 ERA in 71 contests. The 2000 season was curtailed by surgery to remove bone chips in his elbow, limiting him to 13 appearances and eight saves.

Urbina started the 2001 season well, going 2-1 with a 4.24 ERA while notching 15 saves in 45 games before being traded to the Boston Red Sox on July 31. Urbina appeared in 19 games with Boston, saving nine with a 2.25 ERA. Urbina earned his second All-Star berth in 2002, when he recorded 40 saves and had a 3.00 ERA in 61 games.

He signed as a free agent with the Rangers at the end of 2002 and had 26 saves and a 4.19 ERA in 39 games for that team in 2003 before being traded in midseason to the Marlins. For the remainder of that season, Urbina served as a setup man for Marlins closer Braden Looper, going 3-0 with six saves and a 1.41 ERA in 33 games.

Urbina finished his short stint with the Marlins by helping them win the 2003 World Series title, defeating the New York Yankees in six games. In what would turn out to be his only post-season experience in his career, he went 1-0 along with four saves and a 3.46 ERA in ten games in 2003.

Next it was onto the Tigers. In 54 games in 2004, he went 4-6 with 21 saves and a 4.50 ERA. He began the 2005 season in good form, with a 2.63 ERA and nine saves, but then in June found himself on the move again for the third time in his career, traded to the Phillies. Urbina went 4-6 with a 4.13 ERA and just one save in 56 games for Philly. Overall in 2005, he posted a 5-6 record with 10 saves and a 3.62 ERA in a career-high 81 games. He would make what would turn out to be his last major league appearance on Oct. 2, 2005, during a 9–3 Phillies victory over the Washington Nationals at RFK Stadium.

Before the 2006 season came around, Urbina would find himself in jail (see "Ephemera" for more details). A two-time All-Star during his 11 major league seasons, Urbina finished with a 44–49 record, 237 saves, 814 strikeouts, and a 3.45 ERA.

BEST DAY (BY WPA OR OTHER MEASURE): Though he had more statistically impressive days, Urbina's best day might have been on Oct. 15, 2003, in game seven of the National League Championship Series against the Chicago Cubs. Urbina came on in the bottom of the ninth to protect a 9-6 lead. He hit the first batter he faced (Aramis Ramirez), then recovered to strike out Randall Simon and Alex Gonzalez before inducing Paul Bako to fly out to left to send the Marlins to the World Series.

THE WONDER OF HIS NAME: All those U's! The "Oogie" nickname! The "double uniqueness" of his name! The mystery of the origin of his first name!

NOT TO BE CONFUSED WITH: *Boogie Oogie Oogie* (Disco song by A Taste of Honey from their 1978 self-titled debut album), Luis Ugueto (Player that had a couple of cups of coffee for the Seattle Mariners in 2002 and 2003).

FUN ANAGRAMS: "Ugueth Urtain Urbina" turns into "Ugh! Urinate ... ruin tuba!"

EPHEMERA: 1) In November 2005 Urbina was arrested by Venezuelan authorities on a charge of attempted murder for an incident that occurred a few weeks previous. Urbina attacked five farm workers on his property whom he had accused of stealing a gun. The pitcher came after the men with a machete and attempted to pour gasoline on them. On Mar. 28, 2007, Urbina was convicted of attempted murder and sentenced to more than 14 years in prison. He was released in Dec. 2012. 2) He is the only player in major league history with the initials UU or UUU. 3) He pitched an "immaculate inning" (striking out the side on nine pitches) as a member of the Expos on Apr. 4, 2000. Pitching the ninth inning against the Dodgers, he set down F.P. Santangelo, Devon White and Mark Grudzielanek in order on three strikes each. 4) In 1994, Urbina's father was murdered during a robbery attempt. 5) In September 2004, Urbina's mother was kidnapped and held for a $6 million ransom in southwest Venezuela. Urbina's family refused to pay the ransom and an anti-kidnapping unit rescued her in a military-style operation in February 2005. 6) Urbina has a son Juan who pitched in the Mets organization but never made it past short season single-A for the Brooklyn Cyclones. 7) There is at least one more U-named person in the Urbina clan, as Ugueth has a brother named Ulmer.

Dirty Names
Done Dirt Cheap

GENE BRABENDER
Hard-throwing righthanded country boy

BIRTH NAME: Eugene Mathew Brabender
PRONUNCIATION OF DIFFICULT PARTS: BRAH-bender
NICKNAME: His teammates in Baltimore called him "Animal"
HEIGHT/WEIGHT: 6'5" 225 lbs.
BORN: Aug. 16, 1941, in Madison, Wisconsin
DIED: Dec. 27, 1996, in Madison, Wisconsin
POSITION: Pitcher
YEARS ACTIVE IN THE MAJORS: 1966-1970
NAME ETYMOLOGY/DEFINITIONS: "Eugene" is from the Old French form of the Greek name "Eugenios" (from *eugenēs* meaning "noble" or "well-born"). "Mathew" is a variant of "Matthew." It ultimately derives from the Hebrew name "Matityahu" which means "Gift of Yahweh." "Brabender" has German and Dutch origins, as the ethnic name for a native of Brabant (a region in The Low Countries, the Low Land or historically also the Netherlands), or an occupational name for a mercenary. This German family name is fairly common in Wisconsin, especially in Dane County, which turns to picturesque farm country as one travels west of the state capital.

In high school, Gene Brabender was a defensive tackle and running back; and as a punter and kicker, his booming leg got him attention from college recruiters. He didn't start to pitch in high school until his senior year; previously he played first base and outfield.

Brabender gained baseball experience playing in Wisconsin's Home Talent amateur league, where he once broke an opponent's jaw in a game with a pitch that got away. (He broke down and said he would never pitch again before the batter got up, put his arm around Gene, and consoled him.) Major-league scouts took notice of the young fireballer, thanks to Black Earth High coach Don Oscar, who sent letters to all 16 teams alerting them. Eventually he was signed for a $10,000 bonus by the Dodgers.

As a result, Gene quit college. The hulking 19-year-old left in March 1961 for spring training at Dodgertown in Vero Beach. The following month, he headed west for Great Falls, Montana in the Pioneer League (Class C). After posting a record of 2-3 with a 6.33 ERA in his first eight games as a pro, Brabender took a step back to Class D. With Orlando in the Florida State League, he went 4-10, with a 5.01 ERA in 20 games. Control was his major issue: while he struck out 100 batters, he walked 119 in 115 innings (mostly as a starter).

Brabender remained in the Florida State League in 1962. His record was 9-14, his ERA improving to 3.20. He fanned 204 men in 191 innings but was still very wild, walking 139 and unleashing 37 wild pitches. That fall, the Dodgers sent him to the Instructional League in Arizona. In 1963, with Salem, Oregon (Class A), the young hurler showed even greater promise. Gene went 15-10 with a 3.30 ERA and led the Northwest League with 223 strikeouts, though he still walked 108. His 16 complete games also topped the league, but it was all or nothing with Brabender that year, as he averaged only three innings in his other 15 appearances.

He was promoted to Albuquerque in the AA Texas League, making five relief appearances (1-0) and notching eight more Ks in four innings. He remained impressive in the Arizona Instructional League, striking out 38 in 33 frames with a 2-0 record and 1.64 ERA.

Gene's career was interrupted as he spent the 1964-1965 seasons in the Army, where he was an MP and played some baseball at the Aberdeen Proving Ground in northeastern Maryland. Scouts from Houston, Pittsburgh and Philadelphia saw him there, but Aberdeen was in the backyard of Baltimore, and their influential Orioles scout Walter Youse recommended him. When Brabender returned to his baseball career, it was with the Bóer Indians in the Nicaraguan League. The Nicaraguan season began in early November 1965, and on Nov. 29, the Orioles selected him in the Rule V draft.

When Brabender reported to the Orioles camp in spring 1966, pitching coach Harry Brecheen ordered him to throw just fastballs and sliders and to keep the ball down. Orioles manager Hank Bauer, who had previously called Gene a "sleeper," said, "I'm thinking about him as a long reliever now. But if he shows he can get the ball over the plate, he could be a short reliever too. He sure throws the ball hard and he's really tough on righthanders. He might be a lifesaver." By the time Bauer used his rookie, it was May 11, minutes before the roster cutdown deadline. (In those days, clubs were permitted to carry 28 players for the season's first month.)

In his big-league debut, Bender entered in the tenth inning against the White Sox at Memorial Stadium. He pitched a scoreless tenth but a walk, a single and a hit batsman loaded the bases to start the 11th, before he balked home the eventual winning run. He took the loss despite striking out four in his two innings of work.

Brabender's first victory in the majors came on June 8. It was a doubleheader, and the first game went 14 innings. In the nightcap, as the clock struck midnight, a local curfew in Washington, D.C. caused a suspension in the Orioles half of the sixth. Play resumed the next day with Brabender (who had relieved Steve Barber in the third inning) still on the mound. The O's rallied in the eighth to earn Brabender the win. Brabender finished the year at 4-3 with a 3.55 ERA.

From Dec. 1966 through Feb. 1967, Brabender was in Venezuela, with the La Guaira Tiburones. He finished that winter league season at 13-7, 2.45, tying for the league lead in wins with Jim McGlothlin. He also had 147 strikeouts in 161 innings. Luis Tiant defeated Brabender in both Game 1 and Game 4 of the championship series as Caracas took the five-game series 3-2.

Despite his excellent showing that winter, Gene did not make the Baltimore staff to open the 1967 season. He was sent to AAA Rochester near the end of spring training. He went 8-6, 2.77 in the International League. The Orioles recalled him in July as their staff was beset by injuries. Over the rest of the season, Gene was a regular in the rotation (6-4, 3.35 in 14 starts). Dodgers general manager Buzzie Bavasi said that year, "If we ever made a mistake, it was letting Brabender get away."

Gene spent the entire 1968 season with Baltimore, as a swingman (6-7 record, 3.31). His best outing came in his first start, in which he fired a six-hit shutout against the Senators at D.C. Stadium – also connecting off Dennis Higgins for his first of two major-league homers.

In December 1968, the Orioles acquired Mike Cuellar from Houston, a crucial trade that would help establish them as a power in the American League for several seasons. The team already had a lot of good pitching, but now they were even deeper in starters. Thus, near the end of spring training in 1969, Baltimore sent Brabender and Gordy Lund to the expansion Seattle Pilots for Chico Salmón.

One of the reasons Brabender got dealt was that he had reported late to spring training and had gotten little work. In addition, there was concern for Gene's conditioning, which turned out to be the wrong kind of workout: The muscleman had spent the winter hoisting 150-pound crates of carp in Sturgeon Bay, Wisconsin.

Gene got off to a slow start with the expansion Pilots, working mainly in relief. Toward the end of May, though, he rounded into form as a starter: the first time he faced Baltimore after the trade, we went all the way in an 8-1 win. Then in a three-week stretch starting in mid-June, he racked up four more complete-game wins in five starts. In the first of these games, at Yankee Stadium, Brabender and the Pilots won 2-1. Eight days later, versus Kansas City at home, he threw his only shutout of the season – with a beer in the clubhouse between each inning (as a fluid replenishment strategy?). Brabender finished the year as the club's leading winner (13-14 record), pitching a career-high 202 innings with a 4.37 ERA. One reason, in his view, was that Seattle let him bulk up. Whereas he had to keep his weight down to 220-230 pounds with the Orioles, "I weighed about 248," he noted at the start of 1970.

Brabender was mentioned often throughout the pages of Jim Bouton's *Ball Four*: "We were talking about what to call Brabender when he gets here. He looks rather like Lurch of the *Addams Family*, so we thought we might call him that, or Monster, or Animal, which is what they called him in Baltimore last year. Then Larry Haney told us how Brabender used to take those thick metal spikes that are used to hold the bases down and bend them in his bare hands. 'In that case,' said Gary Bell, 'we better call him Sir.' ... Gene Brabender sometimes walks around bellowing 'cowabunga!' ... He looks like if you got a hit off him, he'd crush your spleen."

After just one year in Seattle, the Pilots moved to Milwaukee. Unfortunately, even with family rooting him on at County Stadium and the presence of many local friends, the season was a big disappointment. He suffered an early leg injury and from a sore shoulder. "Big Bra" – articles from this period indulge in dreadful lingerie-based puns – couldn't throw his hard sinker or his slider, as reflected in his 6-15 record and 6.02 ERA.

In January 1971, the Brewers traded Brabender to the Angels for outfielder Bill Voss. The Angels assigned him to AAA Salt Lake City, where he went just 1-4, 8.36. Clearly still hurting, he pitched just 27 innings in 13 games and barely appeared at all after May. His biggest thrill as an Angel was meeting club owner Gene Autry; as a boy, Brabender had idolized "The Singing Cowboy."

In the spring of 1972, Gene returned for a last chance with Salt Lake. Although he said his arm felt great again, a later report said it hadn't really improved. The Angels cut him in early April, and he then retired to "spend more time with family."

BEST DAY (BY WPA OR OTHER MEASURE): The best game of his career came on Aug. 7 of 1967 against the Cleveland Indians in Memorial Stadium in Baltimore, when he pitched a complete-game four-hit shutout and struck out 12 while walking three. All four hits were singles.

THE WONDER OF HIS NAME: "Whoa here he comes ... watch out girl he'll unhook you up ... whoa here he comes ... he's a brabender." A litany of lingerie-based puns can be generated from his name, regardless of the origin of that surname.

NOT TO BE CONFUSED WITH: Ozzie Van Brabant (Canadian-born pitcher who got into nine games for the Phillies in 1954-5), Brandon Braboy (Minor league relief pitcher for the Yankees from 2008-2013), bodice-ripper (A sexually explicit romantic novel, usually in a historical setting and always with a plot involving the seduction of the heroine).

FUN ANAGRAMS: "Eugene Mathew Brabender" turns into "Ahem! Degenerate Web burn!"

EPHEMERA: 1) Gene's father Bernard and his mother Cecilia (née Meier) had seven children. Gene's brothers, Darrell and Deane, were roughly five and eight years his junior. Then came twin sisters, Charyl and Charlene, plus two more girls named Karyn and Caryl. 2) As a young boy, on one visit to County Stadium, Gene predicted to his father, "I'll play here someday." 3) During his military duty he received a furlough to marry Karen Gean Zespy of Beloit and Black Earth. 4) Deane Brabender on how his brother struck fear in minor-league hitters. "He wore those thick glasses, and one game it was so hot, and he was sweating so much that he threw away the glasses because he couldn't see. The batter stepped out. The umpire ordered him back in, and the guy said, "Not until he puts them glasses back on!" 5) Brabender owned Frank Howard during their matchups. Howard went just 4-for-25, with 11 strikeouts. Harmon Killebrew was a different story, though: 8-for-19 with five homers. 5) Brabender became the first Wisconsin native to appear for the Brewers. 6) His 13 wins with the 1969 Pilots set a mark for expansion teams that lasted until 1998, when Rolando Arrojo won 14 for the Devil Rays. 7) Right after retiring from baseball, Brabender got into the mobile-home business in Sturgeon Bay. But the business tanked, and his marriage went kaput. He then established a small construction firm, doing concrete work, siding, and other related jobs along with one of his sister Caryl's classmates.

JOHNNY DICKSHOT
The self-proclaimed 'ugliest man in baseball'

BIRTH NAME: John Oscar Dicksus
PRONUNCIATION OF DIFFICULT PARTS: None
NICKNAME: Ugly
HEIGHT/WEIGHT: 6'0" 195 lbs.
BORN: Jan. 24, 1910, in Waukegan, Illinois
DIED: Nov. 4, 1997, in Waukegan, Illinois
POSITION: Leftfielder
YEARS ACTIVE IN THE MAJORS: 1936-1939, 1944-1945
NAME ETYMOLOGY/DEFINITIONS: "John" is originally of Semitic origin. The name is derived from the Latin "Ioannes" and "Iohannes"," "Oscar" is of Gaelic origin, composed of the elements *os* meaning "deer" and *cara* meaning "friend." The name owes its popularity in Scandinavia and elsewhere to the Ossian poems of James MacPherson. "Dicksus" is still a mystery, as various reference

sources come up empty on that name, but he was of Lithuanian and German roots. According to the Apr. 20, 1936 edition of the *Chicago Daily Tribune*, Johnny's father was once erroneously listed on a Waukegan mill payroll as "Dickshot" rather than "Dicksus," so Johnny decided it was good enough for him to carry into his baseball career. However, this story is contradicted by another in the May 18, 1937 edition of the *Republican-Northwestern* newspaper, which reported it was sportswriters that called him "Dickshot" rather than his given name, but after unsuccessful attempts to correct the writers, he decided to stick with that.

A corner outfielder, Dickshot began his professional career in the early 1930s playing for the Milwaukee Brewers, which was at that time a minor league team. After starting the 1936 season with a brief stint on the major league Pittsburgh Pirates (going 2-for-9), Dickshot was sent to AA Buffalo, where he hit .359 and slugged .562 with 15 triples and 17 homers. Returning to the Pirates in 1937, he hit a mediocre .254/.323/.358 in 82 games, mostly playing in left field. In 1938, he again played for the Pirates but only in 29 games, with 43 plate appearances, hitting .229 with no extra-base hits.

Dickshot returned to the International League in 1939 and won the batting title by hitting .355 for Jersey City. In 1940, for Jersey City again, he managed a "mere" .290 average. He moved to the Hollywood Stars in the PCL in 1941. His slash stats in 1941 and 1942 were quite similar, .298/.390/.434 and .303/.384/.409. In 1943, he hit .352 for the Stars and collected at least one hit in each of the first 33 games of the season.

He joined the White Sox in 1944, batting a subpar .253 in 62 games, but had his best major league season in 1945, his last year in the majors, when he had a .302 batting average (third-best in the American League) with 58 RBIs, 10 triples and 18 stolen bases in 486 at-bats. Still, he lost his job when younger players returned from the war. He finished his baseball career with two more seasons at the AAA level, retiring after the 1947 season at age 37.

BEST DAY (BY WPA OR OTHER MEASURE): On May 4, 1937, against the Brooklyn Dodgers, Dickshot had a career day. With two on and no out in the top of the first against Roy Henshaw, he tripled to score teammates Woody Jensen and Paul Waner. He would score on a flyball one out later. One inning later, with Waner again on base, Dickshot sent the ball out of the park, and ended Henshaw's day in the process. Dickshot flew out to left in the fifth, but in the seventh, with one out and Jensen on third, he grounded out to drive in the run. Dickshot himself would later score in that inning. He ended his day with a groundout in the ninth. Bottom line: 2-5, three runs scored and five driven in.

THE WONDER OF HIS NAME: The 12-year-old in all of us appreciates the "naughtiness" of "Dickshot." Throw in the "Ugly" nickname, add the fact that he changed his last name to "Dickshot," and you have an R-rated, four-star moniker.

NOT TO BE CONFUSED WITH: Richard "Dick" Schott (University of Louisville offensive lineman drafted by the NFL's Minnesota Vikings in 1964), "Big Shot" (Second hit single from Billy Joel's 1978 album *52nd Street*), Marge Schott (Managing general partner, president and CEO of the Cincinnati Reds franchise from 1984-1999, banned from running the team by MLB from 1996 through 1998 due to statements in support of German domestic policies of Adolf Hitler), Johnny-on-the-spot (A person who is on hand and ready to perform a service or respond to an emergency).

FUN ANAGRAMS: "Johnny Oscar Dickshot" anagrams into "SOS! Dirty 'John Hancock'."

EPHEMERA: 1) Some reference sources (erroneously) have his last name at birth as "Dickshot." 2) From the 1928 Waukegan H.S. yearbook: "Although this was John's first year out for football, he played a good game. His ability to recover fumbles made him indispensable to the team." (Obviously in 1928 no one had metrics to tell them that fumble recoveries were a totally random event.) 3) To earn extra money in the early years of his baseball career, he worked at a North Chicago steel mill in the off-season. 4) Upon retirement, he opened a tavern in Waukegan, called the Dugout, which he ran from 1947-1977, and then tended bar in the Lithuanian Hall after selling his tavern. 5) His granddaughter, Michelle McDermott, said he would often call his wife at home from the bar, demanding that she look in his encyclopedia to settle a dispute over baseball trivia. 6) He was selected for the Waukegan Sports Hall of Fame in 1975. 7) He threw out a first pitch in the new Comiskey Park in June 1994.

JACK GLASSCOCK
Best shortstop of the nineteenth century

BIRTH NAME: John Wesley Glasscock
PRONUNCIATION OF DIFFICULT PARTS: None
NICKNAME: Pebbly Jack, due to his habit of picking up and tossing away the many small stones he found on the infield during his playing days
HEIGHT/WEIGHT: 5'8" 160 lbs.
BORN: July 27, 1857, in Wheeling, West Virginia
DIED: Feb. 24, 1947, in Wheeling, West Virginia
POSITIONS: Shortstop, Second Baseman
YEARS ACTIVE IN THE MAJORS: 1879-1895
NAME ETYMOLOGY/DEFINITIONS: "John" is originally of Semitic origin. The name is derived from the Latin "Ioannes" and "Iohannes." "Wesley" is from the surname of the founder of the Methodist Church, John Wesley, and his brother Charles, who was also influential in the movement. Their family must have come originally from one or other of the various places in England called

Westley, meaning "the western wood, clearing or meadow." "Glasscock" has English origins, as the habitational name from Glascote near Tamworth in Staffordshire, named from Old English *glæs* meaning "glass" and *cot* meaning "hut" or "shelter;" it was probably once a site inhabited by a glass blower. It also has Welsh origins, as the habitational name from Glascoed in Monmouthshire (Gwent), named from Welsh *glas* meaning "gray" or "green" and *coed* meaning "wood." This name is also found in Ireland and may also have been brought to the U.S. from there. (Glasscock's parents were Scotch-Irish).

C onsidered by many to have been the best shortstop of the 19th century. His contemporary, Al Spink, founder and editor of *The Sporting News*, wrote of Glasscock: "He was acknowledged by all his fellow players to be the greatest in [sic] his position … one of the greatest players from a fielding standpoint the game has ever known."

At 15 he played for the Buckeye Base Ball Club, one of ten amateur teams in the Wheeling area. Before the 1875 season ended, Glasscock was one of three players who joined the Standards, the top club of Wheeling. In 1876 he hit .369 for the Standards. In 1877 the Standards became an independent professional team, the first pro team in West Virginia. The team paid Glasscock $40 a month to play third base.

Before the summer of 1877 ended, Glasscock, still a teenager, left home to play for more money than he could make in Wheeling. He left with a barnstorming team called the Stars but soon joined the Champion Club of Springfield, Ohio.

The next summer found him in Pittsburgh with the Alleghenys of the International League. When that club disbanded in June, he caught on with an independent professional team in Cleveland called the Forest City Club. In 1879 Cleveland entered the National League. His rookie season split between second and third base, Glasscock batted a paltry .209.

He switched to shortstop in 1880, and Glasscock led National League shortstops in putouts, assists, and fielding average in 1881. He followed up leading the NL in assists and double plays in 1882 and fielding average in 1883. In 1883 he batted third in the order, hit close to .290, and tied for the team lead in runs batted in.

When the short-lived Union Association claimed major league status in 1884, Glasscock jumped to the new league. He batted .419 against inferior pitching. It was here a sportswriter named Harry Weldon bestowed the "Pebbly Jack" nickname on Glasscock.

Following the collapse of the Union Association, the National League assigned Glasscock to the St. Louis Maroons for 1885. He was a standout on an otherwise bad team in the two seasons he played in St. Louis. The Maroons paid him well, $2,200 in 1885, and made him captain. Glasscock rewarded them by hitting .325 in 1886. He set NL records in assists in 1885 and double plays in 1886.

After the Maroons folded following the 1886 season, sports pages speculated about which team would land him. *The Sporting News* predicted, "he will get the largest salary ever paid a player." Glasscock claimed Boston offered $7,500 for him, but, of course, the League wanted no free agents and transferred the St. Louis players to Indianapolis. Glasscock's career peaked in his three seasons with the Hoosiers. His fielding continued to excel. He set new major league records for assists and double plays in 1887, and again led the league in fielding in 1888.

The following year he set new marks with 246 putouts and led the league in assists, double plays and fielding average. The 1889 season was Glasscock's finest. He led the majors with 205 hits, and finished second in batting with a .352 average, the highest yet achieved by a shortstop. He ranked second in doubles and total bases, while scoring 128 runs and stealing 57 bases. He even took over as manager.

The Hoosiers had a wretched 25-43 record when he took over. Under his command they went 34-32. Despite the team's success he did not enjoy managing and never did it again. The Indiana experience seems to have considerable stress for Glasscock: back home in Wheeling, he was jailed for being drunk and disorderly; as a manager he drove his players and baited and bullied umpires. After Indianapolis lost its franchise before the 1890 season, Glasscock was transferred to the New York Giants.

With the Giants he won his only major league batting championship, hitting .336 for the 1890 season. He again led the league in hits, the first time anyone had led in back-to-back years. In 1891 he injured his hand and was never the player he was before. He fielded well again in 1893, but he could not throw as he once did. He could still hit, as his .320 average and 100-plus RBIs in 1893 attested. Transferred to Washington, the Nationals released him in 1895 midway through his seventeenth season. After Washington released him, Glasscock returned to Wheeling where he caught on with Ed Barrow's team in the Iron and Oil League. Batting over .400, he led his hometown team to the league championship. It was Glasscock's first pennant. He continued to play in the minor leagues as a first baseman until 1901.

BEST DAY (BY WPA OR OTHER MEASURE): Individual game logs do not exist for that era in baseball history, however, on Aug. 8 of that splendid 1889 season, Glasscock hit for the cycle and on Sep. 27 of 1890, he put together six hits in six at-bats in a game.
THE WONDER OF HIS NAME: His last name sounds like an amazing anatomical attribute, and it helps from a "sound" standpoint that his first and last names end in "-ck."
NOT TO BE CONFUSED WITH: Pete LaCock (see page 70; Former MLB first baseman/outfielder, and son of long-time *Hollywood Squares* host Peter Marshall), Gamecock (mascot of the University of South Carolina), Jack Glass (A Scottish Protestant preacher, evangelicalist and political activist, most readily associated with his strong views on unionism in Northern Ireland and his anti-Catholic speeches), Jackass Aeropark (A public-use airport located in Amargosa Valley, Nevada, named after Jackass Flats, Nevada, where wild jackasses once gathered to graze on the Nevada Test Site).
FUN ANAGRAMS: "John Wesley Glasscock" turns into "Shags well. Enjoys cock."
EPHEMERA: 1) His Scotch-Irish parents, Thomas Glasscock and Julia A. Collett, named him for the father of Methodism, even though he would attend St. Luke's Episcopal Church for his entire life. 2) After attending Madison Elementary School through the fourth grade, he dropped out of school to become a carpenter like his father, but he did take some correspondence courses. After finally retiring from baseball, Glasscock made a living as a carpenter. 3) He became the first native of West Virginia to play in the big leagues. 4) He and his wife, Rhoda Rose Dubla, raised two sons, John T. and Eugene, and a daughter, Florence. 5) In his career he struck out only once every 33 at-bats. It would be 35 years before Joe Sewell bettered his 1890 average of 64 at-bats per strikeout. 6) He was inducted into the West Virginia Hall of Fame in 1987.

GENE KRAPP
Spitballs and beanballs from this diminutive righty

BIRTH NAME: Eugene Hamlet Krapp[3]
PRONUNCIATION OF DIFFICULT PARTS: None
NICKNAME: Rubber (Arm)[4], for his durability
HEIGHT/WEIGHT: 5'7" 165 lbs.
BORN: May 12, 1887, in Rochester, New York
DIED: Apr. 13, 1923, in Detroit, Michigan
POSITION: Pitcher
YEARS ACTIVE IN THE MAJORS: 1911-1912, 1914-1915
NAME ETYMOLOGY/DEFINITIONS: "Eugene" comes from the Greek *eugenēs* meaning "noble," literally "well-born," from *eu* meaning "well" and *genos* meaning "race, stock, kin." "Hamlet" is of English origins as a variant of "Hamlett," which is from the Norman personal name "Hamelet," a double diminutive of the personal name "Haimo." "Haimo" is the short form of names beginning with the Germanic element *heim* meaning "home." "Krapp" has German origins, as a variant of "Rapp," which is from Middle High German *rapp, rabe* meaning "raven," hence a nickname for someone with black hair, or some other supposed resemblance to the bird. It also has

---

[3] According to SABR biographer Chris Rainey, "Mr. Krapp holds an iconic spot in the legendary halls of baseball journalism. Celebrated baseball writer Fred Lieb wrote in his memoir about the influence that writer Charley Dryden had upon Lieb's career. Lieb was especially impressed with Dryden's ability to occasionally slip a double entendre past an editor. Lieb wrote, "In the 1920's, when Dryden worked in Chicago, the Cleveland club came up with a pitcher named Eugene Krapp. The name intrigued Dryden. He was proud of this one, which he got by the editor: "Krapp squeezed his way out of a tight hole when, with the bases full, he induced Rollie Zeider to line to Bill Wambsganss for an inning-ending double play." This priceless example of literary chicanery has appeared in numerous books and articles since then. Sadly, the gem of a tale suffers from the fact that Krapp played with Cleveland in 1911-12 meaning Wambsganss was never his teammate."
[4] Some current sources indicate his nickname was "Rubber Arm" but contemporary newspapers simply used "Rubber."

Dutch origins, as a variant of "Krabbe," from Middle Dutch *crabbe*, Old Norse *krabbi* meaning "crab," hence a metonymic occupational name for someone who caught or sold shellfish or perhaps a nickname for someone with a peculiar gait.

Gene Krapp began his career as a pitcher just as the spitball was gaining popularity. In later years he also experimented with the emory board and scuffing the ball. Krapp also delivered his pitches both overhand and underhand. One of his catchers, Gus Fisher, claimed that the ball would actually break in two different directions in the course of flight. Krapp's career was plagued by control problems.

He played amateur ball in Detroit and moved up to semi-pro in 1905. In 1906 he joined the Tecumseh Indians in the Class D Southern Michigan League. In 1907, Tecumseh got off to a strong start on their way to the title, but Krapp was beaned in early June and released. He was signed soon after by the Flint Vehicles who were in last place and winless. In his first start for the Vehicles, Krapp beat Battle Creek to make the team's record 1-17. In 1908, the Flint team moved up to seventh place with Krapp as staff ace and outfielder. He played 79 games and batted .232.

In 1909, Krapp focused solely on pitching, leading the league in wins with 23 as Flint barely missed beating out Saginaw for the pennant. The Portland Beavers of the PCL drafted him for 1910 and Krapp cemented his spot in the rotation in the Mar. 28 intrasquad game when he tossed a three-hit shutout and hit a two-run homer.

In the PCL, Krapp's first appearance came Apr. 1 in San Francisco; he shut out the Seals 3-0 and drove in the first run when he coaxed a base-loaded walk in the seventh. The movement on his pitches won praise and his fielding was superb. He followed that performance with a four-hitter against Vernon for a 10-1 victory. For the season, Krapp allowed only 4.7 hits per nine innings. Even with walking a league-leading 177 batters his WHIP was a team-best 0.919 and was best in the league for pitchers with 150 or more innings. He hit 22 batters but later confessed that, "I am only a little fellow and some of those husky hitters crowded the plate so hard. The 'bean ball' certainly helped me..." In a tight race, Krapp pitched three shutouts down the stretch, leading Portland to the pennant.

The American League's Cleveland Naps acquired Krapp for the 1911 season. Naps manager Deacon McGuire needed to rebuild the pitching staff. Cy Young was 44 and no longer useful. Addie Joss took ill and died in April. Krapp made a good first impression in camp, but the wear of 442 innings the previous season led to a sore arm in mid-March.

After a respite from the mound, Krapp showed his stuff and earned a spot on the team. Krapp made his major-league debut against the St. Louis Browns. With a 4-0 lead Willie Mitchell lost sight of the plate in the seventh and walked four straight batters. Krapp was rushed to the hill without much warm-up. He proceeded to toss a wild pitch and then walked Jimmy Austin. A double and sacrifice fly followed to put St. Louis up 5-4. Krapp gained his composure and pitched two strong innings including striking out the side in the ninth. The Naps rallied to win 7-5 giving Krapp his first win.

He spent five weeks in the rotation, then went to the bullpen for a month and a half. He rejoined the rotation in July and went 4-4. That stint included a 1-0 shutout of the Athletics. He pitched 222 innings and had the equivalent of a save to go with 13 wins. Still, his control was an issue, as his 138 walks led the league.

The following year he had a sore arm and posted a 2-5 record. The Naps waived him, and the following season he was back with the Beavers, who took the PCL pennant that year. Krapp led the squad in walks while going 12-13.

Krapp was a holdout in 1914. He had been paid $300 a month the previous year and wanted $400. There was sentiment that he had "outgrown his usefulness." So Krapp signed with the Buff Feds (short for Buffalo Federals) in the newly formed Federal League. Krapp went 16-14 that year, and once again, he led the squad in walks (115).

After training in Virginia in 1914, the Buff Feds went to Athens, Georgia in 1915 for spring training. Krapp injured his back but did not let that deter him from taking his spot in the rotation. He started the second game of the season against the Brooklyn Tip-Tops.[5] Buffalo jumped out to a 3-0 lead, but Krapp allowed two hits and four walks in the second before heading to the showers. Started again only two days later against Baltimore, he surrendered eight hits while walking nine. He ended the month of June with a 2-10 mark. He steadied a bit after that and closed out the year at 9-19 for the sixth-place team.

The Buffalo writers took a liking to Krapp and supplied the fans with insight into his personality. They provided stories about his cigarmaking talents, picked up from his dad, even though he did not smoke cigars. He also was fond of singing in his baritone voice which a writer likened to a hyena and a washing machine full of bricks.

After the Federal League folded in December 1915, the National Commission took until March 1916 to determine the fate of the league's players looking for new pastures. If a player had not been signed by Mar. 1, then their contract reverted to the last team with which they had a valid (non-Federal) contract. This meant Krapp was under the control of Portland. The Beavers passed, making him a free agent. He ended up playing for three different squads that year, none of them on the major league level.

In 1917 Krapp returned to the semi-pro game as a member of the Detroit Hupmobiles[6] in the Detroit Amateur Baseball Association. In the feature game of the season, he suffered a 5-1 defeat against a pitcher named Eddie Standish who struck out 19.

After moving on to another team that same season, Krapp's next team located at Camp Custer, home of the 85th Army Division, and run by Uncle Sam. Camp Custer, located near Battle Creek, Michigan, was built specifically for WWI training. Krapp was assigned to the 160th Depot Brigade. He was never called for service overseas and was discharged in March 1919. He never made it back to the majors.

---

[5] The team was named by owner Robert Ward, who owned the Tip Top Bakery.
[6] Hupmobile was an automobile built from 1909 through 1939 by the Hupp Motor Car Company.

BEST DAY (BY WPA OR OTHER MEASURE): Krapp pitched four complete games of at least 11 innings in his career, including one in which he hurled 13⅓ frames, walked 11, allowed seven hits, but somehow only yielded four runs (he did, however lose the game, 4-3). Aside from those feats of endurance, his best game on the mound may have come on August 19, 1915, as Buffalo hosted the Chicago Whales.[7] Krapp pitched a complete-game shutout, despite allowing five singles, one hit batter and his defense committing three errors behind him. For a change he didn't walk anyone across the nine innings, and he struck three men out. He even helped himself at the plate, going 1-4 with an RBI and a run scored, in the Blues 5-0 win.

THE WONDER OF HIS NAME: I heard his "number 2" was pretty nasty to opposing batters. Too bad Mr. Krapp never dealt with Mr. Head (see page 20), not to mention Tommy John. I'm glad I had the intestinal fortitude to deal with this shit and get his profile down on paper. Now it's over and dung with.

NOT TO BE CONFUSED WITH: Thomas Crapper (19th-century English plumber who founded Thomas Crapper & Co in London, a sanitary equipment company. Crapper held nine patents, three of them for water closet improvements such as the floating ballcock. He improved the S-bend trap in 1880 inventing the plumbing trap [U-bend]), Gene Krupa (American jazz drummer, band leader, actor, and composer known for his energetic style and showmanship. His drum solo on *Sing, Sing, Sing* (1937) elevated the role of the drummer as a frequently used solo voice in the band).

FUN ANAGRAMS: "Eugene Hamlet Krapp" becomes "Page unkempt healer." or "Keen ape ... large thump."

EPHEMERA: 1) His parents were Frederick "Fritz" and Bertha (Hettig) Krapp. The father was born in Wurtemberg, Germany, in 1854. His mother was a native New Yorker whose family had come from the same area in Germany. Bertha gave birth to 12 children, seven of whom survived to adulthood. Gene was the sixth child and the fourth son. The elder Krapp was a cigarmaker. 2) In his years with the Cleveland Naps, Krapp was considered one of the fastest runners on the team, almost as swift as Joe Jackson. 3) In 1918, while still serving in the military, Krapp wed Chloe Hunter on base. The couple had a one-day leave for honeymoon and then Krapp returned to the base. After his military service was over, the couple settled in Grosse Pointe Farm Village, Michigan, located outside of Detroit, where he worked with the family automobile sales business (Krapp Brothers Auto Sale Company – One could only imagine the advertising slogan "Our cars run like Krapp!") and played baseball. 4) In 1922 he was found to be suffering from cancer of the bowels. He underwent surgery in 1923 for an intestinal blockage; the surgery was unsuccessful, and he died in the hospital.

---

[7] What ... you didn't know there were whales in Chicago? Well, the Federal League's Chicago franchise, which had been known as the Federals in their inaugural season, changed their nickname to Whales for what would turn out to be the league's final season in 1915.

RUSTY KUNTZ
Watch how you pronounce that last name!

BIRTH NAME: Russell Jay Kuntz
PRONUNCIATION OF DIFFICULT PARTS: Its "Koonts," NOT "Cunts"
NICKNAME: None
HEIGHT/WEIGHT: 6'3" 190 lbs.
BORN: Feb. 4, 1955, in Orange, California
POSITION: Outfielder
YEARS ACTIVE IN THE MAJORS: 1979-1985
NAME ETYMOLOGY/DEFINITIONS: "Russell" has English, Scottish, and Irish origins: from "Rousel," a common Anglo-Norman French nickname for someone with red hair, a diminutive of "Rouse" with the hypocoristic suffix -el. Americanized spelling of German "Rüssel," from a pet form of any of the various personal names formed with the Old High German element *hrod* meaning "renown." "Jay" is a common given name and nickname. It is the short form of any of the given names beginning with the letter "J" and now often used as an independent given name. "Kuntz" has German origins, from the old personal name "Chunizo," formed with Old High German *kuoni* meaning "bold," "brave," "experienced," or possibly *chunni* meaning "race," "people." It is sometimes taken as a pet form of "Konrad." The expression "Hinz und Kunz" was a German equivalent of "every Tom, Dick, and Harry."

Rusty Kuntz attended Cuesta Junior College in San Luis Obispo, California. He quarterbacked the football team, played center on the basketball team, and patrolled center field for the baseball team. In 1975, the right-handed hitter batted .442 as a sophomore, and was named to the Junior College All-Star team. But after he couldn't land a scholarship with a local four-year college, he went to Cal State-Stanislaus, a fledgling school near Modesto. "I wanted a place where I could play, and Stanislaus was the only one that really gave me a chance," he said.

In 1976, Kuntz's first year with the Cal State Stanislaus Warriors, he primarily played left field before shifting to center field for his senior season. The team got to and won the NCAA Division III World Series championship, defeating Ithaca College, 13-6. The team repeated the feat in 1977. Kuntz was named to the all-tournament team and was selected the tournament's most valuable player.

On June 7, 1977, the Chicago White Sox drafted Kuntz in the 11th round of the amateur draft. The news surprised him. Kuntz said. "I get a letter in the mail that tells me you've been selected by the White Sox in the 11th round. Get your butt on an airplane and fly back to Sarasota, Florida, as quick as you can because the Gulf Coast Rookie League has already started. And I'm going, wait a minute, where are the cameras, where's the action, where's all this hoopla?"

With a $1,000 signing bonus and an airplane ticket, Kuntz's baseball career began. He'd yet to sign his contract when he arrived in Florida. "When I got to Sarasota, Joe

Jones was my first manager," he said. "He slipped my contract under a bathroom stall and says, 'Hey, kid, sign this thing and shove it back underneath.' So, there was my hoopla." Kuntz played two months in the Gulf Coast League and spent the winter in Paso Robles preparing for the neat season.

When he arrived in Sarasota for spring training in 1978, he did well enough to be assigned to AA Knoxville to start the season. His manager that year was Tony LaRussa. After a year with Knoxville, hitting .263 in 113 games, Kuntz arrived in spring training for the 1979 season set to return to Knoxville.

However, in the offseason, the White Sox promoted LaRussa to manager of the AAA Iowa Oaks of the American Association, and Kuntz would make the jump with him.

Kuntz hit .294 for the Oaks with 15 home runs. On Aug. 3, 1979, LaRussa was promoted to replace White Sox player-manager Don Kessinger. "[Sox owner] Bill Veeck at that time loved Tony. So, he called him up at the All-Star break. At the end of the '79 season, I got called up," Kuntz recalled.

Kuntz made his major-league debut on Sep. 1, starting in left field and batting second against the Milwaukee Brewers and right-hander Lary Sorensen at Comiskey Park. It would take Kuntz three weeks to get his first major-league hit. He started 0-for-11 with six strikeouts. At the Seattle Kingdome on Sep. 23, Kuntz stepped to the plate with two out in the top of ninth inning. He'd gone hitless in his previous three at-bats against Mariners starter Rick Honeycutt. "I hit a topper over the mound that just snuck through," he said.

For parts of the next four years, Kuntz was an extra outfielder with the White Sox. He made the club out of spring training in 1980 and '81, and again in '83. (He spent the 1982 season at AAA Edmonton before a September recall.) In 1983, approaching the All-Star break, the White Sox, after a slow start, began to build momentum for a second-half surge. On June 21, 20 days after Kuntz's last appearance on the field, general manager Roland Hemond called him into his office.

They had to make a roster move, and Kuntz was given a choice ... get sent down to AAA or accept a trade to the Minnesota Twins where he would get a chance to play on a regular basis. Kuntz chose to go to Minnesota. Two days later, Kuntz appeared against his former team at Comiskey Park, now as a member of the Twins. Manager Billy Gardner put Kuntz in the leadoff spot against Chicago lefty Floyd Bannister.

"I'm a fourth or fifth outfielder playing sparingly [with Chicago], and now all of a sudden I'm the starting center fielder leading off for the Minnesota Twins," Kuntz said. "So, I walk up to the plate ... and I look out there and Banny's got his glove over his face. And I'm trying not to smile, too, and, oh, my gosh, it's weird. And I look out there and he's looking in. Okay, so now I put my head down and dig into the plate. Well, the first pitch he throws to me is right under my chin. I fell flat on my back. I'm like, oh, my God! And so, as I'm lying there looking up, now I kind of get up, and I'm finding my helmet, I'm finding the bat, I'm looking around," he said. "Well, I put everything on, and I look out there and Banny is like 'Sorry,' you know, one of those it-just-got-away-from-me kind of deals. So now I'm looking around for the helmet. Well, the second pitch that he threw to me was just a fastball [belt high], nothing on it, and I hit a home run. And I hit my first home run against Floyd Bannister."

Kuntz played in just 31 games for the Sox and Twins that year and finished the 1983 season with a combined .211 average, three home runs, and six RBI. In December he was traded to the Tigers for pitcher Larry Pashnick.

"At the end of the season I talked to Billy Gardner, and he said there's a good chance that we might trade you because we got a AA center fielder that we think is going to be better than you,' he said. "And I'm sitting there thinking, you know, just so naive: 'Wait a minute, I've been in the big leagues for about four years now, and you're going to bring a AA guy up that you think's better than me?' You know, that kind of pompous ass kind of stupid talk. And they said, yeah, he's pretty good, and I said, well, all right. And this is after I hit .200. How in the heck could I say anything?

I'm just happy to have a job. But, a AA guy? Okay, I want to see this AA outfielder that's so hot. Of course, it was Kirby Puckett."

The Tigers assigned Kuntz to their minor-league camp in Lakeland, Florida, for spring training in 1984. Sparky Anderson, the Tigers' skipper, told Kuntz that he was never going to start, never going to play more than two games in a row, and never be in the mix of main guys. "You're going to be basically a backup guy, defensive replacement," Kuntz remembered Anderson telling him. "So, if you want it, accept your role and be ready.' That's exactly how he used me."

Kuntz finished the 1984 season with a .286 average, a pair of home runs and 22 RBIs in 84 games. Now, with a 104-win season behind them, Kuntz and his Tiger teammates prepared for the playoffs.

In Game 1 of the American League Championship Series, Kuntz pinch-hit for left fielder Ruppert Jones in the top of ninth inning. Facing left-hander Mike Jones of the Royals, Kuntz flied out to right field. It was his only plate appearance in the series.

Against the Padres in the World Series, Kuntz appeared in Game 2 as a pinch-hitter for Johnny Grubb and struck out against southpaw Craig Lefferts. In Game 5, with Detroit up three games to one, Kuntz again pinch-hit for Grubb – once more against Lefferts. The game was tied, 3-3, in the fifth inning, and the bases were loaded: Kirk Gibson on third, Larry Herndon on second, and Chet Lemon at first. Kuntz lofted a "dying quail" towards right field that second baseman Alan Wiggins had to race back to catch. His throw towards home hit the mound, and Gibson slid into home safely. Kuntz had a sac fly and the go-ahead ribbie. The Tigers took a 4-3 advantage and never relinquished the lead. (So even though Gibson's dramatic rocket shot in the eighth inning off Goose Gossage may have been more emphatic, Kuntz is also credited with the game-winning RBI of a World Series-clinching game.)

Kuntz returned to the Tigers in 1985 but appeared in only five hitless games before spending the rest of the season with Detroit's new AAA affiliate, the Nashville Sounds. He hit only .222 for Nashville and was released in October. He was 30 years old, and never appeared in another major or minor league game.

In the winter of 1987, the Houston Astros hired him as their roving minor-league outfield and baserunning coach, a role in which he served again in 1988. The following season, Kuntz was hired by Seattle Mariners manager Jim Lefebvre to be the team's first-base coach. Kuntz coached in Seattle until 1993, when he took a coaching position with the Florida Marlins (where in 1997 he earned a second World Series ring). Next, he moved to the Pittsburgh organization, first as the Pirates' first-base coach and then as a roving outfield instructor. Kuntz was the Kansas City Royals' first base coach in 2008 and 2009. In 2010 the Royals named him an assistant to the general manager/ field instructor, a role that focuses on player instruction at the big-league and minor-league levels. But during an in-season managerial change, Kuntz was installed as the club's third base or first base coach, jobs he held until 2018 when eye surgery forced him off the field.

BEST DAY (BY WPA OR OTHER MEASURE): Game 32 of the Tigers 1984 season, which took place at Tiger Stadium on May 14, was a lot like the prior 31 games of that magical season. Detroit came out of the gate winning 35 of their first 40 games, the best start to a season in the modern era, on their way to a World Series title. Rusty only started 113 games in his career, but 38 of those games (the most he would start in any season) came during 1984. He would get the start on this particular Monday night in place of the regular right fielder Kirk Gibson against Mariners starting pitcher Ed Vande Berg. Kuntz's first at-bat came in the second inning with the Tigers already up 1-0. Darrell Evans walked to lead off, and Kuntz singled him to second. A balk and a sac fly scored Evans, and Kuntz would score on an Alan Trammell single. In the bottom of the fourth with one out and Detroit now leading 3-2, Kuntz cracked a solo homer (one of only two he'd hit all year, and one of only five in his career). With Detroit up 5-3 in the sixth, Kuntz grounded out to short to lead off the inning. The Mariners would tie the game at five as they moved to the bottom of the eighth. With one out, Kuntz doubled, knocking Vande Berg out of the box. Kuntz would score on pinch-hitter Dave Bergman's triple, and Detroit would add another run in the inning and go on to win 7-5. The win was part of a 16 out of 17 spurt that would bring them to that 35-5 mark. Kuntz's night: 3-4, three runs scored, three hits, one RBI, with a homer and a double.

THE WONDER OF HIS NAME: A 2010 *Bleacher Report* article said that his name was "hands down the best name ever. So many jokes, so little time." In April 2013, *The Big Lead* wrote about the name after a photo depicted Kuntz standing to the right of White Sox first baseman Paul Konerko and Royals baserunner Chris Getz. The resulting image seemed to display the phrase "Konerko Getz Kuntz" on the backs of their uniform jerseys. Of course, this presumes you don't know the correct pronunciation of his last name. On behalf of America, Rusty ... we're sorry not sorry sort of sorry conflicted, yes that's the word, conflicted for the fun we've poked at you for your last name. And that you like them rusty.

NOT TO BE CONFUSED WITH: *Rusty Cage* (Song by the American rock band Soundgarden, released in 1992 as the third single from the band's third studio album,

Badmotorfinger). Dean Koontz (American author whose novels are billed as suspense thrillers, but frequently incorporate elements of horror, fantasy, science fiction, mystery, and satire), Robert Kuntz (Game designer and author of role-playing game publications. He is best known for his contributions to various materials related to Dungeons & Dragons).

FUN ANAGRAMS: "Russell Jay Kuntz" anagrams to "Lazy junk results."

EPHEMERA: 1) Rusty's parents are Chet and Willie Kuntz. Chet worked as a bricklayer and then joined Rusty's uncle in his job as an auto mechanic. 2) After his playing career ended, Kuntz spent the 1986 season delivering packages for UPS in the Stanislaus area. 3) In 1989, Kuntz married the former Salli Elmore. Their son, Kevin, was drafted by the Royals in the 2009 MLB draft, but he chose to play baseball at the University of Kansas. He was selected again by the Royals in the 28th round of the 2013 MLB draft and made it as far as A-ball in 2014. 4) In 2000, Rusty was a member of the first class inducted into the Cal State Stanislaus Hall of Fame.

PETE LACOCK
His dad ruled over the "Squares" while he played on the diamond

BIRTH NAME: Ralph Pierre LaCock
PRONUNCIATION OF DIFFICULT PARTS: None
NICKNAME: None
HEIGHT/WEIGHT: 6'2" 200 lbs.
BORN: Jan. 17, 1952, in Burbank, California
POSITIONS: First Baseman, Outfielder
YEARS ACTIVE IN THE MAJORS: 1972-1980
NAME ETYMOLOGY/DEFINITIONS: "Ralph" is derived from the Old Norse "Raðulfr" (with *rað* meaning "counsel" and *ulfr* meaning "wolf") through Old English "Rædwulf "and the longer form "Radulf." "Pierre" is a French form of the name "Peter." "Pierre" originally means "rock" or "stone" in French (derived from the Greek word *petros* meaning "stone, rock," via Latin petra). "LaCock" has English origins as a variant spelling of "Laycock," an Americanized form of French "Lecocq." Laycock has English origins as the habitational name from "Laycock" in West Yorkshire or possibly from "Lacock" in Wiltshire. Both seem to owe their name to the Old English *lacu* meaning "stream."

P ete LaCock was a first round pick out of high school by the Cubs in the January Secondary Draft in 1970. He put up fairly pedestrian numbers his first two minor league seasons until 1972 when he hit .306 while leading the Texas

League in walks (84) and triples (13). That earned him a cup of coffee with the Cubs at age 20. The following year he hit .297 at AAA Wichita and again earned another cup of coffee with the Cubs. The Cubs had a young first baseman named Andre Thornton ahead of LaCock, so Pete was again sent to Wichita in 1974 where he erupted with a .327 average, 23 home runs and 91 RBIs. He did manage more time in the big leagues that year but hit just .182 in 110 at-bats.

The 1975 season saw LaCock get to stay in the majors for the full year for the first time. He was still relegated to mostly reserve duty, starting only 63 games and compiling a dull .229/.324/.321 line with six homers in 249 at-bats. He did quite well as a pinch-hitter, going 9-for-27.

The following season was practically a carbon copy statistically, as LaCock put up a .221/.327/.373 line with eight homers in 244 at-bats. That winter, the Cubs decided to move him in a three-team trade, in which LaCock ended up with the Royals.

LaCock flourished in his first season in Kansas City, hitting .303 in 218 at-bats and serving as a valuable pinch-hitter, going 8-for-22 (.364) in the role. The Royals won the division title that year but fell to the Yankees in the American League Championship Series. Manager Whitey Herzog was particularly perturbed at the performance of first baseman John Mayberry who reportedly played hung over during Game 4 of that series. Herzog demanded that management get rid of Mayberry, and the Royals traded the slugger that winter, handing the first base job to LaCock.

LaCock responded with his best season ever in 1978, hitting .295 with five home runs, 48 RBIs and a 110 OPS+ in 118 games. He was a contact hitter, striking out just 27 times in 347 plate appearances. (He didn't have much power as a First Baseman, but LaCock kept his job with tremendous bat control, striking out just 171 times in over 1,700 at-bats for his career.) LaCock had a terrific ALCS in 1978, hitting .364 with two doubles and a triple in 11 at-bats, but it wasn't enough to beat the Yankees who beat the Royals for a third year in a row. Pete was again the starter in 1979 and reached a career high in at-bats (408). He hit .277 with three home runs and 56 RBIs but slugged just .380.

The Royals grew dissatisfied with the lack of power they were getting from him, and in the winter of 1979, acquired a power-hitting first baseman by the name of Willie Mays Aikens. LaCock was relegated to the bench in 1980 and hit just .205 in a very limited role. He made an appearance in both the ALCS and World Series but did not get to hit. The Royals did not extend him a contract for 1981, so he ended up signing with a team in Japan. In nine major league seasons (715 games), he had hit 27 home runs with 224 RBIs and a batting average of .257.

In 1981, he played in Japan for the Yokohama Taiyo Whales after signing a two-year contract for $800,000. He said he was not worth that much. He hit .273/.359/.427 in 1981. He was criticized for his refusal to bunt in one game, for going into the Yomiuri Giants clubhouse to talk to Yomiuri outfielder Gary Thomasson, and for making excuses when he made an error. He once gave his bat to the umpire as a dispute for a called third strike, saying "You're taking the bat out of my hands, anyway, so you might as well have it." Due to his poor performance and his behavior, he was released even though the club had to pay his full 1982 salary.

After his playing career ended, LaCock managed and coached at various minor league outlets, including the Niagara Stars of the Canadian Baseball League, the independent American Association's St. Joe Blacksnakes, the Lincoln Saltdogs and the Golden Baseball League's Tucson Toros.

In addition, in 1989, LaCock played for the St. Petersburg Pelicans and Winter Haven Super Sox of the Senior Professional Baseball Association.

BEST DAY (BY WPA OR OTHER MEASURE): Besides the game in which he hit his only major league grand slam (see Ephemera for details), LaCock's best day might have been an otherwise routine contest in the middle of the 1978 season. The Royals were hosting the Athletics on June 24, and Steve Renko started for Oakland. LaCock had been serving in a reserve role for most of the season to that point, starting only eight of the team's first 67 games, hitting .208/.232/.302 in 53 at-bats. But he got the start at first that night. The Royals greeted Renko with a five-run first inning, capped by LaCock's first homer of the season, a three-run shot that scored Darrell Porter and Al Cowens. LaCock's next at-bat came in the third inning with Kansas City up 6-1 and Renko having been replaced by Steve McCatty. Batting with one out and Cowens on first, he laced a run-scoring double to left field. With the Royals up 7-2 in the fifth with two out and a runner on second, the A's intentionally walked LaCock to get to Freddie Patek, who flew out to end the inning. LaCock struck out leading off the bottom of the eighth. Final tally for the day: four plate appearances, three at-bats, one double, one homer, one run scored and four driven in.

THE WONDER OF HIS NAME: No ... as much as the 12-year-old in all of us want it to be, "LaCock" does NOT mean "the cock." But we can still wish it to be the case.

NOT TO BE CONFUSED WITH: *Beat the Clock* (Television game show that involves people trying to complete challenges to win prizes while faced with a time limit. The show was a creation of Mark Goodson-Bill Todman Productions and first premiered on Mar. 23, 1950), Abner Lacock (Early 19th-century American surveyor, civil engineer, and politician from Rochester, Pennsylvania).

FUN ANAGRAMS: "Ralph Pierre LaCock" anagrams to "Phallic porker race," or "Recall happier rock."

EPHEMERA: 1) LaCock is the son of long-time *Hollywood Squares* host Peter Marshall. 2) According to a 1974 story in *The Sporting News*, during a AA game that year, LaCock became angry at Frank Haraway, the official scorer for Denver Bears games. LaCock had been charged with a fielding error after not being given a hit earlier in the game. He picked up a ball and threw it in the press box, narrowly missing Colorado Governor John Vanderhoof who was sitting near Haraway. LaCock was suspended one game for this. 3) On Sep. 3, 1975, during what would turn out to the last game of Bob Gibson's career, LaCock blasted the only grand slam of his career deep to right field off Gibson. Before he left the clubhouse that day Gibson said, "When I gave up a grand slam to

Pete LaCock, I knew it was time to quit." 4) LaCock had a harrowing experience in August of 1978. He was with some friends when three men, including one with a gun, held them up. A scuffle ensued, resulting in the assailant, Alex Clark, getting shot in the head with his own gun. LaCock was cleared of any wrongdoing, and Clark survived and was charged with aggravated assault. 5) As of 2014, Pete was serving as a special consultant for Zinger Bats, a company that has been creating custom bats for professional players since 1998 or as they describe themselves, "Destroying ERAs since 1998."

CHARLIE MANLOVE
He was working on the railroad, then baseball briefly called

BIRTH NAME: Charles Henry Weeks Manlove
PRONUNCIATION OF DIFFICULT PARTS: None
NICKNAME: Chick, origin unknown, but it seems somewhat confusing in a way, given his last name, no?
HEIGHT/WEIGHT: 5'9" 165 lbs.
BORN: Oct. 8, 1862, in Philadelphia, Pennsylvania
DIED: Feb. 12, 1952, in Altoona, Pennsylvania
POSITIONS: Catcher, Outfielder
YEARS ACTIVE IN THE MAJORS: 1884
NAME ETYMOLOGY/DEFINITIONS: "Charles" is derived from the Germanic *karl* (meaning full-grown, a man), which is a cognate of the Old English *ceorl* (meaning a man, freeman, peasant). It is a royal name, being borne by ten kings of France as well as by kings of Hungary, Naples, Sardinia, and Wüttemberg. It was introduced to Great Britain by Mary, Queen of Scots who bestowed it upon her son, Charles James. His son and grandson both rules as King Charles, furthering the name's popularity. "Henry" is of Continental Germanic origin, from *haim* meaning "home" and *ric* meaning "power" or "ruler." "Weeks" is of English origin, as patronymic from the Middle English personal name "Wikke." It might also be a variant of "Wick," or an Americanization of Scandinavian "Vik." "Manlove" has uncertain origins. There was an Old English *lufu* meaning "love;" however, there was also a Norman French *louve*, denoting a female wolf. It is most likely that as a surname, Manlove developed independently from both sources.

Charlie Manlove played for an amateur team named Molineaux in Philadelphia in the early 1880s, before joining Altoona of the fledgling and informal Western Interstate League in 1883.

Manlove really wanted to keep his "regular" job, working at the railroad. His refusal to leave the railroad gig delayed his major league debut until Altoona's last day as a member of the Union Association in 1884. Altoona manager Ed Curtis's persistence

73

finally won Manlove over to saying goodbye to the railroad. With a couple of exceptions, the 1884 Altoona squad was filled with middling, mid-level minor league players masquerading as major leaguers. Given his late signing with the team, Manlove got into only two games for Altoona, going 3-for-7 with a run scored, and handling seven chances behind the plate flawlessly.

After the Union Association season ended, the 1884 National League season was still going, so he joined that league's New York Giants squad. He appeared in three games for them, going 0-for-10 with four strikeouts and making three errors at catcher. With New York, he made his debut catching 20-year-old rookie pitcher Ed Begley in a 1-0 loss. *The Sporting Life* noted: "Manlove ... made his first appearance as catcher with New York but did nothing strikingly brilliant behind the bat." The game's lone run came in the ninth inning when opposing pitcher Charlie Ferguson reached third on an errant throw by Manlove and scored on a sacrifice fly. After his three games with New York, his major league career ended. He then played for several Altoona-based minor league teams and settled in the city permanently.

BEST DAY (BY WPA OR OTHER MEASURE): While individual game logs from that era are not available, it's pretty safe to state that his best game was probably his debut for Altoona on May 31, 1884, where he went 3-for-4 at the plate.

THE WONDER OF HIS NAME: I demand equal time for a "Womanlove" surname (I've checked the Internet and come up empty, at least as far as "names" are concerned). "Manlove" sounds like a gay bar, or same-sex magazine ... unless it's for some reason pronounced "man-loave," in which case it's a guy into bread.

NOT TO BE CONFUSED WITH: USS Manlove (An Evarts-class destroyer escort of the United States Navy during WWII. She was sent into the Pacific Ocean to protect convoys and other ships from Japanese submarines and fighter aircraft), Charlie Manuel (Named hitting coach for the Philadelphia Phillies in August 2019 and a former outfielder, coach, manager, and executive in the majors), Amanda Hugginkiss (Name used in crank call by Bart Simpson in the *New Kid on the Block* episode of *The Simpsons*).

FUN ANAGRAMS: "Charles Henry Weeks Manlove" becomes "Now smear heavenly hecklers." or "He serves melancholy wanker."

EPHEMERA: 1) His parents were Daniel Stevens Manlove and Lydia Elizabeth Manlove (nee Truitt). There was many trials and tribulations in the family, as Daniel and Lydia's children, with the exception of Charles and one other son named Abraham Lincoln Manlove, all died young: sister Mary Elizabeth (died prior to age 1), brother Augustus (died age 5), sister Mary Rebecca (died age 4), brother George (died age 23) and brother Daniel (died age 19). 2) Charles married Minnie Mary Moore in 1885 at age 23 (she was 19). 3) Depending on your reference source Charles and his wife Minnie had as many as seven children: Peter Moore, Charles Henry, Florence May, Bertha Irene, Thomas Reed, Marion Elizabeth and Geraldine. 3) Minnie passed away in 1919, predeceasing Charles by 33 years. 4) One of the players who nearly became a teammate of Manlove on the 1884 Altoona squad was a man named Ed Sullivan. Sullivan was blind in one eye and sported an eye patch. But before he could sign, he was run over by a freight train. As one might infer from the near-signing of a half-blind man, the talent in Altoona was somewhat lacking. 5) Altoona holds the distinction of being the smallest city to ever have a major league franchise. 6) After his minor league playing days were over, Manlove ran a cigar store and worked as a machinist for the Pennsylvania Railroad. 7) Charlie's brother Abraham played under the name Linc Manlove for Altoona and nearby minor league clubs in the late 1880s. 8) At the time of his death at age 89, Charlie Manlove was the last surviving member of the original Altoona major league team.

J.J. PUTZ

When he was good, it was "puts," when he was bad it was "putts"

BIRTH NAME: Joseph Jason Putz
PRONUNCIATION OF DIFFICULT PARTS: puts
NICKNAME: None, although late Mariners announcer Dave Niehaus called him "The Big Guy"
HEIGHT/WEIGHT: 6'5" 250 lbs.
BORN: Feb. 22, 1977, in Trenton, Michigan
POSITION: Pitcher
YEARS ACTIVE IN THE MAJORS: 2003-2014
NAME ETYMOLOGY/DEFINITIONS: "Joseph" has English, German, French, and Jewish origins, from the Hebrew personal name "Yosef" meaning "may He (God) add (another son)." In medieval Europe this name was borne frequently but not exclusively by Jews; the usual medieval English vernacular form is represented by "Jessup." In the Book of Genesis, Joseph is the favorite son of Jacob, who is sold into slavery by his brothers but rises to become a leading minister in Egypt (Genesis 37–50). In the New Testament Joseph is the husband of the Virgin Mary, which accounts for the popularity of the given name among Christians. "Jason" comes from Greek "Iásōn" meaning "healer," from the verb *iáomai* meaning "heal," "cure," cognate with "Iasō," the goddess of healing and *iatros* meaning "healer," "physician." "Putz" has Austrian/Bavarian origins as the topographic name for someone who lived by a well, putz (Latin *puteus*), or a habitational name from a place so named in Luxembourg. *Putz* means "plaster" in German.

J.J. Putz led Trenton H.S. to the 1994 Division 2 state championship. He graduated in 1995 and won the Mr. Baseball award for the state of Michigan. He was first drafted by the White Sox in the third round of the 1995 draft but chose instead to go to the University of Michigan. The Twins selected him in the 17th round of the 1998 draft, but Putz decided to stay in school for his senior year. He was drafted by the Mariners in the 6th round in 1999 and signed with Seattle.

All through the minors, Putz had shown an excellent fastball that topped out at 97 mph, but he had been only marginally successful because his only other pitch was a below-average slider. He spent most of his time in the minors as a starting pitcher, but in the end, Seattle thought his stuff and lack of secondary offerings would play up better in relief. In 2003 he started the transition to the bullpen and made his major league debut with the Mariners on Aug. 11, 2003. In that game he relieved starter Joel Piniero to start the seventh inning. His first major league inning was a spotless 1-2-3, two groundouts and a strikeout of the Blue Jays' Vernon Wells.

He spent the vast majority of 2004 in the big leagues, where he compiled a less-than-stellar 4.71 ERA due to gopheritis (allowing ten homers in 63 innings). He also hadn't found the command really needed to be an effective reliever, walking 3.4 per nine innings against fewer than seven strikeouts per nine. The next season was almost a carbon-copy, statistically (eight homers in 60 innings, with 6.8 strikeouts and 3.5 walks per nine innings).

The big jump in command and statistics came the next year, thanks in large measure to Eddie Guardado. In Spring Training that year, Guardado, who had been the Mariners' closer since 2004, taught Putz to throw a splitter. After mastering the new secondary pitch, Putz abandoned his slider and became a much-improved pitcher, soon taking over the closer's role from Guardado. Putz converted 36 of 43 save opportunities while posting a 2.30 ERA, striking out 104 and walking only 13 in 78⅓ innings of work. He also yielded only four homers that season.

In 2007, Putz again improved his game. He converted 40 saves in 42 opportunities in the regular season with a 1.38 ERA, 0.698 WHIP, 82 strikeouts and 13 walks in 71⅔ innings. On July 14, 2007, Putz broke Eddie Guardado's Mariners consecutive saves record. The streak ended at 30 consecutive saves. He made his first All-Star appearance, and became the first Mariner ever to win the Rolaids Relief Man of the Year award.

The next year, however, Putz turned back into a bit of a pumpkin, or rather, the luck he apparently experienced in 2007 disappeared in 2008. Putz's 2007 BABIP was an unsustainable .200. In 2008, that number flipped over to an unlucky .347. He yielded a hit per inning in 2008, and his command went south. He compiled a 1.597 WHIP while his ERA nearly tripled to 3.88. In December 2008, Putz was part of a three-team, twelve-player trade that sent him to the Mets in exchange for pitcher Aaron Heilman, utility outfielder Endy Chávez, and prospects.

The 2009 season was a mess from the beginning for Putz, apparently because, in his mind, the Mets wasted two months before Spring Training not dealing with what turned out to be a bone spur in his elbow. (Could this have been part of the reason for his decline in 2008? Probably, as he was pitching with it for at least part of the season) As a result, Putz appeared in only 29 games for the Mets in 2009, pitching 29⅓ innings in which he walked as many as he struck out (19).

The Mets declined to exercise Putz's option, and in December 2009 Putz signed a one-year contract with the White Sox. Healthy for the first time in over a year, Putz set a White Sox franchise record by pitching 25 consecutive scoreless outings during the 2010 season.

In December 2010, the Diamondbacks signed Putz to a two-year, $10 million deal with a $6.5 million club option for 2013. Between 2011 and 2012, Putz pitched to a 2.48 ERA while racking up 77 saves for the Snakes, yielding only 86 hits and 23 walks in 112⅓ innings while striking out 126 batters.

The Diamondbacks exercised his option for 2013, but that year Putz dealt with a variety of physical issues which impacted his command. He still managed to post a 2.36 ERA in 40 games. In 2014, the wheels finally came off for the now 37-year-old Putz in 2014, as he appeared in only 18 games and compiled a 6.59 ERA before being released on June 27. That ended his playing career. (Putz subsequently rejoined the Diamondbacks as a special assistant to club president Derrick Hall.)

BEST DAY (BY WPA OR OTHER MEASURE): Well, while not in a save situation, he struck out five of the six Yankees he faced during a perfect two-inning appearance in a 6-0 loss on May 8 of 2004 (He K'ed Enrique Wilson, Kenny Lofton, Derek Jeter in the eighth, then Alex Rodriguez and Jason Giambi in the ninth.) Perhaps one of his best days in a winning situation came in a 10-inning game that saw the teams combine for 19 runs, 34 hits, seven walks and one error, none of which came off Putz. On Sep. 25, 2006, the visiting Oakland Athletics were one win away from clinching at least a tie for the AL West division title. The host Mariners were playing out the string at 75-81. Putz entered the game in the ninth inning with the A's up 9-6. He got Nick Swisher to pop out to third, struck out Mark Ellis, and induced a groundout to second by Marco Scutaro. Then the M's mounted a three-run rally on five hits off A's closer Huston Street to send the game into extras. Putz struck out all three Oakland batters (Jason Kendall, Mark Kotsay and Milton Bradley) swinging. He then watched his teammates piece together the winning run on an Ichiro Suzuki single, a botched pickoff attempt that sent him to second, a strikeout, an intentional walk to set up the double play, then a Willie Bloomquist walk-single to give the M's a 10-9 decision. The A's would have to wait another day to pop champagne.

THE WONDER OF HIS NAME: He can be the chairman of the "If you mispronounce my name it sounds either like an insult or a scatological term" committee (otherwise known as the IYMMNISELAIOAST, an acronym that might need some work). You must feel for a guy who, when he screws up in a game, or in life for that matter, can be put down with just his surname.

NOT TO BE CONFUSED WITH: Putz (A decorative, miniature-scale village often set up during the Christmas season. These villages are rooted in the elaborate Christmas traditions of the Moravian church), Peter Schmuck (American sportswriter who was elected president of the Baseball Writers' Association of America in 2005), Charlie Schmutz (Pitched for the 1914–1915 Brooklyn Robins; see page 78).

FUN ANAGRAMS: "Joseph Jason Putz" turns into "J.J. snoozes up path."

EPHEMERA: 1) Putz shared a dorm with New England Patriots quarterback Tom Brady while at the University of Michigan. 2) He married Kelsey Kollen in 2002, with whom he has four children; twin daughters Lauren and Kaelyn, son Ethan, and daughter Addison. 3) His wife played college softball for the Michigan Wolverines softball team from 1999 -2002. She was selected as the Big Ten Conference Freshman of the Year in 1999 and a first team NFCA All-American in 2002. She was also selected as the first-team All-Big Ten second baseman in 1999, 2001, and 2002.

CHARLIE SCHMUTZ
High school phenom with a very short pro career

SCHMUTZ, TACOMA, N. W. L.

BIRTH NAME: Charles Otto Schmutz
PRONUNCIATION OF DIFFICULT PARTS: Schmuts (rhymes with "puts")
NICKNAME: King
HEIGHT/WEIGHT: 6'1" 195 lbs.
BORN: Jan. 1, 1891, in San Diego, California
DIED: June 27, 1962, in Seattle, Washington
POSITION: Relief Pitcher
YEARS ACTIVE IN THE MAJORS: 1914-1915
NAME ETYMOLOGY/DEFINITIONS: "Charles" is derived from the Germanic *karl* meaning "full-grown" or "a man," which is a cognate of the Old English *ceorl* (a man, freeman, peasant). It is a royal name, being borne by ten kings of France as well as by kings of Hungary, Naples, Sardinia, and Wüttemberg. It was introduced to Great Britain by Mary, Queen of Scots (1542 – 87), who bestowed it upon her son, Charles James (1566-1625). His son and grandson both rules as King Charles, furthering the name's popularity. "Otto" is from the Old High German "Otho" and "Odo," which are derived from *auda* meaning "rich." The name was borne by Otto I (912 – 73), a king of Germany and emperor of the Holy Roman Empire. "Schmutz" is of South German and Jewish (Ashkenazic) origin, as the nickname for a dirty or slovenly person, from German *schmutz* meaning "dirt," Middle High German *smuz*.

A s a child, Charlie Schmutz moved to the Seattle area with his father, Frank, and his stepmother, Alice. He apparently couldn't hit, but had an arm on him. He joined one of the more accomplished high school baseball teams in the area, and that team was good enough that, with Schmutz on the mound, they actually beat the Seattle Giants of the Northwestern League in an exhibition game in 1907.

In the summer of 1907, the Seattle H.S. baseball team went on an unprecedented tour of the East, Midwest and Southwest to help promote the upcoming (1909) Alaska-Yukon-Pacific Exhibition, a world's fair of sorts conceived to tout the economic opportunities in the Pacific Northwest and advertise Seattle as the gateway to the wealth and luck of Alaska. By the time they arrived back home two months later, they had traveled 8,600 miles and played 31 games in ten states and the District of Columbia against an assortment of high school and town teams, business college nines, and professional clubs

As soon as he graduated in 1909, Schmutz agreed to join Tacoma in the Northwestern League. He was listed at 6'1" and called "Big Charlie" in the local papers – not only was he tall for his time, but he carried at least 180 pounds on his frame (and was listed at 195 when he joined the Robins five years later). By the time Schmutz had moved to Vancouver, he also acquired the nickname "King." Schmutz threw a hard fastball and, as a change of pace, a nasty spitball.

Amos Rusie, who convinced Brooklyn to sign Schmutz, said Charlie had greater speed than any pitcher he had ever seen in the minors. An article announcing his arrival in the big leagues said, "Schmutz has one of the most peculiar deliveries ever seen in the big show. He heaves much like a shot putter." Schmutz moved around some during his baseball career – after two and a half years with Tacoma, he was sent to Vancouver in July 1912. His season, covering both teams, resulted in an overall record of 13-17, but he walked only 57 in 261 innings of work.

In 1913, Brooklyn Robins' owner Charles Ebbets purchased Schmutz from Vancouver. Schmutz joined Brooklyn for spring training of 1914. Schmutz was good enough to make the team, but he was pretty much the last guy on the pitching staff. He'd only see action when games were out of hand, or when the Robins were desperate to give a starter a day off. He may have struggled with a shin injury, too – one article suggested that he may have had up to three different surgeries on his shin to address the problem.

This pattern continued into the 1915 season, when the lack of work affected his ability to consistently throw strikes. Schmutz became a nomad, first optioned to Newark, then sold to Salt Lake City, and finally traded to Seattle. That was just the 1915 season. He stayed in Seattle until 1916. However, he held out at the beginning of the 1917 season and was eventually dealt back to Vancouver. Before he could pitch, though, Schmutz registered for the U.S. Army and was soon serving his time with the 362nd Company in Europe. His baseball career had come to an end. His major league career consisted of just 19 appearances, five starts, and a 3.52 ERA to go with his 1-3 record.

BEST DAY (BY WPA OR OTHER MEASURE): On June 18, 1914, Schmutz took over in the second inning for starter Frank Allen and hurled eight innings of quality ball – two runs (both coming in the ninth), four hits, two walks and four strikeouts. It was the longest outing of his brief big-league career.

THE WONDER OF HIS NAME: Charles? That's fine. Otto? A little off the beaten path, but palindromic names are cool. Schmutz? Well, that falls in the "unfortunate"

bin. Having your name mean "dirt" isn't cool. Now, if "dirt" is your nickname (Dick Tidrow) ... that's another story.

NOT TO BE CONFUSED WITH: Schmaltz (excessive sentimentality; chicken fat or drippings used as a schmeer on bread), Schmidt's (brand of beer from the 1860s until the mid-1980s), J.J. Putz (Reliever for the Mariners, Mets, White Sox and Diamondbacks from 2003-2014; see page 75).

FUN ANAGRAMS: "Charles Otto Schmutz" becomes "Much scrotal hot zest." or "Mozart clutches shot."

EPHEMERA: 1) After a two-year hitch in the Army, he returned to Seattle and married Brenda Jenkins in June of 1919. They had a daughter Nancy in 1927, but Brenda passed away in 1938, leaving Charlie a widow and single parent. 2) Schmutz occasionally played semi-professional baseball while working as an electrician. He worked for Graybar Electric Company until he retired in 1957. 3) A story that made the wires said that Schmutz was in a car with former Giant Arthur Bues and Bues' fiancée when they were pulled over for speeding. When they faced a judge, Schmutz offered to do all the talking, and stammered his way through a story about a couple trying to get married using nothing but baseball terms. The judge was sufficiently amused at Schmutz's effort and, instead of collecting the fine, offered to marry the couple instead. 4) According to the *Seattle Post-Intelligencer*, one of Schmutz's teammates on his terrific high school team was a left fielder named ... Ten Million (yes really), along with a speedy centerfielder nicknamed "Wee" Coyle, who had picked up his less-than-flattering moniker from a bully named Maureen.

TONY SUCK
When it came to baseball, the name was totally apt

BIRTH NAME: Charles Anthony Zuck[8]
PRONUNCIATION OF DIFFICULT PARTS: None
NICKNAME: None
HEIGHT/WEIGHT: 5'9" 164 lbs.
BORN: Nov. 11, 1858, in Chicago, Illinois
DIED: Jan. 29, 1895, in Chicago, Illinois
POSITIONS: Catcher, Shortstop, Centerfielder
YEARS ACTIVE IN THE MAJORS: 1883-1884
NAME ETYMOLOGY/DEFINITIONS: "Charles" is derived from the Germanic *karl* (meaning full-grown, a man), which is a cognate of the Old English *ceorl* (meaning a man, freeman, peasant). It is a royal name, being borne by ten kings of France as

---

[8] Though he was born "Zuck," Baseball Reference and other sources list his last name as "Suck." However, it appears that at some point in his early life, for some unknown reason, the Zuck family changed their surname to "Suck" (as per the 1880 Federal Census rolls).

well as by kings of Hungary, Naples, Sardinia, and Wüttemberg. It was introduced to Great Britain by Mary, Queen of Scots who bestowed it upon her son, Charles James. His son and grandson both rules as King Charles, furthering the name's popularity. "Anthony" is the usual English form of the old Roman family name "Antonius," which is of uncertain (probably Etruscan) origin. The spelling with -th- (not normally reflected in the pronunciation) represents a learned but erroneous attempt to associate it with Greek *anthos*, meaning "flower." "Suck" is a bit of a mystery, but perhaps the answer lies in "Zuck," which has German origins, from a Slavic personal name, "Zuk," meaning "beetle." "Zuck" also has South German origins from dialect *sucke* meaning "sow," an occupational name for a hog raiser. It is also an Americanized form of "Zuch" or of Swiss German "Zug."

Tony Suck caught for a bunch of amateur and semipro teams beginning in the late 1870s. In 1883 he got to play for pay with Fort Wayne of the Northwestern League. In his first pro game, starting at catcher in a 7-3 win, Suck made quite an impression on a *Fort Wayne Daily Gazette* reporter who wrote: "Billy Geiss' pitching and Tony Sucks' catching, with any kind of support, (we) will win the championship pennant and Tony Suck will surprise the baseball world before many days. Very few men could have done the great feat he performed in yesterday's game."

Suck was soon summoned to join the National League's Buffalo Bisons. That didn't last long, as he was cut after only two games (during which he went 0-7 with four strikeouts and three errors in the field, a result that would be pretty standard during his career). He then moved to Brooklyn of the Interstate Association for one game at the end of 1883.

Suck then joined the Union Association's (UA) Chicago team, where he shared the catching duties and batted a paltry .149/.204/.160 in 53 games and committed 46 errors across three different defensive positions. He was with the team until it disbanded when it was transferred to Pittsburgh in the middle of the season.

At that point he joined the UA's Baltimore team for what would be his final three games in the majors. He batted .151 and slugged .161 during his brief big-league career. He was even worse in the field, committing 32 errors in 32 games at catcher, 16 errors in 15 games at short and five errors in 13 games in the outfield. He managed to play one errorless game at third, but only because no balls were hit to him.

After bouncing around the minors for a few more years, he took up umpiring in the Chicago City League where he was known for a "casual good style."

Despite his lack of success at the major league level, Suck was so highly considered as a player of integrity that in 1891, rumors circulated around Chicago that he would be included with former major leaguers Silver Flint, Bill Phillips, Rudy Kemmler and Billy Taylor to be the nucleus of a new league that was to be formed by Chicago native and former major leaguer Emil Gross. The Gross plan was to start a new league based in Tacoma, but the league never materialized. Suck played amateur and semipro ball almost to the end of his life.

BEST DAY (BY WPA OR OTHER MEASURE): You're kidding, right?

THE WONDER OF HIS NAME: Quite possibly the worst player, by standard statistical measures, in major league history. He was the Mendoza Line before there was a Mendoza Line, and at least Mario Mendoza could field his position. If ever there was a name that fit the player, this is it.

NOT TO BE CONFUSED WITH: Charles Blow (American journalist, commentator, and op-ed columnist for *The New York Times*), Hendrick Zuck (German footballer who plays as a left winger for 1. FC Kaiserslautern), Jack Sock (American professional tennis player highly ranked in doubles).

FUN ANAGRAMS: "Charles Anthony Zuck" turns into "Hot, clean crazy hunks."

EPHEMERA: 1) According to the Oxford Dictionary of Modern Slang, the verb "suck," unaccompanied by "up," "off," or "around," in its non-sexual connotations, didn't enter the language until 1971. So, Tony Suck can't claim any ownership of that, even if he did suck on the field. 2) He appeared in *Deadspin's* list of "The 100 Worst Baseball Players Of All Time," and came in at number 29 on *Bleacher Report's* "The 100 Worst Athletes in Sports History" 3) He died of pneumonia at the age of 36, and his wife Cora outlived him by 50 years. 4) Baseball historian David Nemec, in his book *Major League Baseball Profiles 1871-1900*, notes that after Suck passed, *The Sporting News* related an (amusing?) story about him. It seems that some years prior to his death, while working as a bartender at Silver Flint's saloon, Suck had grown jealous of all the attention being paid to Flint's gnarled hands from his years of catching. To remind patrons that he too had once been quite a catcher, Suck hacked up his hands with a hatchet and feigned an illness to get time off to heal. But when he returned to the saloon and began flaunting his mangled hands, he was greeted by hoots of laughter and derision rather than the awe and sympathy he had anticipated.

LEDELL TITCOMB
The man with a recently-debunked nickname

BIRTH NAME: Ledell N. Titcomb

PRONUNCIATION OF DIFFICULT PARTS: None

NICKNAME: Posthumous chronicles and reference works about Titcomb refer to him as "Cannonball" (or "Cannon Ball") Titcomb. But in fact, the nickname was never used during his playing days and did not appear in newsprint until Titcomb was 82. In the autumn of 2016, SABR historian and author Bill Lamb published an article in that organization's *Nineteenth Century Notes* newsletter debunking the nickname. After analyzing between 600 and 700 newspaper articles mentioning Titcomb, Lamb discovered that: "For the most part, Titcomb was identified by last name only during his pro career. On at least 17 occasions, however, 'Ledell Titcomb' appeared in newsprint. At no time whatsoever during his professional playing career did the nickname 'Cannon Ball'/'Cannonball' appear in the newspapers that covered Titcomb ... A search for the surname Titcomb in newspapers published from the start of Titcomb's playing days in 1884 until the day before his death in June 1950 via GenealogyBank yielded 10,458 page hits. Linkage of the word 'Cannonball' with 'Titcomb' promptly reduced that number to zero." The nickname first appears in print in 1948, two years before Titcomb's death. The *Haverhill Gazette* published a profile of the long-retired player, and the article included the following passage: "Those who remember Titcomb will recall that his pitches were so fast that the only fellow who could catch them was Bill (sic) Robinson, who later became manager of the Brooklyn Dodgers. His mates at Haverhill nicknamed him 'Cannonball' after he split a plank with a pitched ball." However, the unsubstantiated claim was unattributed in the article. When Titcomb died in 1950, the Gazette repeated the nickname in an obituary which included numerous biographical errors. Thereafter, obituaries appeared in the Associated Press and *The Sporting News*, both of which drew upon the *Gazette* obituary, repeating the erroneous nickname and the factual errors. So, although it would be terrific if he were nicknamed "Cannonball," it just doesn't seem to be true. He was sometimes called "Dell" by his teammates.

HEIGHT/WEIGHT: 5'6" 157 lbs.

BORN: Aug. 21, 1866 in West Baldwin, Maine

DIED: June 8, 1950 in Exeter, New Hampshire

POSITION: Pitcher

YEARS ACTIVE IN THE MAJORS: 1886-1890

NAME ETYMOLOGY/DEFINITIONS: Information on the use of "Ledell" as a given name is sparse, but according to HouseofNames.com its use as a surname was first found in Oxfordshire as "Ledwell," which dates back to the *Domesday Book* of 1086. That book was a manuscript record of the Great Survey of much of England and parts of Wales completed in 1086 by order of King William the Conqueror. In that book, "Ledell" was listed as "Ledewelle" and literally meant "spring or stream called the loud one," having derived from the Old English words *hlyde* and *wella*. "Titcomb" has English origins, as the habitational name from "Titcomb" in Berkshire or "Titcombe" in Gloucestershire.

I n 1884, Ledell Titcomb became a charter member of an amateur ballclub formed in a nearby town called Haverhill. When Haverhill entered the professional Eastern New England League in 1885, Titcomb pitched effectively during the early going. But in August, a lackadaisical performance – perhaps the first hints of attitude and maturity problems that would surface during Titcomb's pro career – led to his indefinite suspension. Titcomb responded by demanding his release by the Haverhill club. In time, club management capitulated, leaving Titcomb free to offer his services elsewhere.

Harry Wright, then in charge of the National League's Philadelphia Quakers, noticed this development. Previously in June, Titcomb had impressed Wright by pitching Haverhill to a 2-1 exhibition-game victory over the Quakers. Once Titcomb became available, Wright signed him for the 1886 season. In May 1886, Titcomb made his major-league debut, holding the New York Giants to three hits while striking out eight. He was hit hard, however, in two of three subsequent starts, all losses.

Then, off-field horseplay with fellow Quakers pitcher Ed Daily left Titcomb sidelined with a broken right arm. He returned to action and suffered a late-season 11-0 clobbering from Detroit and finished the 1886 campaign at 0-5 for a Philadelphia club that went 71-43. Wright retained high hopes for Titcomb and re-signed him for the next year. Titcomb reported for Quakers spring camp in great shape but, with control problems and a lack of pitching savvy, he did not make the club's roster.

Instead, Titcomb began the 1887 season with a local rival, the Philadelphia Athletics of the American Association. He eked out a 10-9 victory over Brooklyn in April to record his first major-league win, but was ineffective the next two times out, and was unconditionally released in early May. Several days later, he signed with the Jersey City Skeeters of the minor International League.

He started well with Jersey City, winning his first three starts. Several major-league clubs took note and expressed interest in him. In late August, he was sold to the New York Giants. On September 2 he made an impressive Giants debut in a 2-1 victory over Detroit. After that, Titcomb's work was sketchy. He finished 4-3 with the Giants, with a 3.88 ERA in 72 innings pitched for the fourth-place club. Still, his showing was enough for New York to retain him for the following season.

Titcomb was the unlikely Opening Day starter for the Giants in 1888, turning in a three-hit, 6-0 victory over the Senators. Titcomb won his next four starts, and settled into a spot starter role, reliably spelling staff aces (and future Hall of Famers) Tim Keefe and Mickey Welch, each of whom hurled over 400 innings that season. On Oct. 10, Titcomb recorded a one-hit, 1-0 victory over Pittsburgh to bring an excellent season to a close. For a NL pennant-winning (84-47) Giants club, he went 14-8, with a 2.24 ERA in 197 innings pitched, and ranked second among league hurlers in strikeouts per nine innings pitched.

He regressed in 1889 and got himself into Giants owner John B. Day's doghouse. With two starting pitchers out with illness or injury, the club was in dire need of a starter for a May 11 game against Boston. But Titcomb and another young, immature hurler were "out of condition" and unavailable, necessitating the use of an infielder to pitch. New York lost, 4-3. A couple of weeks later, the Giants released him. Despite his youth and recent success, there were no major-league bidders for Titcomb's services.

Titcomb signed a contact offered by the minor league Toronto Canucks of the International League. This led to a controversy, as the widely reported $500-per-month salary tendered Titcomb surpassed the $400 IL limit. Titcomb was believed one of the two highest-paid pitchers in the International League and was in the end allowed to keep the money. Pitching for the middling (56-55) Canucks, he posted only a 15-13 mark, but led IL hurlers with a sparkling 1.27 ERA in 245⅔ innings pitched.

He began the 1890 season where he had left off the previous year, pitching in the minors for Toronto. He went 10-11 in 22 games for the Canucks. The International

League suddenly disbanded in mid-July and the first-year Rochester Hop Bitters of the struggling-to-survive American Association grabbed Titcomb. He quickly solidified his status with his new club by winning his first three decisions. Thereafter, Titcomb struggled amid reports that his shoulder had gone lame. Sadly, he ended the season and, as it turned out, his major-league career on a sour note, giving up 19 hits in a 16-11 loss to Baltimore.

From there, he bounced around the minors for a couple of teams in the 1891 season, but although he was still only 24 years old, his professional pitching career was over. In parts of six major-league seasons, Titcomb had gone 30-29 (.508), posting a 3.47 ERA in 528⅔ innings pitched and completed all but one of 62 career starts. Control on the ballfield was as big an issue as it was off the field for him, as Titcomb's career walks/HBP/wild pitches total (298) exceeded his strikeouts (283).

BEST DAY (BY WPA OR OTHER MEASURE): Taking the mound on Sep. 15, 1890 against the Syracuse Stars before a home crowd of 543, Titcomb struck out seven, walked two, and was aided by several brilliant defensive plays behind him in completing a 7-0 no-hitter, one of only two no-hitters thrown in the majors during the 1890 season. On Oct. 11, Titcomb near-repeated the feat, throwing a six-inning one-hitter in a 4-3 win over Baltimore.

THE WONDER OF HIS NAME: Despite losing that great nickname, he still has the relative scarcity of his given name "Ledell" (which increases its coolness factor) and the 12-year-old's "appreciation" of the surname "Titcomb."

NOT TO BE CONFUSED WITH: Ledell Eackles (Former NBA player who was selected by the Washington Bullets in the second round of the 1988 draft), La Belle Titcomb (stage name of Heloise McCeney, an American vaudeville performer known as The Parisian Dancer on Horseback. Her act usually had her riding upon a white horse while singing operatic arias).

FUN ANAGRAMS: "Ledell N. Titcomb" gets you "Cold tent? Bill me!"

EPHEMERA: 1) He was the second of four children born to carpenter Joseph J. Titcomb and his wife, the former Mary Frances Burnell (known as Fannie ... Fannie Titcomb is itself quite the name ... no?). 2) On May 17, 1887, he managed to lose a game in two separate cities on the same date. In the morning he dropped a 3-2 decision to Newark in a game played in Jersey City. That afternoon, the clubs reconvened in the nearby Newark ballpark where Titcomb was an 11-1 loser. 4) Over the winter of 1887, Titcomb apprenticed in a local shoemaking shop, learning the trade that he would pursue for most of his post-baseball life. 5) Looking back on Titcomb's career, a *New York Times* sportswriter observed, "(he) ... did remarkable pitching during the season of 1888. In fact, he was sensational. [But] Titcomb was too much a comedian to take baseball seriously. [Still], the fellow had rare skill and was a puzzle to all big league batsmen when he felt inclined to do his best." 5) In January 1896, Titcomb married 21-year-old Margaret O'Herne. Their marriage would last for 54 years but produce no children.

Sounds Good
to Me

RIVINGTON BISLAND
Good-field, not-even-a-semblance-of-a-hit player

BIRTH NAME: Rivington Martin Bisland
PRONUNCIATION OF DIFFICULT PARTS: None
NICKNAME: None
HEIGHT/WEIGHT: 5'9" 155 lbs.
BORN: Feb. 17, 1890, in New York, New York
DIED: Jan. 11, 1973, in Salzburg, Austria
POSITION: Shortstop
YEARS ACTIVE IN THE MAJORS: 1912-1914
NAME ETYMOLOGY/DEFINITIONS: "Rivington" is a small village and civil parish of the Borough of Chorley, Lancashire, England. "Martin" comes from the Latin name Martinus, which is a late derived form of the name of the Roman god Mars, the protective godhead of the Latins, and therefore the god of war. The meaning is usually rendered in reference to the god as "of Mars," or "of war/warlike" ("martial"). "Bisland" has Scottish origins with variant spellings such as "Billsland," "Bilsland," "Bellsland," and "Belliland." It is a locational name from Bellsland (Kilmaur), or Bellsland (Riccarton) in Ayrshire, deriving from the personal name "Bille" plus the old English pre-7th Century, Old Norse word *land*, hence "Bill's land." The surname dates to the late 16th century.

Ashortstop, he broke in at age 22 with the 1912 Pittsburgh Pirates where he wasn't likely to replace the incumbent, Honus Wagner. Bisland had one at-bat after being purchased by the Pirates from Atlanta of the Southern Association. In 1913 Bisland had 44 at-bats with the St. Louis Browns, a team whose regular shortstop, Mike Balenti, hit .180. The team tried several other players at short, and Bisland had by far the highest fielding percentage. However, he hit only .136. The next year Doc Lavan won the job, even though he had had the worst fielding percentage in 1913 and had hit .141. Bisland moved to the Cleveland Naps in 1914, getting 57 at-bats and hitting .105. Once again, Bisland had by far the highest fielding percentage on the team among the shortstops, but this time he didn't displace regular Ray Chapman.

In the flimsiest batting order of baseball history, Mario "Mendoza Line" Mendoza would hit cleanup and Bisland would bat eighth. In parts of three major league seasons (1912-1914), he had a .118 career batting average with 12 hits (11 singles and one double) in 102 at-bats. His slugging percentage was .127 and his OPS was a wretched .317. Of all non-pitchers with at least 100 plate appearances in their major league career, Bisland's .118 batting average is the third-worst all time (Mike Jordan hit .096 in 1890, and Scotty Barr hit .112 from 1908-1909).

BEST DAY (BY WPA OR OTHER MEASURE): When you go 12-102 in your career, just about any game in which you get a hit is a cause for celebration. Bisland actually had two games in his time in the majors in which he collected not one but two hits.

On May 26, 1914, in a game against the Red Sox, Bisland reached base in all four of his plate appearances, via two singles and two walks.

THE WONDER OF HIS NAME: Of course, it doesn't hurt that it's a "double unique." Quite the whiff of aristocracy with this name, but given his lameness with the bat, perhaps we shouldn't use the word "whiff." But you know, Bisland was made for you and me.

NOT TO BE CONFUSED WITH: Rivington Bruce Bisland III (American League of Legends sports commentator and Player Behavior Specialist for Riot Games, who is reportedly a great-grandson of the ballplayer), Rivington Street (a street in the New York City borough of Manhattan, which runs across the Lower East Side neighborhood, between the Bowery and Pitt Street, named after James Rivington who, under cover of writing one of the most infamous Loyalist newspapers in the American colonies, secretly ran a spy ring that supplied George Washington with information).

FUN ANAGRAMS: "Rivington Martin Bisland" becomes "Born virgins and militant." or "Darn, militant virgin snob."

EPHEMERA: 1) Bisland was hitting .254 in 61 games for the Wheeling Stogies of the Central League when he was seriously injured during a game in late July of 1910. He was spiked in the foot by Fort Wayne Billikens infielder Grover Redden. Bisland developed a severe case of blood poisoning and amputation of the foot seemed a possibility. In late November, Bisland finally left a Wheeling hospital with both feet in good shape. 2) After his baseball career ended, he became the box office treasurer at Madison Square Garden, a job that he held for over 40 years. 3) Bisland married twice, with two sons from his first marriage, Rivington Bruce Bisland and Richard Grant Bisland.

MILTON BRADLEY
His "Life" has been nothing but "Trouble"

BIRTH NAME: Milton Obelle Bradley
PRONUNCIATION OF DIFFICULT PARTS: None
NICKNAME: None
HEIGHT/WEIGHT: 6'0" 215 lbs.
BORN: Apr. 15, 1978, in Harbor City, California
POSITION: Outfielder
YEARS ACTIVE IN THE MAJORS: 2000-2011
NAME ETYMOLOGY/DEFINITIONS: "Milton" has English and Scottish origins, a habitational name from any of the numerous and widespread places so called. The majority of these are named with Old English *middel* meaning "middle" and *tun* meaning "enclosure" or "settlement;" a smaller group, with examples in Cumbria, Kent, Northamptonshire, Northumbria, Nottinghamshire, and Staffordshire, have as their first element Old English *mylen* meaning "mill." "Obelle" is a bit of a mystery, with no listing in the usual genealogy reference books. "Bradley" had English origins as the habitational name from any of the many places throughout England named Bradley,

from Old English *brad* meaning "broad" *and* leah meaning "woodland clearing." It also has Scottish origins as the habitational name from "Braidlie "in Roxburghshire, as well as Irish (Ulster) origins, being adopted as an English equivalent of Gaelic "Ó Brolcháin."

How does a second-round draft pick end up playing for eight different teams in a 12-year career? Milton Bradley just couldn't keep out of trouble, on or off the field. Over his MLB career, Bradley played with the Montreal Expos (2000–2001), Cleveland Indians (2001–2003), Los Angeles Dodgers (2004–2005), Oakland Athletics (2006–2007), San Diego Padres (2007), Texas Rangers (2008), Chicago Cubs (2009), and Seattle Mariners (2010–2011). His career was marred by legal troubles and several notable on-field incidents.

Bradley grew up in difficult circumstances in Long Beach, California, with a single mother who had trouble making ends meet. He has explained that this hardship motivated him to work hard to reach the major leagues, in order to ensure his mother would no longer have to deal with these problems. Bradley attended Long Beach Polytechnic H.S. and was a teammate of Chase Utley. Despite having a 3.7 grade point average, he passed up an opportunity to attend Long Beach State after he was taken by the Expos in the second round of the 1996 draft, six picks ahead of Jimmy Rollins.

Bradley began his professional baseball career in the Gulf Coast League in 1996; in 32 games, he batted .241. The following season, he was named to the postseason New York–Penn League All-Star team. In 1998, he played for the Cape Fear Crocs and the Jupiter Hammerheads, tying for the Croc team lead in doubles with 21 while hitting .302, and batting .287 for the Hammerheads. While playing for the Eastern League's Harrisburg Senators the next season, he was suspended seven games for starting a fight after he had been hit by a pitch. In the final game of the league playoffs, Bradley hit a walk-off grand slam with two outs and a full count, in the bottom of the ninth inning, to give the Senators a 12–11 win. During the next season, after playing in 88 games for the Ottawa Lynx, he was promoted to the major league club, and batted .221 in 42 games.

During the 2001 season, he got into a verbal altercation with Expos owner Jeffrey Loria. Loria saw him in the locker room wearing a tee-shirt on which was written a nasty message, which Loria found unprofessional.

The fracas ended with Loria ordering general manager Jim Beattie to trade Bradley immediately, and on July 31, he was sent to the Cleveland Indians in return for minor league pitcher Zach Day, a poor return for such a talented player. From Cleveland's point of view, Bradley could serve as a possible replacement for Kenny Lofton.

Speaking to the Associated Press about the trade, Indians General Manager John Hart stated, "In Milton Bradley we are getting a top-of-the-order, middle-of-the-diamond player we feel will have a major impact at the major-league level in the near future."

Bradley's 2002 season got off to a rocky start, as he was shelved by an appendectomy in mid-April and then suffered a broken orbital bone and a scratched iris after a batted ball had bounced off the outfield wall and hit him below his left eye while he was trying to make a catch in early May. After a rehabilitation stint with the Bisons, he was reactivated by the Indians and finished the season with a .249 batting average, 38 RBIs and nine home runs.

Bradley spent the entire 2003 campaign with the Indians. Despite being placed on the 15-day DL with a strained right hamstring and missing the final six weeks of the season with a lower back injury, he led the team in stolen bases, with 17. On Aug. 30, while on the DL with a back injury, he was ticketed for speeding in Cuyahoga Falls, Ohio. After being stopped, he refused the ticket and sped away. He pleaded not guilty to speeding and fleeing charges on Sep. 12 but was sentenced to a three-day jail term. (The ruling was upheld by the Supreme Court of Ohio in December 2004.)

During spring training in 2004, he was banned from the Indians' training camp after not running out a pop-up during a game. On Apr. 3, he was traded to the Dodgers for Franklin Gutiérrez and a player to be named later (Andrew Brown); the *Akron Beacon Journal* later reported that manager Eric Wedge had insisted that Bradley be traded. In his first game with the Dodgers, playing center field, Bradley went 2-for-3, with two singles and two walks. On June 1, he was ejected from a game by home plate umpire Terry Craft for arguing over balls and strikes. After being restrained by manager Jim Tracy, he returned to the dugout and threw a ball bag onto the field. Bradley was suspended for four games and Tracy for one game. Dodgers general manager Paul DePodesta had this to say in response to Bradley's suspension: "When we traded for Milton, I think we knew everything that came along with it. We knew the past; we don't necessarily think that everything's going to be completely different because he came to a different place. That's fine. I would take nine Milton Bradleys if I could get them."

On Sep. 28, during a home game against the Rockies, Bradley mishandled a line drive and was charged with an error. A fan threw a bottle at Bradley, who left his position in right field, picked up the bottle and threw it into the stands, yelling at the fan. Bradley was immediately ejected from the game. The next day, MLB suspended him for the remainder of the regular season and fined him an undisclosed amount. He finished the 2004 season batting .267 with 19 home runs and 67 RBIs but was only 15-for-26 in stolen base attempts. Returning for postseason play, he hit .273 with a home run while the Dodgers lost the National League Division Series to the St. Louis Cardinals. During the offseason, Bradley had anger management counseling.

Things were relatively quiet for Bradley during the 2005 season. On Aug. 25, after hitting .290 with 38 RBIs in 75 games, he tore a patellar tendon and anterior cruciate ligament and missed the remainder of the season.

After the 2005 season, Bradley was sent to the A's for minor league outfielder Andre Ethier in a typical *Moneyball* deal: the A's valued Bradley's on-base ability and saw him as underrated because of all the time missed to injuries, while they considered Ethier too much of a free swinger to ever amount to much in the majors. Ethier would blossom into a star in Los Angeles, but Bradley gave the A's an excellent – if abbreviated – season in 2006, hitting .276 with 14 home runs and 52 RBIs in 405 plate appearances over 96 games. During Game 4 of the 2006 American League Championship Series versus the Tigers, Bradley became the third player in MLB history to hit home runs from each side of the plate in a postseason game, joining Bernie Williams and Chipper Jones. For the series, he went 9-for-18 with two home runs and five RBIs.

In June 2007, after appearing in only 19 games that year for Oakland, the A's traded him to the Padres, with cash, in exchange for Andrew Brown; it was the second time those two players had been traded for each other. In July, he batted .364 with four home runs and 12 RBIs in 18 games for San Diego.

On Sep. 23, 2007, his temper resulted in him suffering a bizarre injury. He tore his right ACL while being restrained by Padres manager Bud Black during an altercation with first base umpire Mike Winters. Home plate umpire Brian Runge reportedly told Bradley that Winters said that he had tossed his bat in Runge's direction in a previous at-bat. After Bradley reached first base, he questioned Winters about the alleged bat throwing and subsequent communication with Runge.

According to Bradley and Padres first base coach Bobby Meacham, Winters addressed Bradley with a barrage of profanity. Bradley then moved towards Winters. While restrained by Black, Bradley fell to the ground and injured himself. He missed the final week of the regular season. He had hit .313/.414/.590 with 11 home runs in 42 games for the Padres, but without him in the line-up for the season's last week, they were caught and passed by the Colorado Rockies in the National League Wild Card race. Winters was suspended for the remainder of the season and spent the postseason on the restricted list for the incident, after MLB determined that he had indeed directed obscene language toward Bradley. Bradley was not suspended, since he had not make physical contact with Winters.

After the 2007 season, Bradley agreed to a one-year contract with the Rangers. After a June 2008 game, Bradley attempted to confront Royals television announcer Ryan Lefebvre in the press box for what he believed were unfair comments made on the air. As the Rangers' designated hitter, Bradley watched the broadcast when he was not batting and took offense to a comparison Lefebvre made between him and Josh Hamilton (who had struggled with drug addiction). Manager Ron Washington and general manager Jon Daniels chased after him and stopped him before he got to Lefebvre, at which point he returned to the clubhouse in tears and said. "All I want to do is play baseball and make a better life for my kid than I had, that's it. I love all you guys. ... I'm strong, but I'm not that strong." He was quoted by Rangers radio broadcasters as saying that he never intended to physically harm Lefebvre but did want to speak to him; Daniels said he was upset that someone he didn't know was judging him.

As the Rangers designated hitter for the 2008 season, he led the league in OPS with a .999 mark and OPS+ (162). He was third in batting average (.321) and led the league in on-base percentage (.436). He made his first and only All-Star team that year. On making the All-Star game, he stated, "If I somehow miraculously made it to the All-

Star Game, I would be floored. I'd really be totally humbled by that. I'm just happy right now to play, to produce and to be with a good group of guys."

In January 2009, Bradley signed a three-year, $30 million deal with the Chicago Cubs. On Apr. 16, he was issued a two-game suspension for supposedly making contact with umpire Larry Vanover while arguing a strike call, which was reduced to one game on appeal. In late-June, Cubs manager Lou Piniella told Bradley to leave the dugout and go home after he "went after" a Gatorade cooler in frustration after flying out in a game against the Chicago White Sox. Piniella and Bradley later confronted each other in the locker room and exchanged words. Piniella later apologized to Bradley and reinserted him back into the line-up during the team's next start. On Sep. 20, the Cubs announced that Bradley would be suspended for the remainder of the season after an interview in which Bradley talked about "negativity" on the part of the Cub organization and declared, "You understand why they [the Cubs] haven't won in 100 years here." He also said he was uncomfortable just being on the Cubs. General Manager Jim Hendry felt the comments were disrespectful. Bradley later apologized to the Cubs organization for his remarks.

For the Cubs, Bradley hit .257 with 12 home runs and 40 RBIs before being traded to the Mariners for Carlos Silva and cash in December. Bradley was part of a flurry of off-season moves by the Mariners in hopes of returning to the playoffs, having not reached the postseason since 2001.

On May 4, 2010, Bradley removed himself from a game and left the stadium. He asked the Mariners for help with a personal problem, and the organization responded. He was placed on the restricted list and returned to the team on May 18 after undergoing treatment of an undisclosed nature. He told the Seattle Times on May 25 that he had been harboring suicidal thoughts and that these had compelled him to seek assistance. He continued to undergo counselling aimed at focusing on more positive feelings and not tying his entire identity to his on-field performance. He ended the season on the DL after having been placed on it on July 31 prior to right knee arthroscopic surgery. He finished the season batting .205, with eight homers and 29 RBI over 73 games played.

In April 2011, in a game against the Red Sox, he was involved in yet another controversy. After hitting a double that broke an 0-for-22 slump, he started yelling at first base umpire Todd Tichenor about a close play on which teammate Miguel Olivo was called out at first. He was then ejected by second base umpire Gerry Davis as it was alleged that he had bumped him during the argument; he was later suspended for one game and fined an undisclosed amount by MLB head of on-field discipline Joe Garagiola, Jr. On May 9th, the Mariners decided they had had enough and designated him for assignment. "He's not part of our future and not part of our present," explained general manager Jack Zduriencik. He was hitting .218 with two homers and 13 RBIs in 101 at-bats at the time. Unable to trade Bradley, the Mariners released him on May 16. He never set foot on a professional ballfield again.

BEST DAY (BY WPA OR OTHER MEASURE): Though it came in what was ultimately a losing effort for his team, Bradley's performance on July 21, 2002 as a member of the Indians was spectacular. Cleveland was in Kansas City that day, and Bradley batted fifth and patrolled center field. CC Sabathia started for the Tribe, while Darrell May toed the rubber for the Royals. Cleveland put a four-spot on the board in the very first inning, with the first two batters (Chris Magruder and Omar Vizquel) going yard, and the first five batters all reaching base. Bradley contributed an RBI double to right field as the last of those five. In the top of the second with two out and the score now 5-1, Bradley doubled to right again, scoring Ricky Gutierrez. The Royals plated two in the second and three in the third to tie the game, which Bradley un-tied with a two-run homer in the fourth. In the sixth, with the Indians now up 9-6, Bradley was finally retired for the first time that day on a groundout to first. Carlos Beltran hit a grand slam in the bottom of the inning to put the Royals back in front 10-9. With that same score in the top of the eighth, Bradley notched his fourth hit of the day, a groundball single. The Indians eventually loaded the bases but didn't score. In the top of the ninth, the Indians rallied one more time, scoring three runs on two singles, two doubles and a walk. Bradley chipped in with the go-ahead RBI double to deep center. However, Cleveland's Bob Wickman yielded a game-tying homer in the bottom of the ninth and in the tenth the Royals loaded the based off Heath Murray before Raul Ibanez won it on a walk-off hit-by-pitch of all things. Final score: Royals 13, Indians 12, despite Bradley's 5-for-6 day with three doubles, a single, a homer, two runs scored and five driven in.

THE WONDER OF HIS NAME: So, you took this profile for a spin. You rolled the dice and read it to this point. You didn't have to read any instructions, though obviously this tale was meant for those age eight or older and should be read by no more than two to four people at a time. I hope this didn't monopolize all your free time (whoops, wrong company!).

NOT TO BE CONFUSED WITH: That other Milton Bradley (19th-century American business magnate, game pioneer and publisher, credited by many with launching the board game industry, with the Milton Bradley Company), Milton Barney (Former wide receiver with the Atlanta Falcons. He played college football at Alcorn State University and attended Gulfport H.S. in Gulfport, Mississippi), Arthur "Boo" Radley (Reclusive character in *To Kill a Mockingbird*).

FUN ANAGRAMS: "Milton Obelle Bradley" turns into "Boldly intolerable me."

EPHEMERA: 1) His mother, Charlena Rector, worked as a clerk at a local Safeway supermarket. His father, Milton Bradley Sr., was a veteran of the Vietnam War, awarded a Purple Heart for his service. Bradley was named Milton Bradley Jr. when Bradley Sr. filled out his son's birth certificate without Rector's permission. According to Rector, Bradley Sr. was addicted to cocaine, physically abused her, and was homeless for several years. Bradley Jr. had four half-siblings from her previous marriage. 2) In 2005, Bradley was the Dodgers' nominee for the Roberto Clemente Award for working with the Dodgers Dream Foundation, Children's Hospital Los Angeles, and the Long Beach Boys & Girls Clubs, among other charities. 3) In August 2005, Redondo Beach police received three domestic violence-related calls from Bradley's house. No charges were filed. In January 2011, Bradley was arrested at his home in Encino and charged with making criminal threats to his wife, Monique. When he agreed to participate in an out-of-court hearing process, no charges were filed against him. However, his wife subsequently filed for divorce. In January 2013, Bradley was charged with several crimes stemming from five different domestic incidents in 2011 and 2012. In June 2013, Bradley was convicted by a jury of nine counts of physically attacking and threatening his wife including four counts of spousal battery, two counts of criminal threats, one count of assault with a deadly weapon, one count of vandalism and one count of brandishing a deadly weapon. He was sentenced to 32 months in prison and 52 weeks of domestic violence and anger-management classes and released on bail. Despite his convictions and sentence, Bradley maintained sole custody of his and Monique's two sons. 3) In September 2013, at the age of 33, Monique died at Encino Hospital Medical Center. A death certificate lists the causes as cryptogenic cirrhosis of the liver, hemorrhagic shock and cardiac arrest. 4) In January 2015, a Los Angeles appellate court rejected Bradley's appeal of his 32-month sentence. *Sports Illustrated* reported in May 2015 that, following another unsuccessful appeal, he was ordered to begin serving the 32-month sentence for his 2013 convictions, with the hearing judge stating that Bradley's request for leniency was "breathtaking, frankly, in how callous" it was. 5) In April 2018, Bradley was charged for allegedly assaulting his second wife (named Rachel) during a January incident, at which time Bradley was still on probation for his earlier domestic violence conviction. Bradley pleaded no contest to domestic battery, was sentenced to 36 months of probation, and was required to complete 52 weeks of domestic violence counseling.

ROCKY CHERRY
"Wild" Cherry played that funky reliever, albeit with no rhythm

BIRTH NAME: Rocky Ty Cherry
PRONUNCIATION OF DIFFICULT PARTS: None
NICKNAME: None, but in hindsight "Wild (Cherry)" would have been appropriate given his lack of control
HEIGHT/WEIGHT: 6'5" 225 lbs.
BORN: Aug. 19, 1979, in Dallas, Texas
POSITION: Pitcher
YEARS ACTIVE IN THE MAJORS: 2007-2008
NAME ETYMOLOGY/DEFINITIONS: "Rocky" is mainly of recent United States origin, originally the nickname for a tough individual. The name came to public notice through the American heavyweight boxing champion Rocky Marciano. He was of Italian extraction and Anglicized his original name (Rocco) into a form that seems particularly appropriate for a fighter. Also, the movie *Rocky II* came out a couple of months before Cherry was born. "Ty" is often a shortened form of "Tyler" (which happens to be the name of a major economic hub in northeast Texas and is about 100 miles southeast of

Dallas). "Cherry" is of English origin from the Middle English *chirie, cherye* (cherry), hence a metonymic occupational name for a grower or seller of cherries.

Prototypical big frame guy from Texas, but seemingly no sense of where the ball was going. The Cubs made him a 14th round pick out of the University of Oklahoma in 2002. He was a starter his first three minor league seasons (2003–2005).

Cherry's 2005 season ended after three appearances in the AA Southern League and Tommy John surgery. He became a relief pitcher after that. In 2006, he had a middle finger injury (pitching hand) in mid-July which also required surgery.

He made his major league debut with the Cubs in 2007, but in 22 games with them walked 19 against 23 strikeouts in 31⅓ innings. In August 2007, the Cubs traded Cherry to the Baltimore Orioles. His control worsened, as he walked 13, with only 10 strikeouts, in 16⅓ innings for the Orioles.

The next year, Cherry started on the 15-day disabled list with a shoulder strain. Upon his return, his control was actually even worse than in 2007. All told he walked 16 in 17 innings of work that year, while pitching to a 6.35 ERA in 18 games.

In December 2008, Cherry was selected by the Mets in the Rule 5 draft, but they released him three months later in March of 2009 and the Orioles declined to take him back. He then signed a minor league contract with the Boston Red Sox but was released from that deal five months later. Finally, three days after the Red Sox let him go, he signed a minor league contract with the San Diego Padres. He became a free agent in November 2009, but that's where the roller coaster ended for his baseball career.

BEST DAY (BY WPA OR OTHER MEASURE): After taking the loss in his major league debut on Apr. 23, 2007 (serving up what turned out to be the game-winning homer to the second batter he ever faced, Prince Fielder, in the top of the 12th), Cherry redeemed himself by "earning" his first and only win eight days later. He entered the May 1 game versus the Pirates with his Cubs trailing 5-2 with runners on first and second and one out in the bottom of the sixth. He threw one pitch to Ronny Paulino, who grounded into a force out at second, then Cherry repeated the trick with Jose Castillo. The Cubs then proceeded to score four runs in the top of the seventh to take the lead, which they never relinquished. So, Cherry faced two batters, threw one pitch to each, and snagged what would be the only win in his career, thanks to his teammates' bats.

THE WONDER OF HIS NAME: His name is like some mishmash of terrific alone but terrible together ice cream flavors. You also have the first and last name each having two syllables with sounds ending in -y, which rolls nicely off the tongue.

NOT TO BE CONFUSED WITH: Wild Cherry (American funk rock band best known for their song *Play That Funky Music*), Eli Apple (cornerback for the NFL's New Orleans Saints), Darryl Strawberry (former MLB outfielder with 335 career homers)

FUN ANAGRAMS: "Rocky Ty Cherry" turns into "Cry? Hey! Try rock!"

EPHEMERA: 1) As a kid, Cherry didn't like his first name and when he was 7 or 8 asked his mom if he could change it. His mom's name, by the way? Merry Jo (yes, spelled that way). 2) He was the last visiting pitcher ever to take the mound at the old Yankee Stadium (Version II) while a member of the Orioles on Sep. 21, 2008. 3) After his baseball career, Cherry joined the family business as a vice-president in the Dallas office of Cherry Painting. Extra special cool name bonus: The V.P. of Business Development in their Austin office is named Zip Drain (yes really). 4) During the 2018 season, at one of the adult beverage locations at Cooley Law School Stadium (home of the Lansing Lugnuts, where Cherry once played), there was supposedly a drink called Rocky Cherry.

KIKI CUYLER
Awesome all-around player with a flair for the dramatic

BIRTH NAME: Hazen Shirley Cuyler
PRONUNCIATION OF DIFFICULT PARTS: KAI-kai KAI-lur
NICKNAME: Kiki, "It came from shortening my name," Cuyler explained about acquiring the moniker (which rhymes with "eye-eye") as a minor leaguer in 1923. "Every time I went after a fly ball, the shortstop would holler 'Cuy' and the second baseman would echo 'Cuy' and pretty soon the fans were shouting 'Cuy.' The papers shortened it to 'Kiki.'" According to another story, the nickname had less glamorous origins: It arose as a way to mock Cuyler, who struggled to overcome his stuttering.[9]
HEIGHT/WEIGHT: 5'10" 180 lbs.
BORN: Aug. 30, 1898, in Harrisville, Michigan
DIED: Feb. 11, 1950, in Ann Arbor, Michigan
POSITION: Outfielder
YEARS ACTIVE IN THE MAJORS: 1921-1938
NAME ETYMOLOGY/DEFINITIONS: "Hazen" as a given name isn't prevalent enough to yield a clear etymology or definition. However, as a surname, its meaning has Dutch origins, from "Hasin," a pet form of a Germanic personal name, "Haso," derived from *haswa* meaning "gray" or "black;" or from the plural of Haas. "Shirley" was his mother's maiden name (Anna Rosalind Shirley). "Cuyler" has Dutch origins, probably a variant of "Koole," from a short form of the personal name "Nikolaas." A variant form of the surname in the Netherlands is "Kuilart," suggesting perhaps that these could be occupational names for a potato grower, from *kuilen* meaning "to plant potatoes" (from *kuil* meaning "pit" or "hole").

The Pirates, acting on the recommendation of scout Frank Haller, purchased the outfielder for $2,500 from the Bay City (Class B) club in September 1921. Cuyler made his major-league debut later that month but was optioned to the minors after spring training in 1922. He had a breakout season in 1923 with the Nashville

[9] This story was totally debunked by Cuyler's great-grandson (also named Hazen Cuyler) in an interview I conducted with him for this book.

Volunteers of the Class A Southern Association: named the league's most valuable player, he led the league in runs scored (114) and stolen bases (63) while batting .340.

Cuyler began the 1924 season on the Pirates bench but got 11 hits in 17 at-bats in his first four starts, and soon was batting third in the regular lineup. By Sep. 6, Cuyler was batting .380, helping to keep the Pirates just one game behind the Giants and a half-game behind the Brooklyn Robins in a tight pennant race. Unfortunately, suffering from a sore right shoulder, Cuyler slumped, batting only .211 in the next 17 games, and his team's playoff hopes ended with a three-game series sweep by the Giants at the Polo Grounds. Cuyler led the Pirates in batting (.354, fourth best in the NL) and home runs (9) while scoring 94 runs and legging out 16 triples in 117 games.

In 1925, Cuyler was once again his club's offensive catalyst, and the Pirates won the pennant, finishing 8½ games ahead of the Giants. From Sep. 18-22, Cuyler tallied 14 hits in 16 at-bats, including 10 consecutive hits. Cuyler set a post-1900 NL record with 144 runs scored (since eclipsed by Chuck Klein's 158 in 1930), led the majors with 26 triples among his 220 hits, clouted a career-best 18 home runs, and finished fourth in batting average (.357). He was successful on 41 of 54 attempts in 1925. He finished second in the NL MVP race to Hornsby.

In the 1925 World Series, Cuyler's clutch hitting helped propel the Pirates to victory over the reigning champion Washington Senators. In Game 2, Cuyler belted a game-winning eighth-inning two-run homer off starter Stan Coveleski. In Game 7, a rain-soaked struggle at Forbes Field, Cuyler came to bat with the bases loaded against Walter Johnson in the bottom of the eighth inning with the game tied, 7-7. He hit what appeared to be a home run down the right-field foul line; but the ball dropped in the outfield, buried itself in a tarpaulin, and was ruled a ground-rule double. It gave the Pirates a 9-7 lead, and the championship.

In 1926, Cuyler began the year once again among the league leaders in hitting, and on July 26 the Pirates were in first place. The turning point in the season came to be known as the "ABC Affair." The controversy started when Pirates vice president Fred Clarke, sitting on the bench, made disparaging remarks about star outfielder Max Carey, who was struggling. Veterans Babe Adams, Carson Bigbee, and Carey (the ABC in the Affair) held a team meeting to decide whether Clarke should be allowed to remain on the bench. The Pirates brass responded by releasing all three players, and the team limped to a third-place finish. Cuyler led the league in games played (157), runs (113), and stolen bases (35); but critics pointed to his lower batting average (.321) and drop in home runs (18 to 8) and RBIs (102 to 92) as evidence of a poor season.

In 1927, Cuyler was batting .329 on May 28 when he tore ligaments in his ankle sliding into third. He returned to the lineup on July 9, but tensions flared between the player and first-year manager Donie Bush. Cuyler was upset about being moved from center field to right, and objected to batting fifth and especially second, instead of his customary third position.

The situation came to a head when Cuyler failed to slide during a force play at second base in a game against the Giants on Aug. 6. Bush fined him $50, and Cuyler was then benched, starting only one game for the remainder of the season even though the Pirates were battling for the pennant. *The Sporting News* reported that the team's owner, Barney Dreyfuss, instituted the benching because he still fumed over Cuyler holding out for more money after the 1925 season; others countered that the player was moody and egotistical, and wanted more publicity. Even without Cuyler, the Pirates won the pennant. Cuyler did not play in the World Series (the Pirates were swept by the Yankees).

In November 1927, the Cubs acquired Cuyler in exchange for infielder Sparky Adams and outfielder Pete Scott. In a 1928 preseason exhibition game in Kansas City, Cuyler injured his right hand when he ran into a wall attempting to catch a fly ball. The injury made it difficult to hold a bat and plagued Cuyler the entire season. As an aggressive, first-pitch hitter, he also had difficulty adjusting to manager Joe McCarthy's approach of taking pitches when ahead in the count. Cuyler hit a disappointing .285 for the season, but still led the majors with 37 stolen bases and the team with 92 runs.

In 1929, Chicago had one of the most imposing lineups in NL history with Cuyler and the recently acquired Rogers Hornsby (who would be NL MVP that year). Cuyler's late season surge (he batted .396, scored 51 runs, and knocked in 48 over the last 55 games of the season) helped the Cubs build an insurmountable lead over the Pirates and capture their first pennant since 1918. No player in the NL could match Cuyler's combination of speed and power. He batted a career-best .360, led the majors with 43 stolen bases, mashed 15 home runs, and drove in 102 runs.

In their highly anticipated matchup with the Philadelphia Athletics in the World Series, the Cubs lost Games One and Two at Wrigley Field. With the score tied 1-1 in the sixth inning of Game 3, Cuyler singled to center to give the Cubs the lead and eventual victory.

In Game 4, Cuyler connected for three singles and drove in two runs. In Game 5 he collected his first extra-base hit of the Series (a double). But the Cubs lost both games, and the Series.

In 1930, the Cubs lost Hornsby to a broken ankle in late May, and Cuyler assumed a greater role in his team's offensive juggernaut. Over a 13-game stretch beginning on June 23, Cuyler batted .483 (28-for-58), scored 17 times, and drove in an eye-popping 27 runs to help the Cubs transform a 2½-game deficit into a 1½-game lead in the pennant race. The Cubs increased their lead to 5½ games by Aug. 30 and seemed poised for another NL pennant, but had an epic collapse, losing 14 of 21 games. Manager Joe McCarthy was ousted and Hornsby, who had been jockeying behind the scenes for the managerial position, took the reins for the final four games. Cuyler ended up playing in all 156 of the team's games (the third time he led or co-led the league in games played), scored 155 runs (!), set career highs in hits (228), doubles (50), and RBI (134), and led the major leagues in stolen bases with 37. A "five-tool" player, Cuyler drew comparisons to Cobb, Speaker, and Joe Jackson.

In 1931, Cuyler was one of the few bright spots for the Cubs, whose players bristled at Hornsby's autocratic managing. Batting leadoff through most of June, Cuyler was moved back to the third spot to provide the team with more offense. He batted .330, tied for third in the league with 202 hits, and ranked fourth by scoring 110 runs.

Cuyler's reputation as one of the fastest players in baseball ended with injuries. While rounding third base in April 1932, Cuyler cracked a bone in his left foot, missed six weeks, and struggled after his return. The Cubs occupied first place for much of May and June but fell 5½ games behind by the end of July. Players were increasingly resentful of Hornsby, who was also under investigation by Commissioner Kenesaw Mountain Landis because of his gambling debts.

When affable first baseman Charlie Grimm ("Jolly Cholly") replaced Hornsby as manager on Aug. 4, the Cubs responded by winning 23 of their first 27 games and took the pennant. Cuyler surged under his former Pittsburgh teammate (.373 average with 28 RBIs in the last 28 games) to finish with a .291 average and 77 RBIs in 110 games.

In the 1932 World Series the Cubs lost four straight games to Joe McCarthy's Yankees. There were few Cubs highlights in a Series best remembered for Babe Ruth's supposed "called shot" in Game 3. In that dramatic contest, Cuyler went 3-for-4 with a double and solo home run to deep right field but was otherwise quiet (5-for-18).

Cuyler splintered the fibula bone in his right leg during a spring-training game in 1933 and was limited to just 70 games (batting .317) for the third-place Cubs. In 1934, while the Cubs contended for the title most of the season before finishing in third place, the 35-year-old Cuyler made a remarkable comeback. He ranked third in hitting (.338), led the league with 42 doubles, and added 15 stolen bases.

The Cubs released Cuyler (batting .268) in July 1935 and the Reds outbid at least five other teams to sign the aging star. Playing on a losing team for the first time in his big-league career, Cuyler batted just .251.

Now the oldest regularly starting position player in the NL, Cuyler made yet another comeback in 1936. After batting primarily in the leadoff position through May, he went back to his customary third spot and hit at a .345 clip from June 4 on. He led the fifth-place Reds in hits (185), extra-base hits (47), runs (96), and RBIs (74), and batted .326.

In spring training 1937, Cuyler suffered a broken cheekbone when he collided with teammate Alex Kampouris during an exhibition game. Cuyler was ready to play by Opening Day, but later revealed that the injury bothered his timing all season. He batted just .271 with no homers and 32 RBIs for the NL cellar-dwellers. On Sep. 21 he announced that he was retiring at the end of the season and was granted his release in October.

After considering several minor-league managerial positions, he signed with the Brooklyn Dodgers as a player in February 1938, with the hope of moving into a coaching position. The NL's oldest player, Cuyler started 58 games. He ended his career as a player on Sep. 16 and was a Dodger coach for the remainder of the season.

In an 18-year career (1921-1938), he batted .321, collected 2,299 hits and led the major leagues in stolen bases four times. With his speed and a strong arm, Cuyler was also impressive in the field: six times he ranked among the top five in assists for outfielders.

Cuyler spent the final 11 years of his life in the dugout of minor- and major-league teams, but never achieved his dream of piloting a big-league club. In his rookie season as player-manager of Chattanooga (Class A1 Southern Association), he led the Lookouts to the pennant. He resigned after 2½ seasons with the club to accept a coaching position with the Chicago Cubs, serving under manager Jimmie Wilson through the 1943 season. Cuyler piloted the unaffiliated Atlanta Crackers of the Southern Association for five seasons, guiding them to first-place finishes in his first three years and to the league title in 1946. He spent his final year in baseball (1949) as a member of Joe McCarthy's coaching staff for the Boston Red Sox.

BEST DAY (BY WPA OR OTHER MEASURE): Besides the ground-rule double in the bottom of the eighth inning that helped lead the Pirates to the win in Game 7 of the 1925 World Series, Cuyler's heroics on Aug. 31, 1932 while playing for the Cubs are worth a mention. The Cubs were hosting the New York Giants that day, and the visitors jumped out to a 3-0 first inning lead. Cuyler, batting third in the lineup, hit a two-out single in the bottom of the inning but was left stranded. In the third with the Cubbies now down 4-0 and a man on first, Cuyler lashed a run-scoring triple, and then scored when Riggs Stephenson followed with a double. Down 5-3 in the fifth, Cuyler led off with a single to center, but went no further. Still down by that same score in the eighth, Cuyler led off with a groundout to the third baseman. Moving to the ninth inning, the Cubs had closed it to 5-4, and had runners on the corners with two outs. Cuyler stepped up and tied the game with a single to center to send the game to extras. The Giants put up a four-spot in the top of the tenth, but the Cubs staged another rally in their half. A solo homer and three singles left Chicago down 9-7 with two outs and two on for Cuyler. Kiki hit a game-winning walk-off homer to cap a five-run inning and give the Cubs a 10-9 decision. Cuyler finished the day 5-6 with five RBIs, two runs scored, a triple and a homer.

THE WONDER OF HIS NAME: We're all in for alliteration here. Regardless of the origin of his nickname, the "Cuy-cuy-cuyler" sound is terrific, and his given name including a typically female middle name is a nice bonus.

NOT TO BE CONFUSED WITH: Hazen Pingree (A four-term Republican mayor of Detroit (1889–1897) and the 24th Governor of the U.S. State of Michigan), Christina "Kiki" Cutter (A former World Cup alpine ski racer from the United States, who was the first American to win a World Cup event, a slalom race in Oslo, Norway, on Feb. 25, 1968), Milt Cuyler (A former major league outfielder drafted by the Detroit Tigers in the second round of the 1986 amateur draft, who finished third behind Juan Guzman and winner Chuck Knoblauch for the 1991 American League Rookie of the Year award).

FUN ANAGRAMS: "Hazen Shirley Cuyler" anagrams to "Hey … sure … in crazy hell!"

EPHEMERA: 1) After finishing high school he enlisted in the US Army and served in Company A of the 48th Infantry Regiment, but was not sent to France during WWI. He briefly attended the Military Academy at West Point before returning to Michigan and marrying his high-school sweetheart, Berta M. Kelly. 2) In an era when many ballplayers were considered uncouth for their excessiveness off the field, Cuyler was an exception. Often described as one of the "gentlemen of baseball," he neither drank nor smoke, and rarely argued with umpires or opposing players. 3) His 369 total bases in 1925 still rank as the most in Pirates history. 4) Cuyler was the first player to hit World Series home runs for two different teams. About twenty players have homered for more than one World Series team since, including Matt Williams who homered for three teams. 5) Cuyler suffered a heart attack in 1950, while ice fishing near his home. Two days later, while he was in a local hospital, a blood clot formed in his leg. The likely cause was varicose veins, which plagued Cuyler in his later years. He was sent by ambulance to a hospital in Ann Arbor but died in transit at the age of 51.

SHIGETOSHI HASEGAWA
If Bob Sheppard loved to pronounce your name …

BIRTH NAME: Shigetoshi Hasegawa
PRONUNCIATION OF DIFFICULT PARTS: Shi-ga-toe-shi Hoss-eh-ga-wa
NICKNAME: Shiggy
HEIGHT/WEIGHT: 5'11" 160 lbs.
BORN: Aug. 1, 1968, in Kobe, Japan
POSITION: Pitcher
YEARS ACTIVE IN THE MAJORS: 1997-2005
NAME ETYMOLOGY/DEFINITIONS: His name could have different meanings depending on the kanji (Chinese characters) used. One possible set of definitions would be "Shigetoshi" meaning "luxuriant/verdant benefit" and "Hasegawa "meaning "long-valley-river."

Taught how to pitch by his grandfather, Hasegawa twice led his high school team to the Koshien[10] Tournament, once bringing them to the quarterfinals. As a college all-star he went to the United States and according to the book *The Meaning of Ichiro*, Hasegawa "instantly fell in love with it" due to the freedom and golf courses.

He helped the Japanese national team to a Silver Medal in the 1990 Goodwill Games. A first-round draft pick of the Orix Blue Wave in 1990, Hasegawa went 12-9 with one save and a 3.55 ERA in 1991. He was named Pacific League Rookie of

---

[10] Koshien are two Japanese high school baseball tournaments held at Koshien Stadium: 1) the National H.S. Baseball Championship, or "summer Koshien," which has been held since 1915 and 2) the National H.S. Baseball Invitational Tournament, or "spring Koshien," which has been held since 1924. Summer Koshien is a nationwide tournament to determine the top high-school team in Japan, while Spring Koshien pits the best high school teams against each other. Both tournaments predate Japan's pro leagues by over a decade and attract more attention than any Nippon Pro Baseball event other than the Japan Series. Many players have first achieved their fame nationally in these tournaments.

the Year. Orix pitching coach Jim Colborn taught Hasegawa to use the changeup frequently (most Japanese pitchers did not employ it). Hasegawa mixed it in with his fastball, slider and forkball. In 1992 he went 6-8 with one save and a 3.27 ERA then went 12-6, 2.71 in 1993 and finished fourth in ERA.

In 1994 Hasegawa went 11-9 with one save and a 3.40 ERA, second behind only Hideki Irabu. His three shutouts were most in the league. In 1995, he went 12-7 with a 2.89 ERA as a key member of an Orix staff that took the team to the club's first Japan Series. He tied for third in the Pacific League in victories and made his only All-Star team in his time in Nippon Pro Baseball. Colborn left the team before the year, though, and Hasegawa began requesting that he be allowed to go to the United States to play. He had a dreadful 1996 (4-6, one save, 5.34 ERA) and had the worst year of any starter on an otherwise dominant Orix team as the Blue Wave won their first Japan Series. Given Hasegawa's poor play, the team gave him his shot to play in the States, selling him to the Angels. "Shiggy" had gone 57-45 with four saves and a 3.33 ERA in his time in NPB.

Hasegawa failed to make the Angels as a starter in 1997 but he did join the club in the bullpen and he had a bounce-back season, going 3-7 with a 3.93 ERA (116 ERA+). Due to his role as a middle reliever, the Japanese media pressure was minimal. Shigetoshi had an ERA+ from 116 to 150 in four of his five years with Anaheim.

Troy Percival helped Hasegawa with weight training and his fastball improved from the mid-80s to 93 MPH. He earned his first Major League win on Apr. 15, 1997.

When he tore a rotator cuff in 2001, he left Anaheim and joined the Seattle Mariners as the team's third Japanese player. When Kazuhiro Sasaki was injured in 2003, Hasegawa took over as closer and made his second All-Star team nine years after his one NPB trip. He had a 1.48 ERA in 63 appearances in 2003. He did not fare as well the next two years but remained a solid reliever. Shiggy retired at the end of the 2005 season after 15 years as a pro baseball player. In the United States he had gone 45-44 with 33 saves and a 3.71 ERA in 517 games.

BEST DAY (BY WPA OR OTHER MEASURE): On Sep. 7, 1997, Hasegawa entered a tie game in the bottom of the 12th inning in Detroit and proceeded to shutout the Tigers for the next four innings, yielding only one hit while striking out eight. The Angels would eventually push across a run in the top of the 15th inning, and Hasegawa retired the side in order in the bottom of the inning for the win. It would be the eighth relief appearance of at least three innings for him that season.

THE WONDER OF HIS NAME: Four short yet lyrical syllables in the first name, and four more in the last. The name looks daunting to pronounce but is actually reasonably easy once you hear it a couple of times. And speaking of hearing it, no less a public speaking authority than the late Yankees public address announcer Bob Sheppard deemed Hasegawa's name as one of his favorites to say over the P.A. system.

NOT TO BE CONFUSED WITH: Suzuka Hasegawa (a female Japanese Olympic swimmer who in April 2017 broke the world junior record in the 200 butterfly)

FUN ANAGRAMS: "Shigetoshi Hasegawa" turns into "The Who is gaga, as is he."

EPHEMERA: 1) He received the Japanese Rookie of the Year Award in 1991 and was a teammate of Ichiro Suzuki in Japan. 2) He holds the record for most appearances by an Asian pitcher in Major League Baseball, ahead of Hideo Nomo. 3) He speaks fluent English, even interviewing teammates on an American television show, and he introduced himself in English at his first press conference in the United States. 4) Nowadays he serves as a Senior Adviser to the Orix Buffaloes in the Japan Pacific League. 5) An avid golfer, Hasegawa qualified for the U.S. Amateur Championship tournament in 2017 and has aspirations of joining the PGA Senior Tour. 6) A collection of Hasegawa's interviews, called *My Way to Study English*, became a best-seller in Japan. 7) Hasegawa also wrote a book called *Adjustment* in which he blasted Japanese workloads for young pitchers and the poor weight training there, which he blamed for his 2001 injury. He also said American workloads for pitchers were too lenient, seeking a middle way. 8) He became involved in teaching youth baseball in Japan. 9) In December 2011, he coached an All-Star team of Japanese high schoolers who traveled to Compton, California, for a series of games against players in Major League Baseball's Urban Youth Academy.

DRUNGO HAZEWOOD
A one-of-a-kind name with the raw talent to match

BIRTH NAME: Drungo LaRue Hazewood
PRONUNCIATION OF DIFFICULT PARTS: None
NICKNAME: None
HEIGHT/WEIGHT: 6'3" 210 lbs.
BORN: Sep. 2, 1959, in Mobile, Alabama
DIED: July 28, 2013, in Sacramento, California
POSITIONS: Pinch-runner, Rightfielder
YEARS ACTIVE IN THE MAJORS: 1980
NAME ETYMOLOGY/DEFINITIONS: With regard to "Drungo," the story is that just prior to his being born (he would end up being the second-youngest of ten children), his mother told his eight older siblings that whichever of them won a footrace to the hospital would name the new baby. Her son Aubrey was the victor and named his new brother after the surname of a friend. However, surname reference books come up empty when trying to describe the etymology of "Drungo," as they also do with "Hazewood." "LaRue" is a French topographic name for someone who lived beside a road, track, or pathway, from the Old French *rue* (Latin "ruga," meaning "crease" or "fold"), with the definite article *la*. It means "the street" in French.

A two-sport star at Sacramento H.S., he was offered a full scholarship to USC as a tailback and was a 1977 first-round selection by the Orioles. Cal Ripken Jr., who played with Hazewood for two seasons in the minors in Charlotte, marveled at his abilities: "He was big and fast and something to watch scoring from first on a double." Tremendously strong, he bopped his way through the minors and jumped from AA to the big leagues in 1980.

Unfortunately, he never mastered hitting the curveball and only stuck around for the briefest of cups of coffee with the Orioles. Five hitless at-bats over six games, with four strikeouts ... and he was done in the big leagues. In 1981, Hazewood was back in the minor leagues. He struggled in 18 games with AAA Rochester, going an abysmal 6-for-64 before getting sent to AA Charlotte. Hazewood hit .226 with 11 home runs and 28 stolen bases in 1982. In 1983, his last baseball season, Hazewood hit a combined .247 for two minor league teams.

BEST DAY (BY WPA OR OTHER MEASURE): Given his .000/.000/.000 career slash line in six games, let's assume his major league debut, on Sep. 19, 1980 was his best day in The Show. He was called upon to pinch-run for Rich Dauer, who had walked to lead off the bottom of the ninth in a 5-5 game. A walk moved Hazewood to second. A double play got him to third, but he was stranded there, and then replaced in the next half-inning. He DID score one run in his career, but it came in the ninth inning of a losing effort one week later.

THE WONDER OF HIS NAME: What we call a "double unique" in the name business. There have been approximately 19,000 individuals to have played major league baseball since 1871, and roughly 425 of them have "double unique" names, including Hall of Famers Harmon Killebrew, Tris Speaker and Branch Rickey.

NOT TO BE CONFUSED WITH: Fungo bat (specially designed bat used by baseball and softball coaches for practice), Van Lingle Mungo (see page 121), Mungo Jerry (1970s British rock group with the hit "In the Summertime"), Spencer Haywood (Basketball Hall of Fame member).

FUN ANAGRAMS: "Drungo LaRue Hazewood" becomes "Doze unaware ... drool. (Ugh!)"

EPHEMERA: 1) More from Ripken on Hazewood: After a brawl resulted in Hazewood being ejected, Ripken recalled how Drungo broke a bat using his hands and nothing else. "He threw on some street clothes – no shower – and then stopped in front of a display of two bats mounted on hooks on the wall. He grabbed one and snapped it like a toothpick. ... Drungo didn't snap this bat across anything, and he didn't hit it against anything. He just twisted and snapped it like a toothpick." 2) He had more strikeouts than hits in every major league and minor league season he played. 3) He was a participant in the record 33-inning minor league game that took place in 1981 (Pawtucket outlasted Rochester by a score of 3-2). Hazewood went 0-4 with three strikeouts during the game, which was played in increasingly frigid temperatures. Years later, when asked about the weather during the game, he said "When you opened your eyes, the insides of your eyes got cold." 4) He abruptly stopped playing in 1983, leaving baseball to take care of his mother who was suffering from breast cancer. 5) He later became a truck driver and raised seven children.

SIXTO LEZCANO

Part of not one, not two, but three big multi-player trades

BIRTH NAME: Sixto Joaquin Lezcano
PRONUNCIATION OF DIFFICULT PARTS:
Seesh-toe or Sees-toe (but most American-born
announcers of the era went with "six-toe")
NICKNAME: None
HEIGHT/WEIGHT: 5'10" 165 lbs.
BORN: Nov. 28, 1953, in Arecibo, Puerto Rico
POSITION: Rightfielder
YEARS ACTIVE IN THE MAJORS: 1974-1985
NAME ETYMOLOGY/DEFINITIONS: "Sixto"
literally means "Sixth" and is a Spanish variant of
the Latin name "Sextus." "Sextus" is an ancient
Roman "first name." Its standard abbreviation is
"Sex," and the feminine form would be "Sexta." It
is one of the numeral "names," like Quintus ("fifth") and Decimus ("tenth"). Although
it is sometimes thought that these names originally referred to birth order and were
then handed down through the family line, they may have also been a reference to
the month of birth. "Joaquín" is the Spanish language version of "Joachim." It finds
its origin in Hebrew (Yehoyaqim) and literally means "lifted by Yahweh." "Lezcano"
is probably a variant spelling of Spanish "Lazcano," a habitational name from Basque
Lazkao, a town in Gipuzkoa province.

Sixto Lezcano was signed as an amateur free agent in 1970 by the Brewers.
He spent four seasons climbing the ladder in their minor league system. His
1974 campaign saw him hit .325 with 34 homers[11] and 99 runs driven in for
Sacramento in the PCL, earning him promotion to the big leagues that September.
In his first major league game, he started out with a single against the Orioles' Dave
McNally, and finished in the bottom of the tenth inning with a game-winning single
off reliever Grant Jackson. Lezcano's first home run came ten days later, off John Hiller
of the Tigers. He became the Brewers' starting right fielder in 1975, a job he held for
the next six seasons.

Lezcano developed a reputation for being a "hard head" in his rookie season,
leading to a clash of personalities with Brewers manager Del Crandall. Lezcano felt
Crandall had tried to give him too much advice and had confused him. In early August

---

[11] However, he was only third on the team in round-trippers behind Bill McNulty's 55 and Gorman Thomas'
51. The Sacramento team hit 305 home runs, a large number until you consider that the left-field foul
pole sat a mere 233 feet from home plate. Their home stadium was primarily a football and track and field
stadium and thus not suited for baseball.

Crandall fined Lezcano twice (for $100 and $50) for his poor attitude and benched him for several games. One of the fines was for smashing a water cooler in the dugout and hurting his hand. The friction with the manager came to a head when Crandall suspended Lezcano for a week at the end of the season. After using several pinch-hitters and runners during a game, Crandall asked Lezcano to pinch-run. Lezcano did not respond and continued to stand in place, smoking a cigarette. (Yes, players still smoked in the dugout during games in the 1970s.) Some viewed Lezcano's actions as downright mutiny.

Before the season ended, Lezcano went to Crandall's office and apologized for his behavior. Crandall was impressed with his sincerity. "After all, he knew I was going to be fired, so he didn't have to butter me up," the manager said. Lezcano also had a long discussion with Bud Selig, the Brewers president, and general manager Jim Baumer who related, "He was almost apologetic as he told us he was wrong. He promised us he was going to be a different person and you've got to believe him. He'd never been a problem before in our organization."

During the 1975-76 winter season, he changed his approach at the plate from trying for home runs to looking for a hit by getting good wood on the ball. He adjusted his stance so he could cover more of the plate. He acknowledged advice from his winter-ball teammates Félix Millan, Jerry Morales, Willie Montañez, and manager Jim Bunning. In the 1976-77 winter season, Lezcano led the league in batting (.366) for Caguas Criollos.

Lezcano had a strong throwing arm and led American League outfielders in assists with 18 in 1978. His best offensive numbers came in 1979, when he finished among the top ten in the AL in batting average (.321), home runs (28), slugging percentage (.573) and OPS+ (164). Despite all that, he finished only 15th in the MVP voting, though he was honored with the only Gold Glove of his major league career. He was voted the Brewers' Most Valuable Player.

The Brewers slumped to 86 wins and a third-place finish in 1980. It was Lezcano's worst season to date. He was plagued by injuries and his average dipped 92 points to .229, the largest drop of any major-league regular, making him expendable. Lezcano's attitude also took a nosedive. Teammate Ben Oglivie noted that the team was marked by frustration and fault-finding and that Lezcano was one of the instigators.

After the 1980 season, he was part of his first blockbuster trade. In December, he was sent to the Cardinals with a highly regarded prospect, outfielder David Green, and starting pitchers Dave LaPoint and Lary Sorensen for catcher Ted Simmons and what turned out to be the next two AL Cy Young Award winners, Rollie Fingers and Pete Vuckovich. All three new Brewers were key members of the 1982 pennant-winning team. All four of the new Cardinals (or players traded for them) made contributions to the 1982 Cardinals World Series champions. But Lezcano couldn't consistently crack the starting lineup in St. Louis and batted only .266 with the Cards in 1981.

Major trade number two came after the 1981 season. Lezcano demanded to be traded and Cardinals manager-GM Whitey Herzog obliged. The Cardinals had a chance to unload troubled shortstop Garry Templeton with Lezcano to the Padres for shortstop Ozzie Smith and pitcher Steve Mura. While Templeton was a key cog in the Padres' 1984 NL championship season, Smith was the final piece the Cardinals needed to win the 1982 World Series and the 1985 and '87 NL pennants.

The 1982 season turned out to be a comeback year for Lezcano as he had his second-best offensive season with 16 home runs and 84 RBIs (both second on the team), a .289 batting average, 78 walks, a .388 on-base percentage, and a .472 slugging percentage. Despite missing 24 games to injuries, he tied for the NL lead in outfield assists (16), led in double plays (8) and made only three errors.

However, his numbers fell off with the Padres in the 1983 season, and he lost his job in right field to a youngster named Tony Gwynn. He was eventually part of a third multi-player swap that took place at the end of August. In that one he and a player to be named later were dealt to the Philadelphia Phillies for four players to be named later (one of which turned out to be a young Lance McCullers). Lezcano joined a Phillies team which won the NL pennant in 1983. He platooned with Joe Lefebvre during the postseason and homered off Rick Honeycutt during the 1983 National League Championship Series. He had one base hit in eight at-bats in the Phillies' World Series loss.

He continued to platoon in Philadelphia in 1984 where he had an OBP of .371 and a slugging percentage of .480, before leaving the team as a free agent. He signed with the Pittsburgh Pirates in 1985 and served as one of the team's pinch-hitters. The Pirates released him in spring training before the 1986 season, which ended his major league career. After the majors he played briefly for the Taiyo Whales in Japan in 1987.

Lezcano coached in the Royals and Braves organizations from 1993-2010. In 1994 Lezcano was named manager of his old team, the Caguas Criollos, just four games into the winter season after Mike Easler was fired. Lezcano was later fired as well as Caguas finished in last place.

BEST DAY (BY WPA OR OTHER MEASURE): On July 31 1982, against the Reds at Riverfront Stadium, Martinez put on quite a show. With one out and runners on second and third in the top of the first against Reds starter Tom Seaver, Martinez launched a homer to give San Diego a quick 3-0 lead. Next time up, with the Padres still leading 3-1 with no out and a runner on second in the top of the third, Martinez doubled to left, scoring Garry Templeton. In the top of the fifth, with the score now 4-2, Martinez led off with a double to the left field gap off Seaver. In the seventh, facing Seaver's replacement, Joe Price, Martinez hit his second homer of the game. Martinez ended his day with a ninth-inning walk. Final tally: 4-4 with two runs scored and five driven in a 5-4 Padres victory.

THE WONDER OF HIS NAME: Yes, we now know how to correctly pronounce his first name, but growing up, didn't we innocently think it was "six toe?" And didn't we get a kick out of that, wondering if each of his shoes had a little sidecar on them? There is also the "toe/no" rhyming ending to his names that make it fun to pronounce.

NOT TO BE CONFUSED WITH: Sixto Diaz Rodriguez (Known professionally as Rodriguez, an American singer-songwriter from Detroit. His music career was told in the 2012 Academy Award–winning documentary film *Searching for Sugar Man*), Sixto Castelo López (He was secretary of the Philippine mission sent to the United States in 1898 to negotiate US recognition of Philippine independence).

FUN ANAGRAMS: "Sixto Joaquin Lezcano" becomes "Quiz ace joins tax loon."

EPHEMERA: 1) Félix Delgado signed 16-year-old Lezcano to a contract with the Brewers for $5,000 when he was a student at Fernando Collegio San Jose H.S. in San Jose, Puerto Rico, in October 1970. Four years earlier, Delgado tried to sign him as a 12-year-old, thinking he looked much older. Lezcano wore number 16 while with both the Brewers and Cardinals in honor of his age at the signing of his contract. 2) On May 20, 1977, Lezcano broke the American League record for most putouts by an outfielder in a nine-inning game (10). 3) Lezcano, Gorman Thomas and Cecil Cooper became the first teammates to hit a grand slam in three consecutive games on Apr. 7-9, 1978. 4) In 2014 Milwaukee established the Brewers Wall of Honor with Lezcano being one of the initial honorees along with Hall of Famers Hank Aaron, Robin Yount, Paul Molitor, and Rollie Fingers. 5) Sixto's cousin Carlos Lezcano played two seasons for the Cubs and managed more than 1,800 games in the minor leagues. 6) Sixto was the first player in major league history to hit a grand slam in opening day games in two different years, 1978 and 1980, a feat since matched by Hanley Ramirez.

WARNER MADRIGAL
A debacle of a major league debut, but oh that anagram of his name

BIRTH NAME: Warner Antonio Madrigal
PRONUNCIATION OF DIFFICULT PARTS: None
NICKNAME: None
HEIGHT/WEIGHT: 6'1" 235 lbs.
BORN: Mar. 21, 1984, in San Pedro de Macoris, Dominican Republic
POSITION: Pitcher
YEARS ACTIVE IN THE MAJORS: 2008-2009
NAME ETYMOLOGY/DEFINITIONS: "Warner" has English (of Norman origin) and North German origins, from a Germanic personal name composed of the elements *war(in)* meaning "guard" and *heri, hari* meaning "army." The name was introduced into England by the Normans in the form "Warnier." "Antonio" is of Latin origin. In the English language it is translated as "Anthony." The name derives from "Antonius," a well-known Latin family name, probably of Etruscan origin. The Roman general Marcus Antonius held that the origin of the name was Anthon, son of Hercules. This myth, recorded by Plutarch, was probably created by Marcus Antonius himself, in order to claim divine parentage. "Madrigal" has Spanish origins, as the habitational name from any of various places, for example in the provinces of Avila, Burgos, Cáceres, and

Guadalajara, apparently so called from Late Latin *matricale*, an adjective derivative of *matrix* meaning "womb," "riverbed."

A s a 17-year-old, Warner Madrigal was signed as an outfielder by scout Leo Perez for the Angels in 2001 and began his career in the Dominican leagues. The beefy Madrigal was an All-Star outfielder in the minor leagues but struggled hitting the breaking ball as he moved up the ladder and subsequently became a pitcher. He showed an ability to pitch down in the zone and offered an above-average breaking ball to go with a mid-90s fastball. Two years later, he was in the major leagues as a reliever.

But first, in 2003 he came to the Rookie level Provo Angels in the Pioneer League and put up a very good season, batting .369/.394/.581 with 28 doubles and 75 runs in 70 games. He led the Pioneer League in runs, doubles, hits (103), extra-base hits (39) and total bases (162) and was third in the league in average. He was voted the seventh-best prospect in the league and made the All-Star team as an outfielder – the only All-Star on Provo's championship team.

Warner did not play much the next year, getting into only 26 games for the Single-A Cedar Rapids Kernels, hitting .275/.330/.396. Playing regularly for Cedar Rapids in 2005, Madrigal batted .247/.288/.420 with 15 homers. He slipped to .235/.273/.348 for the 2006 Kernels and was converted to pitching.

He made his mound debut with the Rookie league AZL Angels and went 2-1 with five saves and a 3.75 ERA in 12 games. In 2007, Madrigal went 5-4 with 20 saves and a 2.07 ERA as the Cedar Rapids closer. He struck out 75 in 61 innings and allowed 44 hits and a .202 average. He did not give up a home run after May. He was second in the Midwest League in strikeouts per nine innings and was fourth in saves.

He spent the winter with the Escogido Lions in the Dominican Winter League, throwing 3⅔ scoreless innings across six games. The Angels inadvertently left him off the 40-man roster before the 2007 World Series, and he subsequently became a minor league free agent.[12]

Madrigal signed with the Rangers for 2008 and was assigned to the AA Frisco RoughRiders. He had a 1-0 record with ten saves and a 1.72 ERA in 14 games there and was moved up to AAA with the Oklahoma RedHawks. The right-hander fanned 25 in 20⅓ innings for Oklahoma and saved four games, with a 3.98 ERA. He was then promoted to the majors when Kason Gabbard was put on the disabled list.

Madrigal made his big-league debut at Yankee Stadium on July 2, 2008. It would be a night to forget. He entered in the bottom of the seventh protecting a 7-6 lead, in relief of Joaquin Benoit. Bobby Abreu greeted him with a ground-rule double. He walked Alex Rodriguez. He then yielded a two-run double to Jason Giambi and a run-scoring double to Jorge Posada to make it 9-7. Robinson Cano singled. Madrigal

---

[12] At the end of the 2007 season, the Angels decided to protect Madrigal from the Rule 5 Draft by putting him on their 40-man roster on Nov. 6. However, because Madrigal had spent six years in the minor leagues with one team, he became a free agent at the close of the 2007 World Series on Oct. 29.

finally retired a batter when Wilson Betemit grounded out, scoring Posada. After a wild pitch, Brett Gardner singled home Cano (it was Gardner's first hit in the majors after starting his career 0-for-7). Jamey Wright replaced the ineffective rookie and allowed Gardner to score; Madrigal had been charged with six runs and had only retired one better for a 162.00 ERA.[13] To his credit, the rest of the season he pitched much better: 30 appearances, 35⅔ innings, 31 hits, 13 walks, 22 strikeouts and a 3.28 ERA.

He spent 2009 shuttling between Texas and AAA Oklahoma City. For the Rangers he appeared in 13 games with dreadful peripherals: 12⅔ innings, 18 hits allowed, 14 runs given up, 12 walks and only five strikeouts. That would be the last he would see of big-league parks. He spent all of 2010 in the Rangers minor league system, then started riding the transaction carousel. Prior to the 2011 season, the Yankees signed Madrigal to a minor league contract with an invitation to spring training. In December 2012, he signed a minor league contract with the Diamondbacks. Madrigal signed with the Chunichi Dragons for the 2013 season. He signed a minor league deal with the Washington Nationals in January 2014. All in all, he spent nine years from 2010 to 2018 bouncing amongst teams in AA, AAA, the Dominican Winter Leagues, the Mexican League and the Japanese Central League.

BEST DAY (BY WPA OR OTHER MEASURE): One might think that after the pounding he took from the Yankees in his big-league debut, he might be a little spooked the next time he faced them. Well that wasn't the case when Madrigal got a second shot versus New York on Aug. 6, 2008 in Texas. The Yanks had built a 5-2 lead in the fifth inning and had runners on the corners with one out when Madrigal got the call to relieve starter Tommy Hunter. Madrigal induced a double play ball from Alex Rodriguez to end the threat, then got through the sixth yielding only a one out double to Xavier Nady. He pitched a 1-2-3 seventh, ending it with a Derek Jeter strikeout. He pitched the eighth inning too, yielding only a leadoff single to Bobby Abreu. Though the Rangers would still end up losing the game 5-3, the contest represented Madrigal's longest and probably most successful appearance in his career. He pitched 3⅔ innings, striking out two, allowing two hits and walking none.

THE WONDER OF HIS NAME: You have the word "madrigal," which is a "part-song" for several voices primarily of the Renaissance period. Too bad he didn't use a madrigal as his warm-up music. But the real fun comes here ... if you ignore his middle name, and just anagram his first and last name, you get a perfect description of his

---

[13] Math lesson! If you don't retire any batters in your debut, and you end up getting charged with at least one earned run, your earned run average is "infinity" (because you are dividing a number [earned runs] by zero [innings]). If, like our friend Warner here, you manage to retire one batter while allowing six earned runs, your ERA would be ([6 runs per inning x 9 innings] /.33 inning) or 162.00. Assuming you DO allow six earned runs in ⅓ of an inning, it would take you 8⅔ consecutive scoreless innings from that point forward to bring that ERA down to 9.00, and 17⅔ consecutive scoreless innings to bring it down to 3.00. And ... if you are a reliever who pitches maybe one inning in each appearance, that's a lot of scoreless appearances you have to string together. You've dug yourself some hole.

contribution to the overall success of the Texas Rangers while he hurled for them, namely "marginal reward."

NOT TO BE CONFUSED WITH: Al Madrigal (American comedian, writer, actor and producer. He is a co-founder of the *All Things Comedy* podcast network, alongside Bill Burr. He rose to fame on *The Daily Show* with Jon Stewart as a regular correspondent for five seasons), *Madrigal* (Song by the rock band Rush, from the album *A Farewell to Kings*, also a song by the progressive rock band Yes, from the album *Tormato*).

FUN ANAGRAMS: "Warner Antonio Madrigal" anagrams to "Rewarding, amoral nation," or "Ringworm and a rationale."

EPHEMERA: The only other player in major league history with the first name of "Warner" was a fellow named Warner Anderson back in the 1890s. But he actually went by "Varney" rather than "Warner."

QUINTON MCCRACKEN
From Blue Devil to Devil Ray

BIRTH NAME: Quinton Antoine McCracken
PRONUNCIATION OF DIFFICULT PARTS: None
NICKNAME: None
HEIGHT/WEIGHT: 5'7" 170 lbs.
BORN: Aug. 16, 1970, in Wilmington, North Carolina
POSITIONS: Outfielder, Pinch Hitter
YEARS ACTIVE IN THE MAJORS: 1995-2006
NAME ETYMOLOGY/DEFINITIONS: "Quinton" is taken from the habitational name from any of the places, for example in Gloucestershire, Northamptonshire, and Birmingham, named in Old English as *cwen tun*, from Old English meaning "the queen's settlement." Variants such as the Old French personal name "Quentin" or "Quintin" are from the habitational name from any of the places in northern France named for St. Quentin of Amiens, a 3rd- century Roman missionary to Gaul. "Antoine" has French origins, with those coming from Latin "Antonius," that could mean "beyond praise" or "highly praise-worthy." The name is a cognate of the name Antony. "McCracken" is a hereditary surname derived from Ulster and nearby Galloway, Scotland. It is an Anglicisation of "Mac Reachtain" an Ulster Gaelic variant of the patronymic surname "Mac Neachtain" (commonly Anglicised as "McNaughton").

Quinton McCracken attended South Brunswick H.S. where he was the starting running back and free safety in football, the starting point guard in basketball, and a standout in baseball and track. He played baseball and football (defensive back) for Duke University, where he earned his political science and history degrees in four years.

McCracken was selected by the Rockies in their inaugural draft in 1992 in the 25th round. In the minors he stole 60 bases in 1993 and another 36 in 1994. In 1995 at AAA Colorado Springs he put up a .359/.418/.482 line, which was gaudy even by PCL standards.

He made his major league debut as a September call-up in 1995; in three games, he struck out in his only at-bat. In 1996, he played mostly center field, batting .290 in 283 at-bats. In 1997, he stole a career-high 28 bases and batted .292.

McCracken was then taken by the expansion Tampa Bay Devil Rays in the 1997 Major League Baseball expansion draft. In 1998, playing in a career-high 155 games as the starting center fielder for the Devil Rays, McCracken had his best-ever season, batting .292 with seven home runs and 59 RBIs. He was named the Devil Rays first-ever most valuable player.

McCracken sprained a knee during off-season conditioning coming into the 1999 season, then played only 40 games that year due to a torn ACL. From that point on his base-stealing days were pretty much over, and without his usual burst of speed, his career sputtered. He spent most of 2000 in the minors with AAA Durham, getting into 85 games with them and only 15 for the big-league Devil Rays.

After paying him a total of $3.7 million between 1999 and 2000 and getting only 179 major league at-bats from him, the Devil Rays released him in November 2000. He signed with the St. Louis Cardinals four weeks later but was released in spring training. In April 2001, McCracken signed with the Twins and again spent most of the year in AAA, where he batted .338 with 27 doubles in only 361 at-bats for Edmonton.

For 2002 he signed with the Diamondbacks and spent the entire season with the major league club, hitting .309 with 27 doubles in 400 plate appearances as the team won the NL West. McCracken batted .364 in 11 at-bats in the NLDS, but the D'backs were swept out of the playoffs by the Cardinals.

In 2003, his batting average dropped 82 points to .227 with a .276 OBP. In December 2003, he was traded to the Mariners for first baseman Greg Colbrunn. McCracken did not get much playing time with Seattle, however, and in June 2004 he was released. Two days later, he re-signed with the D'backs and batted .288 in 55 games. McCracken re-signed with Arizona for 2005 but struggled with a .237 batting average.

He signed with the Reds for 2006 but was released in July. The Twins then signed him to a minor league contract on July 21, assigning him to the AAA Rochester Red Wings. After that season, he was not picked up by another team and signed on to play with the independent Bridgeport Bluefish of the Atlantic League. After one season in independent ball, McCracken played for the Dominican Winter Baseball League in late 2007 and retired.

After his playing days were over, McCracken was the Assistant Director, Player Development for the Diamondbacks in 2011-2012. He was Director of Player Development for the Astros in 2013-2017 and a minor-league coordinator for the Marlins in 2018. He was a coach for the Durham Bulls in 2019.

BEST DAY (BY WPA OR OTHER MEASURE): McCracken's best day on the diamond might have been in a game he didn't even start. On July 18, 2005, in a game versus the Marlins as a member of the host Diamondbacks, McCracken came on as part of a double-switch during the top of the fifth inning. With the D'backs trailing 3-2, he led off the bottom of the fifth with a line drive single to center and scored the tying run one out later on a two-base error by right fielder Jeff Conine. One inning later, McCracken grounded another single to center, this time with two outs and Jose Cruz on first. Arizona's Craig Counsell singled Cruz home for a 4-3 lead. In the bottom of the seventh with the Diamondbacks having extended the lead to 5-3 and having loaded the bases with two out, McCracken contributed a two-RBI single to left. Florida tied the game at 7-7 in the top of the eighth and the game eventually went into extra innings. In the bottom of the 11th with one out and Kelly Stinnett on first, McCracken sent everyone home with a walk-off triple to deep center. His final tally for the day: five plate appearances, three singles, a triple, three runs driven in and a run scored. The walk-off hit was the third and last of his career. From 1925-2019, there have been only 101 recorded walk-off triples in extra innings, and McCracken has one of them.

THE WONDER OF HIS NAME: As Jeff Pearlman notes: "If you've never heard of Quinton McCracken, well, shame on you. Because Quinton McCracken may well be the most pleasurable name in the history of the human tongue. Seriously, take a second, stop reaching and just say it aloud – Quinton McCracken. Q-u-i-n-t-o-n M-c-C-r-a-c-k-e-n. See? Fantastic, right? I've always had a soft spot for McCracken, first because his name is Quinton McCracken. Second, because his name is Quinton McCracken. Third, because he was the best player on the expansion Rays. Fourth, because he was the rare Major Leaguer to have played baseball at Duke. Fifth, because of the time I … name-dropped my friend and colleague, Seth Davis, on Quinton and it worked. Sixth, because he was an exceedingly nice guy to deal with and had zero airs about him. McCracken is back working for the Rays, which is cool because now a whole new generation of Tampa baseball fans (all six of them) will be required to say Quinton McCracken."

NOT TO BE CONFUSED WITH: Marshall Quinton (Catcher in the American Association from 1884-1885), Robert "Voros" McCracken (American baseball sabermetrician. "Voros" is a nickname from his partial Hungarian heritage. He is widely recognized for his pioneering work on Defense Independent Pitching Statistics).

FUN ANAGRAMS: "Quinton Antoine McCracken" becomes "Romance incontinent quack."

EPHEMERA: 1) He made history as the first batter to step to the plate for the Devil Rays franchise on Mar. 31, 1998. He also scored their first run, swiped their first stolen base and grounded into their first double play. 2) Quinton married Maggie Moskal in 2005. The couple have a son Isaiah Cicero born in 2008. Maggie was a cast member of VH-1s *Baseball Wives*. 3) He was elected to the Greater Wilmington Sports Hall of Fame.

ODDIBE MCDOWELL
The O is for Oddibe

BIRTH NAME: Oddibe McDowell
PRONUNCIATION OF DIFFICULT PARTS: "owed a bee" or "oh-ta-bee"
NICKNAME: None, though ESPN's Chris Berman called him "Oddibe Young Again McDowell"
HEIGHT/WEIGHT: 5'9" 165 lbs.
BORN: Aug. 25, 1962, in Hollywood, Florida
POSITION: Centerfielder
YEARS ACTIVE IN THE MAJORS: 1985-1990, 1994
NAME ETYMOLOGY/DEFINITIONS: Oddibe's dad was also Oddibe, and his dad was ... Ottie. According to an article in the *Austin American-Statesman* in 1984, "In all probability he should have been Ottie III, inheriting the real name of his paternal grandfather, but when his dad's father left home, some of the letters got scrambled as they were passed down. Hence, Oddibe." The etymology/meaning of "Ottie" is still a mystery, not appearing in any reference book of first names, but it appears to be a unisex name. "McDowell" is a surname of Scottish and Irish origin. It is an Anglicized form of Gaelic "Mac Dubhghaill" meaning "son of Dubhghall," a personal name composed of the elements *dubh* meaning "black" and *gall* meaning "stranger." This was originally a byname to distinguish the darker-haired Danes from the fair-haired Norwegians.

O ddibe McDowell was a two-time All American at Arizona State and won the Golden Spikes[14] award in 1984 when he hit .405 and slugged .788 with 31 stolen bases. He was a member of the United States National Baseball Team at the 1984 Olympics. The team included Mark McGwire and Barry Larkin. McDowell was drafted twice in 1981, twice in 1982, and once in 1983. He finally signed as a first-round selection in the 1984 amateur draft by the Rangers.

Playing only 31 games at AAA Oklahoma City in 1985 – and hitting .400 with eight triples – he was brought up to the Rangers for the rest of the 1985 season. He continued to be a sensation with the Rangers. He was second on the team with 18 home runs and second on the team with 25 stolen bases in 32 attempts. He finished fourth in the AL Rookie of the Year vote, compiling a .239/.304/.431 slash line while playing terrific defense in center.

The next year, 1986, he raised his batting average to .266 and his on-base percentage to .341, but despite playing a full season he only hit 18 home runs, the same as the previous year. He stole 33 bases but was caught 15 times. He scored 105 times but struck out 112 times. It was to be the only season in his major league career when he played in over 150 games.

---

[14] The Golden Spikes Award is given annually, since 1978, to the best amateur baseball player in the United States.

In 1987, he slumped to .241 with 14 home runs. His on-base percentage and slugging percentage remained mediocre. One bright spot was that he stole 24 bases in 26 attempts.

1988 was a disaster. Starting slowly, he was sent to the minors for 18 games in June – back to the Oklahoma City 89ers, where he hit .286. In the majors, he appeared in 120 games during the season, hitting .247 with only six home runs. He stole 33 bases. The Rangers were ready to move him, even though he had just turned 26. In December, they traded McDowell, Jerry Browne and Pete O'Brien to the Indians for thirty-year-old Julio Franco.

Oddibe lasted half a season with Cleveland in 1989 before being traded to the Braves at the start of July for Dion James. With Atlanta, he hit .304, with seven home runs in 76 games, but got caught 10 times in 25 steal attempts.

The following off-season, Bill James commented at length in his *Baseball Abstract* that the trade was an absolute steal for the Braves, given McDowell's tremendous talent and athleticism, but in 1990 he hit only .243 with 7 home runs, and he was released at the end of spring training the following year. He signed with the Baltimore Orioles a couple of weeks later and spent most of the season with the AAA Rochester Red Wings before being released again on July 28.

In the spring of 1992, he signed with the Angels. He played in six unimpressive games with the AAA Edmonton Trappers and was released on May 14. On July 13, 1993, he signed back with the Rangers and finished the season in AA ball with the Tulsa Drillers.

After beginning the 1994 season with the Oklahoma City 89ers, he was called up to the big-league Rangers in late April and spent the duration of the season in the majors, hitting .262 with one home run in 59 games. He still had some speed at age 31, stealing 14 bases in 16 attempts.

His last professional season, 1995, was spent with the Columbus Clippers in the Yankees chain. He appeared in only 14 games, hitting a mere .217 without a stolen base (one caught stealing).

BEST DAY (BY WPA OR OTHER MEASURE): On July 23, 1985, McDowell hit for the cycle, going 5-for-5 with a stolen base, three runs scored and three driven in as he helped the Rangers secure a 8-4 win over the Indians. The 5-for-5 day gave him hits in eight consecutive at-bats over a two-game span.

THE WONDER OF HIS NAME: "McDowell" has an interesting etymology, but let's be real ... "Oddibe" makes the name here. When I originally heard "Oddibe" back in the mid-1980s, I thought of "Oh to be in England!" from Robert Browning's poem, *Home Thoughts, from Abroad*, written in 1845. It has been voted one of the U.K.'s most popular poems. But I'm a bit of a nerd ... your mileage/associations may vary.

NOT TO BE CONFUSED WITH: Jack "Black Jack" McDowell (AL Cy Young winner in 1983), "Sudden" Sam McDowell (Six-time All-Star pitcher)

FUN ANAGRAMS: "Oddibe McDowell" gives us "Bold cow idled me."

EPHEMERA: 1) He is, not surprisingly, the only "Oddibe" in professional baseball history. 2) That cycle he hit for in 1985 was the very first one in Texas Rangers history. 3) Arizona State University inducted McDowell to the university's athletic hall of fame and has retired his number. 4) He was assigned number zero by his college coach, who insisted it was really "0 … for Oddibe." McDowell would wear zero for the first four years of his time in the bigs. The late, great Yankees public address announcer Bob Sheppard refused to utter the word "number" when introducing anyone wearing zero, because he believed it to not be a number. So, when someone like McDowell stepped to the plate at the Stadium, Sheppard would intone "The center fielder, zero, Oddibe McDowell." 5) McDowell is currently the head coach for the McArthur H.S. varsity baseball team in Hollywood, Florida. 6) He was inducted to the National College Baseball Hall of Fame in 2011. 7) Between February 2011 and March 2012, *Deadspin* ran a series of 14 articles which published McDowell's monthly water bill and the amount owed; until that time, water bills were publicly accessible on the Broward County Waste and Wastewater Services department's website.

LASTINGS MILLEDGE
From awkward rookie to baseball mentor

BIRTH NAME: Lastings Darnell Milledge
PRONUNCIATION OF DIFFICULT PARTS: None
NICKNAME: None
HEIGHT/WEIGHT: 5'11" 210 lbs.
BORN: Apr. 5, 1985 in Bradenton, Florida
POSITION: Outfielder
YEARS ACTIVE IN THE MAJORS: 2006-2011
NAME ETYMOLOGY/DEFINITIONS: As for "Lastings," according to Milledge himself, "My mom named me 'Lastings' because she knew I'd be her last child. My brothers are older." "Darnell" is from Old French *darnel*, an annual grass (Lolium temulentum), hence perhaps a topographic name. "Milledge" has English origins, namely as the habitational name from Milwich in Staffordshire, so named from Old English *myln* meaning "mill" and *wic* referring to a "dairy farm;" it could also refer to a "trading settlement."

A t the age of 12, Milledge pitched and played third base and hit third for the Manatee East Little League team that was the national runner-up in the 1997 Little League World Series. He received the win on the mound in the semi-final game of the regional, giving up only one run on a solo home run.

In 2001, he led Team USA to a Gold Medal game victory over Venezuela in the International Baseball Federation's AA World Youth Championships. Later that year, *Baseball America* named Milledge the best 16-year-old player in the United States.

He might have been the top pick in the 2003 amateur draft, but an expulsion from high school for sexual misconduct resulted in him falling to the Mets as the twelfth overall pick in the first round. After prolonged negotiations due to new allegations of additional sexual misconduct in high school, New York finally signed Milledge to a contract with a signing bonus of just over $2.0 million.

He was initially assigned to the Rookie level Kingsport Mets, where he hit .231/.323/.308 and stole five in six tries in seven games. *Baseball America* rated him the 21st-best outfield prospect in baseball. In 2004, he spent most of the season with the Single-A Capital City Bombers, where he hit .340/.401/.580 and stole 23 in 29 tries in 65 games. He also played for the St. Lucie Mets, batting .235/.319/.432 in 22 outings there. He was rated as having the best outfield arm in the South Atlantic League (SAL) by *Baseball America*, which rated him the number two outfield prospect in baseball, behind Delmon Young and just ahead of Jeff Francoeur and Grady Sizemore. The same publication picked him as the third-best SAL prospect behind Young and Ian Stewart.

In 2005, he split the year between St. Lucie (.302/.385/.418, 18-for-31 in SB) and the AA Binghamton Mets (.337/.392/.487, 11-for-16 in SB). He feasted on left-handed pitching, batting .410 against Florida State League (FSL) southpaws and .377 against lefties while with Binghamton. He was rated the number three prospect in the FSL by *Baseball America* (behind Andy LaRoche and Justin Verlander) and number two in the Eastern League (behind Francisco Liriano).

In 2006, he played 84 games with the AAA Norfolk Tides where he hit .277/.388/.440. *Baseball America* named him the most exciting player in the International League and number two prospect, behind Delmon Young. He was promoted to the majors in late May and made his major league debut on May 30, 2006, as the starting right fielder for the Mets.

On June 4 of that year Milledge hit his first major league career homer off Giants closer Armando Benítez to tie up the game 6–6 in the bottom of the tenth inning. When the Mets returned to the field the following inning, Milledge, still excited, high-fived the home fans in attendance at Shea as he returned to his position, raising the ire of his manager and some teammates, not to mention the national sports media.

In late September one of Milledge's Mets teammates placed a sign on his locker which read, "Know Your Place, Rook!" (The sign-placer was identified in published reports as then-Mets closer Billy Wagner). All told he had three separate stints in the majors in 2006, and for the year he compiled a .241 average with four homers and 22 RBIs in 56 games.

While on the disabled list in 2007 for strained ligaments, Milledge was discovered to have used sexist language in a not-yet-released rap CD. The Mets issued a statement that "We disapprove of the content, language and message of this recording, which does not represent the views of the New York Mets." After his rehab from the injury, Milledge was called up by the Mets in mid-July. For the year, he hit .272/.341/.446 for a 104 OPS+ (which would turn out to be his highest OPS+ in his career).

After the 2007 season, the 22-year-old Milledge was sent to the Nationals in a trade for veterans Brian Schneider and Ryan Church. With the Nationals in 2008, he played 138 games, hitting .268/.330/.402 with career highs in doubles (24), home runs (14), steals (24 in 33 tries), runs (65) and RBIs (61). His OPS+ for the year was 92, subpar for an outfielder.

Things got off on the wrong foot in 2009, as he went 4-for-24 in seven games before being sent down to AAA because of what were rumored to be attitude issues. He hit only .253/.277/.316 in 22 games for the Syracuse Chiefs. On June 30, he was traded to the Pirates. He got into 58 games with Pittsburgh the rest of the season, batting .291, although with relatively little power (four homers in 220 at-bats). His .333 OBP and .395 slugging percentage resulted in a 94 OPS+. He began 2010 as the Pirates' starting left fielder. He hit .277/.332/.380 for another 94 OPS+. For a player once praised as a multi-tool threat, he showed little power or speed.

He wound up behind Garrett Jones in playing time in right field for the 2010 Bucs and behind Jose Tabata in left. Though he was still only 25 years old, Pittsburgh had younger outfielders with brighter upsides in 23-year-old Andrew McCutchen and the 21-year-old Tabata. There was little room for Milledge in Pittsburgh.

Milledge signed with the White Sox for 2011 but only went 1-for-4 with a double and a run for them, spending the rest of the year back in AAA with the Charlotte Knights. With Charlotte, he batted .295/.364/.441 with 27 steals in 33 tries and 12 home runs.

Milledge played in 125 games for the Tokyo Yakult Swallows in 2012, hitting .300 with 21 HR and 65 RBIs. He re-signed with the Swallows after 2012, for three years and $4.4 million. Hampered by injuries in 2014-15, he appeared in only a combined 34 games those years. All told in four seasons with the Swallows, Milledge played in 255 games, batting .272 with 39 home runs and 129 RBIs.

In 2017, Milledge played with the Lancaster Barnstormers of the Atlantic League and retired from professional baseball after that the season.

BEST DAY (BY WPA OR OTHER MEASURE): On Aug. 7, 2008, while playing for the Nationals, Milledge tortured pitcher Jeff Francis of the host Rockies. Milledge grounded out against Francis in the second, but leading off in the fifth, Milledge launched a homer to deep left field to give the Nats a 1-0 lead. The very next inning, with Washington now leading 3-0 and one out and Austin Kearns on first, Milledge drove Francis out of the game with another longball to deep left. Milledge punctuated his day with a single to center off Jason Grilli in the seventh, driving in Cristian Guzman. He finished 3-for-4 with two homers, four runs driven in and two runs scored.

THE WONDER OF HIS NAME: It's another "double unique" name! Also, who can beat that origin story of his first name ... his mom could have named him "ThatsIt," "Final," "NoMore" or "TubalLigation."

NOT TO BE CONFUSED WITH: John Milledge (American politician who fought in the American Revolution and later served as United States Representative, 26th

Governor of Georgia, and United States Senator. Milledge was a founder of Athens, Georgia, and the University of Georgia), firsting (according to the Oxford English Dictionary, it is an archaic term referring to a preliminary process in laundering, in which clothes and linen are soaked, rubbed to remove dirt, and then washed in boiling water before further cleansing treatments).

FUN ANAGRAMS: "Lastings Darnell Milledge" transforms into "Strangle smelling idle lad."

EPHEMERA: 1) Milledge was 21 years, 55 days old on the day of his debut – exactly the same age as Darryl Strawberry when he made his debut in 1983. 2) In 2009, Milledge gave up his uniform number, 44 for Adam Dunn, instead wearing number 85 to match his birth year. 3) His brothers Greg and Tony Jr. each played in the minor leagues. 4) Milledge now mentors youngsters in the finer points of baseball at 1st Round Training in Palmetto, Florida. He also recently opened Manatee Innercity Baseball in nearby Bradenton in an effort to afford minority kids an opportunity to learn and play the game. "That's what we're supposed to be doing," Milledge said of black ex-major leaguers like himself, "exposing the game to less-fortunate kids, and letting them know there are other opportunities in other sports than what they know."

VAN LINGLE MUNGO
Temperamental guy who was the subject of a hit novelty song

BIRTH NAME: Van Lingle Mungo
PRONUNCIATION OF DIFFICULT PARTS: None
NICKNAME: None
HEIGHT/WEIGHT: 6'2" 185 lbs.
BORN: June 8, 1911, in Pageland, South Carolina
DIED: Feb. 12, 1985, in Pageland, South Carolina
POSITION: Pitcher
YEARS ACTIVE IN THE MAJORS: 1931-1943, 1945
NAME ETYMOLOGY/DEFINITIONS: "Van" is derived from the English surname Van. It is from the Middle English *vanne* and the Middle French *van*, words denoting a type of old winnowing machine. Alternatively, the name can be a borrowing of the Dutch "Van," an element in family names which means "of, from" and indicates place of origin. Besides happening to be Mungo's mother's maiden name, "Lingle" is possibly an altered spelling of the German "Lingel." "Lingel" is possibly a shortened form of a habitational name from a place such as "Lingelbach." "Lingel" might also be a nickname from the Middle High German linge, meaning "hurried." "Mungo" is of Scottish origin. It was an alternative name for St. Kentigern, the patron saint of Glasgow, who was a 6th-century apostle of southwestern Scotland and northwestern England.

Van Lingo Mungo graduated from South Carolina's Pageland H.S. in 1928 and began his career in 1929, pitching for Fayetteville, North Carolina, in the Class D Eastern Carolina Association, going 10-9. A hard-throwing right-hander who lacked a bit of control, Mungo spent most of 1930 with Winston-Salem in the Class C Piedmont League, going 11-11, and his work impressed "Nap" Rucker, who was scouting the South for the National League's Brooklyn Robins. Brooklyn acquired his contract from Winston-Salem at the end of the season and assigned him to its affiliate in the Eastern League, the Hartford Senators, in 1931.

Mungo's first appearance of the 1931 season was nerve-wracking. In the season opener, on Apr. 27 at New Haven, Hartford's starter, Johnny Krider, got into difficultly in the ninth inning and Mungo came into the game with none out, the bases loaded, and the score 10-4. Van sandwiched two strikeouts around a walk but an error by the shortstop and another walk made the score 10-7, and Mungo's day was over. New Haven continued its rally against two other pitchers and won the game, 11-10. The 20-year-old Mungo recovered from his debut to go 15-5 and lead the league with 151 strikeouts in 191 innings pitched. His 2.12 ERA was third best in the league. At the end of the season, Mungo was called up to Brooklyn, and posted a 3-1 record. He shined in his debut, shutting out the Boston Braves, 2-0, on three hits, while helping himself out at the plate with a single and triple.

Mungo was the only quality pitcher on some very bad Dodgers teams in the 1930s. In his first full season with Brooklyn he went 13-11 in 1932 as the Dodgers finished third in the league with an 81-73 record for new manager Max Carey. In 1933 Mungo went 16-15 with a 2.72 ERA as the Dodgers finished in sixth place with a 65-88 record.

In 1934, Mungo was named to the All-Star team for the first time. Mungo was a workhorse that season, leading the league in games started (38) and innings pitched (315⅓).

After his 18-win season in 1934, Mungo held out for a larger salary increase than the Dodgers were interested in putting forth. He eventually did report and would up posting a 16-10 record, including a league-leading four shutouts in 1935. On Sep. 29 he struck out 15 Philadelphia Phillies in route to his final win of the season. He also wound up the season batting .289 (26-for-90).

Mungo's batterymate was Al Lopez, with whom he had a great rapport. However, Lopez was traded to the Boston Braves over the winter of 1935. The new Brooklyn catcher was Babe "Blimp" Phelps, and Mungo did not think particularly highly of Phelps, who would find himself consistently among the league leaders in passed balls.

The Dodgers offense sputtered to support Mungo during the early part of the 1936 season, and after two June losses took his record to 6-8 (five of the losses by one run), he demanded to be traded. A sportswriter, Eddie Zeltner, smelled a good story, and arranged for airfare to get Mungo out of town, which in this case was Pittsburgh. Mungo, not one to turn down a favor, temporarily left the team on June 10, much to the consternation of manager Casey Stengel. He returned after three days, joining the club in Cincinnati and receiving a $600 fine. From that point on, as noted by Tommy Holmes of the Brooklyn Eagle, Mungo was "likely to become the center of a number of wild reports every time somebody sees him, or thinks they see him, drink a glass of beer."

During the 1936 season, Mungo struck out ten or more batters in a game six times. He started a league-leading 37 games that year, posted an 18-19 record, and led the league with a career-high 238 strikeouts (but also led the league with 118 walks). He was named to his second All-Star team. Despite Mungo's efforts, the Dodgers slogged along to a 67-87 record. It came as no surprise that Casey Stengel did not return as manager for 1937.

Before the 1937 season, Mungo once again expressed dissatisfaction with his contract, before signing for an estimated $15,000. He got to play for his fourth manager in his years with the Dodgers, Burleigh Grimes.

Van's temper would occasionally overshadow his talent. On May 16, in a tight game, the Dodgers and Bees were knotted, 2-2, as the game entered the 11th inning. Teammate Tom Winsett snuffed out Mungo's hopes for his fifth victory in succession. He singled to right field with one out in the top of the inning. The next batter hit what appeared to be a single to right but somehow Winsett lost track of the ball and was forced at second base, stopping the rally in its tracks. The Bees won the game in their half of the inning. Mungo blew his top, going as far as to question Winsett's ancestry. After the game, he walked to a telegraph office and sent the following wire to his wife. "Pack up your bags and come to Brooklyn, honey. If Winsett can play in the big leagues, it's a cinch you can too."

Five days later, he called his wife in Pageland only to find out that his infant son, Van Jr., was critically ill after surgery. The news prompted Mungo to an evening of drinking. Early the next morning, he broke into the hotel room occupied by teammates Woody English and Jimmy Bucher in St. Louis, ostensibly looking for a pinochle game. Bucher confronted Mungo and the latter began throwing furniture over the room. Bucher then sent his fist into Mungo's face, giving him a black eye. Mungo was fined $1,000 for his extracurricular activities. He then returned home for a short spell to tend to his ailing son, who did recover.

On July 4, 1937, while pitching against the Giants, Mungo was forced to leave the game in the eighth inning when he pulled a muscle in his side. He had been chosen for the All-Star team and joined the NL team to Washington. Brooklyn skipper Grimes instructed National League All-Stars manager Bill Terry not to use Mungo in the game. During the game, despite Grimes's instructions, Terry pitched Mungo anyway. Mungo aggravated his injury and developed a sore shoulder while pitching the sixth and seventh innings. To make things worse, Grimes did not rest his star and handed Mungo the ball on July 11. He lasted only four ineffective innings that day and proceeded to lose his last four decisions in 1937.

He did not start from July 19 to Aug. 14, as he had his tonsils removed and he rested in Pageland. At the end of August, not long after he came back, Grimes, skeptical of Mungo's claims of a sore arm, suspended him. Mungo pitched in pain for the balance of his time with the Dodgers, and his blazing fastball was rarely seen again.

Mungo returned to the Dodgers for the 1938 season, promising a return to the form he had displayed before the 1937 All-Star Game. Newly appointed Dodgers executive vice president Larry MacPhail, so convinced that Mungo would be his former self, turned down a trade offer from the Cubs that included four players and $75,000 in cash.

By the end of April, Mungo's arm problems were back. His fastball was M.I.A. as he lost his first three decisions. His first win of the season was a nine strikeout, 7-0 shutout of the Cubs on May 11. Hope was flickering, but he would never again strike out as many as nine in a game.

There was one more glimpse of what might have been. On June 30, 1938, Mungo pitched a one-hitter against the Boston Bees. Reflecting on his effort he stated, "The truth is my arm ached from the first inning to the last. I really wasn't fast. Only occasionally, I would throw a fast one. But when I threw a curve, it was terrible. I thought it would pull the arm out by the roots." When manager Burleigh Grimes sent Mungo out for his next start, on July 4, Mungo retired only one batter before exiting. Mungo finished the season at 4-11, and his salary was cut from $15,000 to $5,000 prior to the 1939 season.

Despite the salary cut, in December 1938, an Associated Press article pronounced: "The Brooklyn baseball club has made the approach of a new year official by issuing its annual announcement that Van Lingle Mungo, the big fireball pitcher with the ailing arm and sultry disposition, will not be sold or traded 'because we expect him to win 20 games for us next season.'

Grimes was dispatched after the 1938 season. During Mungo's final years, his manager would be Leo Durocher. When he took over the managerial reins in 1939, Durocher had hopes that he could "handle" Mungo and see a return to form. On May 4, Durocher used Mungo in relief of "Boots" Poffenberger. Mungo came on in the first inning with one run in, none out, and the bases filled with Cubs. He got out of the jam by striking out two and inducing Billy Herman to hit a popup, and he did not allow a run until the ninth inning, when he showed signs of tiring. The Dodgers won the game, 6-2. Durocher inserted him in the rotation and by the end of May his record stood at 3-3 with a 2.79 ERA. After May, Mungo was largely ineffective and his season ended on July 23, when he broke his ankle sliding into second base while being used as a pinch-runner. His record for the season was 4-5 with a 3.26 ERA in only 77⅓ innings.

The Dodgers were impressed with Mungo's efforts during the season, although he won only four games. He was used as a pinch-hitter and pinch-runner, and even took a turn in left field. For the season, Mungo's batting average was .345. After having his salary slashed the winter before, Larry MacPhail rewarded him with a bonus after the 1939 season.

In 1940, Mungo's role with the Dodgers was that of a relief pitcher. He was doing well in his new role. In his first four appearances, he pitched a total of 14 innings and did not yield a run. But his arm problems came back and his season ended on June 24. After Mungo was dropped from the Dodgers' active list, it was decided that surgery was the best option to restore the strength to his arm. On July 1, 1940, Mungo underwent an operation to remove calcium deposits from his shoulder. He came to spring training in 1941 ready to pitch.

Over a three-day period of Sat., Mar. 8 to Mon., Mar. 10, Mungo made some very bad life choices. He was scheduled to pitch on the 8th, but the game was rained out and he found himself with some idle time. Accompanied by Lady Ruth Vine, the mistress of ceremonies for the floor show at the Hotel Nacional, he went for some "malt and merriment" and became inebriated. (Lady Ruth was not of nobility. She was from a Nashville family and her first name was really Lady.)

After midnight, no longer in the company of Lady Ruth, Mungo, who had pledged to remain sober, found his way into the bar at the Hotel Nacional and offered to buy a round of drinks for everyone there. He told the bartender not to "skip those two fellows up at the end of the bar. They look like a couple of regular guys." Those regular guys, unfortunately for Van, were Durocher and coach Chuck Dressen. Durocher, not in the least amused by the incident, ordered Mungo to retreat to his room. The next day, Mungo went to the ballpark ready to pitch the opener of the Mar. 9 doubleheader against the Cleveland Indians. Larry MacPhail and Durocher had other ideas.

They fined Mungo $200 for drinking and had him banished from training camp. Mungo was assigned to the Dodgers affiliate in the International League and ordered to depart Havana via a Sunday evening boat (along with the visiting Cleveland squad), and to join the Montreal Royals at their Macon, Georgia, training base.

But the Sunday night boat left Havana Harbor without Mungo. After leaving the ballpark that afternoon, he resumed his drinking and set about to destroy everything in sight. After he missed the 7:00 P.M. boat, arrangements were made to have him take a flight out of Havana the following morning. The Dodgers went so far as to have a detective keep an eye on Van as he had dinner and went back to his room to rest up for the 10:00 a.m. flight.

Sometime after midnight, Van was joined once again by Lady Ruth and she brought along Miriam Morgan, the female half of the dance duo of Gonzalo and Cristina. Cristina, prior to taking to a life in show business, had been the petite Miriam Morgan of Wilkes-Barre, Pennsylvania. The trio took in the Havana nightlife.

By 6:00 a.m. on Monday the 10th, the drunken Mungo and the women had found their way to Room 273 of Hotel Nacional, the room of Lady Ruth. Lady and Cristina were on one bed, and Van Lingle Mungo was in the other. Gonzalo was in Room 272. His real name was Francisco Callada Carreno, and in another life, he had been a matador. He was quite annoyed to discover that his wife, Cristina, was not occupying her proper bed.

He made his way to the next room and, by his account, found his wife attired in a blue negligee. The former Dodger ace was in the room with the ladies and had on not a stitch of clothing. A fight ensued and Gonzalo came out on the short end. Van, who had done some prizefighting in his younger days, displayed his skills, despite being somewhat incapacitated by the alcohol he had consumed.

There were many versions of what happened. Robert Sullivan in the *New York Daily News* wrote that the ladies contended that they were "doing a Samaritan act, seeking to sober Van up on milk and other health-giving elements full of Vitamin B-1. This work at last proved so tiring that the ladies, not knowing otherwise how to get rid of Van, dumped him into one of Lady's beds. They fell into the other, knowing nothing more until the before mentioned dawn."

At 10:00 a.m. that same day, Mungo was deposited on an airplane and flown back to the United States. Gonzalo sued Van Lingle Mungo $20,000 for breaking up his marriage. Mungo's Dodger days were effectively over.

He made two brief appearances without a decision before being sent to Montreal on May 15, 1941. Mungo was traded to the Giants' American Association affiliate at Minneapolis before the 1942 season. An 11-3 record with the Minneapolis earned him a call-up to the Polo Grounds, and Mungo proceeded to post a 3-7 record for the big-league club in 1943. He entered the Army early in 1944 and served stateside for nine months, missing the entire season. After nine months in the Army, he received a medical discharge on Oct. 19, 1944.

Mungo returned to the Giants in 1945, once again sober and once again promising to make good – this time at age 33. He did not touch so much as a drop of alcohol in training camp, and he excelled in an exhibition performance against the Yankees in Atlantic City on Apr. 1. With determination, sobriety, and a sinker pitch alleged to contain a certain amount of foreign substance, Mungo posted a 14-7 record in 1945 for the Giants. His 101 strikeouts were his most since 1937.

After his performance in 1945, he elected to hold out. He was re-signed by the Giants for $12,000, but during spring training, his sobriety, which had been a key to his 1945 success, was questioned by manager Mel Ott. Mungo was suspended and subsequently released.

For his career, Mungo was 120-115 with an ERA of 3.47.

BEST DAY (BY WPA OR OTHER MEASURE): The Cardinals and the Dodgers' crosstown archrivals, the Giants, were tied going into the last weekend of the 1933 season. The Giants' last two games were against the Dodgers. On Saturday, Sep. 29, Mungo went the distance, allowing only five hits, to gain his 18th win of the season (against 16 losses) and the Cardinals passed the Giants in the standings. In the 5-1 game, Mungo starred at the plate as well, hitting two singles, scoring the Dodgers' first run and driving in the second, which was all Brooklyn would need. Mungo's ninth-inning performance put the icing on the cake. After the first two batters reached base, he struck out Travis Jackson, George Watkins (who had homered earlier for the Giants' sole tally), and pinch-hitter Lefty O'Doul, all on called third strikes, to end the game. Fifty years later, Mungo looked back on that moment as the highlight of his career.

THE WONDER OF HIS NAME: How many baseball players ever had songs named after them (besides "Joltin' Joe DiMaggio")? Mungo's prosodic name became the title of a novelty song by jazz pianist Dave Frishberg in 1969. He developed the song's melody first, but couldn't settle on lyrics, until he browsed through a copy of a baseball encyclopedia. In the encyclopedia, he found the name of Van Lingle Mungo, a name he found unusual. He later found himself humming Mungo's name to the melody. From there, Frishberg found more names in the encyclopedia that he found interesting. He proceeded to write lyrics for the melody that included only the names of major league players from the 1940s and the words "and" and "big," attempting to order the names in a rhyming fashion. It was subsequently reported that Mungo and his wife both enjoyed the song.

NOT TO BE CONFUSED WITH: Fungo bat (Specially designed bat used by baseball and softball coaches for practice), Drungo Hazewood (see page 105), Mungo Jerry (1970s British rock group with the hit "In the Summertime"), Linda Lingle (governor of Hawaii from 2002-2010)

FUN ANAGRAMS: "Van Lingle Mungo" anagrams to "Vile man, long gun."

EPHEMERA: 1) His parents were Henry Van and Martha Charlotte (Lingle) Mungo. His father, a cotton grower and retailer, had himself been a pitcher, plying his trade in the Sally League during the early years of the 20th century. Van was one of two children. His sister, Lucille, was born in 1908, and as an adult worked as a saleswoman in the family's retail store. 2) Van and Eloise Clamp, a schoolteacher, were married in 1932. They welcomed their first child, Pamela, in 1934. Van Jr., known as Sonny, followed in 1937, and their youngest child, Ernest, came along in 1943. Ernest played outfield in the minor leagues from 1962 through 1964, making it as far as Class A. Eloise went on to teach for 28 years, and was said to remain devoted to her husband, despite the fact that over the years, as legend has it, many females caught the eye of Van Lingle Mungo. 3) During his May 6, 1937 start, the Hindenburg hovered overhead, but the fans took little notice with Mungo pitching. Later that day, in Lakehurst, New Jersey, the airship burst into flames. 4) By his own estimation, Mungo probably paid more in fines than any player of his era, amassing a grand total of over $15,000. As examples, in 1936 he was fined twice by the Dodgers, $25 for a fistfight with a teammate and $200 for "quitting" the team during a series in Pittsburgh. In 1937 the Dodgers fined him $1,000 for getting into another fistfight with a teammate. 5) After he retired, he purchased and operated a movie house called the Ball Theatre, and had a balcony built to accommodate people of color, who had previously been denied access to the facility. The theater was ruined by a fire in 1957. 6) Mungo also continued his family's involvement in cotton, owning a cotton gin, and continued to operate the retail store that had been started by his father. One of his other businesses was a trucking concern. However, the company was not properly insured and when one of his drivers was involved in a major accident, the resulting lawsuits caused the business to fail. 7) Mungo forever remained the pride of Pageland, and if you drive through Chesterfield County, South Carolina, you may very well find yourself on the Van Lingle Mungo Boulevard. 8) In 1974, Mungo was inducted into the South Carolina Athletic Hall of Fame.

BIFF POCOROBA
10-year vet of the Atlanta Braves

BIRTH NAME: Biff Benedict Pocoroba
PRONUNCIATION OF DIFFICULT PARTS: po-ko-ROE-buh

NICKNAME: None
HEIGHT/WEIGHT: 5'10" 175 lbs.
BORN: July 25, 1953, in Burbank, California
POSITIONS: Catcher, Pinch Hitter, Third Baseman
YEARS ACTIVE IN THE MAJORS: 1975-1984
NAME ETYMOLOGY/DEFINITIONS: "Biff" has English origins, from a mid-20th century nickname which was based on the English word *biff*, which means "punch," "hit" or "strike." "Benedict" comes from Late Latin word *benedictus*, meaning "blessed." Etymologically it is derived from the Latin words *bene* meaning "good" and *dicte* meaning "speak," i.e. "well spoken." Pocoroba is a bit of a mystery. One possibility is that it has Corsican origins, with *poco* meaning "little" and *roba* meaning "clothes" or "stuff/goods." Biff's father on the reason for his son's name? "Well, I named him that because I didn't want him to go through life having to answer to Herman, or something."

D rafted by the Braves in the 17th round of the 1971 amateur draft, Biff Pocoroba attracted attention during spring training in 1975 by throwing out 11 straight would-be base stealers, and made his major league debut (as a defensive replacement) that April. His best season was in 1977 when he played in 113 games, with a slash line of .290/.394/.445 to go with eight home runs, 24 doubles and 44 runs batted in, an OPS+ of 115, and a WAR of 1.8. He didn't make the All-Star team that season, but instead made it the following year, when he was compiling a lesser line of .262/.337/.349 prior to the break. Why did he make the All-Star team that year? One reason may have been that teammate Phil Niekro was on that squad, and Niekro's knuckler required Biff's experience in catching that pitch.

Following rotator cuff surgery in 1979, Biff was limited primarily to pinch-hitting duties and very infrequent excursions behind the dish, although Bobby Cox did try him out at third base. Another casualty of the rotator cuff injury was Pocoroba's ability to switch hit. After the injury he batted right-handed only.

He had one postseason at bat, pinch-hitting for Niekro in the seventh inning of Game 2 of the 1982 NLCS, grounding out to second. The Braves were swept in that NLCS by the Cardinals, who went on to win the World Series that year.

Pocoroba played in his final game on Apr. 20, 1984, pinch-hitting, drawing a walk and eventually scoring on a Dale Murphy home run. His final career line was .257/.339/.351 with 21 home runs, 172 RBIs and an OPS+ of 86.

BEST DAY (BY WPA OR OTHER MEASURE): Walk-off hits are cool. Walk-off homers are cooler. Walk-off grand slam homers? Cooler still. Pinch-hit walk-off grand slams? Oh baby. How about a pinch-hit walk-off grand slam homer with two out in the ninth? Well Biff Pocoroba did just that on May 17, 1977 against the visiting Expos. The hometown Braves went into the bottom of the ninth trailing 6-5, and the first two batters were retired with no issue for Expos reliever Bill Atkinson. Then Junior Moore singled, Jeff Burroughs walked and Gary Matthews singled to load the bases. Catcher Vic Correll was due up, but instead manager Dave Bristol sent up Pocoroba. Pocoroba, who would amass only 21 homers in a career of nearly 1,700 plate appearances, proceeded to launch the first pinch-hit homer of his career, giving the Braves the 9-6 win. At the time it was only the seventh pinch-hit walk-off grand slam since those records were first tracked (1945).

THE WONDER OF HIS NAME: Biff! Who doesn't like saying that name? It's short and dramatic and has onomatopoeic qualities to it. In fact, if you remember the fight scenes in the *Batman* TV series of the mid-1960s, "BIFF!!!" punctuated some punches thrown by the Dynamic Duo. Then you add in the lyrical "Pocoroba" with its "po-co-ro" sequence. The complete name is the "Reese's Peanut Butter Cup" of this book. Allow me to paraphrase Reese's great slogan ... "Biff Pocoroba ... two great names that sound great together."

NOT TO BE CONFUSED WITH: Biff Loman (Willy Loman's elder son in *Death of a Salesman*), Biff, the Michigan Wolverine (A live wolverine who served as a team mascot at University of Michigan Wolverines football games and was later kept in a small zoo at the University of Michigan in the 1920s and 1930s. In the mid-1920s, before the acquisition of a live wolverine, the University of Michigan used a mounted and stuffed wolverine, also named Biff, as the team mascot).

FUN ANAGRAMS: "Biff Benedict Pocoroba" turns into "Forbid boob, accept fine."

EPHEMERA: 1) For a high school graduation gift, his dad gave him the choice of a batting cage or a car. Biff chose the batting cage. 2) In 1988 he and his brothers started Sausage World Inc. in Lilburn, Georgia. Pocoroba serves as the President of the company that makes various kinds of sausage including sweet basil Italian sausage, links of pepperoni, bratwurst, knockwurst, kielbasa, and andouille. 3) Clint Courtney, a manager in the Braves minor league system during the early 1970s, had trouble pronouncing "Pocoroba," so he called him "Coca-Cola." 4) Pocoroba married Jody Raymond in 1974 and they have four children, a son Victor and daughters Jenna, Keisa and Angela.

JENNINGS POINDEXTER
"Temperamental," "wild and wooly" lefty pitcher

BIRTH NAME: Chester Jennings Poindexter
PRONUNCIATION OF DIFFICULT PARTS: None
NICKNAME: Jinx[15]
HEIGHT/WEIGHT: 5'10" 165 lbs.
BORN: Sep. 30, 1910, in Pauls Valley, Oklahoma
DIED: Mar. 3, 1983, in Norman, Oklahoma
POSITION: Pitcher
YEARS ACTIVE IN THE MAJORS: 1936, 1939
NAME ETYMOLOGY/DEFINITIONS: "Chester" is from a surname which originally belonged to a person who came from Chester, an old Roman settlement in Britain. The name of the settlement came from Latin *castrum* meaning "camp" or "fortress." "Jennings" has English origins, patronymic from the Middle English personal name "Janyn," or "Jenyn," a pet form of "John." It could also have German origins, patronymic from a pet form of the personal name "Johannes." "Poindexter" has English origins, as the nickname from Old French *poing destre* meaning "right fist." This name is particularly associated with Huguenot refugees who fled from France to England and, from there, on to Virginia.

Jennings Poindexter's first appearance in professional baseball was in the Class-C West Dixie League in 1935 with the Shreveport Sports, a Red Sox farm club. The Sports moved 80 miles west to Gladewater, Texas that June, becoming the Gladewater Bears, and finishing the season in last place in the six-team league. With Shreveport/Gladewater, Poindexter was 7-5 in 14 games, with a 3.06 ERA. He was considered the best lefthander in the league by the managers and writers.

Poindexter started the 1936 season with the Bears (now in the East Texas League) and got off to a terrific 5-0 start, featuring back-to-back shutouts, a 15-strikeout game, a one-hitter, and then another 15-K game. He was then jumped from Class C to the Single-A ball Little Rock Travelers.

In his first game for the Travelers, Poindexter threw a three-hit shutout. In mid-July he set a Southern Association record with 17 strikeouts in a two-hit game. In the end, Poindexter went 12-11 with a 3.56 ERA. Despite only joining Little Rock in midseason, he led the league in strikeouts with 144.

Poindexter's debut with the Red Sox, on Sep. 15 1936, at Cleveland, did not go well. He started the game and faced just six batters, getting only one out. He walked the first four batters, and gave up a single, and was charged with four runs (and the loss). Sporting an ERA of 108.00, he was given another start by manager Joe Cronin.

---

[15] The origin of this nickname is subject to debate. My educated guess would be that it was an amalgam of the J in Jennings and parts of his last name Po(in)de(x)ter.

On Sep. 23 he worked 6⅔ innings in Washington, allowing just one run on five hits (albeit with seven walks). His third and final appearance was another start, on Sep. 27 at Fenway Park. In 3⅔ innings, he doled out five more bases on balls and gave up six runs, three of them unearned. He lost that game, too, finishing the season 0-2 with a gnarly 6.75 ERA and 16 walks in 10⅔ innings.

United Press syndicated a story claiming that Poindexter was "one of the most colorful rookies" in the game, a "wild and wooly Texan." It continued, "Poindexter had a brief trial with the Red Sox, but Joe Cronin sent him back to the Southern Association when he chased a steward off the dining car with a butcher knife." It was apparently a Filipino porter, and writer Bill Dooly quoted Poindexter in print.

The pitcher said he'd asked the porter what city the train was in and that the porter had replied, "What the hell do you care?" Poindexter said he shot back: "'Why you **** heathen, ah'll kill you.' An' ah went for him an' he ran up the steps of the train and ah chased him through two cars and out the back end. He didn't even get back on again when the train pulled out. Yeah, ah guess that was it, because Cronin didn't seem to like me after that."

Writer Red Smith wrote of the time in Minneapolis when Poindexter suddenly came down, late in a key game, with an arm injury the team trainer was unable to diagnose. The trainer, wrote Smith, "shook his head, [and] significantly tapped his forehead."

Alcohol may have had something to do with Poindexter's erratic reputation. Jack Troy wrote in the Atlanta Constitution, "Jinx used to take a sociable highball. In fact, he didn't always stop at one. He'd cheerfully admit it."

Poindexter was back with Little Rock for 1937 and in a full season was 15-10 with a 3.48 ERA. Little Rock won the pennant. In 1938 the Red Sox had him work in AA, with the Minneapolis Millers.

Doc Prothro, who had managed Poindexter back when he was hurling for the Travelers, signed on to skipper the big-league Phillies for 1939, and he was able to bring Poindexter with him, signing him as a free agent in the fall of 1938. Poindexter, starting the season with the Phillies, worked in relief in nine games through April and May, then was given a start on June 3 against the Pittsburgh Pirates. He lasted 2⅓ innings, giving up five runs (three earned). His last appearance in the majors was on June 7, three innings of hitless relief.

Two days later, the Class AA Southern Association Atlanta Crackers traded first baseman Jack Bolling to the Phillies for Poindexter and cash. Poindexter's ERA for Philadelphia was 4.15, with no decisions. In Atlanta he was 10-7, struggling at first but then winning five games in a row; he finished the year with an almost identical 4.17 ERA.

The other Philadelphia team, the Athletics, bought his contract from Atlanta in December 1939, but by the time the 1940 season began, he had been returned to Atlanta, and worked for the Crackers all season (11-7, 3.45), setting a Southern Association record with eight consecutive strikeouts on Sep. 20.

Poindexter began 1941 with Atlanta but was sent to Knoxville during the season. He did spend at least a few hours in the clink after running a red light – and claiming he didn't see it because he was colorblind. He was a combined 12-15 that season.

That December, three days before Pearl Harbor, Knoxville traded Poindexter to the Oklahoma City Indians, taking him back to his home state. Poindexter appeared in only 12 games (with a 3-5 record) between Oklahoma City and Tulsa in 1942.

Poindexter was out of baseball in 1943 and 1944, returning in 1945 by signing with Nashville in March. He appeared in 29 games (21 starts) and, perhaps a little rusty, posted a 7-13 record with a 5.21 ERA.

The final two full seasons of Poindexter's career were with the Texarkana Bears. He won 15 games in 1946 and 10 more games in 1947. He appeared in only 10 games in 1948.

His final ledger in the majors was 14 games pitched (four starts), an 0-2 record, 41 innings pitched, 42 hits, 31 walks, 14 strikeouts, 22 earned runs allowed and a 4.83 ERA.

Going back home to Pauls Valley, Poindexter was the manager of the Raiders of the Class-D Sooner State League for part of 1948, one of two skippers for the seventh-place team.

BEST DAY (BY WPA OR OTHER MEASURE): Not only did Poindexter not win a game in the majors, he only appeared in one game that was eventually won by his team. That event took place on Apr. 22, 1939 as a member of the Phillies against the Brooklyn Dodgers in a game at Shibe Park. With the game tied at one in the top of the fifth, the Dodgers chased starter Al Hollingsworth with a three run, five hit uprising. Poindexter was called in with a runner on third and two out and got Al Todd to ground out to shortstop. He retired Brooklyn in order in the sixth, including a strikeout of Cookie Lavagetto. He pitched a hitless seventh, yielding a two-out walk. He was pinch-hit for in the bottom of the inning with the Phils trailing 4-2 and Chuck Klein on second. Philadelphia put together a three-run rally in the bottom of the ninth, scoring the winning run on a balk. Poindexter's line for the game: 2⅓ innings pitched, no hits, one walk, two strikeouts.

THE WONDER OF HIS NAME: The name/word "Poindexter" has taken on the meaning of a bookish and socially unskilled person, as derived from the character of Poindexter in the late-1950s cartoon series *Felix the Cat*. However, Jennings Poindexter apparently read liquor bottles more than books. It's an aristocratic-sounding name for someone who seemingly was anything but.

NOT TO BE CONFUSED WITH: Buster Poindexter (Pseudonym of American rock musician David Johansen), John Poindexter (A retired United States naval officer and Department of Defense official. He was Deputy National Security Advisor and National Security Advisor for the Reagan administration).

FUN ANAGRAMS: Chester Jennings Poindexter anagrams to "Rejects hindering exponents." or "Jesting, inexpert chosen nerd."

EPHEMERA: 1) His father, William Thomas Poindexter, was a farmer who had moved to Oklahoma from Missouri. His mother, Emma Jane (North), came from Arkansas. The couple had two older sons – George and Carl – when Jennings joined the family. 2) Poindexter married at a young age, about a week before he turned 18, wedding Beatrice Belvin in 1928. Beatrice was born in 1913, thus either 15 or 16 at the time they married. They had two children, Olan Gene and Barbara Nell. 3) After his ballplaying and managing days were over, Poindexter took a position with Phillips Oil.

BILLY JO ROBIDOUX
Of the Massachusetts' Robidouxs?

BIRTH NAME: William Joseph Robidoux
PRONUNCIATION OF DIFFICULT PARTS: Roe-ba-dough
NICKNAME: None
HEIGHT/WEIGHT: 6'1" 200 lbs.
BORN: Jan. 13, 1964, in Ware, Massachusetts
POSITIONS: First Baseman, Leftfielder
YEARS ACTIVE IN THE MAJORS: 1985-1990
NAME ETYMOLOGY/DEFINITIONS: "William" is a popular given name of an old Germanic origin and a derivative of "Wilhelm." It became very popular in the English language after the Norman conquest of England in 1066 and remained so throughout the Middle Ages and into the modern era. It is derived from the Germanic *wil* (meaning "will" or "desire") and *helm* (meaning "helmet" or "protection"). "Joseph" originates from Hebrew. The name can be translated from Hebrew yosef as signifying "Yahweh/Jehovah shall increase/add." In the New Testament there are two men named Joseph: 1) Joseph, the husband of Mary, the mother of Jesus; and, 2) Joseph of Arimathea, a secret disciple of Jesus who supplied the tomb in which Jesus was buried. The form "Joseph" is used mostly in English, French and German-speaking countries. "Robidoux" is a French name probably from an altered form of the personal name "Robardeau," a pet form of "Robert." The first Robidoux recorded in Canada was from Burgos in Spain and seems to have been present in Canada from around 1664. He bore the secondary surname L'Espagnol. Growing up in Cape Cod, Robidoux's father lived next door to a guy named "Billy Joe" and, liking the name (and possibly the rareness of it in that part of the country), named his son that. Billy Jo dropped the "e" from "Joe" to make signing autographs easier and faster (really).

Billy Jo Robidoux was selected by the Brewers in the 6th round of the 1982 Amateur Draft out of Ware H.S. in Massachusetts. Billy Jo reported to Pikeville in the rookie Appalachian League that summer, slashing .287/.389/.359 in 54 games but showing little power.

The next season at Beloit (Single-A Midwest League), Robidoux showed more pop, banging out 30 doubles and ten home runs in a .317/.424/.460 season. In 1984, Robidoux played at Single-A California League entry Stockton, hitting .279/.387/.384 in 401 plate appearances.

That set up his 1985 season at AA El Paso, where the 21-year-old was almost 2½ years younger than league average. Billy Jo pummeled the ball, helped by Dudley Field, one of the top hitting parks in the minor leagues. He played in 133 of 136 games and smacked out league-leading totals in several categories: runs scored (111), hits (176), doubles (46), RBI (132), batting average (.342), and total bases (297). He finished second in the league with 23 home runs, 97 walks, and a 1.020 OPS. Not surprisingly, he earned the Texas League Most Valuable Player award. The Diablos had the best overall record (86-50) but lost to the Jackson Mets in the championship series.

Robidoux made his major league debut for the Brewers on Sep. 11, 1985, pinch-hitting in the eighth inning against the Yankees' Rich Bordi. (He popped up to second baseman Rex Hudler.) He played 18 games that season for Milwaukee, hitting .176/.333/.392 in 63 trips to the plate.

The burly first baseman began the '86 campaign with Milwaukee and had a great start, going 21-for-63 in April, hitting .333/.456/.460, but ended up splitting the season between Milwaukee and the minors, playing 56 games for the Brewers (.227/.344/.287) and 37 games with Beloit and El Paso. Robidoux went back and forth between Milwaukee and in the minors for the next two seasons.

Moving on to the White Sox organization in 1989, Robidoux had a decent season in at AAA Vancouver (.317/.404/.545 in 73 games) but played in only 16 contests for the White Sox. The Red Sox picked him up for the 1990 season, when he split his time between AAA Pawtucket and Boston. At the end of that season he was released and retired from baseball.

In six major league seasons, Robidoux played in 173 games and made 547 plate appearances, hitting .209/.313/.286. He was a good line drive hitter with good patience (71 walks) but could never translate his minor league success to the major league level, perhaps due to a lingering knee injury. Robidoux had been signed by longtime scout Tom Bourque, who stated in a 2008 interview with *Baseball Prospectus*: "Billy Jo was a big, thick-bodied guy, and if he had signed five years later, they would have had him with a personal trainer. What he would do is go home, just like everybody else back then, after the baseball season and not work out, and then go like crazy in January. His problem was that he got tight, and it led to some injuries. If he'd have signed a few years later, he probably would have had a better career, because he would have taken care of his body better."

BEST DAY (BY WPA OR OTHER MEASURE): On Oct. 6, 1985 he went 2-4 with two homers and four RBI in a 9-6 Brewers win.

THE WONDER OF HIS NAME: Guys named Billy Jo are the types you imagine having a couple of cold ones with at the corner watering hole. But you don't often find Billy

Jo's in Massachusetts. Combine that with the rhyming of "Jo," "Ro" and "doux" in rapid succession, and you have a moniker full of joy for public address announcers and fans alike. Given the French origins of his last name, one wonders if, upon hearing about being drafted by Milwaukee, he might have exclaimed "Merci, Brew Crew!" Through 2018, he is one of only 13 major leaguers in history with at least 15 alphabetic letters in his "playing name" to have neither an A or an E in it. (The others are: Robinson Chirinos, Fritz Von Kolnitz, Scott Munninghoff, Billy Southworth, Bobby Livingston, Jimmy Bloodworth, Jimmy Uchrinscko, John-Ford Griffin, Johnny Grodzicki, Johnny Hutchings, Johnny Ostrowski and Julius Willigrod).

NOT TO BE CONFUSED WITH: Billy Joe Hobert (Former NFL quarterback and one-time minor league player with the White Sox), Joseph Robidoux (Established the Blacksnake Hills Trading Post that eventually developed as the town of St. Joseph, Missouri), Rope-a-dope (Boxing fighting style commonly associated with Muhammad Ali in his 1974 "Rumble in the Jungle" match against George Foreman).

FUN ANAGRAMS: "William Joseph Robidoux" turns into "Jail buxom Polish weirdo!"

EPHEMERA: 1) Of Robidoux's name, Dan Duquette, the Brewers scouting director, said, "That's a big-league name, a major league name … That's what everyone liked about him when we drafted him." 2) He is the only person from Ware H.S. to ever be drafted by a major league team and is the only Robidoux to ever play professional baseball. 4) As of 2010, he was working for the highway department in his hometown and umpiring high school baseball games. 5) Robidoux was elected to the Western Massachusetts Baseball Hall of Fame in 2017.

JARROD SALTALAMACCHIA
Longest last name in MLB history

BIRTH NAME: Jarrod Scott Saltalamacchia
PRONUNCIATION OF DIFFICULT PARTS: sal-tuh-la-MAH-kee-yuh
NICKNAME: Salty
HEIGHT/WEIGHT: 6'4" 235 lbs.
BORN: May 2, 1985, in West Palm Beach, Florida
POSITIONS: Catcher, First Baseman
YEARS ACTIVE IN THE MAJORS: 2007-2018
NAME ETYMOLOGY/DEFINITIONS: "Jarrod" is an alternative form of "Jared," which is a name of Biblical derivation, common mostly in North American English-speaking countries. In the Book of Genesis, the biblical patriarch Jared was the sixth link in the 10 pre-flood generations between Adam and Noah. "Scott" is of Scottish origin. It is first attributed to Uchtredus filius Scoti who is mentioned in the charter recording in the foundation of Holyrood Abbey and Selkirk in 1120 and the border Riding clans who settled Peebleshire in the 10th century and the Duke of Buccleuch.

"Saltalamacchia" is Italian in origin, with *salta* meaning "jump over" and *la macchia* meaning "the thicket" or "the spot" (*la macchia* being Southern Italy dialect for a kind of tall shrub).

J arrod Saltalamacchia attended Royal Palm Beach H.S. in Florida, graduating in 2003. The Braves selected Saltalamacchia in the first round (number 36 overall) of the 2003 draft. In 2003, he hit .239/.382/.396 for the Rookie level Gulf Coast League Braves and .214/.267/.286 in nine games with the Danville Braves. In the Gulf Coast League, he led catchers with 35 assists, but also with eight errors. *Baseball America* rated him the number three prospect in the GCL.

In 2004, Jarrod played for the Single-A Rome Braves and hit .272/.348/.437. *Baseball America* ranked him as the number seven prospect in the South Atlantic League and as the 7th-best catching prospect in baseball, between Kelly Shoppach and Russell Martin. In 2005, Saltalamacchia had a breakout season for the Class A Myrtle Beach Pelicans, where the switch-hitting slugger hit .314 with 35 doubles, 19 home runs, and 81 RBIs in 129 games. He made the Carolina League All-Star team, having finished third in average and leading in intentional walks (11). *Baseball America* named him the top catcher in the minor leagues and the top prospect in the Carolina League, ahead of Anibal Sanchez and Nick Markakis.

The prospect struggled in 2006, only hitting .230/.353/.380 for the AA Mississippi Braves. *Baseball America* still rated him the number ten prospect in the Southern League between Sanchez and Miguel Montero. Saltalamacchia ranked 18th in *Baseball America*'s top 100 prospects in 2006, and 36th the following year.

In the 2007 season, Saltalamacchia started at catcher for Mississippi. In 22 games played, he belted seven home runs with a batting average of .373. On his 22nd birthday, he was called up to Atlanta to fill in for an injured Brian McCann. Saltalamacchia's call-up made him the new record-holder of the longest surname in MLB history, at 14 letters, breaking the record of 13 set by many players.

In May, Salty hit his first major league home run, a solo shot off Cole Hamels. Because Saltalamacchia was "blocked" by McCann, who had recently signed a long-term contract with Atlanta, he was the subject of much trade speculation. At the trade deadline that year, he was dealt to the Rangers with Elvis Andrus, Neftalí Feliz, Matt Harrison, and Beau Jones for first baseman Mark Teixeira and reliever Ron Mahay.

In late March 2008 the Rangers sent him to the minors to catch every day instead of sitting as the backup. But Saltalamacchia was soon called back up and got into 61 games with the big-league club that year, compiling a .253/.352/.364 line with only three homers in 230 plate appearances.

The 2009 season didn't go any better for Saltalamacchia. On Apr. 25, he struck out in his 28th consecutive game played, setting a new MLB strikeout streak record for a position player (since eclipsed by three players and as of 2019 held by Aaron Judge at 37 games). In August, he injured his shoulder, and finished the year with a disappointing .233/.290/.371 line.

Saltalamacchia's shoulder forced him back on the disabled list after the second game of the 2010 season. In late April, struggling throwing the ball back to the pitcher, he was assigned to the AAA Oklahoma City RedHawks, and then was traded at the end of July to the Red Sox. Over the entire season, he appeared in only 12 big league games.

Saltalamacchia was Boston's primary catcher in 2011, with veteran Jason Varitek as the backup. Out of the gate, he struggled defensively and hit only .194 through May 5th. But he improved as the season progressed and finished out the year hitting .235/.288/.450 with what were then career highs in homers (16) and RBIs (56) in 103 games played.

In the final months of 2012, Red Sox manager Bobby Valentine moved Saltalamacchia to first base, giving Ryan Lavarnway a look as the team's starting catcher. Saltalamacchia finished the year batting .222/.288/.454 with 25 homers and 59 RBIs in a career-high 121 games played.

Saltalamacchia was the starting catcher in 2013 for the Red Sox, with David Ross and Lavarnway the backups. During the regular season, he had his best year in terms of batting average (.273) while adding 14 homers along with 40 doubles and setting a new career high with 65 ribbies.

In the second game of the 2013 ALCS, Saltlamacchia hit a walk-off single, driving in Jonny Gomes to beat the Tigers 6-5. In Game 2 of the World Series against the Cardinals, he was charged with an error when he dropped a throw from left fielder Jonny Gomes that allowed what turned out to be the winning run to score in the seventh; in Game 3, he made an ill-advised throw in the ninth, trying to retire Jon Jay at third base, starting a string of events that led to Jay scoring the winning run on an obstruction call. He also went 0-3 in both games allowed a total of three stolen bases with none caught stealing. David Ross was then given the starting catcher job for what turned out to be the final three games of the series.

A few months later, Saltalamacchia agreed to a three-year, $21 million contract with the Marlins. He was the starting catcher for the Marlins in 2014, playing 114 games and hitting .220 with 11 homers and 44 RBIs. In 2015, he played only nine games for the Fish before he was released in early May. He was picked up by the Diamondbacks, for whom he had only 171 at-bats; he was productive when he did play, however, hitting .254 with eight homers and 23 RBIs.

In 2016, Saltalamacchia played for the Tigers and hit his 100th career home run, a grand slam off Arquimedes Caminero. He would finish the 2016 season with a .171 batting average in 246 at-bats.

In 2017, Saltalamacchia signed a minor league contract with the Blue Jays that included an invitation to spring training. He made the Opening Day roster as the backup catcher to Russell Martin. After going 1-for-25 in a Blue Jay uniform, he was released on May 3, and signed a new minor league contract with Toronto two weeks later. He was assigned to the AAA Buffalo Bisons but lasted only six weeks there before getting released from his minor league contract.

He decided to retire at that point but changed his mind and signed a minor league contract to return to the Tigers organization. He made a token appearance with the major league club that season, going 0-for-7 in five games. In January 2019, Saltalamacchia announced his retirement for good.

BEST DAY (BY WPA OR OTHER MEASURE): Salty's career day came during an historic run-scoring explosion by the Texas Rangers on Aug. 22, 2007 in Camden Yards. After spotting the Orioles a 3-0 lead through three innings, the Rangers plated five runs in the fourth, nine more in the sixth, ten additional in the eighth and finished it off with a six-spot in the ninth. Final score: Rangers 30, Orioles 3. And this was the first game of a double-header! Jarrod's first plate appearance of the game resulted in an innocent flyball to center leading off the top of the third. From then on ... carnage! With the bases loaded and one out in the fourth, Salty singled in the Rangers first run of the game, and came around to score when the next batter, Ramon Vazquez, homered to deep right. Saltalamacchia led off the sixth inning with a home run, and with the Rangers batting around in that inning, singled in another run with two out. He himself scored two batters later. The Rangers sent 14 men to the plate in that inning. Salty got to bat twice in the eighth inning also. With David Murphy singling to lead off the inning, Saltalamacchia walked and came around to score three batters later. Fast forward to his second at-bat of the inning, which came with the score now 21-3 and two runners on base (they had plated seven runs already, while the Orioles only recorded one out). Salty hit his second homer of the game, the "field goal" pushing the lead to 24-3. Somehow, Saltalamacchia was not a contributing factor in the six-run ninth, as the struck out with one out and runners on the corners. Final tally for the game: seven plate appearances, a walk, two homers, two singles and career-highs with five runs scored and seven RBIs. Teammate Ramon Vazquez also drove in seven, marking the first time since 1962 that two players on the same team reached that mark in the same game.

THE WONDER OF HIS NAME: "Saltalamacchia" sounds like some Italian pasta dish, doesn't it (in the vein of "fish a la name of restaurant")? Given its length, one might think it's really hard to spell for non-Italians, but really the only tricky part is the "double C" in "macchia."

NOT TO BE CONFUSED WITH: Jarrod Dyson (Outfielder most recently for the Arizona Diamondbacks, who previously played for the Kansas City Royals and Seattle Mariners), Salta–Antofagasta railway (Also named Huaytiquina, is a non-electrified single-track railway line that links Argentina and Chile passing through the Andes).

FUN ANAGRAMS: "Jarrod Scott Saltalamacchia" anagrams to "Alas this cold, major cataract."

EPHEMERA: 1) Saltalamacchia attended high school along with future Rangers teammate Kason Gabbard, and the two were friends growing up. 2) He was a member of Team Florida USA and won gold with the team in the 2001 Junior Olympics. 3) On May 19, 2012, in the top of the fourth inning of the Red Sox/Phillies game at Citizen's Bank Park, Will Middlebrooks led off with a homer. Saltalamacchia was the next batter, and he too went yard. The 26 letters in their combined last names set a record for back-to-back homer hitters. (How do I know this? Well, I did the original research and got credited for it on that evening's late edition of ESPN's *Baseball Tonight*). 4) When he banged out 40 doubles in 2013, he became only the 11th catcher to achieve that mark in a season (Yadier Molina also reached the mark that year, and Jonathan Lucroy hit an amazing 53 doubles in 2014). 5) During the second half of the 2017 MLB season, Saltalamacchia worked as a Red Sox studio analyst for NESN and made his debut as color commentator with play-by-play announcer Dave O'Brien. Saltalamacchia was part of the NESN broadcast team for the Red Sox' 2019 season, filling in when regular color commentators Jerry Remy and Dennis Eckersley weren't available. 6) He is married to Ashley Saltalamacchia, his high school gym teacher. They started dating a year after he graduated and have four daughters.

RAZOR SHINES
Favorite son of Indianapolis, with a successful coaching career

BIRTH NAME: Anthony Razor Shines
PRONUNCIATION OF DIFFICULT PARTS: None
NICKNAME: Ray
HEIGHT/WEIGHT: 6'1" 210 lbs.
BORN: July 18, 1956, in Durham, North Carolina
POSITIONS: Pinch Hitter, first baseman
YEARS ACTIVE IN THE MAJORS: 1983-1985, 1987
NAME ETYMOLOGY/DEFINITIONS: "Anthony" is the usual English form of the old Roman family name "Antonius," which is of uncertain (probably Etruscan) origin. The spelling with -th- (not normally reflected in the pronunciation) represents a learned but erroneous attempt to associate it with Greek *anthos*, meaning "flower." As for "Razor," Shines has said it was a family name. Anthony Razor Shines was the third man in his family to be given the middle name Razor (and he passed it down to his son Devin also). Reference books do not provide information regarding "Shines," but if we suppose that its related to "Shine," that name has its possible origin a nickname from Middle English *schene* meaning "beautiful" (Old English sciene).

Razor Shines made the varsity team at Durham H.S. in the tenth grade, and then played baseball for St. Augustine's College for three seasons (1976-1978). In June 1978 he was drafted by the Expos in the 18th round as a catcher. For the first few years of his career, Shines played mostly for Single-A West Palm Beach in the Florida State League. For part of the 1981 season through 1983, he played for AA Memphis in the Southern League.

In 1984, Razor was promoted to AAA Indianapolis, where he would spend most of his time over the next decade, with brief call-ups to the Expos. In Indianapolis,

Razor made his mark on the city and became the player that youngsters growing up in the '80s and '90s idolized. In a 1992 interview, Razor recalled, "I wouldn't go so far as saying this is my town, but I can walk into the same clothing store as [Indianapolis Colts running back] Eric Dickerson or [Indiana Pacers guard] Reggie Miller and sign as many autographs as they do."

His longevity in the town certainly contributed to his legend in the city, as did the way the Busch Stadium announcer called his name when he went to the plate, growling the "R" at the beginning of his name: "Now coming to the plate, Rrrrrrrazor Shines!" "When you win a lot, the city becomes in love with your team, and we won a lot," Razor said. "I loved Indianapolis, and they loved me."

From 1984-1993, Shines played in 793 games for the Indians, with stints in the big-league city of Montreal for parts of 1983, 1984, 1985, and 1987. In Indianapolis he amassed 138 doubles, 404 RBIs, and 68 home runs.

During those years, it was hard to crack the Expos roster. The team was loaded with talented players in the mid- to late 1980s, which made it difficult for a prospect like Shines to get at-bats. Gary Carter, Andre Dawson, Tim Raines, Tim Wallach, and Andres Galarraga (in 1985) were all ahead of Shines in the prospect pecking order.

All the talent surrounding him made an impression on Shines. He noticed the way the players around him took baseball seriously, as a job, and worked at it tirelessly to improve. He said he tried to instill that same impression on the younger players he coached and managed; that "you not only have to be good, you have to work at it."

Shines' last major-league appearance was as a pinch-hitter, in a 10-9 loss to the Reds in Montreal in May 1987, in which he grounded out to the pitcher. He went on to play until 1993, mostly with Indianapolis but also including stops in Buffalo (the AAA affiliate of Pittsburgh at the time), and in Mexico City. In parts of four major league seasons his resume read: 68 games, 81 at-bats, 15 hits, one double, five RBI, one stolen base, five walks, a .185 batting average, .239 on-base percentage and .198 slugging percentage.

After his playing career ended, Shines managed the Birmingham Barons of the Southern League and the Clearwater Threshers of the Florida State League. In 2007, he was back in Major League Baseball, as the third base for the Chicago White Sox. He managed the Phillies single-A Clearwater Threshers team for the 2008 season, piloting the Threshers to a 64-76 record. He served as the first base coach for the Mets for the 2009 and 2010 season. In 2012, he was the hitting coach for the Great Lakes Loons, the A team of the Dodgers. In 2013, he became the manager of the Loons and in 2014 he was promoted to manager of the Chattanooga Lookouts in the AA Southern League. The Dodgers switched AA affiliates for 2015, and Shines became the manager of the Tulsa Drillers of the Texas League. Despite being chosen by *Baseball America* as the best managerial prospect in the Texas League, Shines' contract was not renewed by the Dodgers after the season.

BEST DAY (BY WPA OR OTHER MEASURE): He only started nine games in his big-league career, so the choices for best day are kind of slim. On Sep. 25, 1984, in front of a crowd of about 8,000 at Olympic Stadium, Shines started at first base and managed to amass 20 percent of his career hit total, with three singles in four times at bat.

THE WONDER OF HIS NAME: In 2009, Shines was named by *Maxim* magazine as having "the most bad-ass name of all time." I don't know if I would go that far, but it was and is still a fun one. There is a coolness factor in that the "Razor" name has been in the Shines family for many generations, and how can one not smile when saying the word "Shines." Then you get into the whole "Raines and Shines" dynamic (see below).

NOT TO BE CONFUSED WITH: Tim Raines (Aforementioned teammate during Shines' time in the majors), Razor Ramon (A ring name of American professional wrestler Scott Hall), John Ned "Johnny" Shines (American blues singer and guitarist).

FUN ANAGRAMS: "Anthony Razor Shines" anagrams to "Nosy, harsh, Nazi tenor."

EPHEMERA: 1) He grew up in the projects with his mother, Doris Shines, and his two siblings. Doris made sure her son stayed out of trouble, and as Razor recalled, "I'll never be able to thank her enough. She kept me out of jail." 2) Shines was the second Razor to play in the majors after the Tigers' Ralph Overton "Razor'" Ledbetter, who pitched one inning of one game in 1915. 3) Every time Shines got called up to the Expos, left fielder Tim Raines was there, and thus Montreal had the weather covered ... Raines or Shines. 4) In 1985 Razor married Leann Farris, whom he met somewhat improbably after diving into the stands to catch a foul ball playing a game in Wichita in 1983. He inadvertently knocked a soda into a fan's lap and gave the fan a ball later in the game in between innings. The fan waited outside the ballpark to get Shines' autograph after the game, and invited him to his house for dinner, where he met the fan's wife and two daughters – one of whom was Leann. 5) His son Devin was drafted by the Dodgers in the 38th round of the 2011 MLB Draft. In 2012, Devin played for his dad with the Great Lakes Loons. 6) Shines became a spokesman for Aquafina water during the 2009 season and was featured on its website as "The 3rd Base Coach of Life." Visitors to the site could ask yes or no questions and receive "advice" from Shines.

JOHN WOCKENFUSS
Fan favorite in Detroit during the 1970s and 1980s

BIRTH NAME: Johnny Bilton Wockenfuss
PRONUNCIATION OF DIFFICULT PARTS: None
NICKNAME: None, though locally he was sometimes referred to as "Fuss"
HEIGHT/WEIGHT: 6'0" 190 lbs.
BORN: Feb. 27, 1949, in Welch, West Virginia
POSITIONS: Catcher, First Baseman, Outfielder
YEARS ACTIVE IN THE MAJORS: 1974-1985
NAME ETYMOLOGY/DEFINITIONS: "Johnny" is a variant of "John" which is originally of Semitic origin. The name is derived from the Latin "Ioannes" and "Iohannes," "Bilton"

has Old English origins, as a habitational name from places in Northumberland and Yorkshire named Bilton, from an Old English personal name "Billa" and Old English *tun* meaning "enclosure" or "settlement." "Wockenfuss" is German in origin, and depending on the source you consult, may translate to "weak feet." It could be a variation on "Wockenfoth," which is from a nickname that is common in the Low German area.

John Wockenfuss was drafted all the way down in the 42nd round by the Washington Senators in 1967. Splitting time between the outfield and third base, he toiled year after year in that team's minor league system, even when the franchise relocated to Arlington, Texas and became the Rangers after 1971.

Finally, on June 6, 1973, exactly six years after he had been drafted, the Rangers traded him to the Cardinals as part of a package for pitcher Jim Bibby. Assigned to AAA Tulsa, Wockenfuss remained there for the rest of the season, putting up mediocre batting numbers. Although Wockenfuss failed to impress offensively, he did make an important transition. The Cardinals converted him into a catcher, a move that would greatly increase his odds of making the major leagues.

Then came the second break that Wockenfuss needed. In December 1973, the Cardinals traded him to the Tigers. Detroit didn't have room for him on their Opening Day roster in 1974, but assigned him to AAA Evansville, where he proceeded to hit .275 with ten home runs over the first two-thirds of the season. In August, the Tigers finally called up Wockenfuss, ending his seven-year run of minor league ball. Still only 25, he received some playing time behind the plate, but hit only .138.

The Tigers sent him back to AAA to start the 1975 season, but he was back up by June, playing fairly regularly before settling into a backup role. Once again, he didn't hit much (.229), but he showed some patience at the plate, occasional power, and an aptitude for catching and handling pitchers.

After another subpar offensive season in 1976, Wockenfuss broke through in 1977. Now given a chance to platoon with the lefty-swinging Milt May, Wockenfuss appeared in 53 games, batted a respectable .274, and clubbed nine home runs. Essentially the Tigers' number two catcher, Wockenfuss established himself as one of the American League's most valuable backups.

Over the next three seasons, Wockenfuss continued to develop. Each year, the Tigers gave him more playing time, expanding his role to give him time in the outfield corners and at first base, and each year, he responded with even better offensive numbers. In 1979, he hit 15 home runs, slugged .506, and put up an OPS of .827, all terrific numbers for a part-time player. In 1980, he reached his peak, hitting 16 home runs and OPSing .839. He played in a career-high 126 games that summer, with most of that playing time coming at positions other than catcher. With Lance Parrish firmly entrenched behind the plate, Wockenfuss played first base and the outfield, put in some time at DH, and did some catching, too.

Wockenfuss also became a favorite with fans because of his personality. A native of West Virginia, he acted like, and was perceived as, a fun-loving country boy. Laid back and willing to laugh, he became popular with teammates, too. In 1981, Wockenfuss' hitting fell off, as his batting average dipped to .215, but he bounced back with two more productive seasons in 1982 and 1983. He was clearly the Tigers' best bench player, so good that some felt if he had played for a lesser team, one without a Lance Parrish, he would have been the primary starting catcher.

Wockenfuss' time in Detroit came to an end before the 1984 season. He reported to spring training, expecting to fill his usual role but unhappy because of his low salary. He approached management about the possibility of a trade. Late in spring training, on Mar. 24, the Tigers pulled the trigger on a deal with the Phillies. The four-player trade brought Willie Hernandez to Detroit, along with useful first baseman Dave Bergman. The asking price included touted young outfielder Glenn Wilson – and Wockenfuss. The timing could not have been worse, preventing him from playing for a world championship team in 1984.

Joining the Phillies, which put him closer to his home in Landenberg, Pennsylvania, Wockenfuss played well as a backup catcher, first baseman and third baseman, hitting .289 in 86 games. But then came a downturn. Wockenfuss hit so poorly in 1985, his batting average sinking to .162, that the Phillies released him in August. He contacted several teams, including the Tigers, about a tryout for the 1986 season, but no one was willing to even give him an invite. So Wockenfuss played a season of independent minor league ball before finally giving up playing the game.

In 1987, Wockenfuss joined the Tigers organization as manager of the Toledo farm club. He later managed two seasons in the Pirates organization (1992-1993). In 1996 he managed the Albany-Colonie Diamond Dogs to the Northeast League title.

BEST DAY (BY WPA OR OTHER MEASURE): In the second game of a double-header on Aug. 8, 1979 against the Rangers, Wockenfuss started in left field for the Tigers. He hit a solo homer with one out in the bottom of the second inning to give Detroit a 1-0 lead. The very next inning, he came to bat with two out and the bases loaded and the Tigers now ahead 2-0. He launched his first career grand slam, chasing starter John Henry Johnson from the game. He added a single in the bottom of the fifth before striking out to end the sixth. It was a career-best five RBI day for him. The Tigers went on to win, 10-4.

THE WONDER OF HIS NAME: Come on ... how can one NOT smile when saying the name "Wockenfuss?" It's a three-part last name that starts and ends with cool, unique sounds. Add in a cool middle name of "Bilton" and that his birth name is not John but Johnny, and you have a winner.

NOT TO BE CONFUSED WITH: Magic Bus (Hit song by The Who), Wockenfuss Candies (Baltimore-based chocolatier and chain of candy stores in Maryland), cock and bull story (A fanciful and unbelievable tale).

FUN ANAGRAMS: "Johnny Bilton Wockenfuss" becomes "Now fuck hot, jobless ninny." or "Join stenchful, wonky snob."

143

EPHEMERA: 1) He had one of the most unusual batting stances in baseball history. As a right-handed batter, he used to wrap his left leg back in the direction of the catcher, so that his right leg was actually closer to the pitcher. Additionally, he held his bat well above his head. He also stuck his right elbow out, in the direction of the catcher, while fluttering his fingers on the bat, as if he were playing some sort of musical instrument. In 1980, he explained the stance to Tigers beat writer Tom Gage, "It keeps my shoulder in and keeps my bat level." Ferguson Jenkins had this to say in response to Wockenfuss' stance, "That guy better not get a hit off me the way he stands at the plate ... that stance is out of the caveman days. The last guy who could get away with something like that was Stan Musial, and there ain't no more Stan Musials ..." 2) His defensive versatility made him a favorite of Tigers manager Sparky Anderson. 3) Chicago Cubs broadcaster Harry Carry used to love pronouncing and spelling player's names backwards, including that of Wockenfuss. "Wockenfuss spelled backwards is "Ssufnekcow" (Caray would then chuckle) "boy oh boy that sounds a lot like "holy cow." 4) In 1993, Wockenfuss was inducted into the Delaware Sports Museum and Hall of Fame.

No Focus Group Convened

JAKE ATZ

Did he really change his name for the sake of a paycheck?

BIRTH NAME: According to Atz, he was born John Jacob Zimmermann, but at one point he was playing on a team on which the players were paid in alphabetical order, and one day the team ran out of money before it got to him. So, he decided that would never happen again and had his name legally changed to Atz. Sometimes known as John Jacob Atz in various baseball reference sources, but Atz's wife, in filling out a Hall of Fame questionnaire, listed his name as Jacob Henry Atz.

PRONUNCIATION OF DIFFICULT PARTS: None

NICKNAME: None

HEIGHT/WEIGHT: 5'9" 160 lbs.

BORN: July 1, 1879, in Washington, D.C.

DIED: May 22, 1945, in New Orleans, Louisiana

POSITIONS: Second Baseman, Shortstop

YEARS ACTIVE IN THE MAJORS: 1902, 1907-1909

ATZ, CHICAGO AMER.

NAME ETYMOLOGY/DEFINITIONS: "Jacob" is a biblical name, from the Hebrew "Yaakov" (this may be part of the reason for the supposition of his being Jewish, as we'll see later). It is traditionally explained as being derived from the Hebrew *akev* ("heel") and to have meant "heel grabber," because when Jacob was born "his hand took hold of Esau's heel" (Genesis 25:26). "Henry" is of Continental Germanic origin, from *haim* (meaning "home") and *ric* (meaning "power, ruler"). "Atz" is of South German origin, from the Germanic personal name "Azzo," meaning "noble; noble at birth."

Baseball-Reference.com lists Jake Atz as playing in 1898 for a team in Williamsport, and in 1900 for a New York State League team called the Troy Washerwomen ... really, that was the team's name. Their opponents included squads like the Cortland Wagonmakers and the Schenectady Electricians.

Atz played for the Raleigh Senators in 1901, but his contract was soon sold to the New Orleans Pelicans. Although the Pelicans played in the Southern Association, a higher minor league than Raleigh, a trip to the deep south meant humidity, bad fans and disease – back in those days it was not uncommon for a player to contract malaria while playing in the Southern Association. Like many players of his era, Jake refused to go. That was until he was told he'd be making $125 per month. Atz finished up the year in New Orleans and batted .275 for the Pelicans.

The next year the Washington Senators called him up for a look-see. In front of his hometown fans, Atz got into three games but managed only one hit in ten at-bats.

The Senators sent Jake back down south where he played for New Orleans and then Memphis. Jake then went out to the West Coast where he played for Los Angeles and Portland, all the while hitting around .250.

In 1908 he was back in New Orleans hitting .312 when the big leagues came calling again. The White Sox brought Atz up as a reserve infielder and he hit a lame .194/.311/.209. The next year he was their starting second baseman and improved his batting line to .236/.309/.299, while playing league-average defense.

His major league career was effectively ended when he was hit in the hip by a pitch thrown by Walter Johnson during the 1909 season. In his four major league seasons, Atz played in 209 games, with 132 hits, 21 doubles, three triples, 49 RBIs, 23 stolen bases, and a slash line of .218/.304/.263.

Released to the Providence Grays in 1910, he took over as manager during the second half of the next season. Although the team finished last in the Eastern League, Jake had found his true calling. He was a natural manager.

Atz bumped around the low minors again until he landed a berth as player/manager of the Fort Worth Panthers in 1914. His early years as manager didn't go so smoothly and Atz quit the team in a huff after the owner second-guessed his decision to leave a struggling pitcher in the game instead of going to his bullpen. Atz's popularity was such that the next year the owner was forced out by the minority stockholders and their first move was to bring back Jake. Extremely popular with both fans and players, Atz drove the Panthers to the Texas League pennant every year from 1919-1925.

The Panthers became a dynasty due to the owners, W.K. Stripling and Paul LaGrave, who paid top dollar for the best players they could find. "Jake Atz's Cats," as they were dubbed, were winners. His 109 wins in 1922 and again in 1924 set a Texas League record that still stands. He left Fort Worth after the 1929 season and managed various other teams, mostly in the Texas League until finally retiring after the 1941 season.

All told, Jake Atz managed in the minors for 22 years. His lifetime record of 1,972 wins places him 12th among the most wins by a minor league manager. He held the following minor league records: twenty-two years as a player and manager; eighteen years as manager of one club (Fort Worth); longest continuous service at one club (14 seasons with Fort Worth); and seven successive first-place finishes.

BEST DAY (BY WPA OR OTHER MEASURE): In an Aug. 15, 1908, game versus the Senators, Atz collected the only four-hit game of his career, with four singles in seven plate appearances and a stolen base in what would turn out to be a 5-3, 15-inning win for the White Sox.

THE WONDER OF HIS NAME: Jake Atz. It's very short. Very direct. Very to the point and snappy. And ... subject to some conjecture as to its authenticity/origins.

NOT TO BE CONFUSED WITH: Jay Katz (American physician and Yale Law School professor whose career was devoted to addressing complex issues of medical ethics and other overlaps of ethics, law, medicine and psychology), Stray Cats (American rockabilly trio that had hit singles *Stray Cat Strut, (She's) Sexy and 17*, and *Rock This Town*).

FUN ANAGRAMS: "Jacob Henry Atz" becomes "The crazy banjo."

EPHEMERA: 1) Early baseball researchers thought he might be one of the first Jewish ballplayers, but more recent research (including evidence produced by Atz's descendants) has proven otherwise. 2) In 1946, the Texas League introduced the "Jake Atz Trophy," still awarded at the end of each season to the league champions. 3) In 1963, he was inducted into the Texas Sports Hall of Fame in Waco.

GRANT BALFOUR
Temperamental, Aussie-born record-holding reliever

BIRTH NAME: Grant Robert Balfour
PRONUNCIATION OF DIFFICULT PARTS: BAL-fore
NICKNAME: None
HEIGHT/WEIGHT: 6'2" 200 lbs.
BORN: Dec. 30, 1977, in Sydney, Australia
POSITION: Pitcher
YEARS ACTIVE IN THE MAJORS: 2001, 2003-2004, 2007-2015
NAME ETYMOLOGY/DEFINITIONS: "Grant" has English and (especially) Scottish (of Norman origin), and French origins, as the nickname from Anglo-Norman French *graund, graunt* meaning "tall," "large" (Old French *grand, grant*, from Latin *grandis*), given either to a person of remarkable size, or else in a relative way to distinguish two bearers of the same personal name, often representatives of different generations within the same family. Other English and Scottish origins could be from a medieval personal name, probably a survival into Middle English of the Old English byname "Granta." Probably a respelling of German "Grandt" or "Grand." "Robert" is one of the many French names of Germanic origin that were introduced into Britain by the Normans. It's from Proto-Germanic *hrōd* meaning "fame" and *berht* meaning "bright" or "famous" and had a native Old English predecessor of similar form *hrōdibeorht*. "Balfour" has Scottish origins as the habitational name from any of several places in eastern Scotland named with Gaelic *bail(e)* meaning "village," "farm," "house" and *pùir*, genitive case of *pór* meaning "pasture," "grass." The second element is akin to Welsh *pawr* meaning "pasture." According to the traditional pronunciation, the accent falls on the second syllable, but these days it is found more commonly on the first.

G rant Balfour had an expressive personality and mannerisms. He never entered a game without his madman routine, an expletive-filled sprint from the pen to the mound, complete with a mini-Gatorade shower. Once on the mound, the rage didn't stop, and his intensity ratcheted up pitch after pitch. It often rubbed opposing players the wrong way, but ultimately worked, helping his teams win game after game in which they held the lead.

You always knew what was going on in the fiery Balfour's head. As *Athletics Nation* writer Tim Eckert-Fong put it upon Balfour's retirement, "Balfour is the reason live baseball has a seven second delay, a walking 'F bomb' who swore his way right into our hearts."

One of only a handful of Australian-born players to play in the majors, Balfour was signed by the Twins as an amateur free agent in 1997 and spent that year through 2000 slowly progressing through Rookie and A-level ball. He was primarily a starting pitcher until 2000, when he transitioned to the pen. In 2001, he started his year in AA where he struck out 13 per nine innings with a miniscule 1.08 ERA, then he got the call to The Show. His pitching toolbox primarily featured a four-seam fastball, with an occasional slider, sinker or change-up.

He made his debut relieving starter Kyle Lohse in the fifth inning of a game against the Mariners in the Metrodome on July 22. He pitched 1⅔ innings, allowing a run on one hit with two walks and two strikeouts. He made one more appearance for the big-league club before getting sent back down, this time to AAA Edmonton, where he struggled (28 baserunners in 16 innings in the hitter's paradise that is the PCL).

He spent all of 2002 at Edmonton, appearing in 58 games, and occasionally getting a save opportunity. The next year saw him starting the season with the Rochester Red Wings (another AAA affiliate of the Twins), before getting called up to the majors in early July. He finished the year with the Twins, making one start and 16 relief appearances.

In 2004, things began to come together, as he went 4-1 with a 4.35 ERA in 36 relief appearances for Minnesota. However, Balfour missed the entire 2005 season due to an elbow injury and subsequent Tommy John surgery and recovery. The Twins let him go after that injury, and he spent 2006 in the low minors of the Cincinnati Reds organization.

The Brewers selected him off waivers from the Reds, and then in mid-July 2007, after a two-plus year absence, Balfour made his return to the major leagues. He relieved Chris Capuano in a 2–2 tie with the Arizona Diamondbacks in the top of the eighth, striking out Chris Young, the first hitter he faced. With two outs, he hit a batter and walked another before giving up a three-run home run to Mark Reynolds, giving the Diamondbacks a 5–2 lead. Balfour would finish the eighth and ninth inning and take the loss in relief, having given up three earned runs in the 5–2 defeat. Nine days later the Brewers traded him to the Rays for Seth McClung.

He came into 2008 spring training as a long shot to make the Rays' bullpen. Despite a solid spring training, he eventually lost out on the final spot and was designated for assignment. He cleared waivers and accepted an outright assignment to Durham. He was recalled in late May, and finished 2008 with a 1.54 ERA, a

6–2 record, four saves in five opportunities, 14 holds, and 82 strikeouts over 58 1⁄3 innings in 51 appearances. He helped the Rays win their first divisional title and American League pennant.

During Game 1 of the Divisional Series that year, he exchanged words with White Sox shortstop Orlando Cabrera. With the bases loaded and two outs, his first pitch to Cabrera was outside for ball one. Cabrera then kicked the dirt in front of the batter's box in the direction of the pitcher's mound and told Balfour to "throw it over the plate." (Unaware of Balfour's typical behavior while pitching, Cabrera was under the impression that he was the one being yelled at.) The at-bat ended with Cabrera striking out. Balfour stormed off the mound, yelling at Cabrera as he walked to the dugout. Balfour stated after the game that he told Cabrera to "go sit down" and that he "might have mixed one or two words in with it." There were no further incidents in the series, with Balfour getting the final out as the Rays won three games to one.

In 2009, the Rays finished 84–78, 19 games behind the New York Yankees. Balfour wasn't quite as dominant either, though he pitched in a career-high 73 games. He ended up hurling 67⅓ innings and compiling a 5–4 record with four saves, a 4.81 ERA and 69 strikeouts.

In 2010, he had a 2.28 ERA in 57 appearances and lowered his walk rate, which had been an issue to that point in his career. He hit free agency after the season and signed a contract with the A's.

Before the 2012 season started, and with only 10 career saves under his belt to that point, he was named the Athletics' closer over Brian Fuentes. Balfour held the closer role for the early part of the 2012 season but was demoted to setup man after a few blown save opportunities. In early August, Balfour regained the closer role from Ryan Cook. For the season, Balfour went 3–2 in 75 appearances with 24 saves in 74⅔ innings.

The A's exercised their club option on Balfour for 2013, and he rewarded them with an All-Star season (the first and only one of his career). On July 8, Balfour set the club record for most consecutive saves, earning his 41st over two seasons in a 2–1 win over the Pittsburgh Pirates. In 65 appearances, Balfour finished 2013 38-for-41 in save opportunities, going 1–3 with a 2.59 ERA and striking out 72 in 62⅔ innings. He pitched three scoreless innings in the ALDS against the Tigers, getting one win and one save.

In Game 3 of that 2013 ALDS against the Tigers, Balfour began cursing at Victor Martinez, who then answered back, leading to both benches clearing. Balfour claimed that Martinez gave him a "viral death stare" prior to exchanging words. The A's won the game 6–3 but lost the series.

In early December of that year, Balfour came to an agreement with the Orioles on a two-year, $15 million deal. However, a few days prior to signing the contract it was revealed that the deal was in jeopardy as a result of issues that came up during his physical. The Orioles announced that they would not be signing him and that they would look elsewhere for relief help. Balfour responded that he was perfectly healthy and other doctors who examined him disputed the Orioles interpretation of his physical results. He said he would consider filing a grievance with the players association.

Balfour subsequently agreed to a two-year contract with the Rays, worth $12 million. After starting the 2014 season with a 6.46 ERA in 24 games, Balfour was removed from the closer role in early June. He was designated for assignment by the Rays early in the 2015 season, and several days after the team released him, Balfour signed a minor league deal back with the Rays. He opted out of his contract on May 28, and the following April announced his retirement.

BEST DAY (BY WPA OR OTHER MEASURE): Balfour had 84 saves in his career. He pitched in the playoffs, made an All-Star team. But his most dominant performance might have come in a "hold" situation in an inter-league contest in early July of 2004. Coming into the month, he had an ugly 5.28 ERA with the Twins, with ten walks and 13 strikeouts in 15⅓ innings pitched. But on July 3, pitching in Arizona against the Diamondbacks, Balfour inherited a 6-4 lead in the sixth inning. He got Luis Gonzalez to strike out swinging on a 1-2 count, then struck out Shea Hillenbrand on three pitches, and capped the inning with a first pitch flyout to center by Tim Olson. Back out for the seventh, he got three swinging strikeouts (Alex Cintron, Juan Brito and Chad Tracy). The Twins would go on to win the game 8-4. Balfour had thrown 24 pitches (16 strikes) over two innings, notching five strikeouts and a harmless fly ball. From that game forward, he finished the season with a 3.75 ERA in 24 innings, striking out 29 against 11 walks.

THE WONDER OF HIS NAME: He kinda lived up to his surname, as his control was never a strength. His lowest walks per nine innings figure was 2.8 in 2010, and his career mark was 4.2 free passes per nine. Josh Outman (see page 248) would say, "he was no Josh Outman!" (assuming he liked referring to himself in the third person)

NOT TO BE CONFUSED WITH: *Ball Four* (Book written by former pitcher Jim Bouton), Ed Belfour (NHL Hall of Fame goaltender who helped the Dallas Stars win the Stanley Cup).

FUN ANAGRAMS: "Grant Robert Balfour" turns into "Abort terrorful bang."

EPHEMERA: 1) His father, David Balfour, was the general manager and owner of the Australian Baseball League's Sydney Blue Sox. 2) Grant Balfour holds the following MLB records for Australian-born pitchers: games finished (203), saves (84), innings pitched (539⅔), walks (252), strikeouts (571), WAR (9.2) and wins (30, tied with Graeme Lloyd). 3) He was inducted into the Australian Baseball Federation Hall of Fame in 2015. Other major leaguers so honored include Lloyd, Dave Nilsson and Craig Shipley. 4) Balfour played for Australia at the 2000 Olympics in Sydney. 5) He once landed on the disabled list and missed over a month after suffering an intercostal strain while wrestling with Rays pitching coach Jim Hickey before a game.

LARVELL BLANKS
Part of a pro sports family

BIRTH NAME: Larvell Blanks
PRONUNCIATION OF DIFFICULT PARTS: None
NICKNAME: Sugar Bear, because according to Blanks himself "in the months of August and September [1969], while I was in the Arizona Instructional League, there was a hit single being played on the radio called 'Sugar, Sugar.' Ralph Garr, Darrell Evans and others started calling me 'Sugar Bear' because of my aggressiveness at the plate."
HEIGHT/WEIGHT: 5'8" 167 lbs.
BORN: Jan. 28, 1950, in Del Rio, Texas
POSITIONS: Shortstop, Second Baseman, Third Baseman
YEARS ACTIVE IN THE MAJORS: 1972-1980

NAME ETYMOLOGY/DEFINITIONS: Despite many articles and blog posts written about him, and my own attempts to contact him, there doesn't seem to be a definitive etymology of "Larvell." "Blanks" is a patronymic of "Blank." "Blank" is of Dutch and German origin, as the nickname for a man with white or fair hair or a pale complexion, from Middle Low, Middle High German *blanc* meaning "bright," "shining," "white," or "beautiful" or from Middle Dutch *blank* meaning "fair" or "white."

The Atlanta Braves selected Blanks in the third round of the amateur draft on June 5, 1969, right after his final high school game. His first stop was Magic Valley (Twin Falls, Idaho) in the Pioneer Rookie League. He drove in 60 runs in 72 games, batting .283 with nine homers. He also got married to Rosemary Fay, with whom he would have three children.

He moved up to Class A in 1970, playing for Greenwood in the Western Carolinas League. He batted .277 with 15 homers and 69 RBI in 116 games; the "quiet and coachable" little player was named team MVP.

Promoted to AA Savannah for 1971, he followed that up with 14 more homers and 48 RBIs, though his average slipped to .222 against stronger competition. Sugar Bear (also known as Scooter to his teammates) remained at Savannah to begin the 1972 season. His production returned to more customary levels: .284-6-34 in 83 games.

He made his big-league debut in July and stayed with the Braves for the rest of the season, getting into 33 games. He hit his first big-league home run off Jack Billingham of the Reds in August at Riverfront Stadium.

Blanks made the Atlanta roster in spring training 1973 and spent most of the first two months of the year with the big club, although he started just once. In late May, the Braves sent him down to Richmond, where he played AAA ball for the first time. In the majors that year, he hit .249 with six homers and 35 RBIs.

The Braves sent him down to Richmond near the end of training camp in 1974. He persevered to hit .268 with 13 homers and 47 RBIs, and his 29 doubles led the International League. After the IL playoffs ended, the Braves recalled Blanks, and he got into three big-league games at the tail end of the season.

Blanks made the majors for good in 1975. He took over as the regular shortstop from Craig Robinson, who got sick in spring training. He played in 141 games for the Braves, starting 121 of them at short. His batting line was a modest .234-3-38, and he also committed 25 errors. Near the end of the season, interim manager Connie Ryan said, "I think Blanks is a decent player, but I think he's limited as a regular. I don't think that's his best role."

Dec. 12, 1975, was a busy day for Blanks (and his agent), as Blanks was traded first to the White Sox and then hours later dealt to the Indians. With Cleveland, Blanks enjoyed his two most productive seasons in the majors. He was not a frontline starter, playing along with Frank Duffy at short and Duane Kuiper at second, but he viewed himself as more than a mere utility infielder. He got into 104 games in 1976 and 105 in 1977, amassing 371 and 351 at-bats. His batting lines were also very similar: .280-5-41 and .286-6-38.

When Blanks signed a new contract with the Indians after the 1976 season, manager Frank Robinson called him the toughest man on the club at the plate with men on. (I double-checked this. During 1976, the team hit a collective .277 with men on base. Blanks hit .284 in those situations, no better than sixth on the team amongst semi-regulars and regulars.) Sugar Bear grew disenchanted in 1977, though. According to Cleveland sportswriter Terry Pluto, "Blanks thought he was a better player than Frank Duffy and should have been the regular shortstop."

But Duffy was a reliable glove man; and quite simply, Frank Robinson liked him better, calling him "maybe the most underrated shortstop in the big leagues." The skipper also thought that Blanks' old Braves teammate, Rico Carty, was a bad influence. "I believe that Rico poisoned his mind," said Robinson. "One day I walked in the clubhouse, and Blanks had thrown his uniform, his glove, his bats, everything in the trash because I didn't start him. I fined him. Then he was on the bench wearing a piece of tape over his mouth." Terry Pluto also said in his 1999 book *Our Tribe* that Blanks burned his uniform, though perhaps the story might have gained a little something in the telling by then.

The Indians fired Robinson in June 1977, and traded Frank Duffy and his weak bat to Boston near the end of spring training in 1978. (Rico Carty had been dealt a little over a week before.) So when the 1978 season began, Blanks had won the starting job again. His hitting declined some (.254-2-20 in 70 games), but errors – 13 in just 43 games at short – were really what kept him out of the lineup after mid-May. Cleveland turned to Tom Veryzer, a player much like Duffy who had arrived in trade from Detroit the previous December.

Just after the 1978 season ended, the Indians traded Blanks to the Rangers. Blanks got little playing time in 1979 behind Nelson Norman and Bump Wills; he had his worst big-league season (.200-1-15 in 68 games and just 138 at-bats). In December, the Rangers traded him back to his original team, the Braves. Things didn't get much better for Blanks after he returned to Atlanta for the 1980 season (.204-2-12 in 88 games). He held the third base job for a stretch in April and May, after the Braves demoted Bob Horner to the minors after a dreadful start. Once Horner returned, Blanks then mainly backed up a weak-hitting but good-fielding shortstop in Luis Gómez. Blanks made his last appearance in the majors on Aug. 3, 1980. The following day, the Braves designated him for assignment, and he was released four days later.

In 1981, Blanks took an offer in Mexico from the Azules of Coatzacoalcos. This city, in the state of Veracruz, was not terribly far from Sugar Bear's Del Rio home. Blanks spent part of 1981 with the Mexico City Tigres but returned to Coatzacoalcos for all of 1982. His son Joseph was born soon after the 1982 season to Lisa, the woman who would become his second wife. He split the 1983 season between the Azules and Tabasco, moved on to the Campeche Piratas for 1984, and his final summer in Mexico was divided between Campeche and Aguila-Veracruz. In 451 games across his five seasons south of the border, Blanks hit 21 homers, drove in 194 and batted .295.

He wasn't quite through with baseball. When the Senior Professional Baseball Association started play in the fall of 1989, Blanks joined the West Palm Beach Tropics, but the Orlando Juice obtained his rights. In 52 games, he batted .277 with 2 homers and 28 RBIs, and was a second-team league all-star.

BEST DAY (BY WPA OR OTHER MEASURE): Blanks had a 5-5 day including three doubles for the Indians in a losing effort versus the Orioles on Aug. 8, 1977. His best day in a win came on June 11, 1976 against the White Sox. Blanks went 4-6 with a triple and two runs scored. He singled to center to start a 13th inning rally that helped overcome a 4-3 deficit and propel the Indians to a 5-4 win.

THE WONDER OF HIS NAME: There is the rareness of the first name with its unknown origins. There is the adorable nickname. With a name like "Blanks" he should have been a starting pitcher though … all those missed "Larvell Blanks Phillies" headlines.

NOT TO BE CONFUSED WITH: Larvell Jones (Character played by actor Michael Winslow in the *Police Academy* movie series. Jones was famous for making sound effects with his voice), Kyle Blanks (MLB outfielder and first baseman who played for the Padres, A's, and Rangers).

FUN ANAGRAMS: "Larvell Blanks" doesn't give us anything sensible, but "Larvell Sugar Bear Blanks" rearranges to "Braves arrange skull ball." or "Braver, banal skull glares."

EPHEMERA: 1) Blanks lived much of his life in the border town of Del Rio, Texas. He was one of eight children (five boys and three girls) born to Herbert and Hannah Mae Blanks. 2) Blanks' extended family is athletic, having produced top-level pros in both football and basketball too. Larvell's uncle, Sid Blanks, was a running back in the AFL and NFL from 1964-1970. Sid's son Lance was a guard for three seasons in the NBA starting in 1990. 3) As of August 2018, just 54 men have made it to the majors after appearing in the Little League World Series. One of them is Blanks, who went in 1962 with the team representing the Val Verde County Little League. 4) In 1973, Larvell's cousin Wayne Benson (also a Del Rio native) was drafted in the first round, first in January by the Cubs, then in June by the Yankees. Wayne signed with the Yankees and made it as high as Triple A in 1976. 4) Blanks stayed in the minds of fans thanks to Tom Boswell's January 1987 essay, *99 Reasons Why Baseball is Better than Football*. Reason No. 6: "Baseball has Blue Moon, Catfish, Spaceman, and the Sugar Bear. Football has Lester the Molester, Too Mean, and the Assassin." 5) Blanks served as a teacher and tennis coach at Del Rio High in the late 1990s and early 2000s. 6) In recent years, Blanks has found a new sporting challenge: golf. He now lives between Phoenix and Del Rio, and is currently competing on the Golf Channel Amateur Tour.

DAVE BRAIN
The mind was willing, and the bat could slug,
but the glove was weak

BRAIN, BUFFALO

BIRTH NAME: David Leonard Brain
PRONUNCIATION OF DIFFICULT PARTS: None
NICKNAME: None
HEIGHT/WEIGHT: 5'10" 170 lbs.
BORN: Jan. 24, 1879, in Hereford, United Kingdom
DIED: May 25, 1959, in Los Angeles, California
POSITIONS: Third Baseman, Shortstop, Outfielder
YEARS ACTIVE IN THE MAJORS: 1901, 1903-1908
NAME ETYMOLOGY/DEFINITIONS: "David" is a common name of Biblical Hebrew origin, as King David is a character of central importance in the Hebrew Bible and in Christian, Jewish, and Islamic religious tradition. "Leonard" is a common English, German, Irish, and Dutch given name, originating from the Old High German "Leonhard" containing the prefix *levon* (meaning "lion") and the suffix *hardu* (meaning "brave" or "hardy"). It may also be from the Latin *leo* ("lion"). Leonard was the name of a Saint in the Middle Ages period, known as the patron saint of prisoners. "Brain" is

of Irish and Scottish origin. It is a "reduced form" of the Scottish Gaelic "Mac an Bhreitheamhan" meaning "son of the judge" from "Breitheamh" meaning "judge."

Little is known about Dave Brain's early life, although he appears to have only started playing baseball at the age of 19. Brain's professional baseball career began with Des Moines of the Western League in 1900 at age 21. He played third base, hit .305, and stole 27 bases. Among his 112 hits, 52 were for extra bases, including 13 triples. Later that year, he played third and shortstop briefly for Chicago of the American League, which was a minor league at the time.

With the elevation of the A.L. to major league status in 1901, Dave made his major league debut in Chicago on Apr. 24 of that year. The 22-year-old's fielding was one of the features as the White Stockings won their initial three games. However, Chicago lost its next two games, and Brain's errors were a significant factor. (One wonders if a play-by-play man in that era would have called them ... "brain cramps.") Though he hit well, going 7-for-20, his suspect fielding resulted in his being demoted to St. Paul of the Western League. He was shifted back to third and hit .262 with 11 triples and led the league with 13 homers.

During 1902, Brain had his best professional year while playing third base for Buffalo of the Eastern League. As team captain he produced a .331 batting average with 44 extra-base hits, 247 total bases, and 37 steals. He also led the league with 127 runs scored.

Dave was promptly snapped up by St. Louis of the National League. Despite hitting only .231 in 1903, Brain led the Cardinals with 60 RBIs and 15 triples, the latter being fourth-best in the league, and he stole 21 bases to boot.

Dave's offensive production significantly improved in 1904. He was the team leader in doubles, triples, homers and totaled a career-high 72 RBIs. His seven home runs were second in the league, while his 43 extra-base hits ranked fourth in the National League. During the 1903-04 seasons, Dave played 131 games at short and 76 at third. His versatility was further exhibited in 1904 when he played first, second, and the outfield.

On July 4, 1905, Brain was traded to Pittsburgh, and since Honus Wagner was the Pirates' shortstop, Brain was used almost exclusively at third base. He finished the season hitting .247 with 63 RBIs and 11 triples. On Dec. 15, 1905, the Pirates traded Brain to the NL's Boston squad.

Upon arriving in Boston, his salary was cut; this would be the beginning of serious disputes with the Boston ownership. On the playing field the team produced one of the most dismal seasons in history by finishing 66½ games behind the Cubs (who won 116 games). Dave's offensive numbers took a downturn that season, but his five homers ranked him sixth in the league. He was still error-prone in the field.

In 1907, Brain reached the pinnacle of his career. He led both leagues with ten home runs, all in his home park. In the National League, Brain ranked third with 43 extra-base hits and was fifth in doubles, total bases, and slugging average. He committed 47 errors at third and had a .916 fielding percentage (league average was

.928) but finished first in double plays and second in putouts and assists. Despite Brain's outstanding statistics, he and his 1907 teammates ended the season in seventh place, 47 games out of first.

In the off-season, Boston's President, George Dovey, restructured the team. This involved an eight-player trade with the New York Giants and the slashing of salaries. Several players, including Dave, became holdouts. In mid-May, Brain's holdout ended when he was sold to Cincinnati. His new team was hoping he would supply offense, but in 16 games as an outfielder, Dave hit a paltry .109.

In July 1908, he was sold to the Giants because skipper John McGraw needed a utility player. Brain continued to falter. Brain played four positions with New York, but only had 17 at-bats and a .176 batting average.

In 1909, McGraw sold Dave to Columbus of the American Association, but he refused to go because he wanted a salary of $3200 (what he had been making in New York). The club offered him $1800. Buffalo of the Eastern League did sign him, and he led the league with 15 triples but only hit .234 with two homers. Brain was out of professional baseball after 1910.

BEST DAY (BY WPA OR OTHER MEASURE): On Aug. 8, 1905, while playing for Pittsburgh versus Boston, Brain tripled three times and delivered the game-winning single in a 5-4 decision.

THE WONDER OF HIS NAME: Let's hear it for body part names! And he was described as thoughtful, intelligent and well-spoken, so the name fits.

NOT TO BE CONFUSED WITH: David Hayden Brain (A former Zimbabwean cricketer from 1992-1995), Brain (An extremely intelligent mouse in the cartoon series *Pinky and the Brain* and *Animaniacs*), The Brain (Nickname of both late wrestling manager Bobby Heenan, as well as gangster/gambler Arnold Rothstein), Sara Bellum (a character in the Cartoon Network animated series *The Powerpuff Girls*)

FUN ANAGRAMS: "David Leonard Brain" transforms into "Rid debonair vandal."

EPHEMERA: 1) As of January 2019 he is one of fewer than 50 big league players to have been born in the U.K. 2) He is the only player to win a season's home run title in the American or National League (since 1893) and never have another extra-base hit the rest of his major league career. He led the majors in homers with 10 in 1907 and went without an extra-base hit in 82 plate appearances in his final season of 1908. 3) He is tied with many others for most triples in a game since 1900 and for the all-time record for most consecutive triples in a nine-inning game with three. He shares with three other players the all-time record for most times with three triples in one game during a career with two. He is the only hitter in major league history to have three triples in one game twice in one season. 4) On June 11, 1906, he committed five errors, establishing the major league record for most errors in a game by a third baseman since 1900. 5) After his baseball career ended, Brain moved to California. He married Elizabeth Broderson and had one daughter, Eugenia. 6) He worked for the National

Biscuit Company and then as a credit manager at Standard Oil Company for 20 years. 7) During the Great Depression, David studied to become a chiropractor and passed the required California exam, thus becoming Dr. Brain. 8) He died of congestive heart failure in 1959.

GARLAND BUCKEYE
Early professional "two-sport" performer

BIRTH NAME: Garland Maires Buckeye

PRONUNCIATION OF DIFFICULT PARTS: None

NICKNAME: Gob, referring to his stint in the U.S. Navy, as "gob" was a word for "sailor"

HEIGHT/WEIGHT: 6'0" 260 lbs.

BORN: Oct. 16, 1897, in Heron Lake, Minnesota

DIED: Nov. 14, 1975, in Sand Lake, Wisconsin

POSITION: Pitcher

YEARS ACTIVE IN THE MAJORS: 1918, 1925-1928

NAME ETYMOLOGY/DEFINITIONS: "Garland" is a metonymic occupational name for a maker of garlands or chaplets, perhaps also a habitational name from a house sign. The word is first attested in the 14th century, from Old French, and appears to be of Germanic origin. It can also be a habitational name from a minor place, such as Garland in Chulmleigh, Devon, named from Old English *gara* meaning "triangular piece of land" and *land* meaning "estate." "Maires" is from the Old French *maire*, from Latin *māior* meaning "elder" (mayor). "Buckeye" stems from Native Americans, who called the nut from trees that covered Ohio's hills and plains *hetuck* which means "buck eye" (because the markings on the nut resemble the eye of a deer).

After graduating from Joliet Central H.S. in Illinois, Garland Buckeye broke into the major leagues as a pitcher with the Senators in 1918. Buckeye made his major league debut on June 19, 1918 at the Polo Grounds against the Yankees. He pitched the last two innings of a 9-0 game, allowing three hits, six walks, and four earned runs while striking out two batters. The *New York Times* described his size and delivery, which had "all the motions of a windmill at full speed."

More from the *Times* on Buckeye: "Shaw's successor, a huge lad named Garland Buckeye from Peoria, proved to be the wildest individual that has broken into major league circles in many a day. Buckeye is a southpaw and is just out of high school. He looks strong enough to push over a bridge, but as he was a stranger at the Polo Grounds, he had no idea where the plate was located."

Given his physical stature and athletic ability, he turned his attention to football. In 1920 he was a right guard for the Chicago Tigers of the American Professional Football Association (the APFA, which would become the NFL in 1922). He then played on the Chicago Cardinals from 1921-1924.

In 1925, he turned his attention back to baseball. During that year he had some success as the number five starter for the Cleveland Indians, going 13-8 with a 3.65 ERA. In 1926 he played on the Chicago Bulls of the American Football League (as well as pitching for the Indians that same year).

In 1927 he hurled 204 innings for Cleveland but went 10-17 on a team that finished 66-87. After a slow start with the Indians in 1928 he was released and signed with the New York Giants. He only pitched one game for them, giving up six runs in 3⅔ innings. He finished with a 30-39 record in 108 games in the major leagues.

BEST DAY (BY WPA OR OTHER MEASURE): Buckeye twirled four shutouts amongst his 67 starts in the big leagues. His best shutout may have been his Sep. 19, 1925, assignment against the woeful Red Sox. Going into the game Boston had a record of 43-98, but Buckeye showed no mercy and a surprising amount of control. For a man that walked 214 and struck out only 134 in his career, the baseball gods smiled on him that Saturday at Fenway. Though he only struck out one batter, Buckeye did not walk anyone and scattered six hits (five singles and a triple).

THE WONDER OF HIS NAME: The tree species *Aesculus glabra* is commonly known as Ohio buckeye, American buckeye, or fetid buckeye. Garland Buckeye was built like a tree himself. Then you have the rarity of "Garland" as a given name rather than a surname (like pitcher Wayne Garland), along with the rarity of "Maires" as a middle name.

NOT TO BE CONFUSED WITH: Brutus Buckeye (Mascot of The Ohio State University. Brutus has a buckeye head and block O hat, scarlet and grey shirt emblazoned "Brutus" and "00," red pants with an Ohio State towel hanging over the front, and high white socks with black shoes), Garland Bayliss (A historian and director emeritus of academic services at Texas A&M from 1957-1992).

FUN ANAGRAMS: "Garland Maires Buckeye" anagrams to "Rednecks argue amiably." or "Absurdly American geek."

EPHEMERA: 1) Garland's parents were Knute Buckeye (yes, like footballer Knute Rockne) and Minnie Maiers. The Buckeyes had five children: Garland was the first-born followed by Florence, Esther, Frances and Virginia. 2) On June 12, 1928, while pitching for the New York Giants, Buckeye and 250-pound catcher James Hogan combined for what was then the heaviest battery in major league history. 3) Buckeye was a rarity in that he was a switch-hitting pitcher. On Sep. 10, 1925, he hit a homer batting lefty (off Ed Wells), then in the same game, homered again batting righty (off Jess Doyle), thus becoming became the only pitcher to accomplish the feat. 4) On June 11, 1927, he gave up two home runs to Babe Ruth in the same game. 5) In 1938, Garland was indicted by a Waukesha grand jury on criminal charges of keeping and using slot machines. 6) After he retired from baseball, he managed the Rhinelander Brewery in Wisconsin and then managed a GM auto dealership in Toledo, Ohio. When he retired from those jobs, he spent his time raising and judging bird dogs. 7) Buckeye is the great-grandfather of Drew Pomeranz, who made his major league debut in 2011, as well as Stuart Pomeranz, who came to the majors in 2012.

AMBIORIX BURGOS
A rap sheet longer than his baseball career

BIRTH NAME: Ambiorix Burgos
PRONUNCIATION OF DIFFICULT PARTS: AM-be-OR-icks
NICKNAME: None
HEIGHT/WEIGHT: 6'3" 235 lbs.
BORN: Apr. 18, 1984, in Nagua, Dominican Republic
POSITION: Pitcher
YEARS ACTIVE IN THE MAJORS: 2005-2007
NAME ETYMOLOGY/DEFINITIONS: "Ambiorix" was the co-ruler of the Eburone tribe of Gallia Belgica (north-eastern Gaul, modern-day Belgium) who led an insurrection against Caesar's occupying forces in Gaul in the winter of 54/53 BCE. Nothing is known of his youth or rise to power; he enters and leaves history in the pages of Caesar's Gallic Wars which later historians then drew on for their own accounts of the uprising. Even his name is unknown as "Ambiorix" is a title meaning "Rich King" or an epithet meaning "King in All Directions." "Burgos" has Spanish origins as the habitational name from Burgos, the capital of old Castile.

Signed by the Royals as a 16-year-old starting pitcher in November 2000, Ambiorix Burgos spent the next two seasons hurling in the Dominican Republic. He made his pro debut in 2003 at age 19, getting into two games for the Single-A Burlington Bees of the Midwest League and nine games for the Royals Arizona League team.

In 2004 he went 7-11 in 27 games (26 starts), striking out 172 in only 133 innings (albeit also walking 75) for Burlington. In 2005 he spent part of the season with the AA Wichita Wranglers, relieving in all 12 of his appearances for them. He also made his major league debut for the Royals that year, going 3-5 with a 3.98 ERA and two saves in 59 relief outings for K.C.

He struck out a batter per inning for the Royals in 2005, but also walked one man every other inning and yielded six homers in his 63 innings pitched. He was the Royals closer the following year, notching 18 saves but blowing an amazing 12 more opportunities. He posted a 5.52 ERA while yielding 83 hits (including a stomach-turning 16 homers) in only 73 innings.

After the season, he was dealt to the Mets for Brian Bannister. Burgos split 2007 between the Mets and the minors, going 1-0 with a 3.42 ERA at the big-league level. However, he struggled with arm injuries and had Tommy John surgery late in the season. He made eight minor league appearances in 2008, and never reached the majors again.

BEST DAY (BY WPA OR OTHER MEASURE): In a wild and woolly game that saw the teams combine for ten pitchers used, 18 runs, four errors, 20 hits (six of them homers), ten walks, two wild pitches, two balks and 15 strikeouts, it was Burgos who pitched the absolute best. The game took place on May 8, 2005 at Camden Yards in Baltimore, and Burgos was a member of the visiting Royals. The Royals were off to a wretched start to the season, winning a mere seven of their first 30 games. Meanwhile the Orioles had gotten off to a 20-9 jump to their season. The Orioles took a 1-0 lead in their half of the first and the score stayed that way through the third. Then all hell broke loose. The Royals plated six runs in the fourth and two more in the fifth to take and 8-1 lead, only to see Baltimore post a 7-spot to tie it up in the bottom of the sixth. In the bottom of the seventh the O's loaded the bases with one out when Burgos was summoned from the pen. He struck out Geronimo Gil swinging and caught Brian Roberts looking to end the threat. The Royals pushed across a run in the eighth (on a balk no less), then Burgos went back out on the mound. He sandwiched two flyball outs around a swinging strikeout of Melvin Mora to send the game to the ninth. Mike Sweeney padded the Royals' lead with a solo homer, and Burgos was asked to finish the game. He set down Javy Lopez on a groundout, got Jay Gibbons swinging and induced a groundout from Rafael Palmeiro to secure the 10-8 win for the Royals. Burgos ended up facing eight batters and retired all eight, four via strikeout. It was his first major league win.

THE WONDER OF HIS NAME: Gotta love "Ambiorix," especially since there doesn't appear to be any mention of a nickname for him. No "Ambi" or "Orix" or "Rixie?"

NOT TO BE CONFUSED WITH: Orix Buffaloes (Nippon Professional Baseball team that was formed following the 2004 Nippon Professional Baseball realignment by the merger of the Orix BlueWave and the Kintetsu Buffaloes)

FUN ANAGRAMS: "Ambiorix Burgos" anagrams to "Is buxom? Big roar!"

EPHEMERA: 1) In 2006, Ambiorix was a teammate of the similarly terrifically-monikered Runelvys Hernandez (see page 198). 2) His 12 blown saves in 2006 were the most by a pitcher since Duane Ward accomplished the same feat in 1989. 3) After the 2008 season, Burgos was arrested for assaulting his girlfriend, and a month later, he was indicted in the Dominican Republic following a hit-and-run accident that killed two women. He was ultimately sentenced to nine months in jail for the assault, but the hit-and-run charges were dropped. 4) Burgos faced additional legal problems in 2010, when he was charged with the kidnapping and attempted murder of his ex-wife. 5) He somehow managed to pitch in the Mexican League in 2013, but that was the last time he played organized baseball.

GOWELL CLASET
Career record of 2-0 ... with an ERA of 9.53!

BIRTH NAME: Gowell Sylvester Claset
PRONUNCIATION OF DIFFICULT PARTS: None
NICKNAME: Lefty
HEIGHT/WEIGHT: 6'3" 210 lbs.
BORN: Nov. 26, 1907, in Battle Creek, Michigan
DIED: Mar. 8, 1981, in St. Petersburg, Florida
POSITION: Pitcher
YEARS ACTIVE IN THE MAJORS: 1933
NAME ETYMOLOGY/DEFINITIONS: "Gowell" as a surname has possible English origins, presumably a nickname for a habitual user of the expression "Go well" (from the Old English *gan* meaning "go" and *wel* meaning "well"), or possibly a nickname for a messenger. As it turns out, Claset's mother's maiden name was Gowell. So, we know how the surname became a given name in this case. "Sylvester" is a name derived from the Latin adjective *silvestris* meaning "wooded" or "wild," which derives from the noun *silva* meaning "woodland." As far as "Claset" goes, Gowell's father Charles was actually born "Charles Clesat" and the surname got changed sometime between the 1880 census and the 1910 census.

B ack in the early 1900s, there weren't too many baseball players built like Gowell Claset. He was usually described in the papers of the day as "massive," "big," "giant" or "burly." As a starting pitcher he was wild, but he always took the ball for whatever team he played for in the minors.

From 1928-1932, Claset pitched a total of 1,156 innings in 193 games, quite the workload for a young man who was but 24 when that five-year period ended. It was during the 1932 season, when Gowell went 23-13 with a 3.57 ERA (and 144 walks in 282 innings) in 47 games for Montreal of the AA International League, that Claset caught the eye of legendary Philadelphia Athletics manager Connie Mack. Mack had a thing for large, beefy pitchers, and thought that he could "tame" the wild ones like Claset. Mack had already worked his magic with Lefty Grove, a 6'3" 190 lbs. lefty with a lack of command. Mack saw the same potential in Claset.

Claset would start his major league career in the bullpen and spent most of 1933 there. He appeared in eight games and made only one start. Pretty much every game featured Claset being wild, ineffective or both. The last game he pitched in for the A's, a start on June 7 against the powerful Senators, went about as well (or poorly) as could be expected: one inning plus one batter in the second, six runs, five hits and two walks. He saw ten batters and seven reached base.

Apparently, Mack had second thoughts on Claset, for he was sent to AA Baltimore after that start, and then subsequently traded by the A's after the season to St. Paul of the American Association. He would never again appear on a major league mound. His final major league ledger for 1933: 11⅓ innings, 23 hits, 12 walks, one strikeout, 12 earned runs.

BEST DAY (BY WPA OR OTHER MEASURE): You may be asking yourself how he got two wins if he pitched so poorly (to a 9.53 ERA)? His first win came in a rain-shortened six-inning affair against the Browns on May 24. In that game, Claset came on for the starting pitcher, the equally magnificently-monikered Sugar Cain, in the top of the fourth with two outs, two men on and trailing 4-2. He struck out Jack Burns (the only strikeout of Claset's major league career) to end the inning. He got through the fifth inning yielding only a walk, and then the Athletics rallied for five runs in the bottom of the inning. Claset started the sixth inning, walked the first two batters and then was relieved by Grove, who got out of the jam with no further damage. The game was called due to rain with one out in the bottom of the sixth. The weather that day was so hazardous that lightning started a fire when it struck a corrugated iron runway that served as a ramp to the fence on which the foul line was painted. Claset was credited with the win as the A's took the lead while he was in the game. The other win came six days later in what would now be considered a "blown save" for Claset. He came in in the bottom of the 11th inning to protect an 8-6 lead against the Red Sox. Two singles, a walk and a double later and the game was tied again. The Athletics responded with three runs in the top of the 12th, with Claset helping his own cause with a run-scoring single. Claset stayed in the game for the bottom of the inning, and despite giving up a leadoff triple, and an infield single that didn't score the man from third, he managed to get through the inning unscathed and secured the 11-8 win. His line for the game was two innings pitched, four hits, two walks, two earned runs. So those two wins were probably his best days in the majors, even if he pitched not much better than any other games in his short career.

THE WONDER OF HIS NAME: When your given name is actually your mother's maiden name, you score "cool name" points. The fact that his last name was actually changed, and the original name was an anagram of the new name, scores points too.

NOT TO BE CONFUSED WITH: Larry Gowell (former major league pitcher who played in two games for the Yankees in 1972).

FUN ANAGRAMS: "Gowell Sylvester Claset" turns into "Yellowest, gravest cells." or "Cleverest gallows style."

EPHEMERA: 1) Eddie Rommel, one of the Athletics coaches during the 1933 season, would signal for the "rotund" Claset to come in from the bullpen by holding his arms far apart. 2) During the 1933 season, Gowell married Drusie Eva Corbell Lequesne, who had been born in Québec. About 18 months later, the couple welcomed their first and only child, John Lequesne Claset. John Claset wouldn't grow to be as big as his dad (6'1" and 180), but he did end up playing baseball, pitching five seasons for the Reds and Yankees minor league affiliates. 3) After baseball, Gowell Claset worked as a moulder in a foundry and was a pattern maker for General Electric in Elmira, New York, retiring to Florida in 1973.

HARRY COLLIFLOWER
Pitcher on worst team in baseball history

BIRTH NAME: James Harry Colliflower
PRONUNCIATION OF DIFFICULT PARTS: None
NICKNAME: Collie
HEIGHT/WEIGHT: 5'11" 175 lbs.
BORN: Mar. 11, 1869, in Petersville, Maryland
DIED: Aug. 14, 1961, in Washington, D.C.
POSITIONS: Pitcher, Outfielder, First Baseman
YEARS ACTIVE IN THE MAJORS: 1899
NAME ETYMOLOGY/DEFINITIONS: "James" has English origins from a personal name that has the same origin as "Jacob." However, among English speakers, it is now felt to be a separate name in its own right. This is largely because in the Authorized Version of the Bible (1611) the form James is used in the New Testament as the name of two of Christ's apostles (James the brother of John and James the brother of Andrew), whereas in the Old Testament the brother of Esau is called Jacob. The form James comes from Latin Jacobus via Late Latin Jac(o)mus, which also gave rise to Jaime, the regular form of the name in Spanish (as opposed to the learned Jacobo). "Harry" has English origins (mainly South Wales and southwestern England), from the medieval personal name Harry, which was the usual vernacular form of "Henry," with assimilation of the consonantal cluster and regular Middle English change of -er- to -ar-. It also has French origins: from the Germanic personal name "Hariric," composed of the elements *hari*, *heri* meaning "army" and *ric* meaning "power(ful)." "Colliflower" is the altered form of French "Gorenflo," a habitational name from a village named Gorenflos between Abbeville and Amiens, France. It's also an obsolete form of "cauliflower."

In 1899, 30-year-old Harry Colliflower was a Washington, D.C., carpenter who had gained a bit of local renown as a semipro southpaw hurler with the Eastern Athletic Club. He had some minor-league experience, with Norfolk in 1894 and 1895, moving to the New Haven Texas Steers in 1896 and the Austin Senators in 1896 and 1897, and he'd played for part of 1898 for Oswego.

At the beginning of the 1899 season, he was considering some minor-league offers and almost signed with a Texas club. But on July 21, Colliflower was still pitching for

Eastern when Joe Quinn, whose Cleveland Spiders were in town to face the Senators, signed him to pitch.

The 1899 Spiders were a National League ballclub that was destined to set a record as the worst team in major-league baseball history. But in the decade leading up to that point, the Spiders had been a successful franchise. Ten years prior, the Cleveland National League franchise, then known as the Forest Citys, was purchased by horse-drawn streetcar tycoon Frank DeHaas Robison. Under Robison's leadership, the Cleveland Spiders had won the 1895 Temple Cup[16] and were perennial contenders, featuring future Hall of Famers such as Cy Young and Jesse Burkett.

Things changed overnight for the Spiders when, after the 1898 season, Robison bought the St. Louis ballclub in a sheriff's sale. Robison then decided that St. Louis would be a more profitable baseball city, and essentially robbed his Cleveland club of its best players to support his preferred St. Louis team, which he named the Perfectos.

That left Robison's brother Stanley to run the Spiders as a sideshow, populating the club with a rag-tag collection of minor-league and semipro players, and whomever else Brother Stan could manage to snag on short notice. They won only eight of their first 38 games, when Stanley Robison fired his player-manager, Lave Cross, and did him the favor of exporting him to St. Louis.

Slick-fielding second baseman Joe Quinn picked up where Cross left off, and the results were even worse: the Spiders won just 12 games out of their next 116 (no, that's not a typo!). The team was so bad and so unloved in Cleveland, that after July 1, they gave up playing in Cleveland altogether, playing the rest of their season on the road. Thereafter, the newspapers began referring to them as the Wanderers, or the Exiles.

In his first major-league appearance, Colliflower didn't stink up the joint, giving up only three runs on six hits to lead the Spiders to a 5-3 victory in the first half of a doubleheader. The Washington Post gushed, "Colliflower possesses every quality that is required in a major league twirler. He has fine control of the ball, good speed, and, the requisite amount of nerve."

From there it was all downhill for poor Harry. Staying with the club for the rest of the 1899 season, he pitched 89 innings and gave up 146 hits, went 0-11 and compiled an ERA over 9.00. For their last game of the season (and of the franchise), the Spiders' starting pitcher was a 19-year-old cigar stand clerk they found in Cincinnati named Eddie Kolb. The Spiders lost to the Reds, 19-3.

Colliflower added more to the team as a hitter, finishing the season with a batting average of .303; Quinn put him in center field and at first base a few times just to get

[16] The Temple Cup was the name of a postseason series and trophy awarded to the winner that was conducted for four National League seasons from 1894 to 1897. As there was only one major league at the time, the best-of-seven series was played between the first and second place teams. The cup was the brainchild of William Temple, president of the Pittsburgh Pirates.

his bat into the lineup. The Cleveland club, which finished in last place with a record of 20-134, folded at the end of the season as the National League contracted from twelve teams to eight. Robison may have ruined Cleveland, but he didn't manage to reap any rewards with his St. Louis super-club – they finished the season 18½ games out of first place.

Colliflower drifted during the next few years – after playing for three different clubs in 1900. He then kept busy pitching and/or coaching for one or another of Washington's semipro clubs or in the Virginia State League, umpiring high school games or refereeing in the nascent Professional Basketball circuit. In 1905, he coached Georgetown's baseball team before catching on as a semipro and minor-league umpire, returning in the offseason to work in the D.C. Highway Department.

Beginning in 1906 he umpired for two seasons in the South Atlantic League before American League president Ban Johnson told him to report for duty as an AL umpire in July 1910. He umpired in 46 AL games, 19 behind the plate and 27 at first base. Colliflower umpired in the Southern League in 1911 and returned to D.C. in 1912 as an umpire for the "Departmental League," a collection of ballclubs organized by clerks in the various branches of the federal government.

As his post-playing career progressed, Colliflower spent some time scouting for the major leagues, allegedly discovering Detroit first baseman Lu Blue, but for the most part, he worked as a clerk for his nephew James E. Colliflower's fuel oil and coal company.

BEST DAY (BY WPA OR OTHER MEASURE): Given his career stat line of 1-11, 8.17 ERA and 152 hits allowed in 98 innings, the high points are few and far between. We'll have to simply re-state his big-league debut on July 21 of 1899, in which he pitched a complete game, yielding three runs on six hits to lead the Spiders to a 5-3 victory in the first half of a doubleheader. It was one of only 20 wins for the Spiders on the season, so hopefully it was cherished by the team.

THE WONDER OF HIS NAME: He was kind of a "tomato can" for the Spiders, but then again, it would appear the remnants left of the team were all "tomato cans" after the pilfering by St. Louis. No one on the squad could ... produce. There were no "salad days" for the Spiders. The "side" was often retired in order. (OK I'll stop.)

NOT TO BE CONFUSED WITH: Albert Broccoli (20th century American film producer who made more than 40 motion pictures throughout his career. Broccoli is most notable as the producer of many of the James Bond films), Charles Onions (English grammarian and lexicographer and the fourth editor of the Oxford English Dictionary).

FUN ANAGRAMS: "James Harry Colliflower" turns into "Jolly, warm, heroical serf."

EPHEMERA: 1) His first name was the same as his father's: James, a carpenter. His mother was Catherine Cramer Colliflower. There were four children in the family, an older sister named Lillie, an older brother, Charles, and a younger brother, Robert. 2) In 1906, Colliflower married Lillian Genevieve Rice. (Between "Colliflower" and "Rice," the couple made quite a side dish.) The Colliflowers had three children: Dorothy, Edward, and Harry. 3) Colliflower's nephew earned a bachelor's degree and three law degrees from Georgetown. He is enshrined in the Georgetown Athletics Hall of Fame as a coach of the varsity men's basketball squad from 1911–1914 and 1921–1922. James' brother George was also a college basketball coach, for George Washington University. 4) Harry eased into a graceful retirement from the sporting scene, coming out occasionally to perform Casey at the Bat for athletic club luncheons. 5) Harry passed away at the age of 92 in 1961, leaving behind his wife, Genevieve Rice Colliflower, daughter Dorothy, and son Harry, Jr. He was buried at Mt. Olivet Cemetery in Washington, D.C.

NARCISO ELVIRA
Another Teddy Higuera? Not even close.

BIRTH NAME: Narciso Chicho Elvira
PRONUNCIATION OF DIFFICULT PARTS: None
NICKNAME: None
HEIGHT/WEIGHT: 5'10" 160 lbs.
BORN: Oct. 29, 1967, in Tlalixcoyan, Mexico
DIED: Jan. 28, 2020, in Veracruz, Mexico
POSITION: Pitcher
YEARS ACTIVE IN THE MAJORS: 1990
NAME ETYMOLOGY/DEFINITIONS: "Narciso" is of Portuguese and Spanish origins, specifically from a medieval personal name (Latin "Narcissus," from Greek "Narkissos," the name of a flower). This name was borne, according to classical myth, by a vain youth who was so transfixed by his own beauty that he ignored the blandishments of the nymph Echo and stared at his own reflection in water until he faded away and turned into the pale but lovely flower that bears his name. It was also borne by several early Christian saints. The personal name owes its popularity to saints rather than to the mythological youth. *Narciso* is (also) the Spanish word for daffodil. "Chicho" is the Spanish word for curl or ringlet (of hair). It can also mean "good" when used as an adjective. "Elvira" is believed to be a medieval royal name, of probably Visigothic origin, and debated meaning. It became famous outside Spain after its appearance in Mozart's *Don Giovanni*.

N arciso Elvira said in a 2013 interview, "(Teddy) Higuera and (Fernando) Valenzuela, they were my inspiration," and throughout his time in the minors and early in the majors, Elvira was spoken of as the next Higuera, more for their Mexican heritage than their respective arsenals, as it turned out. Elvira couldn't spin a curve like Higuera did.

Elvira was purchased by the Brewers from the León team in the Mexican League in December 1986 at the age of 19. He got into four games for Beloit in the Single-A Midwest League in 1987, pitching to a 1.000 WHIP in 27 innings. In 1988 he moved to Stockton in the California League (still Single-A). He appeared in 25 games, making 23 starts, and impressed with 10.7 strikeouts per nine innings while allowing only 5.8 hits per 9 innings. (He did walk 79 in 135 innings though). That performance earned him a promotion to AA El Paso in the Texas League to start the 1989 season.

As well as he pitched in Stockton, that's how poorly he pitched in El Paso. In seven starts, he allowed 71 baserunners in 33 innings and struck out only 18.

If his on-field performance wasn't disappointing enough, his friendship with Brewers ace and fellow countryman Teddy Higuera raised some eyebrows. In David Lamb's book *Stolen Season: A Journey Through America and Baseball's Minor Leagues*, he gives some more reasons why Elvira's journey to the majors got slowed down in 1989: "Elvira's desire had gotten sidetracked in spring training, after Milwaukee's million-dollar pitcher, Teddy Higuera, had taken his fellow Mexican under his wing. Higuera had paid Elvira's $3,000 dentist bill, bought his meals in Arizona and, the Brewers had heard, promised him $50,000 to start a new career if his baseball career failed. Higuera had also given Elvira the use of his home and his car in Ciudad de Juarez, just across the Rio Grande from El Paso, and Elvira, age 20, arrived for the Diablos games every afternoon in a chauffeur-driven limousine."

Back in Stockton, Elvira once again dominated. He struck out 135 and allowed only 92 hits in just over 115 innings, and he even improved his walk rate (3.4 per nine innings). In 1990, Elvira spent most of the year shuttling between El Paso and Beloit.

He failed to impress again in El Paso, pitching a total of 18 innings across four starts, and getting tagged for four homers with only 12 strikeouts. In Beloit he pitched better, carding a 2.35 ERA with 45 strikeouts in 38 innings. When the rosters expanded for the big-league club in September of that year, Elvira was called up. by the Brew Crew.

His debut came in a mop-up role in the ninth inning of a contest against the Tigers. Milwaukee was already down 4-0, but Elvira retired Chet Lemon on a flyball to center and he struck out Dave Bergman swinging. Rich Rowland doubled to right and Milt Cuyler followed with another double before Elvira got Darnell Coles to line out. One inning, one run on two hits. All told he got into four games that September and yielded a run in three of those. He ended the season with a 5.40 ERA with five hits allowed in five innings of work, to go along with five walks and six strikeouts.

He started the 1991 season in AAA and got pounded to a 5.96 ERA in 80 innings, allowing 100 hits while striking out only 52. It was obvious at that point that he was not a major league talent. He bounced to the AAA affiliates of the Rangers and Dodgers, pitched in Japan for a few years, and ended up his career in the Mexican League in 2009 at the age of 41.

BEST DAY (BY WPA OR OTHER MEASURE): With only four appearances in the majors, "best day" will have to be redefined a bit. The last game he pitched in the majors was the only one in which he did not yield any runs. On Sep. 27, 1990, at

County Stadium in Milwaukee, the Brewers were playing out the string against the Yankees. Milwaukee starter Teddy Higuera got roughed up for six runs, and Elvira was called in to bail Higuera out of what had become a three-run fourth inning. Rivera caught Jesse Barfield looking with a man on second to end the inning, then pitched the fifth and sixth. He struck out two men to start the fifth, gave up a single to Randy Velarde, then induced a force out from Bob Geren. In the sixth, he yielded a one-out single to Roberto Kelly, who was promptly nailed trying to steal second. Then Elvira issued a four-pitch walk to Steve Sax and a five-pitch free pass to Don Mattingly before getting Barfield to strike out again. And that was Elvira's major league career.

THE WONDER OF HIS NAME: Another "double unique" name! His big-league debut occurred only nine years after the hit song *Elvira* came out, so there was still a chance for a cultural reference there. His given name could conjure up visions of someone very self-absorbed.

NOT TO BE CONFUSED WITH: Elvira (Famous country and pop hit by The Oak Ridge Boys in 1981, now considered one of their signature songs), Elvira – Mistress of the Dark (Television horror movie hostess character portrayed by Cassandra Peterson), Narciso Lopez (Venezuela-born adventurer and Spanish Army general, best known for his expeditions aimed at liberating Cuba from Spanish rule in the 1850s. His troops carried a flag that López had designed, which later became the flag of modern Cuba),

FUN ANAGRAMS: "Narciso Chicho Elvira" turns into "Rich or lavish cocaine." or "Heroic, chronic saliva."

EPHEMERA: 1) He was the Brewers second-ranked prospect by *Baseball America* in 1990 (behind Greg Vaughn) and 1991 (behind Chris George). 2) In 1999, he became just the second Mexican League pitcher with two no-hitters in a year, following Chet Brewer by six decades. 3) He went 1-1 with a 0.82 for Mexico in the 1999 Pan American Games. 4) Elvira pitched a no-no for the Osaka Kintetsu Buffaloes on June 20, 2000. He is the only Mexican to do so in the Nippon Professional Baseball League. 5) In June 2015, Elvira and three of the workers on his ranch were kidnapped in Hueyapan de Ocampo. They were finally rescued in mid-July. 6) In January 2020, Elvira and his son Gustavo were killed while driving on a road near the town of Medellín de Bravo when armed men ambushed their car. Eyewitnesses told local media that the pair tried to flee on foot as the assailants opened fire.

CHONE FIGGINS
Its "Shawn" as in "fawn," not "Chone" as in "phone"

BIRTH NAME: Desmond DeChone Figgins

PRONUNCIATION OF DIFFICULT PARTS: Chone is actually pronounced "Shawn." His father's sister gave Figgins his now famous middle name, because she wanted it to be unique.

NICKNAME: None
HEIGHT/WEIGHT: 5'8" 180 lbs.
BORN: January 22, 1978, in Leary, Georgia
POSITIONS: Third Baseman, Centerfielder, Second Baseman
YEARS ACTIVE IN THE MAJORS: 2002-2012, 2014
NAME ETYMOLOGY/DEFINITIONS: "Desmond" has Irish origins, as the Anglicized form of Gaelic "Ó Deasmhumhnaigh" meaning "descendant of the man from southern Munster," from *deas* meaning "south" and *Mumhain* meaning "Munster," an ancient Irish kingdom named for Mumhu, one of its early kings. Originally a surname, it has passed into common use as a personal name, not only in Ireland. Given the pronunciation of "Chone," it would be reasonable to assume that "DeChone" is a spelling variant of "Deshawn," which consists of the French prefix *de* to the given name "Shawn." "Shawn" is an Anglicized spelling of "Seán," the Irish equivalent of "John," originally meaning "Jehovah has been gracious" in Hebrew. "Figgins" has uncertain English origins; apparently a pet form of "Figg." "Figg" is perhaps a topographic name for someone who lived near a fig tree, or a metonymic occupational name for someone who sold figs, from Old French *figue* (Latin *ficus*).

Chone Figgins attended Brandon H.S. in Florida, where he was a third-team H.S. All-American as a senior. He was drafted in the fourth round of the 1997 draft by the Colorado Rockies, two spots ahead of Xavier Nady (see page 241).

After a slow crawl through the Rockies minor league system (he was in his first year in AA in 2001), he was acquired by the Angels in a trade in June of that year for the also wonderfully-named Kimera Bartee.

Figgins made his major league debut as a pinch-runner in August 2002, and he got his first hit, an RBI single to right field, off Aaron Myette of the Rangers that September. He finished 2-for-12 in his time with the big-league club that season. He split 2003 between AAA Salt Lake, where he hit a robust .312/.379/.509, and the major league club, where he compiled a more representative .296/.345/.367 line in 71 games.

His first full season in the majors was 2004. The Angels used the versatile Figgins at second, third and center. On May 14, 2004, he went 5-for-6 in a 10-inning game against the Orioles and hit his first home run off Kurt Ainsworth. He repeated his .296 batting average from 2003, but added a bit more extra base power, slugging .419.

His breakout year came in 2005, when he was moved to the leadoff spot after the prior leadoff hitter David Eckstein signed with the Cardinals. Figgins used his speed to steal an American League-high 62 bases, the second-most in Angels history. That year, he started at least 35 games at three different positions: second (36 starts), third (48) and center (45). He was named team co-MVP of the 2005 season for the Angels, along with Bartolo Colón.

Eligible for salary arbitration in 2006, the Angels instead signed Figgins to a three-year, $10.5 million deal. Along with third base, Figgins also played shortstop, second base, and all three outfield positions. Although he was initially considered for the center field job in 2006, the Angels decided to move Darin Erstad back to the position. Figgins became the starter at third base.

However, with Erstad on the disabled list for much of the season, Figgins ended up starting 93 games in center. For the year, his batting average slipped to .267, but he did go 52-for-68 in stolen bases.

In a 2007 spring training game against the Diamondbacks, Figgins suffered two broken fingers on his throwing hand while attempting to field a ground ball hit by Conor Jackson. He began the season on the disabled list and did not return till the end of April. That July, Figgins stole his 187th base as an Angel, breaking the 20-year-old club record previously held by Gary Pettis, who was in attendance that day as a coach for the visiting Rangers. For the year, he batted a career-high .330, good for sixth-best in the American League.

In 2008 he was limited to 116 games due to leg issues that dogged him in May and June. He stopped playing in the outfield to save his legs. He stole "only" 34 bases that year and legged out just one triple (he had as many as 17 triples in a season, doing that in 2004). He hit an empty .276/.367/.318.

In 2009, Figgins was selected to his first All-Star Game. He finished the season with an AL-best 101 walks and finished tenth in AL MVP voting. Although Figgins stole 42 bases in 2009, he was caught 17 times – tied for the most in the majors.

On December 2009, Figgins and the Seattle Mariners agreed to a four-year contract worth approximately $36 million. In 2010, he was moved full-time to second base and had his worst year to date, batting just .259, though he did match his previous season stolen base total of 42.

In 2011, Figgins converted back to third base, but halfway through the 2011 season, he was replaced by Adam Kennedy as the everyday third baseman. Appearing in only 81 games, with only 288 at-bats, Figgins finished the season batting only .188.

At the start of the 2012 season, Figgins was allowed the opportunity to bat leadoff for the Mariners in the hopes that the return to the spot in the lineup where he thrived during his time with the Angels would jump start his bat. On May 4 of that season, manager Eric Wedge announced that Figgins would no longer be an everyday player. He ended the 2012 season batting .181 with 166 at-bats in 66 games and was designated for assignment by the Mariners in November.

In February 2013, he signed a minor league contract with the Marlins, but he did not make the team out of spring training and was released. After sitting out the 2013 season, Figgins signed with the Dodgers for 2014. In 38 games with the Dodgers, he appeared as a utility player/pinch-hitter and hit .217, though he had a .373 OBP due to drawing 14 walks in 76 plate appearances. He was placed on the disabled list in mid-June with a hip injury and then spent an extended time with the AAA Albuquerque Isotopes on a rehab assignment. The Dodgers released Figgins in August and he was not signed by another team. In March 2016, Figgins announced his retirement from professional baseball. He signed a one-day contract with the Angels in order to retire with the team.

BEST DAY (BY WPA OR OTHER MEASURE): Figgins tied the American League record of six hits in a nine-inning game when he got a six-pack on June 18, 2007 against the Astros in Anaheim. Figgins batted second in the order that night against Astros' starter Chris Sampson. Figgins singled to right in the first, had an RBI single to left in the second, singled to right and subsequently scored in the fourth, doubled to right in the sixth, had an RBI single back to reliever Chad Qualls in the seventh, and capped the game with a walk-off RBI triple to break a 9-9 tie off of Trevor Miller. Final tally: 6-for-6 with a double, a triple, a run scored and three driven in. Oh, and he also stole a base for good measure. It was part of a remarkable month of June that saw him go 53-for-115 (.461).

THE WONDER OF HIS NAME: Really now ... how is anyone supposed to see "Chone" and at first glance think the "Ch" is pronounced "Sh?" It's just not instinctual when seeing that letter grouping. On the other hand, there is "Michonne," a character on "The Walking Dead" and the name is pronounced "Me-shone" ... so go figure. Add in that Chone Figgins is a "double unique" and you have a distinctly memorable name, if you remember how to pronounce "Chone."

NOT TO BE CONFUSED WITH: Alan Wiggins (Second baseman and outfielder for the San Diego Padres and Baltimore Orioles between 1981-1987), John Riggins (Former NFL running back who played professionally for the New York Jets and Washington Redskins. Riggins had his greatest success in the postseason and was named the Most Valuable Player of Super Bowl XVII. Riggins was inducted into the Pro Football Hall of Fame in 1992.), "Pinky" Higgins (MLB third baseman, manager, front office executive and scout, who played for three teams and served as manager or general manager of the Red Sox from 1955-1965).

FUN ANAGRAMS: "Desmond DeChone Figgins" makes "I'm defending chosen gods."

EPHEMERA: 1) Figgins and his wife, Claudia, had a son, Desmond, Jr., in 2015, and Chone appears to be content to be a full-time dad now. 2) Two of his uncles and his older brother, Demetrius, coached baseball at Blake H.S. in the Tampa area. His mother, Eva, and his father, Charles, often played on coed softball teams comprising all the Figginses and their relatives, and which participated in weekend and other tournaments. 3) Charles was a former semipro ballplayer from Georgia, who later barnstormed through Florida on weekends with a competitive slow-pitch softball team when he wasn't working odd jobs to support his family. To make ends meet his mother worked for the county as a coordinator of services for seniors. 4) Figgins became the fifth Angel to hit for the cycle on Sep. 16, 2006, at Rangers Ballpark in Arlington. Against the A's at Angel Stadium on Sep. 29, 2006, he hit his first career inside-the-park home run.

HILLY FLITCRAFT
Quaker who barely got to sow his baseball oats

BIRTH NAME: Hildreth Milton Flitcraft
PRONUNCIATION OF DIFFICULT PARTS: None
NICKNAME: None
HEIGHT/WEIGHT: 6'2" 180 lbs.
BORN: Aug. 21, 1923, in Woodstown, New Jersey
DIED: Apr. 2, 2003, in Boulder, Colorado
POSITION: Pitcher
YEARS ACTIVE IN THE MAJORS: 1942
NAME ETYMOLOGY/DEFINITIONS: "Hildreth" has Northern English origins, probably from a Middle English personal name, perhaps a variant of Eldridge. "Milton" has English and Scottish origins, as the habitational name from any of the numerous and widespread places so called. The majority of these are named with Old English *middel* meaning "middle" and *tun* meaning "enclosure" or "settlement." "Flitcraft" is an altered spelling of the English "Flitcroft," a Lancashire surname, which is probably a habitational name from a lost or unidentified place named with Old English *croft* meaning "paddock."

A s a kid, Hilly emulated his idol, Bob Feller, who was known for having honed his skills throwing a ball through a hole in a barn. Flitcraft told an interviewer: "On the dairy farm where I was raised, we had a milk house with a cinder block wall. I practiced throwing at specific cinder blocks with various pitches."

By the age of 13, he was playing ball with adults in the college-level Salem County League. After graduating from high school in 1940, Hilly enrolled at the New Jersey Agricultural College, part of Rutgers University. As a 17-year-old he played on the freshman baseball team. The next year he made the varsity squad. In the summer Flitcraft returned to play in the Salem County League; on the team was his former high school baseball coach, Woody Litwhiler, who noticed Hilly's increased speed and improved curveball.

Woody's brother, Danny Litwhiler, played with the Philadelphia Phillies and, after seeing Flitcraft play, Danny arranged for Flitcraft to try out for the big league team. The audition led to the Phillies inviting him to work out with the major-league club for a couple of weeks and pitch batting practice during a swing through the West. Flitcraft also pitched for the Phillies in two exhibitions. After the road trip, the Phillies signed Flitcraft to a two-year contract for $250 per month. The contract also allowed him to continue his studies at Rutgers and rejoin the Phillies when the school year ended in early May.

Flitcraft's major-league debut came on Aug. 31, 1942, in Cincinnati. Manager Hans Lobert called on him with the Phillies trailing the Reds 7-1 in the seventh. Perhaps as a test, Lobert wanted the lefty Flitcraft to take on righthanded hitters Frankie

Kelleher, Frank McCormick, and Eric Tipton. (It might appear unusual from today's perspective for the Phillies to bring a player with no real professional experience to the majors. However, the Phillies were already short on talent, having finished last in the previous four seasons and five of the previous six. To make things worse, the war hit them harder than most, with 17 players lost to military service before the start of the 1943 season.)

Flitcraft's second appearance was not as successful as the first. He faced five batters and retired only one while yielding two hits, two walks, and a wild pitch. Flitcraft rebounded somewhat in his final appearance of the year, on Sep. 17. This time, he went two innings, allowing one run on four hits while recording a strikeout.

He had turned 19 that August, making him eligible for the draft, and his family were Quakers who were morally opposed to war. The family dairy farm was considered a vital war industry and working there would earn Flitcraft a draft deferment. So, before the start of the 1943 season, Hilly officially retired from baseball and returned to the farm in Woodstown.

In the spring of 1945 Flitcraft took himself off the voluntary-retirement list and went to Wilmington, where the Phillies and their farm teams held a combined spring training because of wartime travel restrictions. Upon hearing he wouldn't make the big-league club, he asked for an assignment to the Class-B Wilmington Blue Rocks instead of the higher-level team in Utica, New York, so he could be close to home. The Phillies traded his contract to Wilmington.

Flitcraft's 1945 season was his most successful. He compiled a 15-4 record and was selected for the league's all-star team. His best game of the year came on a day tinged with personal loss: Before a scheduled start on June 29, Flitcraft was informed that his mother had died. He went out that night and pitched a two-hit shutout in which he fanned seven Lancaster hitters. Then he went back to Woodstown for the funeral.

Besides his baseball career, Flitcraft continued to help out on the dairy farm. One day in May he injured his back on the farm, resulting in a bulging disk. After consulting with doctors, who wanted to operate, Flitcraft managed to get the surgery postponed until after the season. In total, he missed only two weeks of playing time prior to surgery. Doctors operated on Flitcraft's back in December 1945. The following spring, he attended spring training but was still not feeling up to par. A second operation was prescribed; that took place in June and kept him off the field for all of 1946. The second operation was more successful than the first, but Flitcraft's back bothered him the rest of his life.

The spring of 1947 saw Flitcraft back in spring training. Initially tabbed for the Phillies' top farm club, in Utica, but with his back still causing him problems, Flitcraft wound up being sent all the way down to Class-D Carbondale (Pennsylvania). His results were respectable, but he was effectively done for the season by the end of July, because of his back problems.

After being released by the Phillies, Flitcraft returned to Rutgers for the spring 1948 semester. However, he was offered another chance at baseball. This time, the

Philadelphia A's wanted him to play first base for their Class D entry in Portsmouth, Ohio. By August he was batting .327, but he broke a finger and thought his season was over. However, the A's asked him to fill in at their Class-A team in Lincoln, Nebraska. It would be Flitcraft's last role in professional baseball. When the season ended, Flitcraft again returned to Rutgers for good, completing his degree in 1950. While there he met Janice Devine, a local girl and student at Douglass, the University's women's college. They married in 1950 and had one daughter, Dana.

BEST DAY (BY WPA OR OTHER MEASURE): Flitcraft's major league experience was all of three games, and the last two of those were less than stellar. So, we're left going with his big-league debut on Aug. 31, 1942. The sad sack Phillies came into the game with a record of 36-87, 49 games out of first place. Down 7-1 in the seventh inning, Flitcraft got Frankie Kelleher to pop to short, Frank McCormick to ground out to the second baseman, and he enticed a pop out to first by Eric Tipton. He was the only Philadelphia pitcher to not allow a baserunner that day, as the Phillies eventually lost 8-1.

THE WONDER OF HIS NAME: "Hilly," and more specifically "Hildreth" is rather unique in baseball annals. The only other "Hilly" to play in the Majors was Hilly (Hillary) Hathaway in 1992-1993. Flitcraft is wholly unique in baseball history.

NOT TO BE CONFUSED WITH: Hilly flanks (The upland areas surrounding the Fertile Crescent of Southwest Asia, including the foothills of the Zagros Mountains, the Taurus Mountains, and the highland parts of the Levant), "Flitcraft parable" (A "digression" that appears about one-third of the way through Dashiell Hammett's *The Maltese Falcon*. In it, Sam Spade tells Brigid O'Shaughnessy the story of Flitcraft, who "left his real-estate office, in Tahoma, to go to luncheon one day and never returned." Hilly Flitcraft came to the majors in 1942, one year after *The Maltese Falcon* became a movie).

FUN ANAGRAMS: "Hildreth Milton Flitcraft" becomes "Deft thrill, romantic filth."

EPHEMERA: 1) Flitcraft was a Quaker who played for the Philadelphia Phillies. The original version of the Phillies franchise was named the Quakers (1883-1889). 2) Hilly's parents, Hildreth Milton (who generally went by his middle name) and Edna Crispin Flitcraft, operated a large dairy farm and creamery serving the Delaware Valley. In addition to Hilly, their family consisted of four other boys and a girl. 3) After graduation from Rutgers, Flitcraft spent several years in the insurance business in New Brunswick, New Jersey. 4) In 1956, he became a food marketing agent for the Cooperative Extension Service at Rutgers. There, he helped teach 4-H club members about purchasing and preparing beef and eggs, taught marketing to farmers, and wrote an educational pamphlet on food costs. 5) In 1961, he returned to Woodstown to work in a local insurance agency. He later bought the agency and operated it until his retirement. 6) In 1993, he was inducted into the South Jersey Baseball Hall of Fame. 7) Flitcraft remained an active supporter of youth sports throughout his life. In New Brunswick he and Janice organized a local swim club. When he returned to

Woodstown, he helped organize the local Little League, becoming the league's first president. He was later instrumental in building the league a new field as a member of the Rotary Club. 8) Upon his retirement from the insurance business in 1991, Flitcraft moved to Colorado to be closer to his daughter and her family. He died of complications from surgery in a hospital there on Apr. 2, 2003.

CHARLIE FRISBEE
Demonstrably affectionate towards his bat

BIRTH NAME: Charles Augustus Frisbee
PRONUNCIATION OF DIFFICULT PARTS: None
NICKNAME: Bunt, due to his frequent and adept bunting[17]
HEIGHT/WEIGHT: 5'9" 175 lbs.
BORN: Feb. 2, 1874, in Dows, Iowa
DIED: Nov. 7, 1954, in Iowa Falls, Iowa
POSITION: Centerfielder
YEARS ACTIVE IN THE MAJORS: 1899-1900
NAME ETYMOLOGY/DEFINITIONS: "Charles" is derived from the Germanic *karl* (meaning full-grown, a man), which is a cognate of the Old English *ceorl* (meaning a man, freeman, peasant). It is a royal name, being borne by ten kings of France as well as by kings of Hungary, Naples, Sardinia, and Wüttemberg. It was introduced to Great Britain by Mary, Queen of Scots who bestowed it upon her son, Charles James. His son and grandson both rules as King Charles, furthering the name's popularity. "Augustus" has Latin origins, from the adjective *augustus* meaning "great" or "magnificent" (from augere meaning to "increase"). "Frisbee" has English origins as a variant spelling of "Frisby," which is of Old Norse origin, and is a locational name from places so called in Leicestershire, for example Frisby on the Wreake or Frisby by Gaulby, deriving from the Old Norse *Frisir* meaning "Frisians," plus *byr* meaning "farm" or "settlement."

Charlie Frisbee attended Iowa State[18] in 1894-1895 and caught for their team. After the 1895 college season, he joined the C-level Illinois-Iowa League's team in Ottumwa,[19] Iowa as a catcher-outfielder. By 1898 he had

---

[17] Until the late 1890s, the catcher could position himself along the foul lines if he wanted to, in order to hinder a batter's attempts to bunt. Of course this would only be done with no one on base. In 1899, a rule was put in by the National League restricting where the catcher may stand. According to Major League Baseball official historian John Thorn the rule was amended in 1901 and 1902 to: The catcher must stand within the lines of his position whenever the pitcher delivers the ball to the bat and within 10 feet of the home base.
[18] Some newspaper accounts and reference books list Iowa State as the college he attended. Other sources (like Baseball Reference) list Grinnell College.
[19] If Ottumwa rings a distant bell, it was the home city of the fictional Radar O'Reilly from *MASH*.

made it to A-level Kansas City of the Western League where he hit .315. In early September of that year, *The Sporting Life* stated "Jimmy Williams, Jimmy Slagel (sic) and Charley Frisbee are covering themselves with glory and receive liberal as well as favorable mention wherever they go."

It was with Kansas City that he first demonstrated some unusual affection for his bat. He would on occasion caress and serenade it while on the bench and then kiss the end of it each time he stepped to the plate (eat your heart out Yasiel Puig). The *Ohio State Journal* referred to his behavior as "idiotic," but Frisbee paid it and similar opinions no mind.

In 1899 he hit .362 in 148 games and was in line to lead the Eastern League in batting when he was promoted to the big league to replace injured Billy Hamilton for the Boston Beaneaters. Although Frisbee hit .329 for Boston, he was loaned out late that year to Grand Rapids in the Western League (obviously a step down from the bigs). Frank Selee, the Boston manager, engineered the loan in order to acquire catcher Billy Sullivan from Grand Rapids. The deal was terminated early the following year when Grand Rapids transferred its club to Cleveland of the new American League and Boston successfully lobbied to the National Board of Control (a ruling body that settled player ownership disputes) that Frisbee didn't have to report to Cleveland and was therefore still property of the Beaneaters.

Frisbee's return to Boston didn't last long. Upon reclaiming him, the Beaneaters sold him and Charley Hickman to the moribund New York Giants. One day after opening the season for the Giants and going 1-3 in right field, Frisbee messed up his knee in a collision on the basepaths and was out until mid-May. He played two more games for the Giants in Chicago upon his return, and then ended up on the shelf again, this time with a split finger. Lo and behold, while he was convalescing from the finger injury, the National Board piped up again, this time reversing its original decision and awarding Frisbee to Cleveland. The Giants didn't protest this time, as Frisbee was damaged goods. Frisbee reported to Cleveland in poor shape due to his long layoff, and upon hitting a lackluster .232 for them in 60 games, Cleveland released him.

Still tending to the knee that he dinged up the prior April, Frisbee sat out the 1901 season. He played for Worcester of the Eastern League in 1902, then joined New Orleans of the Southern League in 1903, where he played center field and batted leadoff. He moved to Toledo of the American Association in 1904.

Frisbee was one of three managers of the Burlington Flint Hills of the Iowa State League in 1905. The Flint Hills had gone by the Burlington River Rats in 1904 and amassed a last place 36-73 record with that nickname. Besides managing, Frisbee also played in 68 games for the Flint Hills in 1905, and the team as a whole got a bit worse, going 37-83 and finishing in last place again that season. They once again changed their name to the Burlington Pathfinders, and got a new manager (tossing the Frisbee away) and went 83-36 in 1906.

Meanwhile, Frisbee moved on to become one of the two managers of the Waterloo Microbes of the Iowa State League in 1906. Frisbee played in 24 games for the Microbes, but it didn't help, as they finished seventh in an eight-team division with a 48-76 record in 1906. Thus, ended Frisbee's managerial career. He finished his playing career with Greenville of the North Texas League in 1907.

BEST DAY (BY WPA OR OTHER MEASURE): Unfortunately, detailed play-by-play game logs are not available from that era in baseball history. We only have linescores for each player and summaries of miscellaneous data below the boxscore in some newspapers. I can tell you that Frisbee had quite a good day for himself in one of his first games for the Beaneaters, against the Baltimore Orioles on July 5, 1899. In that contest, won by Boston 5-4, Frisbee went 2-5 with two runs scored and two stolen bases, as well as two putouts and an assist on defense.

THE WONDER OF HIS NAME: The Frisbee flying disc didn't officially come into existence with that name until 50 years after Charlie ended his career. Nonetheless one would think, given Charlie's fun times with his bat, that he might have embraced the notoriety of the disc. Had he been playing in the early 1960s, one could imagine his team having "Frisbee Frisbee Day" giveaways (though given the probability of fans tossing their souvenir discs on the field and the resulting game delay, perhaps not).

NOT TO BE CONFUSED WITH: Frisbee (Flying disc toy that is generally plastic and roughly eight to ten inches in diameter with a pronounced lip. In June 1957, Wham-O co-founders Richard Knerr and Arthur Melin gave their flying disc the brand name "Frisbee" after learning that college students were calling their "Pluto Platter" disc by that term, which was derived from the Connecticut-based pie manufacturer Frisbie Pie Company, a supplier of pies to Yale University where students had started a campus craze tossing empty pie tins stamped with the company's logo), Frisbee curve (A slider that is reminiscent of the distinctive sideways and downward slide at the end of a typical toss with a Frisbee; also, a slow curveball), "Yo-Yo" Davalillo (Venezuelan-born shortstop for the Washington Senators in 1953), Lonnie "Skates" Smith (The only man to play in the World Series for four different teams – the Phillies (in 1980), the Cardinals (in 1982), the Royals (in 1985) and the Braves (in 1991 and 1992)).

FUN ANAGRAMS: "Charles Augustus Frisbee" anagrams to "Huge fascists abuse ruler."

EPHEMERA: 1) Charlie was born to Francis Palmer Frisbee and Ellen Frisbee (nee Young). Charlie had one sister, Laura Hannah Frisbee. 2) He is the only major league player in history born in Dows, Iowa. 3) Charlie married Luella Florence Caitlin, and they had two children, Frank and Nellie. 4) In 1950, he had the honor of throwing out the first pitch at a new athletic field in Garner, Iowa. The newspaper account stated he pitched for three teams in the majors back in the early 1900s, but I could find no record of any appearance on the mound during his time in the bigs. If he had done so, one wonders if he would have thrown a "frisbee curve."

DEBS GARMS

If they gave an award for being managed
by the most Hall of Famers

BIRTH NAME: Debs C. Garms
PRONUNCIATION OF DIFFICULT PARTS: None
NICKNAME: Tex
HEIGHT/WEIGHT: 5'9" 165 lbs.
BORN: June 26, 1907, in Bangs, Texas
DIED: Dec. 16, 1984, in Glen Rose, Texas
POSITIONS: Outfielder, Third Baseman
YEARS ACTIVE IN THE MAJORS: 1932-1935, 1937-1941, 1943-1945
NAME ETYMOLOGY/DEFINITIONS: Debs Garms was named after Eugene Debs, a founding member of the Industrial Workers of the World and a five-time candidate of the Socialist Party of America for President of the United States. "Garms" is a reduced from of "Garmens," which is a variant of "Garmen" and that is a patronymic of "German."

D ebs Garms' first glimpse of major league baseball was after having driven his sister Maye to Philadelphia in the spring of 1926 to be with her husband, William Jennings Bryan Harriss, otherwise known as "Slim," a pitcher for the A's. Garms attended Howard Payne University, and played on its baseball team as well as on its track team as a sprinter. He was soon noticed by a big-league scout and signed to play for the Abilene Aces (West Texas League).

In 1928, Garms' first year with Abilene, he hit .313 and played shortstop. That season would prove typical for Garms: he hit for a solid average with speed on the bases, but with little power, and there were complaints about his fielding. (Garms later told his son that his play that year at shortstop caused fans seated behind first base to be on the lookout whenever he let loose a throw.)

Garms worked his way up through the minors and was moved to center field to take advantage of his speed. In 1932 Garms had a breakout year for the Wichita Falls Spudders (Texas League) and was called up to the St. Louis Browns (the weakest franchise in baseball) in August. Immediately inserted into the starting lineup, he hit .284 in his first big league season. Garms was now making a salary of $5,000 per year, which he thought was a lot of money, especially during the Great Depression.

With the Browns in last place in early 1933, team owner Phil Ball fired manager Bill Killefer and replaced him with Rogers Hornsby. Hornsby would be the first of five Hall of Famers Garms played for. Years later, Garms recalled that while he never played for a bad manager, he did not care for Hornsby. "He was egotistical, and he thought everyone should be a great hitter, just because he was."

In mid-August, leading the team with a .317 average, Garms jumped for a ball and landed awkwardly, injuring his knee. Garms later recounted: "I was really in pain. They brought out a stretcher for me and carried me off the field. Hornsby told me to go to the clubhouse and be ready for the second game of the doubleheader. Well I missed the rest of the year." He had damaged the cartilage in his knee and a tendon; those injuries would bother Garms for the rest of his career.

In 1934 Garms came back to hit .293, but his career with the Browns was all but over. Pegged by Hornsby as a singles hitter on a team devoid of power, he would play in little over half the games.

When the 1935 season started Garms appeared a few times, mostly as a pinch-hitter, and was soon farmed out to the San Antonio Missions of the Texas League. With the Missions, Garms hit .294 and led the league in triples. The next year he batted .316 and led the league in hits, earning himself a trip back to the majors when the Boston Bees drafted him in September 1936.

Guided by Bill McKechnie (who would win the Manager of the Year Award), the Bees finished a surprising fifth in 1937. While their pitching and fielding ranked at the top of the National League, their offense was dead last. What little offense they had was not helped by Garms' powerless .259 average. He did receive repeated praise for his willingness to play third and all outfield positions when others were hurt or slumping.

In 1938, the Bees hired Casey Stengel to replace McKechnie (who had departed to manage the Reds). As Garms recalled, Stengel approached him at the start of spring training to discuss his hitting technique: "They tell me there's a man on that infield you like pretty well.' I knew he [Stengel] meant the second baseman. I must have hit 150 or 200 balls down that way the previous year. Then Case said: 'Young man, if you're ever going to make a living up here in the big leagues, you've got to learn to bunt and to hit the ball by the third baseman....' Casey told me to make the third baseman my target, and hope that I missed him."

After being a pull hitter throughout his career, Garms worked on going with the pitch to left if it was outside and pulling it if it was inside. Under Stengel's guidance he also sought to improve his bunting skills, and within a few years he would be among the premier bunters in the National League. Nevertheless, when the season started, he found himself on the bench.

In mid-May, Stengel put Garms into the lineup against Brooklyn Dodgers' knuckleball pitcher Forest "Tot" Pressnell. While Pressnell limited the Bees to four hits, Garms collected three of them. Stengel began to use Garms more as the Bees went on a seven-game winning streak. With Garms playing an instrumental part, the team climbed from seventh place to third. Several weeks later, Stengel reflected on Garms' performance with Vic Stout, a sportswriter covering the Bees: "Garms is a fine example of why managers grow old and grey-haired in a hurry. Down South [spring training] it looked as though [Eddie] Mayo, [Gil] English and even [Harl] Maggert ranked way ahead of Garms for my third base choice. And even after nearly a month of the league games it looked as though Garms was the worst of our rather poor lot of third base prospects. I'll admit the fellow has fooled me completely. It looks now as if the best move I've made since managing this club came the afternoon in Brooklyn a couple of weeks ago when I put him out there on third base. I shudder every time I think how I might have unloaded him."

Garms continued to hit well the rest of the season, with Stengel, a pioneer in the use of platooning, playing him against right-handed pitchers. He finished at .315, seventh in the league.

As the 1939 season began, Garms was assured for the first time in his career of opening the season as a regular. During spring training, baseball's patriarch, Connie Mack, approached him and said, "Young man, you can hit the ball," after watching Garms take batting practice. Garms came close to matching his performance from the prior season, hitting .298. But the Bees finished in seventh place and, with lagging attendance and in financial straits, they sold players to raise cash.

Upon arrival at spring training in 1940, Garms was informed the Pirates had purchased his contract. The new Pirates manager, Frankie Frisch, had been impressed by Garms while broadcasting for the Bees and purchased him even though he did not have a spot in the lineup for him. Frisch noted, "Garms will be available for infield and outfield duty. I like his style, especially his spirit."

Observations on Garms' defense were almost always negative, but he hit .472 in spring training and was named opening day right fielder, replacing Paul Waner. Later he would recall, "That whole year, the baseball looked as big as a grapefruit coming up to the plate."

Garms suffered a knee injury in early May that for the kept him out of the lineup for the better part of two months. He reentered the lineup in a game against the Giants on June 16 and got three hits to help the Pirates win, only to reinjure his knee the next day. While occasionally pinch-hitting the next several weeks, he did not start regularly until July 20. By then the Pirates were in sixth place. Frisch, disconcerted because of indifferent play, made several changes to the lineup including replacing the slumping Lee Handley at third with a now healthy Garms. Making the most of his opportunity that day, Garms got four hits to drive in five runs as the Pirates beat the Bees.

Garms continued to hit well. Now batting third in the lineup, he hit .400 in July, raising his average to .345 as the Pirates climbed into fourth place on the strength of an eight-game winning streak. During those eight games Garms hit .480. Little notice was made at the time that Garms' rising season batting average had moved past Giants catcher Harry Danning, who was listed in newspapers as the National League leader in batting.

In late August, Charles "Chilly" Doyle, sports reporter for the *Pittsburgh Sun-Telegraph*, observed that although Garms had the highest average in the league he would have to have 400 at-bats to be the legitimate champion, difficult to achieve given his early season injuries. It was the first time Garms' name was associated with the batting race. The next day Doyle noted that Garms might fall short of the requirement, not because of having missed so many games but because the 400 at-bat requirement did not take into account his walks. At that point Frisch, thinking Garms needed 400 at-bats to qualify for the title, began to bat him leadoff. Garms ended August at .369, well ahead of second baseman Bama Rowell of the Bees who at .329 was listed as the league leader in virtually all baseball publications.

The assumption continued that to lead the league one needed 400 at-bats. Shirley Povich, in his *Washington Post* column, *This Morning*. observed, "Both big leagues two years ago passed a rule at the behest of the Baseball Writers Association demanding that a player must go to bat 400 times in a season before he can win the league batting championship ... that rule this year eliminates Debs Garms of the Pirates, who is leading National League hitters ..."

Soon after, the Reds came to New York to play the Giants. In an interview with Reds manager (and Garms' former skipper) Bill McKechnie, a reporter asked McKechnie if Garms was as good as his batting average. McKechnie replied that Garms had not performed that well for him but conceded that his high average "must account for something." McKechnie then asked the reporter, "What's this I hear about a batter having to be at bat 400 times to be eligible for the championship?" The reporter replied: "That's all wrong. I asked Ford Frick [president of the National League] about that and he said that so far as he knows that is an American League rule and has not been adopted by the National League." After that interview (on Sep. 16), the Times began to list Garms as the leader. Garms at .380 was now 63 points ahead of Ernie Lombardi. On Sep. 19, Bill Brandt, spokesperson for National League Commissioner Ford Frick, confirmed that there were no rules governing qualifications for the league batting title, but added that Frick "thought 100 games would be a sufficient prerequisite for the championship."

For the season Garms ended up playing 103 games and had 358 at-bats, finishing with a .355 average, 36 points ahead of Ernie Lombardi who had 376 at-bats in a season that was also injury-shortened. Garms was 38 points ahead of Chicago's Stan Hack, who had played in 149 games. He also led the majors, squeaking by Joe DiMaggio's American League-leading .352 mark. He struck out only six times and, despite being regarded as a singles hitter, finished sixth in slugging with a .500 mark.

Garms' controversial title would not immediately force a change in rules governing how batting championships were determined, but it served notice that guidelines were lacking. Two years later Lombardi was awarded the title based on even less playing time. Rules for qualifications were eventually changed, first to 400 at-bats, then to the present requirement of 3.1 plate appearances per game.

Despite his successful season, Garms came into the 1941 season without the guarantee of a regular position. "Debs Garms will play a lot," commented Frisch, but in the same interview he announced his third baseman was Lee Handley and his outfielders were Vince DiMaggio, Bob Elliott and Maurice Von Robays. Garms played third, left field and pinch-hit until the middle of May when he tore the cartilage in his knee. Relegated to pinch-hitting for much of the rest of the year, he ended the season batting .264. The Pirates finished fourth for the second year in a row, a disappointment which triggered a look toward the future and younger players.

On Dec. 5, 1941, the Pirates announced the sale of the now 34-year-old Garms to the Cardinals, who assigned him to the Sacramento Solons (PCL). Two days later Pearl Harbor was bombed, marking the country's entry into a war that would eventually bring Garms back to the major leagues. In coming to the PCL, Garms was joining a league considered on a near par level with the majors. During the 1942 campaign, Garms hit .316 while driving in 96 runs, tied for the league lead in triples, and became close friends with Sacramento's manager, Pepper Martin.

By the start of the 1943 season over 200 major leaguers were in the armed services. The Cardinal outfield had been particularly hard hit, shorn of two starters, Terry Moore and Enos Slaughter. To help fill their roster, the Cardinals called up Garms. (He had come full circle in returning to St. Louis, breaking in with the lowly Browns and now joining the World Champion Cardinals.)

Despite losing players to the military, the 1943 Cardinals were still deep in talent thanks to the largest farm system in baseball. Garms would join the Cardinals as a part-time player and he would often be the oldest player on the team. He was regarded as a steadying influence on younger players, impressing them with his attitude toward the game as well as helping them develop their skills.

That year the Cardinals won 105 games and the pennant, beating the second-place Reds by 18 games. Stan Musial had a breakout year winning his first batting title and Most Valuable Player Award, and Mort Cooper led the National League with 21 wins. Garms filled in at third, left and right and even played a game at shortstop. Showing he could still pinch-hit, he batted .300 coming off the bench. The Cardinals met the Yankees in the World Series, losing in five games. Garms appeared in two games, going hitless in five at-bats and making the last out of the Series.

The 1944 National League pennant race was almost identical to the one in 1943. The Cardinals again won 105 games, winning the pennant by 14½ games. Garms, seeing less playing time, hit just .201. In the World Series the Cardinals played against Garms' former team, the Browns, winning in six games. Garms went hitless in two at-bats as a pinch-hitter.

In 1945, the Cardinals they lost Musial to the Navy and finished second to the Cubs. Garms, who believed Musial was the best ballplayer he ever had played with, thought his absence cost the Cardinals their fourth straight pennant. Toward the end of the season as the war was ending and it became clear veterans would return to play in 1946; the team's manager, Billy Southworth, called Garms into his office and asked if he wanted to manage in the Cardinal farm system. Despite knowing he would be released after the season, Garms declined the offer. In his last season, Garms hit .336 in 74 games, pinch-hitting at a .385 pace. He had not played enough to qualify, but his .336 batting average would have placed him third in the league.

Garms' last major league game was on Sep. 25, with an eighth-inning pinch-hit run-scoring triple against the Cubs. It was Garms' 54th career pinch-hit, then placing him sixth all-time; his .273 pinch-hitting average placed him fifth all-time. Playing in just over 1,000 games, he finished his career with a .293 average. He was released that December.

Garms would have retired to his ranch except for the pleas of Pepper Martin that he come back for one more season to play, this time with the San Diego Padres in the PCL. In that final minor league season, Garms hit .270 while playing third and the outfield. During the season Garms was taken ill, and doctors diagnosed a possible heart attack. Although that prognosis was never verified, Garms was told to give up smoking. He was soon back in the lineup with a new diet at the behest of his wife. Toward the end of the season he decided to retire.

BEST DAY (BY WPA OR OTHER MEASURE): On Sep. 21, 1940, Garms collected the first and only five-hit game of his career, notching four singles and a double with three runs scored in six at-bats in a 8-7 Pirates win. Those would be the last hits he would garner that season, finishing the year in an 0-for-23 slump that took his average from .379 down to .355.

THE WONDER OF HIS NAME: I have to admit that when I first happened upon his name, I thought his parents might have wanted a girl. So much for my knowledge of 20th-century Socialists.

NOT TO BE CONFUSED WITH: Clint Barmes (middle infielder for the Colorado Rockies during the mid-2000s), Krebs cycle (the sequence of reactions by which most living cells generate energy during the process of aerobic respiration).

FUN ANAGRAMS: "Debs C Garms" isn't long enough to generate any wonderful phrases, but "Debs C Garms Socialist" turns into "Bigot's classic dreams." or "Scold scares bigamist."

EPHEMERA: 1) Garms' parents, not content to name just him after a prominent socialist, subsequently named his younger brother after socialist Victor Berger. Although Debs was chagrined at his parents' choice for his name, he kept it, subsequently showing his independence by deciding he would be known as Debs C. Garms, the C. in honor of a friend whose name was Charlie. 2) After Garms retired, he turned down minor league managerial offers and instead purchased a ranch in Glen Rose, Texas. Garms lived at the ranch until the 1950s, when the severe Texas drought forced him to sell it and move into town, where he worked as foreman for a lime quarry operation. 3) In 2004, Garms was inducted into the Texas Baseball Hall of Fame.

JIMMY GOBBLE
Batters stuffed their stat sheets when he entered the game

BIRTH NAME: Billy James Gobble
PRONUNCIATION OF DIFFICULT PARTS: None
NICKNAME: None
HEIGHT/WEIGHT: 6'3" 190 lbs.
BORN: July 19, 1981, in Bristol, Tennessee
POSITION: Pitcher
YEARS ACTIVE IN THE MAJORS: 2003-2009
NAME ETYMOLOGY/DEFINITIONS: "Billy" is a pet form of "William," which is of an old Germanic origin and a derivative of "Wilhelm." It became very popular in the English language after the Norman conquest of England in 1066 and remained so throughout the Middle Ages and into the modern era. It is derived from the Germanic *wil* (meaning "will" or "desire") and *helm* (meaning "helmet" or "protection"). "James" is a modern descendant of "Iacomus," the Latin form of the Hebrew name "Jacob." "Gobble" is of English origins, possibly as a variant of "Goble" or "Gobel." Its perhaps an Americanized spelling of French "Gobeil." "Gobel" is of German origins as a pet form of the Old High German name "Godebert," composed of the elements *god* meaning "good" or "god" and *berht* meaning "bright" or "famous."

Billy James Gobble attended John S. Battle H.S. in Bristol, Virginia. He led the team to three state tournament appearances and compiled a 32-8 record and 512 strikeouts. As a senior, he went 10-1 with a 0.49 ERA, striking out 151 while allowing just 23 hits in 71 innings of work, while compiling a .493 batting average.

Gobble was drafted by the Royals with the 43rd pick in the 1999 draft. He was the Royals' second-rated prospect in 2002 at the age of 20, behind Angel Berroa. As a prospect he had an average fastball, good command, a nasty breaking pitch and an average change-up. Gobble made his major league debut with the Royals in 2003. That year, he pitched 52⅔ innings and compiled 31 strikeouts, while giving up just 15 walks and posting an ERA of 4.61. Not bad for a 21-year-old in his first professional season. He was a part of manager Tony Pena's team that had a seven-game division lead at the All-Star break before ultimately finishing third behind the White Sox and Twins.

2004 was supposed to be the start of a new era in Kansas City. In 2003 the Royals posted their first winning record since 1994 and were labeled as "contenders" in the AL Central. They had some young pitching, the returning AL Rookie of the Year at shortstop in Angel Berroa, the Gold Glove and All-Star center fielder Carlos Beltran, and newly acquired Juan Gonzalez and All-Star DH Mike Sweeney. But the Royals finished the year 58-104 and in last place in the AL Central. For his part, Gobble scuffled through 148 innings that season and struck out just 49, while walking 43. He was the only starting pitcher to finish with a winning record, even if it was only 9-8 with an ERA of 5.35. (He was one of three starting pitchers on the staff to end the year with an ERA over 5.00.)

Moved to the bullpen, Gobble spent half of 2005 with AAA Omaha and finished it with the Royals, posting a 5.70 ERA in 53⅔ innings. His walk rate increased from three to five per nine, and he was still giving up more than a hit per inning.

The next season, used as a setup man, the Royals fiddled with Gobble's mechanics, getting him to try a side-arm approach as a way of creating deception with his delivery to throw off lefty hitters. He appeared in 60 games, cut his walk rate back to three per nine innings, and even collected his first two saves, all despite an ERA still north of five.

In 2007, his best season, Gobble was arguably the Royals' second-best reliever (behind Joakim Soria), posting a 3.02 ERA in 53⅔ innings, giving up just six home runs, striking out 50 while walking just 23. In his LOOGY role, he appeared in 74 games, the most on Kansas City's staff and tied for fifth in the American League.

Gobble's 2008 season was the last with the organization. Appearing in 39 games, he posted an 8.81 ERA in 31⅔ innings, striking out 27 while walking 23.

The Royals released him after that season, and the following year the Rangers signed Gobble to a minor league contract and invited him to spring training. He was released nine days later. A week after that, the White Sox signed Gobble to a minor league contract and assigned him to the AAA Charlotte Knights. He got the call back to the big leagues in mid-May but compiled a 7.50 ERA in 12 appearances and was designated for assignment in early July.

In 2010, Gobble signed a minor league contract with the Rockies with an invite to spring training. He did not allow a hit in three Cactus League outings and appeared to have locked up a spot as the team's left-handed specialist before suffering an injury. He appeared in two games for the AAA Colorado Springs Sky Sox before retiring.

BEST DAY (BY WPA OR OTHER MEASURE): First, here is most likely his worst day, which I include only because of its total overload of despair. On this particular day, he would set a Kansas City franchise record for the most runs surrendered in a game by a relief pitcher. On July 21, 2008 at Kauffman Stadium in Kansas City against the Tigers, Gobble came into the game in the seventh inning with the bases loaded, two out and the Tigers already winning 8-0. He walked in a run, then got the last out. He came back out for the eighth, and this happened: single, single, RBI double, run-scoring wild pitch, RBI single, single, three-run homerun, flyball out to deep center, popfly to deep short, walk, single, walk and walk to force in a run. At that point Gobble was finally taken out of the game. His replacement, Juan Carlos

Oviedo promptly yielded a two-run double and an RBI single. In all, Gobble was charged with ten runs (seven he gave up on his own, and the three more he was responsible for that Oviedo allowed in). Gobble's line for the day: one inning, seven hits, four walks, one homerun, ten runs allowed (all earned). He entered the game with an ERA of 7.99 and left with a mark of 11.31. In terms of his best day, we'll go with the only complete game Gobble ever pitched. On Sep. 5, 2004, his Royals played in Minnesota. Kansas City came into the game with a record of 47-87 and sat 29.5 games behind the division-leading Twins. But every dog (or turkey) has its day, and this day was Gobble's. He set down the first six Twins in order, issued a walk to Michael Cuddyer leading off the third, a single to Jacque Jones leading off the fourth, and a ground-rule double, walk and run-scoring double in the fifth (by which time the Royals had built a 6-0 lead). It was 12-1 when the Twins got to Gobble for two harmless runs in the ninth. Final line: a career-high 124 pitches (83 for strikes), to go along with three runs, six hits, two walks and four strikeouts. Of the 34 batters he faced, 23 ended in ground balls.

THE WONDER OF HIS NAME: The player's last name is the sound made by a turkey, which is kind of appropriate given that he was a "sandwich pick"[20] in the amateur draft. (Mmmm … turkey sandwich!). Many of his pitching performances were turkeys also.

NOT TO BE CONFUSED WITH: Gobbles (A fictional turkey in the *South Park* episode *Helen Keller! The Musical*), Gobbledygook (Speech that is (or appears to be) nonsense. The term gobbledygook was coined by Maury Maverick, a former congressman from Texas and former mayor of San Antonio. When Maverick was chairman of the Smaller War Plants Corporation during WWII, he sent a memorandum that said: "Be short and use plain English. ... Stay off gobbledygook language.," Joseph Goebbels (German Nazi politician and Reich Minister of Propaganda of Nazi Germany from 1933-1945).

FUN ANAGRAMS: "Billy James Gobble" turns into "Smelly, big, able job."

EPHEMERA: 1) After he was called up to the major leagues by the Rangers in 2012, reliever Justin Grimm told ESPN.com that he was inspired as a kid by Gobble. Grimm was a little-league pitcher at the time when Gobble visited a game. Both were born in Bristol, Tennessee, and went to high school across the state line in Bristol, Virginia. Gobble had just been drafted by the Royals when he was at Grimm's game. As kids surrounded Gobble, asking him for autographs, Grimm looked to his parents and simply said: "I want to be that someday." 2) Gobble had been an assistant baseball coach at John Battle from 2012-2018 and took over as head coach in 2019. 3) He founded the Washington County Express, a travel-ball organization which fields four teams in various age groups, in 2017. 4) He and his wife Julie have three sons.

---

[20] "Sandwich pick" is a type of draft pick awarded to teams for the loss of certain free agents. A sandwich pick is a pick that takes place in the supplemental round between the 1st and 2nd round of the MLB amateur draft each June and is usually noted as round 1a.

PURNAL GOLDY
Not the heir apparent to Al Kaline

BIRTH NAME: Purnal William Goldy
PRONUNCIATION OF DIFFICULT PARTS: None
NICKNAME: None
HEIGHT/WEIGHT: 6'5" 200 lbs.
BORN: Nov. 28, 1937, in Camden, New Jersey
DIED: Sep. 21, 2009, in Denver, Colorado
POSITIONS: Rightfielder, Pinch Hitter
YEARS ACTIVE IN THE MAJORS: 1962-1963
NAME ETYMOLOGY/DEFINITIONS: It turns out that Purnal's father's name was Purnal, and his father's name was Purnal, and his father's name was Purnal, and his father's name was ... Champion. "Purnal" doesn't come up as an entry in any naming reference books, but it may be a variation of "Purnell" or "Parnell." "Parnell" as a surname has English origins (mainly Devon), from the medieval female personal name "Peronel," "Pernel," "Parnell," a vernacular form of Latin "Petronilla." "William" is a popular given name of an old Germanic origin and a derivative of "Wilhelm." It became very popular in the English language after the Norman conquest of England in 1066 and remained so throughout the Middle Ages and into the modern era. It is derived from the Germanic *wil* (meaning "will" or "desire") and *helm* (meaning "helmet" or "protection"). "Goldy" is a variant spelling of English "Goldey" or Scottish and English "Goldie." "Goldey" has English origins, from an Old English female name, "Goldgifu," which is not independently attested but is found as an element of place names.

Purnal Goldy played college ball at Temple, hitting .335 as a junior. At age 20 he signed with the Tigers and in 1959, his first professional season, he hit .305/.360/.489 in 94 games, mostly with the Erie Sailors of the New York-Penn League.

Goldy moved up to the Knoxville Smokies of the Sally League in 1960 and hit .342/.387/.555 in 138 games, with 36 doubles, 10 triples, 20 home runs and 106 RBIs. In 1961 he split time between Double- and AAA and hit a combined .338/.381/.486. What was also noticed by the bosses in Detroit was the lack of walks: In 1,513 minor league plate appearances, he drew only 95 walks (against 175 strikeouts).

Nonetheless, Goldy received a non-roster invitation to camp in 1962. He was the early talk of camp, carrying a .500 average for a few days and amusing teammates and beat writers alike by running out his home runs. Tigers manager Bob Scheffing was asked if Goldy excited him.

"Darn right he excites me ... Goldy looks like money in the bank to me. Do you know, he reminds you a little of Joe DiMaggio the way he runs ... He takes those long, loping strides like Joe ... I don't think he'll ever be a big home-run hitter ... He'll probably hit line drives like Al Kaline."

Reality (or regression) started to come to light as pitchers figured out that Goldy would chase bad balls. Scheffing said, "I like everything he does except swing at too many low pitches. Once he learns to lay off them and wait for his pitch, nothing will stop him." Goldy was sent to the Denver Bears of the American Association, where his teammates included future Tigers stars Bill Freehan and Mickey Lolich.

On May 26 in old Yankee Stadium. Al Kaline, the Tigers' star right fielder, broke his collarbone on a game-ending diving catch, and was expected to miss eight weeks. The Tigers were still a potent team, coming off a 101-win season in 1961, and expected to contend.

Their outfield, one of the best in the game, was down a key cog. They still had 40-homer man Rocky Colavito in left and three-time NL stolen-base leader Bill Bruton in center. With Kaline's injury, the Tigers cycled through their fourth and fifth outfielders without much success. Out of a bit of desperation, Detroit finally reached down to AAA Denver for Purnal Goldy. He was hitting .304 with three home runs in 48 games when he joined the Tigers in New York on June 12.

Spring training duplicated itself in those first days. He hit in each of his first seven games, going 12-for-30. He went into the June 24 home game against the Yankees still hitting .310/.310/.524 but notice the batting average matching the on-base percentage, signifying zero walks to that point. That game with the Yankees was a bellwether moment for Goldy. In a game that lasted 22 innings, he went 1-for-10 (the one being a homer in the first inning).

The next day he took an 0-for-4. Then Goldy missed a few days with a strained elbow. When he returned, Scheffing gave him two more starts, during which he went a combined 0-for-7, and then hit the bench. When Kaline was reactivated, Goldy headed back to Denver. He was not recalled again, not even when rosters expanded in September.

Back in camp the next year, Goldy said he understood he had to wait for a pitch in the strike zone in order to succeed. Not only did he have to wait for a pitch, he'd have to wait for another shot in the big leagues. There was an impressive list of outfielders ahead of him. Among them were Jim Northrup (116 OPS+ in 1,392 major league games), Mickey Stanley, a Gold Glove center fielder, Willie Horton, a four-time All-Star who hit 325 home runs in the major leagues, and Gates Brown, who achieved great renown as a platoon player and pinch-hitter. Goldy made the team as a reserve, but barely played before being sent down again, this time to the AAA Syracuse Chiefs.

Goldy was unhappy in Syracuse, in part because he had become engaged to marry the daughter of one of the Bears' owners and pined for Colorado. He hit only .261/.299/.436 (with 21 walks in 503 PAs).

When he failed to make the Tigers roster in spring of 1964, Goldy asked to be sent back to the Bears. The problem was that Denver was now a Braves affiliate. The Tigers graciously allowed the Braves to borrow him and play him at Denver in return for the loan of outfielder Mack Jones to Syracuse.

Goldy hit only .245/.291/.353 with only eight homers in 127 games at Denver. Given the thin air in Colorado, it's extremely difficult for a man of Goldy's supposed strength to slug a mere .353. Goldy was now 27 and his shot at the majors had passed.

Back at Syracuse for a final time, he hit .260/.307/.385 in 105 games and was often booed for not hustling, though he contended that, "Because I'm such a tall, gangling guy, the fans get the idea that I'm not really trying. But actually, I'm doing the best I can, all the time. That's the only way I know how to play ball." His final major league averages were .231/.237/.385 in 80 PAs. He never did draw a walk in the bigs.

BEST DAY (BY WPA OR OTHER MEASURE): He went 2-for-4, with those two hits being his first two major league homers, in the first game he ever started. That came in the first game of a double-header on June 17, 1962 against the Red Sox. With one out and one on in the bottom of the first, he took Don Schwall deep. Two innings later, he tacked on a solo homer against Schwall. Goldy's post-game comment? "Don't ask me what Schwall was throwing. I was too busy swinging."

THE WONDER OF HIS NAME: You have the "double unique" factor, and the fact that he was the fourth generation to be named "Purnal." "Goldy" sounds more like a nickname (as we'll see) than a surname.

NOT TO BE CONFUSED WITH: Goldy McJohn (Born John Raymond Goadsby, best known as the original keyboardist for rock group Steppenwolf), Goldy (Rapping stage name of Mhisani Miller, an American rapper from The Dangerous Crew), Goldy (nickname of Paul Goldschmidt, first baseman for the St. Louis Cardinals).

FUN ANAGRAMS: "Purnal William Goldy" becomes "Proud gay man, ill will."

EPHEMERA: 1) When he was playing baseball at Temple University, they suited him up at catcher, all 6'5" of him. The Tigers wisely moved him out from behind the plate when he joined the organization in 1958. 2) Upon leaving Temple, he had a better offer from the Yankees, but he thought he'd have less competition in Detroit. 3) When asked during Spring Training in 1962 why he ran out his home runs, Goldy stated, "I'm used to college and semi-pro parks where they don't have fences … you have to run fast or sometimes you don't make it." 4) Immediately after retirement, he took a job with Celebrity Sports Center in Denver, "one of Walt Disney's many enterprises." 5) Goldy and his wife had four children, none named Purnal.

SCARBOROUGH GREEN
His claim to fame is five stolen bases in one game

BIRTH NAME: Bertrum Scarborough Green. Green started going by his middle name (which was his mother's maiden name) when he got to the minor leagues. At that time, he stated "When I got to training camp in St. Petersburg, they put all the names of everyone on the team up on this board. I noticed there were all these strange names that I had never heard of. Guys like Aldo Pecorilli, Yudith Ozorio and Placido Polanco. And then here I am with Bert. So I changed my name to Scarborough, my middle name. That way, I'd fit in with all those funny names. Initially it was just a joke, but it ended up sticking. I like it because it's kind of unique." After his baseball career ended, it appears he went back to his original given name.

PRONUNCIATION OF DIFFICULT PARTS: None

NICKNAME: None

HEIGHT/WEIGHT: 5'10" 170 lbs.

BORN: June 9, 1974, in Creve Coeur, Missouri

POSITIONS: Outfielder, Pinch Runner

YEARS ACTIVE IN THE MAJORS: 1997, 1999-2000

NAME ETYMOLOGY/DEFINITIONS: "Bertrum" is a variant of "Bertram," which is a Germanic given name from *berht* meaning "bright" and *hramn* meaning "raven," and a surname. "Scarborough" has English origins as a habitational name from Scarborough on the coast of North Yorkshire, so named from the Old Norse byname "Skarði" and Old Norse *borg* meaning "fortress" or "fortified town." "Green" has English origins as one of the most common and widespread of English surnames, either a nickname for someone who was fond of dressing in this color (Old English *grene*) or who had played the part of the Green Man in the May Day celebrations, or a topographic name for someone who lived near a village green, Middle English *grene* (a transferred use of the color term). In North America this name has no doubt assimilated cognates from other European languages, notably German *Grün* (see *Gruen*).

S carborough Green was taken by the St. Louis Cardinals in the tenth round of the 1992 amateur draft as a shortstop. It soon became apparent, via 87 errors in only 215 minor league games, that he wasn't going to cut it at that position. Moved to center field in 1996, he started to make real strides (no pun intended). His speed was an asset in patrolling center field, and he had a bit of plate discipline, although the bat was (still) pedestrian.

After making it up to AAA Louisville in 1997, he made his big-league debut with the Cardinals on Aug. 2, 1997. He ended up appearing in 20 games for St. Louis that season, managing a mere three hits (all singles) in 31 at-bats.

He got sent back to the minors for all of 1998, splitting time between Double and Triple-A. He appeared in only 44 games between the two teams, as his season was interrupted by a hand ligament injury. But even with that limited sample, it was apparent the bat still wasn't quite major league quality (.360 in AA, but .198 in AAA).

In early September of 1998, the Texas Rangers claimed Green off waivers from the Cards. He spent the vast majority of 1999 with the Rangers AAA squad in Oklahoma City, where he hit an underwhelming .248/.316/.351 and stole 26 bases in 38 attempts. He had sporadic trips to the big leagues during the year, getting into 18 games primarily as a late-inning defensive replacement. He managed only 13 at-bats with the Rangers that year.

Green started 2000 back in Oklahoma City but got his most significant shot at the big leagues when he was called up in early May. He stayed with the Rangers for the rest of the year, appearing in 79 games (37 starts). He played error-free ball in the outfield, but the offensive profile still wasn't there (now in his age-26 season): He slashed .234/.291/.258 with only two extra base hits in 124 at-bats. He was released by the Rangers after the season, and never made it back to the majors though, retiring after spending 2001 back in the minors.

BEST DAY (BY WPA OR OTHER MEASURE): Green's big day occurred on Sep. 28, 2000, at Seattle, where the Mariners were in a dogfight for the AL West title. Starting behind the plate for the M's was veteran Joe Oliver, who happened to be in the third year of a steep decline in his caught stealing percentage. On the mound was lefty Jamie Moyer, who just by being a lefty should have been able to control the running game. Green, despite getting caught in five of nine attempts to that point in the season, had other plans. He led off the game and singled to right. On the second pitch to the next batter, Royce Clayton, Green swiped second. He would eventually score on a Rafael Palmeiro sac fly. With the Rangers up 2-0 and runners on second and third with two out in the second, Green singled to centered, driving in two and advancing to second on the throw home. Righty Brett Tomko replaced Moyer at that point, and on a 2-2 count, Green stole third, but Clayton left him stranded there. Rangers starting pitcher Rick Helling gave up a five-spot in the bottom of the third, but Texas rallied in the fifth, with Green jump-starting the inning with a walk and his third stolen base. A Chad Curtis single drove Green in to tie the game, and Texas tacked on one more in the frame to go up 6-5. Moving to the top of the sixth, with one out and a runner on second, Green singled again, putting runners on the corners. Green then stole his fourth base of the day, moved to third on a sacrifice fly and would score on a Ricky Ledee double. By the top of the seventh, Texas had a 10-6 lead. Green worked a two-out walk, this time off righty Kevin Hodges. He successfully stole his fifth base of the game on the ensuing 1-1 pitch to Clayton. With Texas holding a 13-6 lead in the top of the ninth, Green was finally retired for the first time in the game, grounding out to second. His final tally: three hits in four at-bats, two walks, three runs scored, two driven in, and a franchise record five stolen bases.

THE WONDER OF HIS NAME: "Scarborough" is just a wicked-awesome name by itself. "Scarborough Green" sounds like the name of a British detective from the 1930s. On another note, if they had full replay review back in Green's playing days, the play-by-play man might paraphrase a Simon and Garfunkel lyric by stating, "is that ball by Scarborough fair?"

NOT TO BE CONFUSED WITH: Scarborough Green Label Semillon (Dry white wine grown in Australia), Chuck Scarborough (television journalist and author. Since 1974, he has been the lead news anchor at WNBC, the New York City flagship station of the NBC Television Network).

FUN ANAGRAMS: "Bertrum Scarborough Green" turns into "Stubborn cough, rare merger."

EPHEMERA: 1) Scarborough Green was the Cardinals' ninth-rated prospect in 1998, according to *Baseball America*. 2) Green successfully executed a straight steal of home on May 26, 2000, against opposing pitcher Eric Milton of the Twins and his batterymate Matt LeCroy. 4) According to *The Tennessean*, Green was arrested for "theft over $1,000 and under $10,000" on Sep. 7, 2003. 5) Following his career in baseball, Green pursued a collegiate football career at NCAA Division II Harding University in Searcy, Arkansas. Green then transferred to Division III McMurry University in Abilene, Texas, to play football. While serving as the football team's punter, wide receiver, and in other positions, Green also participated in track and field for McMurry. Green had a strong leg on the 2007 National Champion McMurry University 4 x 100 relay team, and he added to his All-American titles by running in the 4 x 400 relay.

DOUG GWOSDZ
Competent backup catcher, bad Scrabble draw

BIRTH NAME: Doug Wayne Gwosdz
PRONUNCIATION OF DIFFICULT PARTS: Goosh
NICKNAME: Eyechart
HEIGHT/WEIGHT: 5'11" 185 lbs.
BORN: June 20, 1960, in Houston, Texas
POSITION: Catcher
YEARS ACTIVE IN THE MAJORS: 1981-1984
NAME ETYMOLOGY/DEFINITIONS: "Doug" is a shortened form of "Douglas," which is a Scottish name which originated from the surname Douglas. The Scottish surname Douglas was borne by one of the most powerful families of the Kingdom of Scotland (the Earls of Douglas, Angus, Morton, Dukes of Hamilton and others). Linguistically, Douglas is derived from the Gaelic elements: *dubh*, meaning "dark, black;" and *glas*, meaning "stream" (also a derivative of glas, meaning "green"). "Wayne" is from an occupational surname meaning "wagon maker," derived from Old English *wægn* meaning "wagon." "Gwosdz" is a variant of the (rare to begin with) surname "Gwozdz," and *gwozdz* is the Polish word for "nail" (which seems to be a good sign if you aspire to be a major league catcher).

D oug Gwosdz was taken in the second round of the 1978 draft by the Padres as compensation for losing Merv Rettenmund to the Angels via free agency. After a "cup of coffee" with the Padres in 1981, Gwosdz got a chance to start a few games in early 1982 thanks to an injury to their regular catcher Steve Swisher. The Padres won each of the first four games he started.

In the 1983 season, he had to wait 40 days for his first hit, and it was the last week of July when he tallied his first extra-base hit and run batted in on the season. He finished the year at .109 in 55 at-bats. However, in the first 11 games he started that year, the staff ERA was under 2.00.

After bouncing back and forth between AAA and the majors in 1984, the Padres left him off their 40-man roster that off-season, and the Giants picked him up. They left him down in AAA for all of 1985 before releasing him in December. The Mets picked him up before the 1986 season, then traded him to Seattle later that year. From there it was onto Cincinnati's AAA club in 1988 and 1989. Bottom line: he never saw the majors again after 1984, and his major league "slash line" in 69 games (24 starts) was .144/.244/.202.

BEST DAY (BY WPA OR OTHER MEASURE): On Aug. 21, 1983, Gwosdz started the game and in the third inning launched what would be the only homer in his career, a three-run shot that helped lead the Padres to a 5-2 victory over the Montreal Expos.

THE WONDER OF HIS NAME: He possesses an unremarkable first name (I can find no record of his first name being anything other than Doug. You didn't even think to name him "Douglas," Mrs. Gwosdz?). He also has a relatively non-descript middle name. These however are overcompensated by his "consonant jambalaya" of a last name. The only other ballplayers whose last name start with "Gw" are the Gwynns (Tony Sr., Tony Jr. and Chris), and a "Marcus Gwyn." There are few if any English words that start with "gw" (one is "gweduc," but even that is a variant of the more popular "geoduck," which is an edible clam).

NOT TO BE CONFUSED WITH: Lyndon LaRouche (Frequent Presidential candidate for the Labor Party), Ebby Calvin "Nuke" LaLoosh (Tim Robbins' hotshot pitching prospect character in *Bull Durham*).

FUN ANAGRAMS: His name doesn't anagram into much of anything special, but if you try "Doug Gwosdz San Diego Padres," it turns into "Good god as Nazi drudge spews!"

EPHEMERA: 1) Though he only started 24 games behind the plate in his big-league career, San Diego compiled a 19-5 record in those games. 2) In a 1983 *Sports Illustrated* article, Padres reliever Gary Lucas felt one reason for Gwosdz's success was that his smaller size (regular catcher Terry Kennedy was a hefty 6'4" 220) enabled "Doug to give a lower target." 3) In July 1989, while toiling for the Nashville Sounds, Gwosdz proclaimed to have overtaken Biff Pocoroba for second place on the all-time list of batting practice hits. In first place according to Gwosdz? Stan Musial. 4) Gwosdz is one of only eight people from Madison H.S. in Houston to ever get drafted, and the only one to ever make the majors. 5) Doug had a brother, Anthony, who got into two games for the minor league Walla Walla Padres 6) Eight picks after Gwosdz was taken in that 1978 draft, the Orioles took an infielder named Cal Ripken, Jr. 7) Doug has been a supervisor at UPS since 1990.

PINK HAWLEY
A hero in his hometown of Beaver Dam, Wisconsin

BIRTH NAME: Emerson Pink Hawley
PRONUNCIATION OF DIFFICULT PARTS: None
NICKNAME: None
HEIGHT/WEIGHT: 5'10" 185 lbs.
BORN: Dec. 5, 1872, in Beaver Dam, Wisconsin
DIED: Sep. 19, 1938, in Beaver Dam, Wisconsin
POSITION: Pitcher
YEARS ACTIVE IN THE MAJORS: 1892-1901
NAME ETYMOLOGY/DEFINITIONS: "Emerson" is more often a surname, derived in the Middle Ages from a name from a father, meaning "son of Emery." "Pink" is normally descriptive of a color intermediate between red and white, as of coral or salmon. In Hawley's case, Emerson was born one of two twins, the other being named Elmer. People had trouble telling the twins apart so the nurse who assisted in their birth pinned a blue ribbon to one and a pink one to the other. This resulted in Emerson being given the middle name Pink, and the brothers were known thereafter as Pink and Blue. "Hawley" is of English and Scottish origins, as the habitational name from any of various places called Hawley. One in Kent is named with Old English *halig* meaning "holy" and *leah* meaning "wood" or "clearing" and would therefore have once been the site of a sacred grove. One in Hampshire has as its first element Old English *h(e)all* meaning "hall" or "manor," or *healh* meaning "nook" or "corner of land." However, the surname is common in South Yorkshire and Nottinghamshire, and may principally derive from a lost place near Sheffield named Hawley, from Old Norse *haugr* meaning "mound" and Old English *leah* in this case meaning "clearing."

I n 1892, disregarding his father's orders against playing baseball, Pink Hawley paid his own way to the training camp of the Chicago White Sox. Sox manager Cap Anson was quite impressed with the right-hander but couldn't find room for him on his roster. Anson then spoke with the Fort Smith Maroons, a semi-professional team located in Fort Smith, Arkansas. The Maroons told Anson they needed pitching and Anson immediately recommended Hawley.

Pink headed to Fort Smith where he helped build the ballpark, organize a team and pitch, as well. Among the games he pitched for the Maroons was a 1-0 loss to Krebs, Oklahoma. In this game he struck out at least 22 batters. In August of that year Pink reported to the St. Louis Browns of the American Association where he made his major league debut on Aug. 13. He pitched 20 games for the Browns that year going 6-14 with a team leading ERA of 3.19. He also spent the 1893-1894 seasons with the Browns.

In 1893, Hawley pitched in 31 games, including 24 starts. He struggled to a record of 5-17 with an ERA of 4.60 for a team which finished tenth in the 12-team National League. (In 1893, he began a string of eight straight seasons of hitting 20 or more batters with pitches.) In 1894, he appeared in 53 games (41 starts), throwing nearly 400 innings. He finished the season 19-27, leading the league in losses.

Following the 1894 season Hawley pitched for the Browns in an exhibition game against the Milwaukee Brewers of the Western League. The Browns, led by Hawley's 14 strikeouts, won the game 14-0. Pittsburg player-manager Connie Mack witnessed the performance and told Pirate officials he just had to have Hawley, and a deal was worked out which accomplished that.

In what would turn out to be his best season, Pink appeared in a league-high 56 games (50 starts) for the Pirates in 1895. He led the league in innings pitched (444⅓). He led the league with four shutouts, while his 31 wins (a franchise single season record that still stands) were good for second in the league. He also hit .308 and drove in 42 runs in just 185 at-bats.

From 1896-1897, Hawley went 40-39 in 82 starts, 70 of which were complete games. The Pirates finished no higher than sixth either season. After the 1897 season, Hawley was shipped to the Cincinnati Reds.

Pink won his first nine games of the 1898 season. He went on to finish 27-11. The Reds finished third in the league with a 92-60 record. In 1899, Hawley's record fell to 14-17 and he pitched fewer than 300 innings (250) for the first time since 1893.

In March 1900, Hawley was sold to the New York Giants where Buck Ewing, who had managed the Reds in 1899, was now the manager. For the 1900 season, Pink hurled 329 innings across 38 starts for New York. He finished with a record of 18-18 and led the league with 34 complete games.

Following the 1900 season, Pink jumped to his home-state Milwaukee Brewers, an entry in the newly formed American League. Now 28 years old, Hawley's numbers sank to 7-14 with a 4.59 ERA in just 182 innings over 26 games. The Brewers, who finished dead last in the eight-team AL, released Hawley in September and his major-league career was over.

Hawley decided to keep pitching, this time back in the minor leagues. He appeared for Milwaukee of the American Association and Buffalo of the Eastern League in 1902. While pitching for Buffalo, the now 29-year-old Pink met Katherine Langen whom he later married. Katherine gave birth to their only child, Emerson Jr. in 1905.

Also, in 1905, he helped organize the Wisconsin State League, which was a Class D League. He managed the La Crosse Pinks to league titles in 1905 and 1906. Hawley went 19-9 as a pitcher for the Pinks in 1905 and 7-4 in 1906. For the 1907 season, the team was renamed the La Crosse Badgers and Hawley managed them to a third-place finish. In 1908 the Eau Claire Tigers moved to Rockford, Illinois, and the league was renamed the Wisconsin-Illinois League. Hawley managed the La Crosse entry to a third-place finish before moving to take over the Oshkosh Indians for the 1909 season, his final one as a manager.

BEST DAY (BY WPA OR OTHER MEASURE): Individual game logs from that era are hard to come by, but that game he pitched for Fort Smith in which he struck out at least

22 batters must be in consideration for his best day. (Hawley's obituary in the Milwaukee Sentinel states that he struck out 27 that day!). Regardless of how many he struck out, he still went toe-to-toe that day with Hall of Fame pitcher "Iron Man" Joe McGinnity.

THE WONDER OF HIS NAME: Given that he was one of a set of twin boys, it's interesting they bestowed upon him a typically "girls" colored-ribbon and thus name. From the writings of the time, it seems he wasn't picked on for his name.

NOT TO BE CONFUSED WITH: Pink (stage name of singer Alecia Moore, also stylized "P!nk"), Pink Floyd (English rock band that achieved international acclaim with their progressive and psychedelic music), Emerson Hart (songwriter, vocalist, guitarist and producer; lead singer and songwriter of the alternative rock band Tonic), Red Ruffing (Hall of Fame pitcher named for his hair color).

FUN ANAGRAMS: "Emerson Pink Hawley" turns into "His keen, manly power." or "Homely, wanker penis."

EPHEMERA: 1) His roots went back to the nation's earliest days as it was his ancestor, Major Joseph Hawley, who ordered the Boston Tea Party. 2) The Hawley twins had an older brother, Fred, and the three of them became legends in their local Beaver Dam baseball community. Pink was the pitcher, Blue the catcher and Fred the First Baseman. The twins were known as the Pink and Blue battery and both appeared to have bright futures as Blue was every bit as talented as his twin. Blue's life was cut short by pneumonia in 1891. 3) While pitching for the Pirates, Hawley earned the nickname "Duke of Pittsburgh" because of his stylish dress and good looks. He was known to wear diamonds and other items of high fashion and developed a reputation like that of a matinee idol in Pittsburgh. Later a cigar was named Duke of Pittsburgh after Hawley. Boxes of these cigars featured his picture. 4) At one point during his tenure with the Pirates, Hawley refused to accept a bribe from a gambler who offered him $20,000 to throw a game. The gambler told Hawley if he didn't take the bribe, he would go back to his room a $2,400 a year pitcher. Hawley replied that he would, but he'd be able to sleep at night.. 5) Throughout his baseball career, Pink spent his off seasons in Beaver Dam where he spent much of his time hanging out at Charley Miller's Book Store, which was the social center of the small town. 7) Immediately after he retired he moved to La Crosse, Wisconsin, where he opened a cigar store. 8) Later on, he and his wife, Katherine, settled in his hometown of Beaver Dam, where Hawley ran the local bowling alley for years.

RUNELVYS HERNANDEZ
One of his own managers called him an asshole

BIRTH NAME: Runelvys Antonio Hernandez
PRONUNCIATION OF DIFFICULT PARTS: ROON-ell-vees
NICKNAME: None
HEIGHT/WEIGHT: 6'3" 185 lbs.

BORN: Apr. 27, 1978, in Santo Domingo, Dominican Republic
POSITION: Pitcher
YEARS ACTIVE IN THE MAJORS: 2002-2006, 2008
NAME ETYMOLOGY/DEFINITIONS: "Runelvys" is a truly unique name. A thorough search of name reference books and on-line sources turned up no information on the genesis of that name. "Antonio" is of Latin origin, derived from "Antonius," an old Roman family name of unknown etymology. "Priceless" and "of inestimable worth" are popular folk definitions of the name. "Hernandez" is of Spanish (Hernández) and Jewish (Sephardic) origins, as the patronymic from the personal name "Hernando." This surname also became established in southern Italy, mainly in Naples and Palermo, since the period of Spanish dominance there, and as a result of the expulsion of the Jews from Spain and Portugal at the end of the 15th century, many of whom moved to Italy.

Relying primarily on a four-seam fastball and slider, while also mixing in a sinker, change-up and curve, Runelvys Hernandez seemingly had the tools to be an effective major league hurler. But his attitude frequently got in the way. After starting with the Royals' Burlington (Single-A) club in 2001, Hernandez spent the early part of 2002 in AA, before making his major league debut in July 2002. He had a respectable rookie season ... a 4–4 record with a 4.36 ERA in 74⅓ innings of work over 12 starts.

The Royals were bad enough going into 2003 that he was their opening day starter. He pleasantly surprised by spending the first five weeks on the leaderboard in almost every pitching category, but then he faltered as he tried to pitch through pain. His season ended after 16 starts with a 7-5 record and a 4.61 ERA. He missed the entire 2004 season with Tommy John surgery.

Hernandez made it back onto the mound for the 2005 season. On July 17 of that year, Hernandez ignited a bench-clearing brawl by hitting Detroit Tigers shortstop Carlos Guillén in the head leading off the bottom of the sixth inning after Guillén claimed that Hernandez's first pitch of the inning had hit his foot. The two continued to exchange words down the first base line, and Hernandez threw down his glove and went after Guillén. In all, seven players were ejected, most notably Kyle Farnsworth, who tackled Jeremy Affeldt to reignite the situation that had been settling down. Hernandez was suspended ten games by Major League Baseball for that. He finished the season with an 8-14 record and a bloated 5.52 ERA, yielding over a hit per inning.

In 2006, Hernandez reported to spring training woefully out of shape and overweight, and the Royals banished him to the minors for three weeks to try to get in game shape. In September of that year, Hernandez got into a scuffle with batterymate John Buck in the dugout during a game, possibly over pitch-calling during the game. After compiling a 6-10 mark with a terrible 6.48 ERA in 21 games (including 22 homers allowed in 109 innings), Hernandez was released by the Royals.

He signed a minor-league contract for the 2007 season with the Red Sox. The contract included an opt-out clause that would become effective if he was not on the major league roster by June 1. He exercised that option and signed a minor league contract with the Yankees, who in turn released him a month later. On July 17, he signed a minor league contract with Pirates, who also released him after less than a month.

For the 2008 season, Hernandez signed a minor league contract with the Astros, and actually made it into four games with the big-league club during that Summer. But he was torched for 32 hits and 11 walks in only 19 innings in those four games.

In September 2008, Hernandez received a 50-game suspension for testing positive for an amphetamine-based substance. However, weeks later the Office of the Commissioner of Major League Baseball announced that it had withdrawn the suspension because it was a first offense.

After the 2008 season ended, Hernandez signed with the Samsung Lions in South Korea's Korean Baseball Organization, but he sought and was issued his release on July 9, 2009. His final major league ledger: 25-36 with a 5.50 ERA in 82 games (all starts).

BEST DAY (BY WPA OR OTHER MEASURE): Hernandez's first and only complete game was also his first and only shutout, which took place on Aug. 26, 2006 as a member of the Royals. Kansas City was in Toronto to face the Blue Jays. Hernandez came into the game with a 3-8 record and a 7.50 ERA. He had given up 93 hits and 60 runs, while walking more than he struck out, in his last 65 innings pitched. But on this day, he was special. He needed 121 pitches to complete the nine innings, and he did allow seven hits and a walk against only four strikeouts, but he got the outs he needed when he had to have them. He even outdueled the great Roy Halladay, who had come into the game with a 16-3 record. The Royals got to Halladay for solo homers in the first and second innings, and Hernandez made them hold up.

THE WONDER OF HIS NAME: "Hernandez" is extremely common and unremarkable, but if you don't know the proper pronunciation of "Runelvys," it sounds like an exclamation to Mr. Presley to channel his inner Forrest Gump. Then again, given his lifetime ERA, perhaps his first name should have been "Earnedrunelvys."

NOT TO BE CONFUSED WITH: *Calling Elvis* (Song written by Mark Knopfler and performed by Dire Straits. It first appeared on the final studio album by the band, *On Every Street*), Flying Elvis (A logo unveiled in 1993 by the NFL's New England Patriots, involving the gray face of a minuteman wearing a red, white and blue hat that begins as a tricorne and transitions into a flowing banner-like design. It became popularly known as the Flying Elvis due to many observing its resemblance to the profile of a young Elvis Presley).

FUN ANAGRAMS: "Runelvys Antonio Hernandez" becomes "Honored Nazi rants unevenly."

EPHEMERA: 1) In 2006, Runelvys was a teammate of Ambiorix Burgos (see page 161). He became the opening-day pitcher in 2004 by winning Royals' manager Tony Peña's coin toss against left-hander Jeremy Affeldt. 3) Buddy Bell was Hernandez's manager in 2005 and 2006, and supposedly once told him, "you're not good enough to be this much of an asshole."

SMEAD JOLLEY
Came along too early to be a DH

BIRTH NAME: Smead Powell Jolley
PRONUNCIATION OF DIFFICULT PARTS: None
NICKNAME: Guinea (put on him in his rookie year by teammate Ted Lyons, who'd watched him devour an entire $6 guinea hen), Smudge, Happy
HEIGHT/WEIGHT: 6'3" 210 lbs.
BORN: Jan. 14, 1902, in Wesson, Arkansas
DIED: Nov. 17, 1991, in Alameda, California
POSITION: Outfielder
YEARS ACTIVE IN THE MAJORS: 1930-1933
NAME ETYMOLOGY/DEFINITIONS: "Smead" appears to have been bestowed upon him by his parents, honoring a prominent lawyer and friend of the family in his hometown of Wesson, Arkansas. "Smead" has English origins, possibly from Middle English *smethe* meaning "smooth," hence a topographic name for someone who lived on a piece

AL27.

of smooth, level ground, or a nickname from the same word used in a transferred sense for someone of an amiable disposition. "Powell" is of Welsh origin, as an Anglicized form of *ap Hywel* ("son of Hywel"), a personal name meaning "eminent." "Jolley" is a contraction of "Jolliffe," which derived from the Middle English or Old French *jolif* or *joli* meaning "merry" and "lively" and was originally given as a nickname to one of cheerful disposition. Perhaps the word ultimately derives from the Old Norse *jol*, a midwinter festival when people celebrated the gradual lengthening of the days.

Smead Jolley broke into the minor leagues in 1922 pitching for the Greenville (Mississippi) Bucks in the Class D Cotton States League, compiling a 12-7 record. The following season he struggled at a higher level of the minors, going 2-8 for the Shreveport Gassers (Class A Texas League).

In 1924, Jolley was back in D ball, pitching for the Texarkana Twins (East Texas League). He went 9-9 in 21 games as a pitcher while also leading his team in hitting with a .371 average, mostly while playing outfield in another 91 games. During the year, he also played for the Western Association's Class C Bartlesville/Ardmore Bearcats, but never on the mound. In 45 at-bats for Bartlesville, he hit .511 with four homers. Perhaps his bat was more valuable than his pitching arm?

Jolley became a full-time outfielder in 1925. Spending most of the year with the Corsicana Oilers of the D-level Texas Association, he hit .362 in 127 games. Sold mid-season, Jolley then hit .447 in 34 games for the San Francisco Seals, knocking the cover off the ball in the PCL (Double A, the highest minor-league level of the day).

Jolley stayed with the Seals for the next four seasons, 1926-1929, with batting averages of .346, .397, .404, and .387 and a total of 138 homers. In 1927 he led the PCL in hitting (.397) and RBIs (163). In 1928, Jolley led the league in almost every offensive category, winning the Triple Crown (.404-45-188, though the Seals played 191 games that season.) In 1929, he amassed an amazing 314 hits, his second straight season over 300. He averaged over 30 assists in his four full seasons with the Seals, but also tallied 55 errors in the same period.

Jolley caught the eyes of major-league scouts, but was passed up more than once because of the good hit/no field reputation, as well as the $50,000 price tag the Seals put on him. The Seals had a great outfield in Jolley and his fellow outfielders Earl Averill and Roy Johnson, and each one of the three was ultimately sold for that reported price, first the other two and then Jolley a year later. Bessie Largent, baseball's first full-time professional woman scout, recommended to the Chicago White Sox that they sign Jolley, and the new White Sox manager, Donie Bush, badgered the tightfisted owner, Charles Comiskey, until it finally happened.

On Opening Day, Apr. 17, 1930, at Comiskey Park, in his major-league debut, he batted fourth against the visiting Indians, going 2-for-5 and scoring twice. The next day's *Chicago Tribune* enthused that Jolley "gives promise of becoming one of the club's hardest hitters." On the defensive side however, by May 9, Jolley had already committed three errors in the field. He also wasn't fast on the bases, and pitcher Ted Lyons often came in to run for him if it was late in the game and Jolley reached base. In his first season with the Pale Hose, Jolley drove in 114 runs and batted .313. Jolley's first year turned out to be his best year.

In 1931, he was saddled with injuries and maladies and got into only 54 games, hitting an even .300. He was often a pinch-hitter and was very effective in that role, hitting .448, including a home run and six doubles. The White Sox finished in last place, and Donie Bush was replaced by Lew Fonseca.

Fonseca thought about trying to take Jolley out of the outfield and converting him to a catcher during spring training of 1932. There was so much rain that spring that Jolley had little time to work at the position. When he did, he acquitted himself well enough and the Mar. 31 *Sporting News* enthused, "Finally Finds Proper Niche" with a picture of Smead wearing his gear.

He was good as a receiver, but just could not deal with foul popups. Jolley consulted Yankees catcher Bill Dickey and told Fonseca that Dickey had given him a few tips, so Fonseca gave him a little more time but finally called off the experiment in early April.

Jolley appeared in 12 games with the White Sox that April, hitting .357 and driving in seven runs, but Fonseca swapped him (plus Johnny Watwood, Bennie Tate, and $7500) to the Red Sox in order to acquire utilityman Jack Rothcock and catcher Charlie Berry. The White Sox manager acknowledged that it was a mixed bag: "I really hated to let the big ape go. With that bat and rifle arm, I know there'll be days when this deal will haunt me. But what could I do? Every time a ball went to him in the garden I shuddered. I tried to make a catcher out of him. But a fly ball is still a fly ball in the outfield, or behind the plate, and Smead was allergic to 'em. ... He's a swell guy to have around but I just can't afford to give away all those runs."

As bad as the ChiSox were, the Red Sox were worse. The 1932 BoSox were the worst team in their club's history (43-111, a .279 winning percentage). Jolley hit well, finishing second on the Red Sox with a .309 mark. He got into 137 games, with 18 homers and 99 RBIs. His defense in the outfield was still a disaster. On May 23, he staggered under a high fly ball that landed behind him while Heinie Manush scrambled around the bases for an inside-the-park Griffith Stadium home run. In mid-June in Cleveland, Jolley turned two line drives (by Bill Cissell and Earl Averill) into doubles; the Red Sox lost, 9-2, and the manager, Shano Collins, quit.

Owner Bob Quinn reportedly took Marty McManus out of church on a Sunday morning and had him take the reins. Three days later, Jolley's baserunning cost his new skipper a game in Detroit when he held up at second on a ball Urbane Pickering hit that should have been a double. Seeing Pickering approaching, Smead suddenly broke for third and was tagged out.

During the final two weeks of the season, Jolley started five games behind the plate. He made no errors, but there were the four Senators stolen bases against him and Ivy Andrews on the 20th.

The Red Sox penciled Jolley in as catcher on their 1933 roster, but he dislocated a finger on Mar. 15 while catching, and that was the last time McManus actually asked him to catch. He appeared to have a somewhat less adventurous year in the outfield, committing only nine errors in 118 games, but his fielding percentage actually declined, while his batting average fell to .282. In his final major-league appearance, he went 1-for-5 against Babe Ruth (in a 1933 game that was also the last that the Babe ever pitched).

Jolley continued in the minors through 1941. In retrospect, he had a lengthy 16-year minor-league career wrapped around four years with the White Sox and Red Sox. Jolley hit .367 lifetime in the minor leagues and a very respectable .305 as a major-league batter, with some power (46 homers in 473 major-league games and 336 more in his 2,228 minor-league games). He was always lacking defensively as an outfielder but had success coming off the bench as a pinch-hitter. Had he come along in the 1970s, he would have been a perfect designated hitter.

BEST DAY (BY WPA OR OTHER MEASURE): On June 23, 1930, playing against the A's in the second game of a double-header, Jolley hit two three-run homers, added a double, scored two runs, drove in six and threw a runner out at third. His White Sox lost the contest 17-9.

THE WONDER OF HIS NAME: "Smead Jolley" is another "double unique" name in the baseball annals. You have the rareness of "Smead," which sounds like the more-common surname Snead but isn't. Then you add in the alternate spelling of "jolly." There's also something clunky and "unfun" about the word "smead," and its juxtaposed with the fun and fun to say "jolley."

NOT TO BE CONFUSED WITH: Doug Jolley (NFL tight end who caught a touchdown pass in the 2002 AFC Championship Game and hauled in five more catches in that year's Super Bowl). Samuel Smead (American newspaper editor and Wisconsin state senator in the early 1890s).

FUN ANAGRAMS: "Smead Powell Jolley" becomes "Oops! Well-made jelly!" or "Dope as mellow jelly."

EPHEMERA: 1) Various sources list him having either eight or ten siblings, but they seem to agree that he was the last to be born into the family. 2) Smead's father owned a 640-acre farm and was kept busy farming cotton and never saw his son play in the major leagues, but Schoolboy Rowe, the major-league pitcher, said that old man Jolley was a "baseball nut" and could rattle off every base hit his son ever made. 3) Smead had an uncredited cameo appearance in a 1935 film, *Alibi Ike*, based on the short story of the same name by Ring Lardner. The film is about an ace baseball player nicknamed "Alibi Ike" due to his penchant for making up excuses. After falling in love with the beautiful sister-in-law of the team manager, he is kidnapped by gangsters who want him to throw the last game of the season and the pennant. 4) One of the larger players by height and weight for his era, he swung a 40-ounce bat. 5) He met his future wife during a minor league game when he was patrolling the outfield and she was a fan in the bleachers. He was reportedly almost late to his wedding when his car ran out of gas. 6) For at least 25 years after his time with the White Sox, a loyal group of White Sox bleacherites convened the Smead Jolley Boosters, a fan club in his honor. Their 1959 dinner attracted some 800 attendees. 7) After baseball, Jolley worked for many years as a house painter for the Alameda Housing Authority. 8) Jolley had some good fortune in that oil was discovered on his Arkansas property in the mid-1970s. 9) In 2003, he was inducted into the PCL Hall of Fame.

DAX JONES
Well, he can say he played next to Barry Bonds

BIRTH NAME: Dax Xenos Jones
PRONUNCIATION OF DIFFICULT PARTS: None
NICKNAME: None
HEIGHT/WEIGHT: 6'0" 180 lbs.
BORN: Aug. 4, 1970, in Pittsburgh, Pennsylvania
POSITION: Centerfielder
YEARS ACTIVE IN THE MAJORS: 1996
NAME ETYMOLOGY/DEFINITIONS: "Dax" is a thoroughly modern given name with an ancient origin. Dax is the transferred use of an early English surname with Anglo-Germanic origins derived from a nickname. The Germanic word *dachs* means "badger" (the burrowing nocturnal animal kind). The nickname was most common in the ancient Anglo-Saxon kingdom of East Anglia (mostly populated by the Angles,

a Germanic tribe from modern-day Northern Germany). It would have been used as a sobriquet describing a person with nocturnal habits or one with a streak of gray or fair hair against black (like the striped black/white markings of a badger's head). The earliest recording of the surname came in the early 13th century in Germany, rendered as "Dach." "Xenos" has Greek origins, from *xenos* meaning "stranger" or "newcomer" (equivalent to English name of "Newman"). "Jones" has English and Welsh origins as a patronymic from the Middle English personal name "Jon(e)." The surname is especially common in Wales and southern central England. In North America this name has absorbed various cognate and like-sounding surnames from other languages.

D ax Jones was selected out of high school in the 49th round of the 1988 draft, but didn't sign. Instead he attended Creighton University from 1989-1991. The Creighton Bluejays baseball team had several future major leaguers there at the time, including Dan Smith, Mike Heathcott, Scott Stahoviak, Kimera Bartee and Alan Benes.

The 1991 Bluejays, coached by future major league general manager Jim Hendry, finished with a 51-22 record and reached the College World Series. That team had the nation's top offense, hitting a school-record .355 during the year. Every Creighton regular hit .330 or higher, and the team also broke and still holds school records for runs, hits, RBIs, doubles, triples, home runs, total bases and slugging percentage (a whopping .601). Jones, playing center field, did his part, stealing 32 of 38 bases and batting .366/.451/.612 with 21 doubles, 11 triples and eight homers in 71 games. His draft lot improved with his three seasons at Creighton, as he was taken in the eighth round by the Giants.

Jones signed a contract and went off to play in the Northwest League in 1991, compiling a .306/.393/.483 line in 53 games with the Everett Giants. He spent most of 1992 in the Midwest League with the Clinton Giants (79 games, hitting .298/346/.376 while stealing 18 of 23 bases) and then played for the AA Shreveport Captains in 1993 (118 games with a .284/.329/.378 line). At the plate he was profiling as a decent bat with minimal plate discipline and not much power. His defensive statlines to that point showed him to be a speedy center fielder with good range but somewhat error prone.

His progress from that point stalled a bit, as he spent the next two-plus seasons at AAA with the Phoenix Firebirds. Despite being in a traditionally hitter-friendly league, he batted only .278/.316/.396 in 1994 and .267/319/.349 in 1995, and his base stealing success across the two seasons was only 60 percent.

In 1996, he started with the Firebirds again, got off to a good start to the tune of .309/.352/.477 in 74 games, and finally got called up to the Giants in early July. His major league debut came as a pinch-hitter with two out in the ninth inning of a game the Giants were losing 8-3. Jones grounded out weakly to shortstop. He started one game the following week and was otherwise mostly a late-inning defensive replacement. He hit the first and only homer of his career at Philadelphia's Veterans Stadium, a line drive that turned into an inside-the-park job when Phillies center fielder Ricky Otero dove and missed the ball. (Otero injured himself, bruising his face in the process, and had to leave the game). During his time with the Giants that season, Jones appeared in 34 games, starting 12 of them. He was usually the center fielder with Barry Bonds in left and Glenallen Hill in right. He got 67 plate appearances across those 34 games and batted a meager .172/.269/.293 with two triples, a homer, eight walks and 12 strikeouts.

If Jones had thoughts of garnering the starting center field job with the big-league club in 1997, those hopes were squashed when San Francisco inked 32-year-old center fielder Darryl Hamilton to a free agent contract in the off-season. Jones returned to the Firebirds in 1997, and though he walked at a greater rate than he had in the past, his batting average dipped to .255 and he was caught stealing in ten of 19 attempts. He was let go by the Giants after the season and signed to a minor league deal by the Astros for 1998. He played for the New Orleans Zephyrs that year, was out of pro ball in 1999, and his last go-round was in independent ball in 2000.

BEST DAY (BY WPA OR OTHER MEASURE): Jones's best day, from a box score perspective, would probably have to be what turned out to be the final game he ever played in the majors. That took place on Sep. 28, 1996, at Coors Field in Colorado. The Giants had been playing out the string for a while, coming into the game at 67-93. It was also a Saturday day game after a Friday night game. Consequently, they fielded their "B" squad against the Rockies. Jones would be leading off in center against Colorado's Bryan Rekar. In his first at-bat, he swung at the first pitch and grounded out back to Rekar. The teams traded runs that inning, and Jones came up in the second inning with runners on first and second and two out and took a four-pitch walk to load the bases. The Giants stranded all three runners. Down 2-1 in the fourth with two out and a runner on second, Jones laced a triple to right to tie the game. He would score when Bill Mueller followed with a single to give the Giants a 3-2 lead. The teams traded the lead back and forth into the sixth inning, with San Francisco now winning 5-4. Jones led off the inning with a lineout to short, but his teammates pieced together another two-run rally to go up 7-4. Still up by that score in the eighth, Jones led off with a walk, and after Mueller reached on an error, Jacob Cruz singled Jones home to make it 8-4. Ellis Burks pulled the Rockies within three with a solo homer leading off the bottom of the eighth, but the Giants held on for an 8-5 win. Jones's final line: five plate appearances, two walks (career high), two runs scored (also a career high), a triple (one of two in his career) and an RBI.

THE WONDER OF HIS NAME: Perfectly ordinary last name, so where did "Dax Xenos" come from? Jones' parents were Charles and Kimberly. No information readily available on how/why they chose "Dax Xenos." There was a character named Dax Xenos in a film called *The Adventurers*, which was released four months prior to Jones' birth. He does have a rather unique monogram on his towels "DXJ."

NOT TO BE CONFUSED WITH: Dax (A xenomorphic character in the fictional *Star Trek* universe. The Dax life form is a Trill symbiont – one that lives inside humanoid hosts), Max Jones (American professional ice hockey forward who is currently playing for the San Diego Gulls of the American Hockey League as a prospect of the Anaheim Ducks of the National Hockey League), Dow Jones (Or simply "The Dow;" A stock market index that indicates the value of 30 large, publicly owned companies based in the United States)

FUN ANAGRAMS: "Dax Xenos Jones" turns to "Joann sexed Sox."

EPHEMERA: 1) In 2011, Jones was working with the State Department demonstrating the finer points of baseball to youth from other countries. 2) In 2016, the 1991 Creighton baseball team was inducted as a unit to the University's Athletics Hall of Fame. 3) He spends much of his time these days coaching a successful youth baseball team in Arizona. 4) Jones is one of only 25 players whose only career home runs of the inside-the-park variety (thanks to *Baseball Reference* for their assistance in determining this).

MALACHI KITTRIDGE
Cantankerous catcher with managerial aspirations

BIRTH NAME: Malachi Jeddidah Kittridge
PRONUNCIATION OF DIFFICULT PARTS: None
NICKNAME: Kit, Mal, Jed
HEIGHT/WEIGHT: 5'7" 170 lbs.
BORN: Oct. 12, 1869, in Clinton, Massachusetts
DIED: June 23, 1928, in Gary, Indiana
POSITION: Catcher
YEARS ACTIVE IN THE MAJORS: 1890-1899, 1901-1906
NAME ETYMOLOGY/DEFINITIONS: "Malachi" has Jewish origins as the name of a Biblical prophet, meaning "my messenger." However, given that Kittridge's parents were from Ireland, it's likely that this is the variant spelling of the Irish name "Malachy." St. Malachy (1095-1148 A.D.) was the Bishop of Armagh who adopted the name from the Hebrew prophet. "Jeddidah" is one of the multiple variants of "Jedediah," which is derived from the Hebrew name "Yedidyah," meaning "friend of God." In the Hebrew Bible, Jedidiah was the second or "blessing" name given by God through the prophet Nathan in infancy to Solomon, second son of King David and Bathsheba. "Kittridge" is a variant of "Kittredge," which has English (East Anglian) origins, from a Middle English personal name, "Keterych." This may be a blend of the Old Norse name "Ketill" (or the word *kettle*) with the common Old English name element *ric*, as in Burridge.

M alachi Kittridge began as a stocky second baseman on the independent Fitchburg Rollstones while still in high school. He spent three years there, was moved to catcher, and by 1888 had advanced to Portsmouth, New Hampshire of the New England Interstate League.

He went west the next year and caught 111 games for the Quincy, Illinois, team that became the Central Interstate League champions. The National League's Chicago team (then called the Colts) brought him in for the 1890 season. There he worked well with their staff ace Bill Hutchison, serving as his batterymate for consecutive 40-win seasons. Unfortunately, Kittridge hit worse than most pitchers. He often batted at the bottom of the order and was sometimes pinch-hit for by a pitcher.

In September 1891, manager Cap Anson suspended him for oversleeping, and handed his job over to Bill Schriver. Perhaps coincidentally, the Colts then blew a 6½-game lead with 17 games to play. Anson and Kittridge eventually ironed out their differences, to the point where the rest of the Colts viewed Kittridge as Anson's pet until mid-1895. At that point, Anson did away with "personal catchers" for pitchers and slated each catcher to appear in a strict rotation. Between 1892-1897, the Colts finished no higher than fourth in the 12-team league, and Anson was let go after the 1897 season in which the club ended up in ninth place.

Kittridge hoped to replace Anson as manager, but Tom Burns got the job instead. Burns tried to protect his managing interests by having Kittridge demoted to Omaha of the Western League, but other NL teams refused to waive on the catcher. He remained on the Chicago roster for two months, collecting full play while sitting idle, until his transfer to another NL team, the Louisville Colonels, in June 1897.

Kittridge played full-time for the Colonels, and they subsequently compiled the best second-half season of their short NL history. Manager Fred Clarke made his new catcher his "first lieutenant." But when Kittridge grew critical of Clarke the following year, he was benched after an 0-for-24 skein, and Clarke accused Kittridge of backstabbing.

On June 30, 1899, Kittridge was released to another NL team, Washington. Kittridge batted a mere .150 in 44 games for Washington in 1899. Then he subsequently left the National League on his own terms.

In 1900 he invested in the Worcester franchise in the Eastern League, named himself manager, and caught 127 games while batting .297. The performance earned him a contract from manager Frank Selee of the National League's Boston Beaneaters in 1901. When Selee moved to Chicago in 1902, Kittridge badmouthed his replacement, Al Buckenberger, and ended up getting sold to the American League's Washington Senators in July 1903. He finished the season in D.C. and invested in Worcester's team again the next spring.

Washington's owners, with some managerial personnel troubles to deal with, refused to let Kittridge go to Worcester and even named him interim manager. The team opened the year 0-13, and general manager Bill Dwyer rewarded Kittridge by giving him his first paycheck in nickels and dimes. Kittridge then pluckily informed the local press he had sprained his ankle carrying the bag of coins, causing him to miss a train out of New York on May 5. Dwyer than suspended him for being AWOL in Philadelphia, but the catcher, in his dual role as manager, rescinded the suspension with a telegram to league president Ban Johnson. Kittridge then used the same tactic to try to trade himself to the New York Highlanders (the precursor to the Yankees), along with star outfielder Kip Selbach for two prospects. The deal was quickly voided, and Kittridge remained with Washington until he was loaned to Cleveland in 1906.

In Cleveland he coached and was an emergency catcher. Returned to Washington in mid-August, he went to the Montreal Royals of the Eastern League instead as player-manager. Between squabbles with front-office personnel, Kittridge was a successful player-manager in the minors for several years, finishing in 1911 with the Southern League's Saginaw Krazy Kats.

BEST DAY (BY WPA OR OTHER MEASURE): On Aug. 16, 1890, in an 18-5 win over Pittsburgh, Kittridge's teammate Burns cracked a fifth-inning grand slam and Kittridge hits his own grand slam in that same inning (part of a 13-run explosion), marking the first time in major league history a team hit two "grand salamis" in the same inning.

THE WONDER OF HIS NAME: His parents were from Ireland, but his naming is based largely on variants of Hebrew names. "Malachi Kittridge" is flavorful enough, and then you add in the middle name "Jeddidah."

NOT TO BE CONFUSED WITH: Malachi Throne (American stage and television actor, noted for his guest-starring roles on *Star Trek*, *Star Trek: The Next Generation*, *Voyage to the Bottom of the Sea*, *Lost in Space*, *Batman*, *Land of the Giants*, *The Time Tunnel*, *Mission: Impossible*, and *The Six Million Dollar Man*, and best known as Noah Bain on *It Takes a Thief*).

FUN ANAGRAMS: "Malachi Jeddidah Kittridge" anagrams to "Deathlike jihad, grim addict." or "I might jail traded dickhead."

EPHEMERA: 1) According to the 1870 U.S. Federal Census, Malachi was the youngest of seven children born to James and Bridget (O'Toole) Kittridge. Malachi's parents were born in Ireland and could neither read nor write English at the time of the census. 2) Kittridge's 0-13 start to his managerial career is a major league record. 3) After baseball he took a sales job with the National Cash Register company. He later sold peanut and popcorn vending machines. 4) He died at age 58 of a cerebral hemorrhage while on a sales trip and left a wife named Annie.

NAP LAJOIE

So beloved in Cleveland, they briefly named the team after him

BIRTH NAME: Napoleon Lajoie
PRONUNCIATION OF DIFFICULT PARTS: Lah-ZHWA or LAJ-way
NICKNAME: Larry (bestowed upon him by a teammate that couldn't pronounce "Lajoie"), Poli
HEIGHT/WEIGHT: 6'1" 195 lbs.
BORN: Sep. 5, 1874, in Woonsocket, Rhode Island

DIED: Feb. 7, 1959, in Daytona Beach, Florida
POSITIONS: Second Baseman, First Baseman; Manager
YEARS ACTIVE IN THE MAJORS: 1896-1916 as player; 1905-1909 as manager
NAME ETYMOLOGY/DEFINITIONS: "Napoleon" is of French (Napoléon) and Spanish (Napoleón) origins, from a Corsican personal name "Napoleone." Occasionally bestowed in modern times in honor of the French emperor Napoleon Bonaparte, who was born in Corsica into a family that was ultimately of Italian origin. "Lajoie" is of French-Canadian origin, as a common secondary surname. It has also been used independently since 1784, from *la joie* ("joy"), hence a nickname for a happy, cheerful person.

N apoleon Lajoie was the youngest of eight (surviving) children of Jean Baptiste and Celina Guertin Lajoie. During Napoleon's early years, Jean worked as a teamster and a laborer, but his premature death in 1881 forced his children to find employment as soon as they were physically able. After attending school for only eight months, Napoleon found work as a card-room sweeper in a local textile mill.

By age 20, he was playing part time with the semi-pro Woonsockets baseball team. Lajoie soon discovered that other semi-pro teams wanted him to play for them in critical games. He was earning $2-$5 per game, plus round-trip carfare from these teams. In 1896 Lajoie joined the Fall River (Massachusetts) club in the Class B New England League, which offered him $500 for the five-month-long season.

Lajoie's career with Fall River lasted only until Aug. 9, when he and teammate Phil Geier were purchased by the Philadelphia Phillies for $1,500. Manager Billy Nash installed the rookie, who was usually a center fielder, at first base.

In 1898 Phils manager George Stallings made sweeping defensive changes. The most important was shifting Lajoie to second base, where he would achieve his enduring fame. Over his final three seasons with Philadelphia, Lajoie, blessed with excellent speed, quick reflexes, and soft hands, became one of the game's best second basemen.

At the plate, he was a force to be reckoned with. From 1896-1900 he never batted lower than .324. He led the league in slugging in 1897 and doubles and RBIs in 1898. He posted a .378 batting average in 1899, though an injury following a collision with Harry Steinfeldt limited him to just 77 games.

He had a temper. In 1904 he was suspended for throwing chewing tobacco into umpire Frank Dwyer's eye. After one ejection, Lajoie, stubbornly refusing to leave the bench, had to be escorted from the park by police. And in 1903, Nap became so infuriated by an umpire's decision to use a blackened ball that he picked up the sphere and threw it over the grandstand, resulting in a forfeit.

Lajoie jumped his contract with the Phillies to join the insurgent American League in 1901. Prior to the 1900 season, Lajoie had been assured by Philadelphia owner John Rogers that he and teammate Ed Delahanty would receive equal pay. After the season began, however, Lajoie discovered that his salary of $2,600 was actually $400 less than Delahanty's. Incensed, he jumped to Connie Mack's Philadelphia Athletics of the upstart American League during the off-season.

In so doing, he almost single-handedly legitimatized the AL's claim to major league status. Rogers, however, immediately moved to block the deal, suing for the return of his "property." While the case worked its way to the Pennsylvania Supreme Court, Lajoie, capitalized on the golden opportunity of playing in a new league with a weak talent pool. Nap punished the American League's overmatched pitchers in 1901, becoming just the third triple crown winner in baseball history with a line of .426-14-125. He also led the league in hits (232), doubles (48), runs scored (145), on-base percentage (.463), and slugging percentage (.643). Despite those gaudy stats, the Athletics could only finish in fourth place.

Going into the 1902 season, Rogers succeeded in getting an injunction from the Pennsylvania Supreme Court which prevented Nap from playing ball in the state for any team other than the Phillies. Meanwhile, Lajoie moved to the Cleveland franchise and circumvented the ruling by skipping all the club's games in Philadelphia.

In the peace agreement brokered between the two leagues following the 1902 season, Rogers dropped his claim on Lajoie, and Nap remained with Cleveland. During what would be his 13 years with Cleveland, Lajoie became such a powerful symbol of the franchise that the press soon took to calling the team the Naps, thus making Lajoie the only active player in baseball history to have his team named after him.

In 1903-1904 Lajoie solidified his reputation as the league's best hitter, winning his third and fourth consecutive batting titles. In 1904 he slashed .376/.413/.552. The Naps still finished a disappointing fourth, and manager Bill Armour resigned in September. After the season, Lajoie formally accepted the position as field manager for 1905.

Lajoie inherited one of the league's most talented rosters. Their pitching rotation was anchored by a trio of young pitchers: Addie Joss, Earl Moore (who had won 52 games in his first three seasons), and Bob Rhoads, who would post a record of 38-19 for the Naps in 1905 and 1906. Despite this rotation and other young talent, under Lajoie's leadership the Naps only twice challenged for the American League pennant, losing out to the White Sox by five games in 1906 and the Tigers by .004 percentage points (one game in the loss column) in 1908.

Midway through the 1909 season, with the team languishing in the standings, Lajoie resigned as manager. Free to once again focus exclusively on his on-field performance, Nap batted over .300 every year from 1909-1913. From 1910-1912 he batted better than .360 every season, with a .384 mark in 1910.

In 1914 Lajoie struggled to a .258 batting average, as bad eyesight gradually diminished his effectiveness. Following the 1914 season, Lajoie's contract was purchased by the Philadelphia Athletics, and Nap was reunited with his old friend and manager, Connie Mack. In 1915 and 1916, Lajoie played out the string as Eddie Collins's replacement at second base, posting batting averages of .280 and .246, respectively, while the A's plummeted into the American League cellar. Following Philadelphia's 36-117 ledger in 1916, Lajoie announced his retirement from the majors.

On Jan. 15, 1917, he signed as playing manager of the International League's Toronto Maple Leafs. Toronto won the pennant and Lajoie captured the batting title with a resounding .380 mark. The following year he signed as player-manager for Indianapolis of the American Association, batting .282 and leading the Indians to a third-place finish in the war-shortened campaign.

For his career, Lajoie batted .338, topping the .300 mark 15 times and leading the league five times. He amassed 3,243 hits, 657 doubles, scored 1,504 runs, and drove in 1,599.

BEST DAY (BY WPA OR OTHER MEASURE): On Oct. 9, 1910, about 10,000 fans watched the awful St. Louis Browns play the sub-.500 Naps in a doubleheader. Most were on hand to see if Lajoie could mount a last-ditch batting title challenge to the hated Ty Cobb. Lajoie tripled in his first at-bat of the opener, then, depending on one's definition of the term, "bunted" over and over. Lajoie went 4-for-4 in a loss and 4-for-4 with a sacrifice in a victory. Lajoie kept dropping or pushing or dumping balls in front of Browns rookie infielder Red Corriden, who kept positioning himself ultra-deep, presumably on orders from his manager, Jack O'Connor. Cleveland's *Plain Dealer* acknowledged that something had smelled at Sportsman's Park: "St. Louis Papers Say Browns Made It Easy for Nap Slugger." After the *Plain Dealer* article described how excited fans were to see Lajoie pile up the hits, the case for the asterisk was summarized: "But Larry's triumph is tinged with a charge of illegitimacy. St. Louis sporting writers assert that Lajoie was favored by opposing fielders. They say that the St. Louis pitchers pitched the ball where Larry could hit it to best advantage. They maintain that Corridon [sic], the Brown third baseman, did not field to the best of his ability when the Cleveland champion drove the ball into Corridon's territory. They insist that other fielders abetted him and aided Lajoie in his race for highest honors." If the opposition had laid down for Lajoie, why had they done so? They, like many other players – including, to a certain extent, Cobb's own teammates – disliked the irascible Cobb. If the down-to-earth Lajoie could be the foil, all the better.

THE WONDER OF HIS NAME: Beyond having your baseball team renaming itself after you? Well, there is the infrequent (by American standards) first name along with the frequently mispronounced last name. In fact, one of the more popular Cleveland Indians blogs out there is called "Its Pronounced Lajaway."

NOT TO BE CONFUSED WITH: Bill Lajoie (General manager of the Tigers from 1984 [when they were World Series champs]-1990), Napoleon LeBrun (American architect known for several notable Philadelphia churches)

FUN ANAGRAMS: "Napoleon Lajoie" doesn't really work, but "Nap Lajoie Cleveland Indians" anagrams to "An idle, clean and jovial penis."

EPHEMERA: 1) Lajoie married the former Myrtle I. Smith, a divorcée, in 1906. They purchased a small farm of about twenty acres in the Cleveland suburb of South Euclid and this remained their residence until they moved to a smaller home in Mentor, Ohio in 1939. 2) Long popular in Cleveland, Lajoie was put up as the Republican candidate for sheriff of Cuyahoga County. Losing that election, he was named commissioner of the old Ohio and Pennsylvania League. He also dabbled around in a rubber company, sold truck tires, and finally set up a small brass manufacturing company. In 1943 the Lajoies made a permanent move to Florida, eventually settling in the Daytona Beach area. 3) His career hit total was the second-most in MLB history at the time of his retirement, behind only Honus Wagner (3,420). 4) He was among the second group of players elected to the Hall of Fame in 1937. 5) Myrtle passed away in 1954 and Nap in 1959. The couple had no children.

MARK LEMONGELLO
"My head was messed up"

BIRTH NAME: Mark Lemongello
PRONUNCIATION OF DIFFICULT PARTS: le-MAHNJ-ul-oh
NICKNAME: None
HEIGHT/WEIGHT: 6'1" 180 lbs.

BORN: July 21, 1955, in Jersey City, New Jersey
POSITION: Pitcher
YEARS ACTIVE IN THE MAJORS: 1976-1979
NAME ETYMOLOGY/DEFINITIONS: "Mark" is derived from old Latin "Mart-kos," which means "consecrated to the god Mars," and also may mean "God of war" or "to be warlike." "Lemongello" is most likely of Italian descent and has mysterious origins. It may be a variation of "Limengello" or "Limongello." Some reference material for Mark Lemongello points to the possibility that his family name may have originally been "Limengello" or "Limongello."

H is pitches weren't overpowering, but on occasion he could put the ball where he wanted. The problem with Mark Lemongello was that he was known throughout his career for his erratic, sometimes violent behavior, which sometimes overshadowed his on-field accomplishments. He would often furiously slap himself in the face after a bad inning, and after bad games Lemongello was known to destroy locker room equipment such as hair dryers and light fixtures in fits of anger. He once admitted to reporter Allen Abel: "My head was messed up."

Lemongello was signed ten days before his 18th birthday in 1973 by the Tigers as an undrafted free agent out of Bridgewater-Raritan H.S. in New Jersey. He tread water in the Tigers' farm system until a seven-player trade in December 1975 sent him to Houston.

While going 3-1 in four starts for the Astros in 1976, Mark impressed with a 2.79 ERA. He started the 1977 campaign 1-11 despite a decent 4.28 ERA. He rebounded, going 8-3 with a 2.90 ERA the rest of the way, finishing his age-22 season at 9-14 with a 3.48 ERA as the Astros went 84-78 for the year.

Mark repeated his 9-14 record in 1978 with an ERA of 3.94, as the Astros lost six more games that year than the year before. After spending three seasons with Houston, where he compiled a 21–29 record, Lemongello was traded to the Blue Jays, almost immediately getting the Toronto fanbase upset with him in asking if Canadians "spoke American."

His tenure with Toronto was disastrous, as Lemongello spent half a season with the club going 1–9 with a bloated 6.29 ERA. In his final start on June 3, he fired a baseball at manager Roy Hartsfield when Hartsfield came to remove him from the game. Lemongello continued making occasional relief appearances until late July, when he was sent down to the minors after a screaming match with Hartsfield. When informed he was being sent down to Syracuse, he threw an ashtray at the head of Blue Jays GM Peter Bavasi, barely missing him. Lemongello never appeared in another major league game.

Posting a 3-0 record in 25 innings and four starts for the Syracuse Chiefs didn't keep Toronto from selling Mark's contract to the Cubs in April 1980. His playing career ended that same year with the AAA Wichita Aeros, compiling a 6-10 record in 27 appearances (17 starts) and a 5.13 ERA.

BEST DAY (BY WPA OR OTHER MEASURE): On Apr. 15, 1978, he pitched a complete game 6-1 victory for the Astros over the Reds, taking a no-hitter into the eighth inning. Johnny Bench led off the top of that inning with a long home run, dashing Mark's dream of baseball immortality. It is unknown if he threw a tantrum after losing the no-no. He ended up with a three-hitter, walking two and striking out four.

THE WONDER OF HIS NAME: You have the long history of the mispronunciation of his surname. It's NOT "lemon jello" ... but given the general public's hold on that pronunciation, the name is exquisitely memorable. Throw in the temper tantrums, and he becomes a definite "name to know."

NOT TO BE CONFUSED WITH: Limoncello (Italian lemon liqueur mainly produced in Southern Italy, especially in the region around the Gulf of Naples, the Sorrentine Peninsula and the coast of Amalfi, and islands of Procida, Ischia, and Capri), Mello Yello (Highly-caffeinated, citrus-flavored soft drink produced and distributed by The Coca-Cola Company that was introduced in 1979 to compete with PepsiCo's Mountain Dew), Blancmange (Sweet dessert commonly made with milk or cream and sugar thickened with gelatin, corn starch or Irish moss, and often flavored with almonds).

FUN ANAGRAMS: "Mark Lemongello" becomes "Make me roll long." or "OK roll, mangle me."

EPHEMERA: 1) In 1982, Lemongello and a ballplayer friend by the name of Manny Seoane were arrested on kidnapping charges and armed robbery. They had abducted Mark's cousin, Peter Lemongello and Peter's brother, Mike Lemongello, and forced them into a van at gunpoint at Feather Sound, a subdivision they were building north of St. Petersburg, Florida. The kidnapping and robbery was the climax of a dispute between

Mark Lemongello and his cousins over a finder's fee for a home construction job the brothers were doing for Astros' pitcher Joe Sambito under the auspices of their Heron Development Corp. Sambito and a landscaper were at the home under construction at the time of the abduction. When the two suspects arrived and began fighting with the brothers, Sambito tried to intervene but backed away when Mark Lemongello pointed a .32-caliber revolver at him. When the suspects left with the cousins in a van, the landscaper called the police. While Peter Lemongello was held in the van by Seoane, Mark accompanied Mike inside a bank where Mike was forced to withdraw "more than $50,000" in cash from a safety deposit box. The brothers had offered Mark a $10,000 finder's fee, but he wanted $45,000, claiming he had invested that much in the development company. After obtaining the money, Lemongello and Seoane were accused of taking the brothers to a wooded area north of St. Petersburg and eventually releasing them. Mark Lemongello and Seoane were both freed on $10,000 bond, and, pleading no contest, were ultimately sentenced to seven years probation. Mark and Seoane were also ordered to perform 200 hours community service, stay away from Peter Lemongello, and to make restitution to Peter if a lawsuit were brought against them by the victim and a judgment rendered. At the time, Mark's attorney told media outlets that his client would work with a little league at his home in Arizona to fulfill his community service. 2) Mark's cousin Peter is an American singer known for his double album *Love '76*, the first album to be sold exclusively through television advertising. Peter's brother Mike was a professional bowler and is a member of the Professional Bowlers Association Hall of Fame. 3) While in the minor leagues at Detroit's Evansville affiliate, Lemongello roomed with Mark "The Bird" Fidrych. Lemongello mentioned that even back then, Fidrych talked to the baseball before pitches and manicured the mound between innings. 4) Following the 1979 season, Mark married the former Diane Dickerson, with the newlyweds taking up residence in Phoenix.

BRIS LORD
Not named after a religious service

BIRTH NAME: Bristol Robotham Lord
PRONUNCIATION OF DIFFICULT PARTS: Row-both-am
NICKNAME: The Human Eyeball, the origin of which remains unknown, but supposedly it was because of his keen vision
HEIGHT/WEIGHT: 5'9" 185 lbs.
BORN: Sep. 21, 1883, in Upland, Pennsylvania
DIED: Nov. 13, 1964, in Prince Frederick, Maryland
YEARS ACTIVE IN THE MAJORS: 1905-1907, 1909-1913
POSITION: Outfielder
NAME ETYMOLOGY/DEFINITIONS: "Bristol" is likely derived from the city in Southwest England of the same name. It is from the

Old English *brycg*, meaning "bridge" and *stow*, meaning "assembly place." "Robotham" is an alternate spelling of *rowbotham*, meaning a depression in the ground inhabited by deer, such as found near Ashton-under-Lyne, England. "Lord" itself derives from Old English *hlaford*, earlier *hlaf-weard*, literally "loaf-keeper," since the lord or chief of a clan was responsible for providing food for his dependents. "Lord" is (among many things) a man of high rank in a feudal society.

I n the early part of the 20th century, Connie Mack was the owner/manager of the Philadelphia A's. Bris Lord had played for Mack from 1905-1907 before Mack grew tired of a lack of improvement at the plate (he batted .239, .233 and .182 respectively in those years), and eventually sold him to the Cleveland Naps.

Flash forward three years. During a Philadelphia/Cleveland game in July 1910, Mack witnesses the poor outfield play of his fielders while Lord, blessed with a cannon arm and all-around fielding acumen, throws out three of Mack's baserunners. The next day Mack tells the Naps' club secretary "Give me Bris Lord for Morris Rath and I'll surrender my rights to Jackson." That Jackson was in fact a 20-year old relative unknown named Shoeless Joe Jackson. Lord did help the A's get to (and subsequently win) the World Series in 1910 and 1911, compiling an OPS+ of 136 and 120 respectively in those years.

Lord managed the Southern Association's Mobile Sea Gulls to a second-place finish in 1914 and the league's Memphis Chicks to a third-place record in 1915.

BEST DAY (BY WPA OR OTHER MEASURE): In the first game of a double-header on July 26, 1910, against the same Cleveland Naps team that had just dealt him to Philadelphia three days earlier, Lord went 4-for-5 with two triples, three runs scored and a stolen base. The A's won 6-4.

THE WONDER OF HIS NAME: The shortened form of his first name is a Jewish religious rite. His last name is a Judeo-Christian god. Throw in the "Robotham" middle name, which despite my whimsical desire is not a porcine cyborg, add a disturbing yet memorable nickname, and you have an all-around All-Star name.

NOT TO BE CONFUSED WITH: Jack Lord (Actor on the original *Hawaii Five-O*), Del Lord (Director of many *Three Stooges* films), Bristol Lord Mayor (Title for the first "Citizen of the City and County of Bristol"), Brisket King (An annual BBQ brisket competition held in New York City).

FUN ANAGRAMS: "Bristol Robotham Lord" becomes "Thrill, stardom or boob?"

EPHEMERA: 1) After his baseball career, he wanted to keep involved with the game, but a series of bad business ventures and lack of opportunities sidetracked him. Lord worked for a year as a Probation Officer in Media, Pennsylvania. He also for a time owned a car dealership in partnership with his brother, as well as a pool hall in Chester, Pennsylvania. 2) In 1920, Lord took over the coaching duties of the then-Pennsylvania Military College baseball team, succeeding the equally terrifically-monikered Si Pauxtis. 3) In the 1940s he worked for the State Highway Department in Pennsylvania. 4) Some reference books and many of the "baseball cards" of the day (mistakenly) list

Lord's first name as "Briscoe." Lord's father was Bristol Lord Sr., ergo the ballplayer was Bristol Lord Jr. 5) In September of 1918, in the waning days of WWI, Lord registered for the Draft. In a section of the registration card titled "Description of Registrant," there was the following question: "Has person lost arm, leg, hand, eye, or is he obviously physically disqualified?" "Small Finger Right hand" is written in as a response. Nothing about his eyes, despite his nickname. 7) He was inducted into the Delaware County Hall of Fame in 1956.

GROVER LOWDERMILK
His wildness begat an eponym

BIRTH NAME: Grover Cleveland Lowdermilk
PRONUNCIATION OF DIFFICULT PARTS: None
NICKNAME: Slim
HEIGHT/WEIGHT: 6'4" 190 lbs. (hence the nickname)
BORN: Jan. 15, 1885, in Sandborn, Indiana
DIED: Mar. 31, 1968, in Odin, Illinois
POSITION: Pitcher
YEARS ACTIVE IN THE MAJORS: 1909, 1911-1912, 1915-1920
NAME ETYMOLOGY/DEFINITIONS: "Grover" has Anglo-Saxon origins as the surname of a family having resided in the area that was referred to as the grove. The surname is derived from the Old English *graf* which meant "of the grove."

"Cleveland" is predominantly a surname with English origins. It is derived from the regional name from the district around Middlesbrough named Cleveland (meaning "the land of the cliffs"), from the Old English *clif* meaning "bank" or "slope" and *land* meaning "land." It's also an Americanized spelling of Norwegian "Kleiveland" or "Klevland," habitational names from any of five farmsteads in Agder and Vestlandet named with Old Norse *kleif* meaning "rocky ascent" or *klefi* meaning "closet" (an allusion to a hollow land formation) and *land* meaning "land." "Lowdermilk" is the Americanized form of the German "Lautermilch," which is a metonymic occupational name for a dairy farmer, from Middle High German *luter* meaning "clear" or "pure" and *milch* meaning "milk." Grover Cleveland Lowdermilk, in a fashion that was somewhat common at the time, was named after the then-president, in this case Grover Cleveland.

During his teenage years, Grover Loudermilk and his younger brother, Lou, a left-handed pitcher, were starring on the Illinois local sandlots. Both would make it to the majors; Lou made 20 appearances with the St. Louis Cardinals in 1911-12.

Grover signed his first professional contract with the Decatur Commodores of the Three-I League at the age of 22 in 1907, but after just one lackluster appearance, he was sent to the Mattoon Giants of the low-level Eastern Illinois League. He was the ace of the Giants' pennant-winning staff, going 33-10 with an ERA of 0.93. He also struck out a whopping 458 batters in 388 innings, including 17 in one game, and the velocity on his pitches clearly made him the class of the league.

Called back to the Commodores in 1908, Lowdermilk went 12-10 but also walked 124 in 217 innings, exhibiting the wildness that plagued him for the rest of his career. Batters learned to be patient and wait for him to throw one across the plate. In 1909 the St. Louis Cardinals were intrigued enough by Lowdermilk's potential, they purchased his contract for $2,500 in July.

Lowdermilk had a rough major-league debut, on July 3 in the second game of a doubleheader against the Cincinnati Reds, walking four batters and recording a wild pitch in 2⅓ innings. In seven appearances for St. Louis, he finished with an 0-2 record, a 6.21 ERA, and 30 walks in 29 innings.

After he had a poor spring training with the Cardinals in 1910, manager Roger Bresnahan sent him to the Springfield (Illinois) Senators of the Three-I League. Under manager Dick Smith, Slim responded with a superb season for the pennant-winning Senators, going 25-9 and lowering his walk rate to just 3.8 batters per nine innings. This earned him a promotion back to the Cardinals in 1911.

Used sporadically and almost exclusively in relief by St. Louis, Lowdermilk appeared in just 11 games. He did throw one shutout but was mostly unimpressive (0-1, 7.29 ERA), and lack of control as usual was his downfall (33 walks in 33⅓ innings). After the season, he demanded a trade and Bresnahan sold his contract to the Louisville Colonels of the American Association, where he found steady work as a starter over the next three seasons, winning an average of 18 games a year from 1912 through 1914.

The Chicago Cubs, in the heat of a pennant race and desperate for pitching, gave Lowdermilk a brief opportunity to return to the majors in August 1912. But he struggled in his only two games (0-1, 9.69 ERA). In December the Cubs included him in an eight-player deal that sent future Hall of Fame shortstop Joe Tinker to the Cincinnati Reds. But weeks later, the Reds sent Lowdermilk back to where he started the season, Louisville, in order to acquire another former Cubs great, Mordecai "Three Finger" Brown.

While Lowdermilk found steady work with the Louisville Colonels, his control never really improved. Nonetheless his velocity and strikeouts (254 Ks in 284 innings in 1914) continued to earn him more shots in the majors. In 1915 St. Louis Browns manager Branch Rickey became the latest to try to tame him. Rickey gave the 30-year-old Lowdermilk his first extended opportunity to make good in the majors, and Lowdermilk responded well, recording a 3.12 ERA and 14 complete games over 29 starts.

A typical Lowdermilk start came in his second appearance, on April 19 against the Indians: He struck out seven and allowed just two hits in a complete-game 7-2 win, but he also walked five and hit three batters. He could have sued his teammates for non-support, as that 3.12 ERA still led to a 9-17 won-loss record. In September the Tigers picked him up for the stretch run. They won all five of his starts but finished 2½ games behind the Boston Red Sox for first place in the American League. The Tigers brought in personal coaches in 1916 to help Lowdermilk gain better control of his fastball, but nothing seemed to work.

In midseason, Detroit traded him to Cleveland, but he made just 10 appearances with the Indians before he was sent down to the PCL's Portland Beavers. Grover disliked playing on the West Coast and quit the team after going 1-4 in seven games; he went home to Illinois before the season ended.

His old teammate Joe Tinker, now managing the American Association's Columbus Senators, persuaded Lowdermilk to return to baseball in 1917. At the age of 32, he put up his best full season in some time: a 25-14 record, a 1.70 ERA, and 250 strikeouts in 355 innings pitched. He also allowed just 128 walks, or 3.2 per nine innings.

In September the St. Louis Browns re-acquired Lowdermilk on waivers from Cleveland and in his first start back in the American League, he pitched a four-hit shutout against the New York Yankees, without issuing a single walk.

In the postseason City Series between the Browns and Cardinals, Lowdermilk had a great day on Oct. 7, when he pitched both ends of a doubleheader and didn't allow a single run. In his opener, which was Game 5 of the series, Lowdermilk shut out the Cardinals 2-0 on seven hits. Then he held them scoreless again through nine innings in Game 6 until it was called for darkness in a 0-0 tie. Lowdermilk pitched all 18 innings and walked only two batters.

After battling injuries in spring training of 1918, Lowdermilk couldn't hold onto the form he had shown the previous season. He went 2-6 in just 13 appearances with an ERA of 3.15. Still, in May 1919, the White Sox, short on pitching depth, purchased Lowdermilk's contract from the Browns and added him to their starting rotation. He pitched solidly for the White Sox, finishing 5-5 with a 2.79 ERA in 20 appearances. The team went on a late-season tear and cruised to the AL pennant.

The White Sox were favored to win the World Series against the Reds, and with Eddie Cicotte and Lefty Williams anchoring the rotation, Lowdermilk didn't figure to see much playing time in October. But in Game 1, Cicotte was knocked out early after allowing five runs in the fourth inning and Lowdermilk was sent in for mop-up duty at the end. He allowed an RBI triple to pitcher Dutch Ruether and walked a man and hit another in the eighth inning as the Reds won 9-1. Although Cicotte and Williams struggled to pitch effectively throughout the Series, Gleason never turned to Lowdermilk again. A year later, it was revealed that Cicotte, Williams, and six other White Sox teammates had conspired to throw the World Series to the Reds. Later, Lowdermilk said he often wished he could forget the whole Series. "I don't think we could have beaten Cincinnati anyway," he said. "The Reds had a great ball club."

Lowdermilk didn't see much playing time with the White Sox in 1920, either. He made three relief appearances and didn't appear to be in Gleason's pitching plans in the immediate future. In mid-May, the White Sox reportedly turned down a $5,000 offer for Lowdermilk from Joe Tinker's Columbus Senators, but a week later they released him to the Minneapolis Millers of the same league.

He spent the next two seasons with the Millers, winning 14 games in 1920 and 11 more in 1921 before calling it a career at the age of 37 after a short stint with his old team in Columbus in 1922. Between the majors and minors, Lowdermilk won 204 games but his true legacy was, of course, his lack of control. In 590⅓ major-league innings, he surrendered 376 walks against 296 strikeouts, and he hit 37 batters. He finished with a won-lost record of just 23-39 in the majors, but his lack of control wasn't as much of a hindrance in the minors, where he won 181 games in 12 seasons. Still, Lowdermilk frustrated managers and teammates who expected more from a pitcher whose fastball was often compared with Walter Johnson's.

BEST DAY (BY WPA OR OTHER MEASURE): On July 4, 1915, Lowdermilk fashioned the low-hit game of his career. In a start at home for the Browns versus the Cleveland Indians, he limited his opponents to one hit (a triple by Elmer Smith) in a complete game 2-0 shutout. He was customarily wild, walking five, but he kept the big bats of Ray Chapman, Shoeless Joe Jackson and Jack Graney quiet. In fact, Lowdermilk out-hit the Indians all by himself, notching a single and double in three plate appearances. He had come into the game batting a paltry .100 (four hits in 40 at-bats). The game took a tidy one hour and 26 minutes to complete.

THE WONDER OF HIS NAME: "Lowdermilk" sounds like a demand from someone who doesn't like quiet udder-squeezing. Throw in the then-president's name as a given and middle name, and you have one odd combination.

NOT TO BE CONFUSED WITH: Powdered milk (A manufactured dairy product made by evaporating milk to dryness. One purpose of drying milk is to preserve it; milk powder has a far longer shelf life than liquid milk and does not need to be refrigerated, due to its low moisture content), Grover Cleveland Land (A backup catcher from 1908 through 1913 for the Cleveland Naps almost exclusively as a backup catcher. In 1914 and 1915 he was the primary catcher for the Brooklyn Tip-Tops of the Federal League).

FUN ANAGRAMS: "Grover Cleveland Lowdermilk" becomes "Love wrinkled, calm groveler."

EPHEMERA: 1) The Lowdermilk family's presence in the United States is older than the nation itself. Their patriarch, Jacob Lautermilch Sr., was born in Baden, Germany, in 1716 and emigrated to the American colonies sometime before 1750. After settling in Maryland, he was a distinguished soldier in the Revolutionary War, a second lieutenant in the Continental Army. His descendants spread westward with the new nation and the family name became Americanized thereafter. 2) In his first year of professional baseball, Lowdermilk set a record that has stood for more than a century: His 465 strikeouts for two minor-league teams are the most in a season by any pitcher at the 60'6" distance. 3) During the 1907 season, he married Honora "Nora" Soulon, the daughter of a French-born blacksmith who had settled in Odin. They had two daughters, Ruth and Irma. After his baseball career ended, the couple returned to Odin, where Grover found work in the coal mines. He lived in retirement on his pension as a miner. 4) Both Grover and his brother Lou Lowdermilk's names reappeared in the news during the baseball card boom of the late 20th century. Grover's 1910 Broadleaf Tobacco Co. card has been valued at several hundred dollars and only about 100 are said to exist. Meanwhile, Lou's T207 tobacco card from 1912 is one of the rarest in the world and sold for more than $3,800 in a 2014 online auction. 5) Author Paul Dickson has noted that "Lowdermilk" had entered the baseball lexicon to describe a pitcher given to acute wildness.

CON LUCID

Questions and conflicting stories surrounding his life ... and death

BIRTH NAME: Cornelius Cecil Lucid
PRONUNCIATION OF DIFFICULT PARTS: None
NICKNAME: None
HEIGHT/WEIGHT: 5'7" 170 lbs.
BORN: Feb. 24, 1874, in Dublin, Ireland
DIED: June 25, 1931, in Houston, Texas
POSITION: Pitcher
YEARS ACTIVE IN THE MAJORS: 1893-1897
NAME ETYMOLOGY/DEFINITIONS: "Cornelius" has similar origins be it Dutch, Danish, or German ancestry, that being from a personal name borne by a 3rd-century Christian saint and pope, Latin Cornelius, an old Roman family name, probably derived from *cornu* meaning "horn." "Cecil" is of Welsh origin. The name was associated with Monmouthshire and derives from the Old Welsh personal name "Seisyllt." The name may be related to that of the local celtic tribe (Silures) and the successor kingdom (Essyllwg). The spelling has been modified greatly as a result of folk etymological association with the Latin name "C(a)ecilius," a derivative of *caecus* meaning "blind." "Lucid" has Irish (County Kerry) origins, but is of uncertain derivation, perhaps a variant of "Lucey."

A fter his family moved to the United States, Con Lucid discovered baseball. He started playing organized ball as a 16-year-old in 1890, then made it to the big leagues at age 19 in 1893, pitching in two games for the Louisville Colonels of the National League. His next stop was the NL's Brooklyn Grooms in 1894, where he achieved a 5-3 record in 10 games despite a 6.56 ERA (runs were plentiful back then).

He split the 1895 season between Brooklyn and the Philadelphia Phillies and posted a composite 16-10 record despite walking more than twice as many as he struck out, as well as hitting 16 batters. He split time between the majors and minors in 1896 and 1897, and so appeared in a total of only 11 more major league games between those two years. His final career record was a pedestrian 23-23 with an ERA of 6.02. If a story by Bill Hallman in the *Pittsburgh Press* in 1905 is to be believed, Lucid apparently scuffed the ball while on the mound:

"I often noticed at the beginning of the game (Con) Lucid never rubbed the ball in the dirt or mud or resorted to any of the usual tricks to blacken the ball or rough it. When the new ball was tossed out to him at the beginning of the game Con would rub it in his glove with all his might. As he came from the box one day, I discovered the secret. Half hidden in his glove was a piece of coarse, new sandpaper. 'What's that for Con?' I asked, innocently pointing to his glove. 'Oh,' said Lucid, 'that's a little invention of my own. You've no idea what a grip I can get on a new ball when it has been in juxtaposition with that little piece of sandpaper for a few times."

So, on the surface, there isn't too much remarkable about Lucid's baseball career. However, it was what he purportedly did off the field that made him memorable – when he was acting as a scout and not a player. The story goes that Lucid was nursing a sore arm early in the 1897 season. The Phillies asked him to go to Paterson, New Jersey, to watch a minor league game between teams in the Atlantic League. He was instructed to watch a player on one of the teams, a guy with the first name of John, who was 5'11" and 200 pounds (fairly hefty for a baseball player at the time). Lucid's report was not a positive one – other than the observation that the player was a "good hitter." "He's big and clumsy" he wrote, "too awkward to play big league ball." Most people at that time agreed with that assessment – but, unfortunately, it was Con Lucid's name that went down in history with that report. Because the player he suggested that the Phillies not sign was named John Peter Wagner… better known by his nickname Hans… or Honus, as in Honus Wagner. Wagner of course went on to be one of the greatest baseball players to ever put on a uniform.[21]

The problems with this story are that 1) Lucid wasn't with the Phillies major league team in 1897, he was with the St. Louis Browns. He was a member of the Reading, Pennsylvania minor league team for part of 1897 and also part of the Atlantic League, so perhaps there was a working arrangement between the big league club and Reading and Lucid was asked to pass on his thoughts about playing against Wagner, and 2) many other "scouts" with better player evaluation pedigrees dismissed Wagner, including Gene Stallings, then-outfielder/manager of the Phillies, as well as Wagner's future Louisville club president Harvey Pulliam and manager Fred Clarke.

---

[21] The Phillies starting first baseman at the end of 1896 was a rookie by the name of Napoleon Lajoie – yes, *that* Napoleon Lajoie, who had a fabulous career as a second baseman starting in 1898, spending most of his career with the Cleveland AL team. But, could you imagine – if the Phillies has signed Wagner, they might have had one of the greatest keystone combinations in the history of the game.

BEST DAY (BY WPA OR OTHER MEASURE): Unfortunately, there are no individual game logs from that era, and frankly, given his career stat line, Lucid didn't have many highlight games.

THE WONDER OF HIS NAME: Many people named "Cornelius" would go by "Con," "Connie" or something similar. As far as "Lucid" … well the player's life story is far from that. But it's still a cool name.

NOT TO BE CONFUSED WITH: Shannon Lucid (American biochemist and retired NASA astronaut. At one time, she held the record for the longest duration stay in space by an American, as well as by a woman), *Silent Lucidity* (Single by the American progressive metal band Queensrÿche from the 1990 album *Empire*).

FUN ANAGRAMS: "Cornelius Cecil Lucid" turns into "I sliced cruel council."

EPHEMERA: 1) One of only 47 players in major league history to be born in Ireland, and one of only five born in Dublin (of those for which we have city of birth). 2) He received his education at Notre Dame. 3) According to the 1920 U.S. Census, Con took a wife (Ina Brooks) and together they had three children (Ina Mary, Margaret and Travis Brooks). Ina wasn't his first wife though. He had previously married a woman named Grace in 1893, and together they bore a child. He apparently subsequently abandoned them to pursue a baseball career, and Mrs. Lucid secured a divorce in 1899. 4) After his baseball career ended, he managed some minor league ball before coaching college baseball at Rice Institute, the University of Texas and Texas A&M. He also worked as a Commissary Manager for an oil company. 5) While pitching for the Phillies in 1896, Lucid's shortstop was a man named Billy Hulen. Hulen wasn't a very good shortstop, even allowing for the era. He committed 51 errors in 73 games and had below-average range. It may have been that Hulen couldn't get to a lot of balls because – believe it or not – he was left-handed. A left-handed shortstop? There's a reason lefties don't typically play short – it's an awkward turn to get the ball over to first, as well as having their glove on the same side as the right-handed third baseman. They both cover the hole between third and short; Hulen must have let a lot of singles get by him up the middle, because he would have to backhand those. 6) In another one of his life story contradictions, one of his obituaries stated that in 1892, while playing for Spokane, he rescued a heavily depleted pitching staff by hurling 30 consecutive games over 30 days. However, Baseball Reference lists him as appearing in only 26 games that year (of which he pitched in 24, making 21 starts). 7) That obituary, and others at the time, noted that he passed away after a short illness, rather than by suicide, as was listed in a few different sources. His death certificate lists "angina pectoris" for his demise. None of the sources that mention suicide note how he took his own life. Furthermore, SABR historian Bill Deane, who compiled a list of players who died by suicide based on research done by Hall of Fame historian Lee Allen, responded to my inquiry regarding this by stating, "… this suggests there is something at the National Baseball Library which pointed to that – maybe a questionnaire completed by a descendant decades after Lucid's death. Whatever it is, I'd say the death certificate trumps it."

PADDY MAYES
Half-Irish, half-Indian, and an Oklahoma legend

BIRTH NAME: Adair Bushyhead Mayes
PRONUNCIATION OF DIFFICULT PARTS: None
NICKNAME: Supposedly nicknamed "Paddy" because of his St. Patrick's Day birthday, but he was in fact half-Irish and half-Indian.
HEIGHT/WEIGHT: 5'11" 160 lbs.
BORN: Mar. 17, 1885, in Locust Grove, Oklahoma
DIED: May 28, 1963, in Fayetteville, Arkansas
POSITIONS: Pinch Hitter, Rightfielder
YEARS ACTIVE IN THE MAJORS: 1911
NAME ETYMOLOGY/DEFINITIONS: He may have been named "Adair" because that is a city in in his home state of Oklahoma, roughly 20 miles from his Locust Grove birthplace. Perhaps not so coincidentally, Adair is a town in Mayes County, Oklahoma. "Adair" is derived from the Old English personal name "Eadgar" (Edgar). The middle name of "Bushyhead" may have been in tribute to Dennis Wolf Bushyhead, a leader in the Cherokee Nation after they had removed to Indian Territory. Born into the Wolf Clan, Bushyhead was elected as Principal Chief, serving two terms, from 1879-1887 (in other words, he was the Chief when Mayes was born). The community of Bushyhead, Oklahoma, was named after Dennis and had a post office from 1898-1955. "Mayes" has English origins as a patronymic from the personal name "May," which has origins as a short form of the personal name "Matthias" or any of its many cognates.

P addy Mayes was a legend in Oklahoma when it was still a territory. The half Irish, half Muskogee (Creek) Indian began his professional career with the Muskogee Redskins in the Oklahoma-Kansas League in 1908. Even then he was already considered one of the area's best players.

He stayed with Muskogee the following season when the club joined the Western Association as the Navigators. Despite hitting just .261, his legend grew. The *Muskogee Times-Democrat* said he was "One of the best outfielders the association ever boasted." His manager George Dalrymple said, "He is the fastest fielder and the best hitter in the Western Association. He is a youngster that in a few years should be in the big leagues."

In 1910, he joined the Shreveport Pirates in the Texas League. He hit .260 in Shreveport, but his speed and fielding ability attracted the interest of Philadelphia Phillies, who purchased his contract. Mayes quickly made an impression during spring training in Birmingham, Alabama, in 1911. The *Philadelphia Inquirer* said: "That Paddy Mayes, the Indian outfielder, will prove a greater find than Zack Wheat is the opinion of Southern ballplayers ... Mayes, the half-breed outer garden candidate is fast as a bullet on his feet, a good fielder and has a wonderful whip. If he can prove that he can hit good pitching, he will probably stick."

Despite the buildup, Mayes didn't make the club and was sent to the Galveston Sand Crabs in the Texas League, but he refused to sign and never played for them. In June, with Phillies outfielder John Titus injured, Mayes was sold back to Philadelphia for $500. In his major league debut, Mayes was 0-3 and was struck out twice by pitcher Bill Steele. Mayes never caught up to the "speed of the big league." In eight plate appearances over five games, he was 0-for-5 with a walk, hit by pitch and a sacrifice. He also scored a run. Mayes' final appearance with the Phillies was just six days after his first.

BEST DAY (BY WPA OR OTHER MEASURE): Since he went hitless in his big-league career, there isn't much to choose from. In his third game in the majors, on June 13, 1911, he went in as a pinch-hitter, drew the only walk of his career and scored his only run.

THE WONDER OF HIS NAME: Half-Irish/half-Indian is an interesting ancestry, and the resulting Irish "Paddy" with Indian "Bushyhead" makes for a wonderful mix.

NOT TO BE CONFUSED WITH: Samuel Houston Mayes (Principal Chief of the Cherokee Nation from 1895 to 1899), "Paddy" Mayne (British Army soldier and a founding member of the Special Air Service, a special forces division of the British military).

FUN ANAGRAMS: "Adair Bushyhead Mayes" turns into "Ha ha! Buy diseased army!"

EPHEMERA: 1) He was the first ballplayer from Oklahoma to make the majors after Oklahoma achieved statehood in 1907. 2) After his baseball career ended, he was an employee of Continental Oil Company in Ponca City, Oklahoma. 3) Mayes had the distinction of having his major league debut become the subject of a story told by humorist Will Rogers. Rogers used Mayes to talk about Mexican calf ropers. The two men had met up after Mayes' first game and apparently talked about rope handling and the cattle business generally. Mayes was quoted by Rogers as saying that professional baseball with the Phillies was what he expected – a lot of really good baseball players. Rogers said that the same applied to his expectation of meeting and watching the Mexican calf ropers – he figured they'd be really good at it.

CAL MCLISH
His father went overboard on the naming

BIRTH NAME: Calvin Coolidge Julius Caesar Tuskahoma McLish

PRONUNCIATION OF DIFFICULT PARTS: None, but you would be advised to take a deep breath before pronouncing his full name

NICKNAME: Bus or Buster, with the origin story for "Bus" being that his father reportedly stated upon Cal's birth "he's as a big as a bus!"

HEIGHT/WEIGHT: 6'0" 179 lbs.

BORN: Dec. 1, 1925, in Anadarko, Oklahoma

DIED: Aug. 26, 2010, in Edmond, Oklahoma

POSITION: Pitcher

YEARS ACTIVE IN THE MAJORS: 1944, 1946-1949, 1951, 1956-1964

NAME ETYMOLOGY/DEFINITIONS: He has stated that the origin of his lengthy name is that his father was given permission to name the newborn, and he took full advantage of the opportunity. McLish said. "There were eight kids in the family, and I was number seven and my dad didn't get to name one of them before me. So, he evidently tried to catch up." His father was three-quarters Choctaw Indian. McLish once related, "I don't know why he named me Calvin Coolidge. He never voted Republican in his life, in fact, he was a Democrat. Just like the name, I guess. And I suppose that's why he slipped Julius Caesar in there, too." Tuskahoma means "red warrior" in the Choctaw language and is a community in Oklahoma.

Cal McLish played shortstop while at Central H.S. in Oklahoma City. In 1944 he was signed by Brooklyn Dodgers scout Tom Greenwade, who saw that McLish had terrific velocity on his throws. Fresh out of high school, with virtually no pitching experience, and no minor-league experience, the teenage McLish made the Brooklyn Dodgers' roster to start the season. Due to the shortage of players because of WWII, the 1944 Dodgers were a mix of players from opposite ends of their baseball careers. There were young, unproven players like McLish and Gene Mauch, and players whose better years were definitely behind them, including Paul Waner and Johnny Cooney.

McLish won his first major-league game on May 31, beating the Pittsburgh Pirates 8-4. Less than three months later, he got the call to report for active military duty. At that point he had a 3-10 record with a 7.82 earned-run average. He served in the 3rd Infantry Division in Europe, earning two battle stars, before he was discharged in August 1946, having missed the equivalent of two major league seasons.

McLish returned to baseball, pitching in one game for the Dodgers against the Cardinals in St. Louis on Aug. 25, and facing just two batters. He didn't retire either and allowed two earned runs. That was his only appearance in 1946, and after the season, he was part of a five-for-one deal with Pittsburgh for outfielder Al Gionfriddo and $100,000.

When a player returned from the service in those days, he had to be kept on a major league roster for one year. McLish pitched one inning for the Pirates on May 25, 1947, against the Cardinals and allowed two earned runs. After the year was up, McLish was optioned to the Kansas City Blues of the American Association, a Yankees AAA team, as part of a deal that sent pitcher Mel Queen to the Pirates from the Yankees. McLish compiled a 6-7 record in Kansas City, pitching 92 innings.

The next season, McLish pitched one inning in a game against the Cincinnati Reds on Apr. 25 before he was sent down to the American Association, where he posted a 12-9 record for the Indianapolis Indians. McLish was called up by the Pirates in September and started a game on the 25th against the Reds in Pittsburgh. He pitched four innings and allowed five runs on seven hits, uncorked a wild pitch, but got no decision as the Pirates won, 8-6.

December 1948 saw him on the move again as he was dealt to the Chicago Cubs. He pitched sparingly for the Cubs: 23 innings in 1949, with a 1-1 record. He spent most of the year on the mound for their top farm team, the Los Angeles Angels of the PCL. A lack of control (6.2 walks per nine innings) led McLish to an 8-11 record.

Cutting his walk rate to 3.6 per nine innings in 1950, he went 20-11, while also leading the team in ERA (3.60) and innings pitched (260). McLish, a switch-hitter, also swung a mean stick, batting .317.

McLish gained major league experience in 1951 at the back end of the starting rotation for the last-place Cubs (62-92). He got into 30 games for Chicago, making 17 starts and went 4-10 that season.

Back in the PCL pitching for a mediocre Angels team (87-93) in 1952, he further limited his walks, now down to 2.5 per nine innings. He won 16 games in 1953, with an even lower walk rate (2.3 BB/9). In 1954, he compiled a 13-15 record. Early in the 1955 season McLish was sold to San Diego, a Cleveland affiliate, for $5,000. There he blossomed under manager Bob Elliot, cutting his ERA to 2.86 with the Padres and winning 16 games. That winter, his pro career changed for good: "I was in Venezuela (playing winter ball) when I heard I had been bought by a big-league club. When I found out it was Cleveland, I couldn't believe it," he said in 1979. "Of all the places to try and make a ballclub! They had superstar pitchers."

Those superstars? Herb Score, Bob Lemon, Early Wynn, and Mike Garcia. McLish wouldn't crack that rotation, so he competed for bullpen playing time with Art Houtteman, Bob Feller, Ray Narleski, and Hank Aguirre. He increasingly earned manager Al Lopez's trust as the Tribe finished in second place, nine games behind the Yankees. His record of 2-4 and his 4.96 ERA wasn't really indicative of his value to the team as a steady and trustworthy middle reliever and "game finisher."

Lopez departed Cleveland after the 1956 season, and the front office promoted Kerby Farrell to replace him. McLish's role didn't change though, as he was again used mainly in middle relief. His innings did jump from 61 to 144. He compiled a 9-7 record and lowered his ERA to 2.74 as he yielded a mere 118 hits in those 144 innings.

Indians General Manager Frank Lane was anything but patient, changing managers and trading players at a brisk pace. In 1958 Farrell was replaced by Bobby Bragan. Bragan put McLish in the starting rotation. But then Bragan was in turn was replaced by Joe Gordon on June 27. McLish stayed in the rotation. At the age of 32, McLish had finally found a steady spot and responded to Gordon's confidence by winning the first five games he started for Gordon. After losing a game to the Senators, McLish strung four more victories together. He ended the year with a 16-8 record and a 2.99 ERA. He led the team in wins, innings pitched (225⅔) and complete games (13). He was grateful to Gordon for the opportunity: "Joe Gordon is an ideal manager. He showed he had confidence in me after I won my first game for him. He didn't say so. He just kept starting me regularly and giving me a chance to prove that I could win. It was wonderful to know that I'd finally found a guy who didn't look at statistics. Joe saw me work, liked what I did and proved it by sending me to the box in my regular turn."

McLish took over as the ace of an otherwise young rotation in 1959. Besides McLish, there were youngsters Jim Perry, Mudcat Grant, and Gary Bell. Cal was 13-4 at the midseason break and was rewarded by being named to the All-Star Game on Aug. 3 at the Los Angeles Coliseum. The Indians fielded a good hitting team as well and went toe-to-toe with Chicago for much of the season, eventually finishing in second place. McLish led the team with 19 victories. Perhaps sensing that they were playing with house money in a soon-to-be 34-year-old starter, Cleveland dealt Cal along with Billy Martin and first baseman Gordon Coleman to Cincinnati for second baseman Johnny Temple after the 1959 season.

McLish's 1960 season in the Queen City was horrendous. He posted a 4-14 record for the sixth-place Reds. He struck out a paltry 56 batters over 151⅓ innings pitched. It didn't help that McLish didn't receive any run support. The Reds mustered only 3.4 runs an outing for McLish in 1960.

Cal moved again after the season, this time to the White Sox with pitcher Juan Pizarro for infielder Gene Freese. On Chicago's South Side he was reunited with Al Lopez. In 1961, McLish scuffled to a 10-13 mark. It was later learned that he had been suffering from a double hernia, which required surgery at the end of the season.

Once more, McLish was swapped after the season. On Mar. 24, 1962, he headed to Philadelphia, to complete a trade between the two clubs from the previous December. Again, he was reunited with a familiar face, Phillies skipper Gene Mauch. On the surface, it appeared that McLish pitched well for the Phillies, going 11-5 in 1962. But Mauch picked the spots for him to pitch, and of those 11 victories, six came at the expense of the two expansion teams, the Houston Colt .45s and the New York Mets.

McLish pitched well in 1963, winning 13 games. But soreness at the top of his right shoulder ended his season two weeks early. The same soreness, which was later diagnosed as tendinitis, developed again the following season. After two appearances in 1964, the 38-year-old McLish ended his career when he was released by the Phillies in July.

Mauch then added McLish to his coaching staff, naming him as the Phillies' pitching coach, replacing Al Widmar. "Widmar and McLish are both real good men," said Mauch. "But we think the organization will benefit more with Cal working with the Phillies and Al with the kids in the minors." McLish followed Mauch to Montreal after Philadelphia, serving as pitching coach from 1969-1975. He joined the staff of Alex Grammas in Milwaukee in 1976, and served under managers Grammas, George Bamberger, Buck Rodgers, and Harvey Kuenn. In 1982, McLish's last season as pitching coach, the Brewers won the American League pennant, besting Mauch's California Angels three wins to two in the American League Championship Series. Under McLish's tutelage, Milwaukee had two Cy Young Award winners, Rollie Fingers in 1981 and Pete Vuckovich in 1982.

BEST DAY (BY WPA OR OTHER MEASURE): On May 5 of 1951, McLish tossed the first complete-game shutout of his career, limiting the Braves to five hits in a 2-0 victory. He also went 1-for-3 at the plate that day.

THE WONDER OF HIS NAME: His is by far the longest full name in major league baseball history, but it is NOT the longest in professional sports history (that most likely goes to former NBAer Dikembe Mutombo's 49-letter entry of "Dikembe Mutombo Mpolondo Mukamba Jean-Jacques Wamutombo"). McLish's full name still gives us a U.S. president, an emperor, and what had been an Indian territory in Oklahoma.

NOT TO BE CONFUSED WITH: Cal McVey (Fine hitter during the 1870s), Rachel McLish (Female bodybuilding champion), Christian Frederick Albert John Henry David Betzel (Known as "Bruno Betzel" in the big leagues. He was a long-time minor league manager), Johann Gambolputty de von Ausfern-schplenden-urstein-crasscrenbon-fried-digger-dingle-dangle-dongle-dungle-urstein-von-knacker-thrasher-apple-banger-horowitz-ticolensic-grander-knotty-spelltinkle-grandlich-grumblemeyer-spelterwasser-kurstlich-himbleeisen-bahnwagen-gutenabend-bitte-ein-nürnburger-bratwustle-gerspurten-mitz-weimache-luber-hundsfut-gumberaber-shönedanker-kalbsfleisch-mittler-aucher von Hautkopft of Ulm (Underappreciated composer in a *Monty Python's Flying Circus* sketch)

FUN ANAGRAMS: His full name gives us "Oh Jesus! Unlavish, tragicomical, social lame duck." or "Lovesick, high-class, miraculous, mad ejaculation."

EPHEMERA: 1) He was the seventh of eight children born to John and Lulu McLish. John McLish, who worked as a farmer, was part Choctaw and Lulu was part Cherokee. 2) McLish homered in three different games as a reliever but didn't homer in any of his 209 games as a starter. 3) He set a major league record, since surpassed, with 16 consecutive road wins over the 1958-59 seasons. 4) In 1950, he married his hometown girlfriend, Ruth Iris Lamer. They had five children: Cal Jr., John, Luanne, Ruth Ann, and Thomas. 5) In his retirement, Cal enjoyed playing golf and writing poetry. 6) In 2009 he was inducted into the Jim Thorpe Oklahoma Sports Hall of Fame.

JOUETT MEEKIN
The fastball pitcher who became a fireman

BIRTH NAME: George Jouett Meekin
PRONUNCIATION OF DIFFICULT PARTS: Jew-et
NICKNAME: Jo
HEIGHT/WEIGHT: 6'1" 180 lbs.
BORN: Feb. 21, 1867, in New Albany, Indiana
DIED: Dec. 14, 1944, in New Albany, Indiana
POSITION: Pitcher
YEARS ACTIVE IN THE MAJORS: 1891-1900
NAME ETYMOLOGY/DEFINITIONS: "George" is derived from the Greek "Geōrgios" through the Latin "Georgius." Its popularity is due to the widespread veneration of the Christian military saint Saint George. The Greek name as given in the Roman era

may ultimately derive from the name of "Zeus Georgos," an epithet of Zeus in his aspect as the god of crops. The noun *georgós,* meaning "husbandman, farmer," and the verb *georgéo,* meaning "to be a farmer; to plow, till, cultivate," are found in the works of Plato and Aristophanes. "Jouett" is a variant spelling of the English "Jewett," which has English origins from the Middle English personal name "Juwet," "Jowet." These originated as pet forms (with the Anglo-Norman French suffix -et(te)) of "Juwe," "Jowe," variants of "Jull," a short form of "Julian," which were borne by both men and women. "Meekin" originally appeared in Gaelic as "O Miadhachain," which is derived from the word *miadhach*, meaning "honorable."

Jouett Meekin initially made his mark on the diamond in his early 20s as a catcher with New Albany's local semipro team, the Browns. He switched to pitching ostensibly on a lark when New Albany's regular pitcher was unavailable for a game in the spring of 1889 and Meekin showed so much velocity that the catcher who replaced him was unable to hold him.

New Albany is situated just across the Ohio River from Louisville, and Meekin, like most of his Browns teammates, grew up a fan of the Falls City[22] American Association (AA) club. He joined the St. Paul Saints of the Western Association in July 1889 just a few weeks after turning to pitching. He was still with them in 1891, and a sad 4-8 when Louisville's manager, Jack Chapman, induced him to jump his contract and go up against American Association hitters.

It did not take Meekin long to realize his mistake in fulfilling his boyhood ambition by signing with Louisville.[23] Little more than a year after he debuted with them, manager Fred Pfeffer weighed his 17-26 career record and 4.19 ERA to that point and released him. By then the American Association had folded and the two major leagues had merged.

When Meekin wanted to sign with Cincinnati, his next best choice in proximity to his hometown he was instead assigned to Washington, a team deep in the National League basement, as punishment for his "jumping leagues." He finished the 1892 season a composite 10-20.

Bill James posited that "[Amos] Rusie, Cy Young, and Jouett Meekin, who all threw harder than anyone had ever seen before, forced the National League in 1893 to move the pitching mound back from fifty feet (where it had been since 1881) to sixty feet and six inches." (James is incorrect, at least in that the pitcher's mound itself wasn't introduced until 1893; before that there was a 4' wide by 5½' foot long box on flat ground; the pitcher could put his back foot anywhere along the 4' back line of the box, which was 55½' from home plate, to start his pitch.)

In any case, the changes didn't impede Meekin much: in 1893 his 10-15 record turned out to be the best on the last-place D.C. club. Taking notice was New York

---

[22] Louisville is nicknamed "Falls City" because it is situated at the Falls of the Ohio River.
[23] In doing so, he ran up against the National Agreement.

player-manager John M. Ward. After Ward told the club's principal stockholder, Eddie Talcott, "Get me one battery like Meekin and Farrell and the Giants will be hard to beat," another of the Giants' part-owners, William B. Wheeler, arranged to send two players and $7,500 to the Senators for Meekin and catcher Duke Farrell in February 1894. Meekin then proceeded to win 33 games and help to carry the Giants to their 1894 Temple Cup[24] triumph over the Orioles.

In a 1940 Sporting News interview, Meekin credited his sudden ascension to being one of the top pitchers in the game to Farrell, his chief catcher early in his major-league career. He related that "Farrell really taught me to pitch. He spent hours studying the weaknesses of the batters. And then he'd go over them with me until we had those weak points down pat." In that interview, he neglected to mention that Farrell had also had a hand into turning him into something of a head-hunter. Meekin once stated that when facing a good hitter, the first two pitches should come "within an inch of his head or body."

In 1895, Meekin dropped to 16 wins and a 5.30 ERA after tearing a muscle in his forearm early in the season. Soon after the injury he "took one for the team" in a June game against St. Louis, giving up 30 hits in a 23-2 loss. This was after the Giants' new owner, Andrew Freedman, requested that he pitch that day even though he had hurled a full game the previous afternoon, and he foolishly agreed to it after extracting Freedman's promise not to let player-manager George Davis remove him from the contest regardless of the score.

The forearm injury gradually left him unable to throw his curveball without terrible pain by the end of 1895. But over the winter he healed sufficiently to go 26-14 the following year while the rest of the staff was a weak 38-53. Meekin fashioned his third and final 20-win season in 1897 and then slipped below .500 (16-18) the following year.

Collecting a mere five wins in his first 18 starts in 1899, Meekin was sold to Boston for a reported $5,000. However, many sources believed the second-division Giants gave Meekin to Boston gratis in order to get rid of a high-priced player and help Boston in its pennant bid against Brooklyn. There was also speculation that Boston owner Arthur Soden owned $50,000 worth of stock in the Giants and Meekin's dispersal was yet another evil of "syndicate ball."

Boston failed to overtake Brooklyn for the 1899 pennant, and even though Meekin remained with the Beaneaters, it may only have been because New York no longer wanted him back. In March 1900, Boston released him. That June, Pittsburgh owner Barney Dreyfuss signed Meekin to a conditional contract and predicted that he was "far from being a has-been and will be heard from before the snow flies," but he was cut a few weeks later after being hammered for 21 runs in just 13 innings. In his big-league finale, on July 8, 1900, at St. Louis, Meekin left after the fifth frame with his club trailing 13-0.

---

[24] The Temple Cup was awarded yearly from 1894-1897 to the winner of a best-of-seven, post-season playoff tournament in the National League.

The following year he quit the game altogether after a brief excursion with the Louisville Western Association club, but returned later that season to pitch a few games for Grand Rapids of the Western Association. Seven starts and a 3-3 record with Memphis of the Southern Association in 1902 capped Meekin's professional playing career.

BEST DAY (BY WPA OR OTHER MEASURE): With individual game logs practically non-existent prior to 1900, its difficult to pin down Meekin's best day. That being said, for all his pitching success, it was a hitting rarity for which he has been noted in baseball record books. No pitcher in baseball history has ever collected a trio of three-baggers in one game except for Meekin, who did this on July 4, 1894. And he had a little assistance that day as long balls hit into the overflow outfield crowd went for three bases. Three triples were accomplished more frequently in those days – a couple of players even hit four triples in a game prior to 1900.

THE WONDER OF HIS NAME: It's another "double unique," admittedly helped by the player going by his middle name. Regardless, it's got symmetry in that each of his first, middle and last names have six letters. And you must admit ... "Jouett" is a LOT more interesting than "George."

NOT TO BE CONFUSED WITH: John "Jack" Jouett, Jr. (May be best known for a 40-mile ride during the American Revolution. Sometimes called the "Paul Revere of the South," Jouett rode to warn Thomas Jefferson, then the outgoing governor of Virginia (and the Virginia legislature who had fled the new state's capitol before electing his successor) that British cavalry had been sent to capture them), Thomas Doodputlee McMeekin (British sailor and Olympic Champion. He competed at the 1908 Summer Olympics in London and won a silver medal in the six-metre class), Frank "Dad" Meek (Catcher who played in six games for the St. Louis Browns of the American Association in 1889-90).

FUN ANAGRAMS: "George Jouett Meekin" becomes "Eerie joke to mug gent."

EPHEMERA: 1) His father, James Meekin, was a renowned riverboat pilot. On the night of Mar. 25, 1856, nearly the entire town of New Albany turned out on the local wharf or up on the Silver Hills look-out to cheer the arrival of Captain James Meekin's Baltic. The New Albany-built boat beat the pride of Louisville, the Diana, up from New Orleans by two hours and seven minutes. James Meekin had so commanding a lead by the time he reached his hometown that he swung the Baltic wide toward the New Albany bank and triumphantly tooted his horn for her many rooters. The townspeople, in turn, fired a cannon in salute. 2) In the fall of 1894, a novel was published with him as its hero that *The Sporting News* maintained was "not a dime novel." Not only was Meekin's biography used in the book but its title was *The Mighty Meekin*. 3) After his baseball playing career ended, Jouett Meekin umpired briefly in the Three-I League after first working as a guard at the Indiana Reformatory. Meekin then served in the New Albany fire department until his forced retirement in 1939 after a major surgical procedure.

HENSLEY MEULENS
First player from Curaçao,
made a name for himself as a coach

BIRTH NAME: Hensley Filemon Acasio Meulens
PRONUNCIATION OF DIFFICULT PARTS: None
NICKNAME: Bam-Bam, from hitting home runs left-handed (he's a natural righty) while playing softball as a teenager. His friends compared his power to a cartoon character on *The Flintstones*.
HEIGHT/WEIGHT: 6'4" 200 lbs.
BORN: June 23, 1967, in Willemstad, Curaçao
POSITIONS: Leftfielder, First Baseman, Third Baseman
YEARS ACTIVE IN THE MAJORS: 1989-1993, 1997-1998
NAME ETYMOLOGY/DEFINITIONS: "Hensley" is probably a habitational name from either of two places in Devon: Hensley in East Worlington, which is named with the Old English personal name "Heahmund" and Old English *leah* meaning "(woodland) clearing," or Hensleigh in Tiverton, which is named from Old English *hengest* meaning "stallion" (or the Old English personal name Hengest) and *leah*. Its possibly also a variant of "Hemsley." "Filemon" derives from the Ancient Greek "Philēmōn," meaning "kindly, affectionate." Philemon was an early Christian in Asia Minor who was the recipient of a private letter from Paul of Tarsus. This letter is known as Epistle to Philemon in the New Testament. "Acasio" is the name of the second municipal section of the Bernardino Bilbao province, in the department of Potosí, Bolivia. As far as "Meulens" is concerned, the surname was first found in Holland, where the name became noted for its many branches in the region, each house acquiring a status and influence which was envied by the princes of the region. The name was first recorded in North Holland, a province of the Netherlands.

"It was my fault ... I was a highly touted prospect who never figured it all out. That's on me."
  — Hensley Meulens in July 2011

Atop New York Yankees prospect in the late 1980s, Hensley Meulens never lived up to his potential but still played seven seasons in the bigs and several more in Japan.

While having great success hitting minor league pitching, Meulens never attained a permanent spot in the New York lineup, despite spending the entire 1991 season on what was a very mediocre Yankees roster. Averaging a strikeout every three at-bats in the majors, as Meulens did, will doom a prospect.

Originally a third baseman, Meulens was signed by the Yankees in 1985 and made his pro debut the following summer in Rookie ball with the Gulf Coast League Yankees. With the Single-A Prince William Yankees in 1987, he batted .300

with 28 home runs and was named Carolina League Player of the Year by *Baseball America.*

After a more challenging 1988 split between the AA Albany-Colonie Yankees and the AAA Columbus Clippers, he repeated the two-team cycle again in 1989. He earned a late season call up to New York in August of that year. He made his big-league debut on Aug. 23, starting at third against the Boston Red Sox, going 1-for-3 with a run scored and his first major league hit coming off Mike Boddicker. Overall, in eight games for the Bronx Bombers that year, he hit .179.

Moved to the outfield in 1990, Meulens was back in Columbus with the Clippers, hitting .285 with 26 home runs and 96 RBIs, and was named International League MVP. He was then with New York again in September, hitting .241 in 23 games with his first big league homer coming off Charlie Hough of the Texas Rangers on Sep. 12.

He was with the Yankees for the full 1991 campaign and hit .222 with six home runs in 96 games as the team's fifth outfielder. However, he was back at Columbus for the majority of 1992. Despite an excellent season, hitting .275 while leading the league with 26 homers, 100 RBIs, and 96 runs scored, he only appeared in two big league games in late September, going 3-for-5 with a home run.

After splitting 1993 between Columbus and New York, he was released. Meulens went to Japan in 1994, playing for the Chiba Lotte Marines. He then spent the next two years with the Yakult Swallows. In his three seasons there, he hit in the .240s each year with at least 23 homers each season.

Returning to the U.S., Meulens signed with the Atlanta Braves in late 1996 but was released during spring training. He then caught on with the Montreal Expos, spending most of the 1997 season with the AAA Ottawa Lynx, hitting .274 with 24 homers for the club. He was back in the majors for a September call-up with the Expos and hit .292 with a pair of home runs in 16 late-season games.

After being let go by Montreal during that off-season, he soon signed with the expansion Arizona Diamondbacks. He spent most of 1998 with the AAA Tucson Sidewinders, going 1-for-15 in a brief cup of coffee in the majors, before ending the season in the Chicago White Sox chain. That would be his last taste of the majors in the States.

From 1999-2002, Meulens played in Korea, the Mexican League, and the independent Atlantic League. During that time, he also played for Dutch National Team in the 2000 Olympics, the 2001 Baseball World Cup, and the 2002 Intercontinental Cup. Now in his mid-30s, he hung up his spikes, and began a coaching career.

Meulens was a coach for the Bluefield Orioles in 2003 and 2004 and a member of the Dutch team's coaching staff at the 2003 European Championship, 2003 Baseball World Cup and the 2004 Olympics. After serving as hitting coach of the Indianapolis Indians from 2005-2008, he was a member of the Dutch staff at the 2009 World Baseball Classic and was the hitting coach of the Fresno Grizzlies that year as well. He was named hitting coach of the San Francisco Giants before the 2010 season. He was named manager of the Dutch team for the 2013 World Baseball Classic, guiding them to the final four for the first time. He was named bench coach for the Giants beginning in 2018, and for the New York Mets beginning in 2020.

BEST DAY (BY WPA OR OTHER MEASURE): Perhaps it says something that Meulens' best game as a pro came not as an uber-prospect for the Yankees, but four years later as a late-season callup for the Expos. In the next-to-last game of 1997, Meulens got the start in left field, batting third against Jim Crowell, a rookie making his second big league appearance. Down 1-0 with two out in the bottom of the first, Meulens worked an eight-pitch walk off Crowell but was left stranded. Still down 1-0 in the third, with runners on second and third and one out, Meulens singled to left, driving in Expos starter Mike Thurman as well as Mark Grudzielanek to make it 2-1. In the fifth, with the game tied at 2-2, Meulens led off the bottom of the inning by lining a 2-1 pitch over the wall in left-center to put Montreal back on top. In the bottom of the sixth, Montreal was clinging to a 4-3 lead and had one out with Orlando Cabrera on first. Meulens doubled Cabrera in, and then scored on a Brad Fullmer double. In the eighth, he flew out, the only time that day he was retired. Montreal won 8-5, as Meulens went 3-4 with four RBIs, a double, a homer, a walk and two runs scored.

THE WONDER OF HIS NAME: Another "double-unique." It's got a melodic rhythm to it also ... Hens-ley Meu-lens ... rolls off the tongue. The nickname adds a few points to the quality of the overall name.

NOT TO BE CONFUSED WITH: Henry Rollins (American singer, songwriter, musician, actor, presenter, comedian, and activist. He currently hosts a weekly radio show on KCRW, is a regular columnist for *Rolling Stone Australia*, and was a regular columnist for *LA Weekly*), Clay Hensley (Former pitcher for the San Diego Padres, Florida Marlins, and San Francisco Giants).

FUN ANAGRAMS: "Hensley Filemon Acasio Meulens" becomes "So masculine ... hymeneal felonies."

EPHEMERA: 1) Meulen's mother is Dominican and his father is Dutch. 2) He was the first major leaguer from Curaçao. 3) Meulens speaks five languages: English, Spanish, Dutch, Papiamentu and Japanese. 4) He is married to Gyselle Meulens Petronia and has four daughters, two from a previous marriage – Michelle Marlise Aimee Meulens-Ebecilio, Danielle Marie Antonia Meulens-Ebecilio, Mia Valentina Turya, and Evangelina Cristina Vuri. In addition to the two daughters he has with his current wife Gyselle, he also has a son, Elijah Gabriel Ludwig. 5) On Apr. 27, 2012, Meulens was awarded the order of Knight in the Order of Orange-Nassau by Queen Beatrix. A ceremony was held at AT&T Park on July 13, 2012, where he was introduced as "Sir" Hensley Meulens. The award ceremony highlighted his role in victory by The Netherlands in the 2011 Baseball World Cup. 6) In 2016, he was inducted into the International League Hall of Fame, based on his 1990

MVP season and 1992 home run title in that circuit. 7) He runs the Dutch Antilles Baseball Academy in Curaçao.

KEVIN MMAHAT
Hat's all, folks!

BIRTH NAME: Kevin Paul Mmahat
PRONUNCIATION OF DIFFICULT PARTS: Mama-hat
NICKNAME: Hat
HEIGHT/WEIGHT: 6'5" 220 lbs.
BORN: Nov. 9, 1964, in Memphis, Tennessee
POSITION: Pitcher
YEARS ACTIVE IN THE MAJORS: 1989
NAME ETYMOLOGY/DEFINITIONS: "Kevin" is the anglicized form of the Irish given name "Caoimhín," composed of Irish *caomh* meaning "dear; noble" and *gin* meaning "birth." "Paul" has existed since Roman times. It derives from the Roman family name "Paulus" or "Paullus," from the Latin adjective meaning "small" or "humble." "Mmahat" is a total mystery, except it is Turkish in origin.

K evin Mmahat was born in Tennessee but adopted at four weeks old by a Turkish family from New Orleans. Mmahat attended high school there and graduated from Tulane University, where he pitched for the Green Wave baseball team.

Mmahat's pro career began in 1987, taken in the 31st round (805th overall) of the draft out of Tulane by the Rangers. He played just one season in the Texas system, in the rookie Gulf Coast League. In June of 1988, the Yankees purchased him from Texas. He played at Single-A Fort Lauderdale and got six starts at AA Albany-Colonie. Between them, he went 9-10, with a 4.09 ERA. With Fort Lauderdale, Mmahat made the league All-Star team.

Mmahat split 1989 between Albany and AAA Columbus. He went 8-5, with a 2.97 ERA between them. He then got his call to the Bronx in September. Years later, Mmahat recalled his initial arrival at Yankee Stadium. "I could smell the fresh grass cut. It was in the House that Ruth built. It was emotional. I am walking in Yankee Stadium. I was crying."

Mmahat debuted with the Yankees on Sep. 9 of that year, coming into the game late in a 7-0 loss to the A's. He picked up two outs, one on a strikeout, and gave up one hit. He didn't get his second outing until 12 days later, a 3⅓ inning effort where he gave up four earned runs in what would turn out to be a 14-1 blowout loss to the Brewers. Mmahat also got ejected from that game for hitting a batter after an earlier brawl (not of his doing) and a warning.

Then came his first major league start, on only three days rest, Sep. 25 at Fenway Park against the Red Sox. Mmahat was given some simple advice before the game, he told the Associated Press afterward. "Our pitching coach, Billy Connors, told me to go out there and have fun – but it wasn't much fun." Mmahat ended up lasting only 1⅔ innings, giving up five earned runs on four hits and five walks and getting pinned with the loss. Mmahat's second major league start would come six days later at home versus the Tigers. He only made it through two innings, giving up two earned runs on three hits and two walks. The Yankee defense didn't help him out, committing two errors while he was in the game, and six overall, in a 5-3 loss.

For the 1990 season, Mmahat returned to Columbus, going 11-5 in 20 starts. It was Columbus again for 1991, though he got just 11 starts, 12 total outings. One of those 1991 outings, though, was a gem: a no-hitter against Louisville, in spite of a sore shoulder.

"I didn't really think about it," Mmahat told the AP afterward of the no-hitter. "I was more concerned about my shoulder, which really didn't feel good tonight."

Mmahat played just one more season, getting seven starts over three levels, ending his career. His final major league line: four games, of which two were starts, a total of 7⅔ innings pitched, 13 hits allowed, 12 runs yielded (11 of them earned), eight walks, three strikeouts and two homers given up.

BEST DAY (BY WPA OR OTHER MEASURE): His big-league career was just four games and he was scored upon in all but his debut outing. The "best" day, then, would have to be his debut on Sep. 9, 1989. Mmahat entered the game with the Yankees already down 6-0 with one out in the eighth. He struck out Mark McGwire looking, gave up an RBI single to Dave Henderson, then got Tony Phillips to fly out to right.

THE WONDER OF HIS NAME: Last names that start with double consonants are exceedingly rare (see Ephemera). "Mama hat" sounds like baby talk ... but if that's the way to remember how to pronounce his name, go with it.

NOT TO BE CONFUSED WITH: *MMMBop* (Song written and performed by the American pop rock band Hanson, released in 1997 as the lead single from their debut album, *Middle of Nowhere*), Mmamabula (A planned coal mine and coal-fired power station to the east of the main road and rail corridor in Botswana between Gaborone and Francistown and south of the Serorome River. The power station would be near to the village of Mmaphashalala), Al Mamaux (who pitched a dozen seasons in the majors, winning 21 games with the Pirates in 1915 and 1916 and appearing in the 1920 World Series for the Brooklyn Dodgers), MAGA Hat (Headwear with the phrase "Make America Great Again" embroidered on it).

FUN ANAGRAMS: "Kevin Paul Mmahat" becomes "Hmm ... a valiant puke!"

EPHEMERA: 1) If you throw the word "Mmahat" into Google Translate and ask it to detect the language, it doesn't come back as Turkish, but Igbo. Igbo is the principal native language of an ethnic group in southeastern Nigeria. In Igbo, "Mmahat" translates to "break out." 2) He is married to the former Gina Tedesco with whom he has three children (Gabrielle, Abigail and Garrett). 3) After his baseball career ended, Mmahat returned to Louisiana. In 2007 he discovered TEX-COTE® a coating system that promised to "protect homes better than paint while keeping them beautiful – without costly maintenance." He founded expert coating company Mid South Coatings to bring his discovery to homeowners and business owners across the Gulf Coast, including Covington, Louisiana, and the surrounding areas. 4) Though not a part of Yankee gatherings like Old Timers Day and fantasy camp, Kevin has participated in MLB Players Association Alumni events in Louisiana. 5) Mmahat is one of only six players in major league history with a duplicated consonant to begin their surname. The other five are Winston Llenas, Clem Llewellyn, Graeme Lloyd, Kyle Lloyd and Pop Lloyd.

FENTON MOLE
A cup of coffee with the Yankees at the beginning of their dynasty

BIRTH NAME: Fenton Leroy Mole
PRONUNCIATION OF DIFFICULT PARTS: None
NICKNAME: Muscles, due to his build and considerable power in the minors
HEIGHT/WEIGHT: 6'1" 210 lbs.
BORN: June 14, 1925, in San Leandro, California
DIED: Feb. 20, 2017, in Danville, California
POSITION: First Baseman
YEARS ACTIVE IN THE MAJORS: 1949
NAME ETYMOLOGY/DEFINITIONS: "Fenton" (more often a surname than a given name) has English origins as the habitational name from any of various places, in Lincolnshire, Northumberland, Staffordshire, and South Yorkshire, so called from Old English *fenn* meaning "marsh" and *tun* meaning "enclosure" or "settlement." "Leroy" is both a given name and a family name of Norman origin. As a surname it is one of the most common in northern France. This family name originated from the Normans, the descendants of Norse Vikings from Denmark, Norway and Iceland who later migrated to Normandy. The derivation is from *le roy*, meaning "the king." The Normans brought this surname to England, which in medieval times was used as a nickname either for one who behaved in a regal fashion, or who had earned the title in some contest of skill. *"Le Roy le vault"* ("The King wills it"), is a Norman French phrase still used in the British Parliament to this day as royal assent. The surname Mole was first found in Roxburghshire, where they held a family seat as a Clan and conjecturally descended from Eustace the Sheriff of Huntingdon who held his lands of Molesworth in Huntingdon from Countess Judith a relative of Duke William of Normandy at the taking of the Domesday Book survey in 1086 A.D.

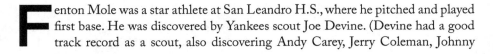

Fenton Mole was a star athlete at San Leandro H.S., where he pitched and played first base. He was discovered by Yankees scout Joe Devine. (Devine had a good track record as a scout, also discovering Andy Carey, Jerry Coleman, Johnny

Lindell, Cliff Mapes, Charlie Silvera and Leo Righetti). After serving in the Air Force from 1943-1945, Mole signed with the Yankees and spent the 1946 season with the Norfolk Tars of the Piedmont League (B-Level ball), for whom he batted .280 and slugged .420 with six homers in 128 games.

Despite the run-of-the-mill stats, Devine was giddy when speaking of Mole. In February of 1947, Devine issued this praise: "This boy is the apple of my eye ... He's big – stands 6' 2½" tall and weighs 212 pounds. He hits that ball just like Babe Ruth did in his younger days ... Mole is a switch hitter and ambidextrous fielder. He plays first base and is a fine fielder. They don't need to worry about that first base spot. Send Tommy Henrich back to the outfield – Mole will fill the bill."

Also, in speaking of Mole and pitching prospect Don Johnson, Devine said: "It just happens that these two boys just can't miss. If they don't make it, I'll be deeply disappointed. They definitely are a pair of the greatest prospects I have ever run across."

In 1947 Mole spent most of the year with the AA Beaumont Explorers of the Texas League, where he batted a pedestrian .254 with a .399 slugging percentage and only five homers in 378 at-bats. At the end of the season he got into two games with the Yankees AAA team in Newark.

It was in the 1948 season that the now 23-year-old first baseman announced his presence. Mole slugged 22 longballs and banged out 34 doubles in 713 plate appearances for the PCL's Portland Beavers. In so doing, he may have attracted the attention of Casey Stengel who was managing the Oakland Oaks in the same league.

The 1949 season was Stengel's first as skipper of the Yankees. Due to injuries to key players, Stengel used seven different First Basemen in all, with Tommy Henrich (who played more often in the outfield) starting in the most games of the seven. Johnny Mize, who came to the Yankees in late August that year, also appeared in six games at first base.

Meanwhile, Mole spent most of 1949 back with Newark, launching 16 homers in 357 at-bats and batting .269/.351/.462 in 107 games. The big-league Yankees finally turned to Mole in September of that year. He started eight games and appeared in two others in the last month of the season. He went 5-for-27 with two doubles, a triple, no homers, three walks and five strikeouts, batting .185/.267/.333. The Yankees went on to win the 1949 World Series, but Mole was not on the roster for it.

As the 1950 season approached, the press wondered who would line up at first for the Bombers. Would Mole get a chance to show what he could do with regular playing time? In a January interview, Stengel seemed to have an answer: "First base? We just have the best first baseman in Tom Henrich. He's also the best right fielder. . ... I think Johnny Mize will be able to help. . ... Fenton Mole could help us and so could (Joe) Collins, who's coming up from Kansas City."

In reality the answer as it pertained to Mole was "no." Mize (70 starts), the rookie Collins (50 starts) and Henrich (30 starts) got the vast majority of playing time at first base that year. Yankee first basemen combined to hit over 30 homers and drive in over

110 runs in 1950. Meanwhile, Mole served as "insurance" back in AAA. Splitting his time between two different AAA clubs that season, Mole whacked (not to be confused with "Whack-a-Mole") 26 homers in only 420 at-bats, but never got a call-up.

In 1951, Mole split the season between AAA San Francisco, where he batted a paltry .198 with two homers in 86 at-bats, and AA Beaumont. His career was slipping away. 1952 turned out to be his final year playing pro ball, as he split time across two AAA clubs but batted only .223. At age 27, he was done.

BEST DAY (BY WPA OR OTHER MEASURE): With a major league career consisting of ten games, we'll go with the game in which he secured his first big league hit. After going 0-2 with two walks in his debut on Sep. 1, 1949 against the woeful St. Louis Browns, he got his next chance two days later against the equally woeful Washington Senators. With veteran starting pitcher Ray Scarborough on the mound for the Senators, Mole grounded out to first base in the second inning. In the top of the fifth, Mole led off with a double to left field, and subsequently scored his first major league run when the next batter, Charlie Silvera, singled him home.

THE WONDER OF HIS NAME: Its always cool to have a last name that reminds one of an animal, a unit of measure, or a spy. Combine that with the rare but elegant "Fenton" and you have an intriguing name.

NOT TO BE CONFUSED WITH: Mole Day (An unofficial holiday celebrated among chemists, chemistry students and chemistry enthusiasts on Oct. 23, between 6:02 a.m. and 6:02 p.m., making the date 6:02 10/23. The time and date are derived from Avogadro's number, which is approximately 6.02×10^{23}, defining the number of particles, be it atoms or molecules, in one mole of substance), Fenton Hardy (A private investigator in the popular *Hardy Boys* novels, and the father of Frank and Joe Hardy), Hans Moleman (A recurring character on the animated television series *The Simpsons*. His appearance usually comes in the form of a running gag, in which, as a bystander to disastrous events, he suffers unfortunate, often seemingly fatal accidents, only to return in later episodes completely unharmed).

FUN ANAGRAMS: "Fenton Leroy Mole" doesn't generate anything sensible, but "Fenton Mole Yankees" anagrams to "Annoy meekest felon."

EPHEMERA: 1) He was the fourth of five children born to Walter and Irene Mole. 2) Don Johnson, Devine's other "can't miss" prospect from 1947, pitched both as a starter and in relief during his long, well-traveled career. His career totals include a record of 27-38 in 198 games, 70 games started, 17 complete games, five shutouts, 62 games finished, and an ERA of 4.78 with more walks than strikeouts. 3) According to a San Leandro appreciation group on Facebook, Mole apparently roomed with Joe DiMaggio during his short stay with the Yankees in 1949. 4) Mole was one of no fewer than 23 men that played first base for the Yankees in the 2,130 games immediately after the end of Lou Gehrig's streak. 5) After his baseball playing days were over, Mole went back to San Leandro and did various jobs including electrician. He organized a Little League in the neighborhood and worked on the local PTA. 6) In 2019 he was selected for the San Leandro Sports Hall of Fame.

XAVIER NADY

His father was Xavier, and HIS father was Xavier, and HIS father ...

BIRTH NAME: Xavier Clifford Nady (the sixth)
PRONUNCIATION OF DIFFICULT PARTS: X-avier NAY-dee. (Nady's father pronounced his first name "Zay-vee-yer.")
NICKNAME: None
HEIGHT/WEIGHT: 6'2" 215 lbs.
BORN: Nov. 14, 1978, in Salinas, California
POSITIONS: Outfielder, First Baseman
YEARS ACTIVE IN THE MAJORS: 2000, 2003-2012, 2014
NAME ETYMOLOGY/DEFINITIONS: "Xavier" is from the surname of the Spanish soldier-saint Francis Xavier, one of the founding members of the Society of Jesus (the Jesuits). Xavier probably represents a Hispanicized form of the Basque place name "Etcheberria" (meaning "the new house"). The Spanish "x" was pronounced in the Middle Ages as "sh," now closer to "h." "Clifford" is the transferred use of the surname, recorded as a given name from the 17th century. It has Old English origins as *clif* meaning "cliff, slope, riverbank" and *ford* meaning "ford." "Nady" is a bit of a mystery but given the long history of the Nady clan in France (see Ephemera), it could very well be of French origin.

Xavier Nady hit .619 as a high school senior. The Cardinals took him in the fourth round of the 1997 amateur draft, but he did not sign. The next year, he batted .404 and slugged .776. He was a second-team All-American at second base according to *Baseball America*, the only freshman on their three All-American teams. He was named the *Baseball America* Freshman of the Year. He set University of California records for doubles (28) and slugging and set a school record with 173 total bases. He set a university freshman home run record (15).

In 1999, Nady had a fine encore performance by batting .374 and making first-team All-America according to *Baseball America*, which named him the top third baseman in the country. He again was an All-Conference selection and his 23 homers were second in the Pac-10. At age 21, Xavier had a disappointing (for him) .329 year and fell to third-team All-American at third base. He was again an All-Conference choice.

He had been rated by many as the top college prospect entering the year, but the relatively poor season and his contract demands led to his sliding down to the 49th pick of the 2000 amateur draft, where the Padres took him and signed him for $1.1 million. Overall, he had set Cal records for career RBIs (191), total bases (479) and homers (57) and set a Pac-10 record for slugging (.729), breaking Mark McGwire's record.

Signing a contract late, Nady became the first player to go straight to the majors since Darren Dreifort six years prior and went 1-for-1 for the 2000 Padres. He went to

241

the Arizona Fall League but was sidelined by elbow problems. *Baseball America* rated him as the #7 prospect in the Padres chain.

In 2001, he was moved to first base and played well for the Single-A Lake Elsinore Storm, hitting .302/.382/.527 with 96 runs, 38 doubles, 26 homers and 100 RBIs. He led the California League in extra-base hits (65), total bases (276) and fielding percentage at first (.989). He made the league All-Star team at first, was named Rookie of the Year and Cal League MVP. *Baseball America* rated him the #4 prospect in the Padres system and the top power prospect, top batting prospect and best defensive first baseman in the California League.

In 2002, Xavier switched positions again, this time to the outfield. He hit .278/.382/.580 in 45 games with the Storm and .283/.329/.422 with the AAA Portland Beavers, drilling 23 homers between the two clubs. *Baseball America* rated him the #6 prospect in the California League and the #12 outfield prospect in baseball.

Nady batted .265/.329/.471 in 37 games for Portland in 2003 and .267/.321/.391 in 110 games in the majors in a somewhat disappointing performance. Nady returned to Portland for most of 2004, putting up a .333/.394/.632 line in 74 games and .247/.301/.416 in 34 games with San Diego; overall, he had 25 homers.

In his first full season in the big leagues, the 26-year-old hit .261/.321/.439 for the 2005 Padres. That winter, San Diego shipped him to the Mets for outfielder Mike Cameron. Xavier began the 2006 campaign with a .264/.326/.487 line for New York. On July 30, Mets set-up man Duaner Sánchez was injured when the cab in which he was a passenger was broadsided. The Mets' pitching corps was already depleted with star pitcher Pedro Martínez on the disabled list. Desperate for pitching, the Mets were forced to give up Nady, their starting right fielder, to the Pirates in exchange for pitchers Óliver Pérez and Roberto Hernández. It was a move that got mixed reviews on both sides.

Installed as a regular in Pittsburgh, primarily at first base, he hit .300/.352/.409 the rest of the way, showing improved contact but poor power. Nady suffered hamstring problems repeatedly in 2007 but remained Pittsburgh's most consistently productive hitter throughout the season. He hit 20 home runs for the first time in the majors and finished the season with a .278/.330/.476 batting line and 107 OPS+.

Despite more injury problems, Nady thrived with the Pirates in 2008, hitting .330/.383/.535 after 89 games and was fifth in the NL in average. His 141 OPS+ was 34 points higher than in any prior season. Hoping to sell high, Pittsburgh dealt him with Damaso Marte to the New York Yankees for Ross Ohlendorf, Jeff Karstens, Daniel McCutchen and José Tabata. He fell back towards his career norms with the Yanks, hitting .268/.320/.474 for a 105 OPS+ in 59 games for them. On the year, he hit .305/.357/.510 with 37 doubles, 25 home runs and 97 RBIs.

Re-signed by New York in 2009, Nady only went 8-for-28 with four doubles and a walk before an elbow injury resulted in a need for Tommy John surgery and he missed the rest of the campaign, then became a free agent.

He signed with the Cubs in 2010 and got into 119 games as a semi-regular, spending most of his time at first base. He hit .256 with six homers and 33 RBIs. His bags were packed for another move in 2011, this time to the Diamondbacks. In August, he was hit by a pitch thrown by Dillon Gee of the Mets, breaking his left hand. He was hitting .248 in 82 games at the time and did not play again that season.

He started 2012 with the Nationals but only hit .157 in 40 games and was released at the end of July. He landed on his feet again, finding a job with the San Francisco Giants in time to be part of their run to a World Series title; he hit .240 in 19 games, then went 0-for-5 in the NLDS in his only postseason action that October.

Unable to land a major league job in 2013, Nady went back to the minor leagues, playing 124 games between the Omaha Storm Chasers in the Royals organization and the Colorado Springs Sky Sox, the Rockies' AAA affiliate. He hit .309 in 71 games for Omaha and .278 in 53 games for Colorado Springs, for a combined batting line of .296/.360/.456, with 26 doubles, 15 homers, 69 runs and 65 RBIs.

In 2014, his original team, the Padres, brought him back as a sub, but only got 42 plate appearances during the year. The following year, his playing career over, Nady replaced Rod Barajas as hitting coach of the Lake Elsinore Storm. He continued in that role in 2016 but was not on their staff the following season.

BEST DAY (BY WPA OR OTHER MEASURE): The 2008 season-opener for the Pirates turned into a late-inning slugfest against the Braves at Turner Field. Nady was penciled in as the right fielder, batting fifth against Braves' lefty and future Hall-of-Famer Tom Glavine. Nady started his day slowly, weakly grounding out to third in the top of the second inning and getting caught looking by Glavine to end the third. With the Pirates down 4-2 in the top of the sixth, Glavine was relieved by Chris Resop. Nady greeted Resop with a line drive double to right, and eventually scored on an RBI groundout by Jose Bautista. With the score tied at four in the eighth, Nady took new pitcher Manny Acosta out of the yard, and the Buccos would add on three more in the frame. In the ninth, Nady led off against Jeff Bennett with a single to center, was wild pitched to second, moved to third on a single to left, and then was squeeze-bunted home to make it 9-4. Then the Pirates bullpen (Damaso Marte and Matt Capps) blew the entire five-run lead in the bottom of the ninth, thanks to four walks (including one with the bases loaded) and two two-RBI singles. With one out and a runner on second in the top of the tenth, Adam LaRoche was intentionally walked by reliever Rafael Soriano to pitch to Nady. Xavier struck out. The game stayed tied at nine until the 12th inning. With two out and two on in the top of the inning, Nady launched his second homer of the game, this one off Blaine Boyer. Pittsburgh's bullpen decided to make even that lead tenuous, as Franquelis Osoria (who may have had a melodious name but was an odious pitcher in his career) yielded a solo homer, a run-scoring single and left the tying run on first to end the game. Nady's contribution to the Pittsburgh's 12-11 win: seven at-bats, four runs, four hits, four RBIs, two homers and a double.

THE WONDER OF HIS NAME: As of the beginning of the 2019 season, there had been only eight major leaguers in history with a first name starting with "X." Nady's pronunciation of his name (an "EX" sound rather than a "ZEE" sound) is a bit unusual, and then you throw in the mystery of the Nady surname.

NOT TO BE CONFUSED WITH: Xavier Hernandez (reliever who pitched in the major leagues from 1989-1998 for the Blue Jays, Astros, Yankees, Reds and Rangers), Dick Dadey (Longtime executive director of the Citizens Union, a group that advocates for openness and fairness in government).

FUN ANAGRAMS: Xavier Clifford Nady turns into "Foxy, fervid cardinal."

EPHEMERA: 1) The actual first Xavier Nady lived in the 1500s in a French hamlet in the Alsace region of France. This current line of Nadys now spans at least seven generations and stretches back more than 150 years, to when Xavier's great-great-great-grandfather (whom the family calls "X the first") moved his family from eastern France to raise horses on a 660-acre patch of farmland in southeastern Iowa. 2) Nady and his wife, Meredith, had their first child, (of course named Xavier, the seventh) in 2008. Their second son, Brayden Chase Nady, was born in 2011. 3) His uncle is boxing referee Jay Nady. 4) Xavier is the first player in MLB history with a first name starting with X to hit a homer (Apr. 2, 2003 off Damian Moss). 5) In late June 2005, Nady became the first Padre since Greg Vaughn in 1998 to homer in four consecutive games. 6) Since 2000, he is one of only two players (Mike Leake being the other) to go directly to the big leagues after being drafted. 7) Nationals outfielder Bryce Harper, a rookie during the 2012 season, later named Nady among the veteran teammates from whom he learned early on in his playing career. 8) Nady donated a package full of signed cards, photos, baseballs and a pair of batting gloves he used as a pro to a 10-year-old Northern California boy named who lost his prized baseball memorabilia collection, including 51 signed baseballs, in the fast-moving Camp Fire in 2018.

JOHNNY NEE
Not much of a player, but a hell of a scout

BIRTH NAME: John Coleman Nee
PRONUNCIATION OF DIFFICULT PARTS: None
NICKNAME: None
HEIGHT/WEIGHT: 5'11" 220 lbs.
BORN: Jan. 18, 1890, in Thayer, Missouri
DIED: Apr. 22, 1957, in St. Petersburg, Florida
POSITION: Non-player (Scout)
YEARS ACTIVE IN THE MAJORS: None
NAME ETYMOLOGY/DEFINITIONS: The name "John" is the English form of "Iohannes," the Latin form of the Greek name ("Ioannes"), itself derived from the Hebrew "Yochanan" meaning "YAHWEH is

gracious," from the roots *yo* referring to the Hebrew God and *chanan* meaning "to be gracious." "Coleman" is most likely of Irish origin. It is the Anglicized form of Gaelic "Ó Colmáin" meaning "descendant of Colmán." (In fact, John's father was from Ireland and his first name was "Colman.") This was the name of an Irish missionary to Europe, generally known as St. Columban (c.540–615), who founded the monastery of Bobbio in northern Italy in 614. "Nee" is of Irish or Scottish origin, as a reduced Anglicized form of Gaelic "Ó Niadh" (descendant of Nia) or "Ó Niadh" (son of Nia).

J ohnny Nee was a minor league player-manager who later became a successful major league scout. He started playing minor league baseball in 1907 at the age of 17, often finding himself ten years younger than his teammates. In 1912, at the tender age of 22, Nee was chosen to skipper the Terre Haute team as a player-manager.

From 1912-1926, he was a player-manager for every team he suited up for except for the 1915 season. During his final season as the skipper of Virginia League Kinston Eagles (1926), one of his young players was future Hall of Fame member Rick Ferrell.

Starting in 1927, Nee began a long career as a major league scout for the Yankees and was credited with discovering many future major leaguers including Bill Dickey, Gene Bearden, Marv Breuer, Ben Chapman, Atley Donald, Tommy Henrich, Chink Outen, Billy Werber, Johnny Allen, Dixie Walker, Spud Chandler, Billy Hitchcock and Willie Jones.

He left the Yankees for the Phillies in 1946. At the end of the 1949 season, Nee was named head of the Phillies farm system, a position he held until July of 1956.

BEST DAY (BY WPA OR OTHER MEASURE): Since he never made it to the big leagues, I'd say that any day in which a player he scouted made his major league debut would be a good day.

THE WONDER OF HIS NAME: The shortened form of his first name flows right into his surname. Otherwise "Johnny Nee" sounds a bit repetitive. It must have been torturous making reservations though.

NOT TO BE CONFUSED WITH: Nenê (Basketball player for the Houston Rockets of the National Basketball Association. His birth name was Maybyner Rodney Hilário, but he legally changed it to Nenê in 2003), "Here's Johnny" (Introduction of Johnny Carson offered by sidekick Ed McMahon every night on *The Tonight Show*), Wounded Knee (Located on the Pine Ridge Indian Reservation in southwestern South Dakota and the site of two conflicts between North American Indians and representatives of the U.S. government).

FUN ANAGRAMS: "John Coleman Nee" anagrams to "Enhance lemon, Jo!"

EPHEMERA: 1) Nee died due to severe burns suffered when he fell asleep in bed holding a lit cigarette. The same thing had happened to him six weeks prior, but that time he escaped with only minor burns. 2) He had a daughter named Beatrice – which means she could have been the "Nee's Bea."

THE ONLY NOLAN
A "name" with a mysterious origin story

BIRTH NAME: Edward Sylvester Nolan
PRONUNCIATION OF DIFFICULT PARTS: None
NICKNAME: None
HEIGHT/WEIGHT: 5'8" 171 lbs.
BORN: Nov. 7, 1857, in Canada[25]
DIED: May 18, 1913, in Paterson, New Jersey
POSITIONS: Pitcher, Outfielder, Third Baseman
YEARS ACTIVE IN THE MAJORS: 1878, 1881, 1883-1885
NAME ETYMOLOGY/DEFINITIONS: "Edward" is derived from the Anglo-Saxon form "Éadweard," composed of the elements *ead* meaning "wealth, fortune; prosperous" and *weard* meaning "guardian, protector." It has been one of the most successful of the Old English given names. "Sylvester" is a name derived from the Latin adjective *silvestris* meaning "wooded" or "wild," which derives from the noun *silva* meaning "woodland." "Nolan" is of Irish origins (Leinster and Munster). It is the Anglicized form of Gaelic "Ó Nualláin" meaning "descendant of Nuallán," a personal name representing a diminutive of *nuall* meaning "famous" or "noble."

So how did he get to be "The Only Nolan?" No one is positive, but one story comes with some sense of plausibility, as determined by official MLB historian John Thorn "In the period following the Civil War, a wildly successful minstrel performer of the day, named Francis Leon, rose to prominence performing a burlesque act while simultaneously in both blackface and drag. His popularity prompted many imitators. In response, Leon began billing himself and his act as 'The Only Leon.' The theory follows then that Ed Nolan somehow reminded an observer of Leon, thus sparking the similar nickname."

Another angle to the nickname could be that in early Spring of 1877, Nolan was pitching for the Indianapolis club, and the team won eleven straight games, six of them shutouts, with Nolan pitching them all. After that he became not Edward J. Nolan [the record books, in which his date and place of birth are in some disarray, have him as Edward S. Nolan] but simply "The Only Nolan," and that was the name for the rest of his career.

Baseball historian Peter Morris adds "[Here is] what seems to me to be the most plausible source of his nickname, an article in the Chicago Tribune on May 5, 1878, describing how the Indianapolis team president had publicized the team by plastering the city with large photos of Nolan and his catcher, Frank "Silver" Flint, that bore the inscriptions 'The Only Nolan' and 'The Champion Catcher of America.'"

---

[25] Subject to debate. Some say he was born in New Jersey.

The Only Nolan was an eccentric 19th-century pitcher who appeared for five different major league teams in five different seasons across eight years. He wasn't very successful on the mound: a lifetime pitching record of 23–52 and an ERA well above league average.

At the age of 16, he began to play baseball for the Paterson Keystones. He moved on to the Columbus Buckeyes in mid-1875 and starred for them in 1876. In February 1877 Nolan, fresh off a dazzling season with Columbus, accepted an offer of $2,500 from club owner W.B. Pettit to pitch for Indianapolis.

In 1877 Nolan won more games by shutouts than most top-flight pitchers, in a single season nowadays. He pitched seventy-six complete games, won sixty-four, and tied eight. No man at any level of professional baseball, before or since, has won 64 games. And he set another record that still stands: thirty shutouts in one season. One of the thirty shutouts was a no-hit no run job against Columbus. And two of them came on the same day, Apr. 26, 1877, when he blanked Syracuse in both ends of a doubleheader, the first pitcher ever to accomplish such a feat.

He came into his rookie year with Indianapolis in 1878 presuming he would pitch every game (perhaps yet another origin story for "The Only" moniker ... he wanted to be the only pitcher). He was but 20 years old, and his season was notable principally for two separate suspensions – the first when he was accused of game-fixing (he was cleared); the second for lying about a sick brother so he could get time off to visit a prostitute. The Chicago Tribune remarked: "'The Only' Nolan owes his downfall to the fascinations of a beautiful habitue of an avenue assignation house, who has ruined more men in this city that she can count on the jeweled fingers of both her hands." On top of all that, he quickly gained a reputation as a head-hunter on the mound.

Nolan's 13 wins were hardly enough to keep the new Indianapolis franchise afloat in the National League beyond its first season. His indiscretions kept him out of the majors the next two seasons. Nolan played in 1879 with the Knickerbocker club and in 1880 with the Unions and then the Bay Citys, all in the San Francisco region. He resurfaced in the majors with Cleveland in 1881, where he went 8–14. One of ten players blacklisted by the league on Sep. 29 for "confirmed dissipation and general insubordination," he returned after a year's suspension for a partial season in 1883 with Pittsburgh of the American Association, for whom he posted a record of 0–7.

In 1884 he was 18–5 with Wilmington of the Eastern League when that club joined the Union Association. In the UA Wilmington went 2–16, with Nolan accounting for one of its victories. The next year he returned to the NL with Philadelphia, where his major league career ended after seven games. He pitched a few games for Savannah and Jersey City in 1886, but then he was done.

THE WONDER OF HIS NAME: Nowadays, only professional wrestlers can get away with a moniker as grandiose as "The Only Nolan." The name is also special because its origin, to this day, is subject to some (educated) conjecture.

NOT TO BE CONFUSED WITH: The Nolans (Irish girl group who formed in 1974 as The Nolan Sisters, before changing their name in 1980. They are best known for their U.K. hit single "I'm In the Mood for Dancing"), The Only (first single from industrial metal band Static-X's third album, Shadow Zone), Gary Nolan (starting pitcher who played with the Reds and Angels).

FUN ANAGRAMS: "The Only Nolan" becomes "Hello to nanny." while "Edward Sylvester Nolan" anagrams to "Lavatory lewdness nerd."

EPHEMERA: 1) After his baseball career ended, Nolan became, of all things, a policeman in his hometown of Paterson, New Jersey. He rose in the ranks, becoming a sergeant. In May 1913, at the age of 55, he died suddenly from illness, possibly nephritis, brought on by strenuous activity during the famous Paterson Silk Strike. 2) Bill James and Rob Neyer report Nolan having thrown an unusually fast (for his day) underhand fastball and a combination of curveballs. Nolan claimed he originated a pitch called the "inshoot," a form of the modern-day screwball. 3) One fan commemorated Nolan's time on the 1883 Pittsburgh Alleghenys by manufacturing a line of T-shirts remembering Nolan, Buttercup Dickerson, and the Alleghenies as "The Hardest Drinking Team of All Time." 4) One day in 1884, in a game against the Boston team, Nolan caused a Boston outfielder to muff a fly by yelling "look out for the fence," although there was no fence nearby. He was fined $10, and when he gave lip to the umpire, the fine went up to $150. 5) He married Mary Coyle around 1882 and they had two children, Marguerita (born 1891) and Edward (born 1895).

JOSH OUTMAN
Great name for a pitcher; quirky delivery

BIRTH NAME: Joshua Stephen Outman
PRONUNCIATION OF DIFFICULT PARTS: None
NICKNAME: None
HEIGHT/WEIGHT: 6'1" 205 lbs.
BORN: Sep. 14, 1984, in St. Louis, Missouri
POSITION: Pitcher
YEARS ACTIVE IN THE MAJORS: 2008-2009, 2011-2014
NAME ETYMOLOGY/DEFINITIONS: "Joshua" means "God is salvation" in Hebrew; it is borne in the Bible by the Israelite leader who took command of the Children of Israel after the death of Moses and led them, after many battles, to take possession of the Promised Land. It is derived from the Hebrew "Yehoshua." The name was a common alternative form of the name "Yēšūă" which corresponds to the Greek "Iesous," from which, through the Latin "Iesus," comes the English spelling "Jesus." The name "Stephen" (and its common variant "Steven") is derived from Greek "Stéphanos," a first name from the Greek word *stéphanos*, meaning "wreath, crown" and by extension "reward, honor, renown, fame," from the verb *stéphein*, meaning "to encircle, to wreathe."

"Outman" is the Americanized form of Dutch Uitman or North German Utmann, from Middle Low German *utman* meaning "stranger," "newcomer," or possibly from the South German cognate *Ussmann*, from Middle High German *uzman*.

J osh Outman and his brother, Zach, were taught to throw a baseball by their father, Fritz Outman. Fritz developed the "Outman Methodology," which strives to deliver a pitch on a purely "vertical plane" and to avoid side-to-side casting of the pitching arm. Josh Outman would start his motion with his pitching arm cocked vertically over the back of his head and just launch himself at the batter with his arm above his head, using no windup or leg kick. He had success in high school and junior college doing this. His fastball velocity was over 90 as a high school senior and as a junior college pitcher, and he had solid peripherals while using his dad's methodology. Outman spoke to David Laurila of *Baseball Prospectus* in 2009 regarding the benefits of his dad's teachings (Warning ... physiology talk ahead):

"Using a vertical arm position freed up my rotator cuff and enabled the use of the larger pectoral and abdominal muscle groups rather than the smaller deltoids and various other shoulder muscles. It used my lats to slow my arm down rather than just the posterior deltoids, and because those are larger, stronger muscles that can withstand more force, it took a large workload off my shoulder muscles. And eliminating the leg kick in lieu of a normal walking step, I was expending less energy to get the same production from my body, while sparing my throwing arm much of the wear and tear associated with pitching."

However, he was told that he would go undrafted unless he changed his mechanics to something a little more conventional. So, after junior college and upon arrival at the University of Central Missouri, he adopted a traditional wind-up and set position for the first time in his life, posting pretty solid statistics while doing so, despite the fact that he was really learning to throw all over again.

Outman was part of a stellar Central Missouri staff in 2005 as they recorded a NCAA-record 16 shutouts; they fell short in their title bid, finishing second in the 2005 Division II College World Series. Outman was 10-2 and had successfully adjusted his motion to a very conventional one during the season so he would be more draftable. Outman would in fact get drafted, by the Phillies in the 10th round that year.

Josh debuted with the Batavia Muckdogs later that year and was 2-1 with a 2.76 ERA, striking out over a batter per inning. In 2006, he went 14-6 with a 2.95 ERA for the Lakewood BlueClaws, striking out 161 in 155⅓ IP, allowing only 119 hits (and a .213 batting average allowed). He only yielded five home runs in those 155 innings. He was second in the South Atlantic League in strikeouts, behind teammate Matt Maloney, third in wins (two behind Maloney) and fourth in ERA. *Baseball America* ranked him as the league's #20 prospect, one spot behind Maloney. With those two left-handers and right-hander Carlos Carrasco, Lakewood went on to win the league pennant for the first time.

Outman was even better in 2007. Pitching for two different teams that season, he led Phillies farmhands in strikeouts (151) and ERA (2.99). He went 10-4 with a 2.45 ERA for the Clearwater Threshers and 2-3, 4.50 for the Reading Phillies. He led the Florida State League (FSL) in ERA and was named to the league All-Star team; *Baseball America* rated him the #14 prospect in the FSL. Outman joined Team USA for the fall as they won the 2007 Baseball World Cup, their first Baseball World Cup Gold Medal in over three decades.

Outman began 2008 back with Reading, going 5-4 with a save and a 3.20 ERA while pitching primarily out of the bullpen. He fanned 66 in 70⅓ innings. In July of that season he was traded with Adrian Cardenas and Matt Spencer to the A's in exchange for Joe Blanton. He was 2-0 in nine games for the Midland RockHounds and Sacramento River Cats following the trade. He was called up by the A's when rosters expanded on Sep. 1 and made his debut the next day, pitching two scoreless innings in relief in Kansas City.

After a successful first half of the 2009 season starting 12 games for the Athletics. Outman was placed on the disabled list with an injury to his pitching elbow. He underwent Tommy John surgery, ending his season on June 30 and his recovery lasted the 2010 season.

He finally made it back in 2011, pitching a total of 58⅓ innings (starting nine games), with a 3-5 record, 35 strikeouts and 3.70 ERA. In Jan. 2012, Outman, along with pitcher Guillermo Moscoso, was traded to the Rockies for outfielder Seth Smith. The year got off to a "(w)retched" start (see Ephemera) for him and when he finally made it back off the disabled list, he made only 27 appearances in the majors, including seven starts as part of the Rockies' unusual four-man rotation. In 40⅔ innings, he was 1-3 with an ugly ERA of 8.19.

Things went a lot better in 2013, as he made 61 appearances, a personal high, all in relief, with a record of 3-0 and a 4.33 ERA, striking out 53 batters in 54 innings. That December, the Indians acquired him as part of a complete overhaul of their bullpen.

That's when the wheels started to fall off for him. His control, which was never exemplary (3.6 walks per nine innings prior to 2014), started to really become a problem. In 28⅔ innings for Cleveland in 2014, he struck out 26 but also walked 16. That June, the Indians designated Outman for assignment. He was acquired by the Yankees on Aug. 28 and pitched strictly as a LOOGY, logging only 3⅔ innings across nine appearances. The Yankees designated him for assignment on Sep. 22.

From there Outman elected free agency and signed a contract for 2015 with the Braves organization, but after a total of nine appearances across four Atlanta affiliates (GCL Braves, Class A Rome, Class A-Advanced Carolina Mudcats, AA Mississippi), he was released in early August. Over the next three years there was (deep breath) a contract with the New Britain Bees of the Atlantic League of Professional Baseball, a minor league deal with the Pirates, a minor league contract with the Nationals, a deal with Acereros de Monclova of the Mexican Baseball League, a trade to Pericos de Puebla of that same league, a trade to Rieleros de Aguascalientes still in that same league, another stint with New Britain Bees, then his contract was purchased by Pericos de Puebla. (Remember them?)

BEST DAY (BY WPA OR OTHER MEASURE): He spent most of his career as a middle reliever, with no saves in 129 relief appearances. He was the finishing pitcher in only 20 games in the big leagues. Finding a "best day" might be tough if we limit it to his days as a reliever. However, there were a couple of starting assignments that were pretty darn good. The best of these would have to be the game of June 15, 2011, when Outman pitched for the host A's against the Royals. His defense behind him helped him out during the game. Outman yielded a bunt single to Melky Cabrera in the first, and Cabrera was caught stealing. He walked Matt Treanor leading off the third, and he was immediately erased on a double play. Alcides Escobar then reached on another bunt single but Outman got Alex Gordon to ground out to end the inning. With the game still scoreless with one out in the top of the sixth, Escobar got the first hit to the outfield against Outman, a single to center. Then Gordon grounded into a 3-6-3 double play. The A's pushed across a run in the bottom of the sixth and Outman started the seventh up 1-0. He got Cabrera to pop to second, then Eric Hosmer singled to right. Outman attempted to pick Hosmer off, but threw the ball away and the error moved Hosmer to third. Billy Butler walked to put runners on the corners but Outman recovered to get Mike Moustakas to pop out to third to end the threat and his day at the office. The A's plated an insurance run in the bottom of the inning, which was good because reliever Brian Fuentes gave the run back to the Royals in the eighth. Andrew Bailey nailed down the save with a 1-2-3 ninth, and the A's had a 2-1 win. Outman's line: seven innings, four hits, two walks, two strikeouts, no runs allowed. The game took only 2:14 to complete, a duration you rarely see anymore.

THE WONDER OF HIS NAME: What better name could a pitcher have than "Outman?" It's certainly better than Grant Balfour (see page 149) or Bob Walk ... or Ivegotnoclu Weritzgoin (OK, I made that last one up, but you'd totally buy that jersey, right?).

NOT TO BE CONFUSED WITH: Josh Inman (American rower born and raised in Hillsboro, Oregon. In the 2008 Summer Olympics, he won a bronze medal in the men's eight), Rick Outman (Republican politician from the state of Michigan. He serves in the Michigan Senate and currently represents the 33rd Senate district), The National Safeman's Organization (One of North America's largest trade associations of safe and vault technicians. It provides technical training at periodic "Penetration Parties").

FUN ANAGRAMS: "Joshua Stephen Outman" becomes "Oh Jesus! A potent human!"

EPHEMERA: 1) Outman suffered a highly unusual injury which put him on the disabled list at the start of the 2012 season. Suffering from a case of food poisoning during spring training, he vomited so violently that he strained an oblique muscle, putting him out of action. 2) Outman's brother Zach was selected by the Blue Jays in the 28th round of the 2009 Major League Baseball Draft, out of Saint Louis

University. He never made it past Short Season A-ball and was out of baseball by 2011. It is unknown if he used his father's method for pitching while with the Blue Jays. 3) Outman was one of five Central Missouri players drafted in the 2005 MLB Draft, but the only one to reach the majors.

ANGEL PAGAN
I'll take "Antonym-sounding Names" for $400, Alex

BIRTH NAME: Angel Manuel Pagan
PRONUNCIATION OF DIFFICULT PARTS: AYNE-jil pah-GAHN
NICKNAME: Crazy Horse, given by his teammates during his early years as player for Las Lomas Potros in Rio Piedras
HEIGHT/WEIGHT: 6'2" 200 lbs.
BORN: July 2, 1981, in Rio Piedras, Puerto Rico
POSITION: Centerfielder
YEARS ACTIVE IN THE MAJORS: 2006-2016
NAME ETYMOLOGY/DEFINITIONS: "Angel" has English origins from Middle English *angel* meaning "angel" or "messenger" (from Latin angelus), probably applied as a nickname for someone of angelic temperament or appearance or for someone who played the part of an angel in a pageant. As a North American surname, it may also be an Americanized form of a cognate European surname. "Manuel" has Spanish, Portuguese, French, and German origins from the personal name Manuel, a short form of "Emanuel." It also has Catalan and Spanish origins as possibly also a habitational name from Manuel in Valencia province. It is the Americanized form of any of various other European family names derived from Emanuel. "Pagan" has Spanish (Pagán) origins: Castilianized spelling of Catalan "Pagà," from the Late Latin personal name "Paganus," which originally meant "dweller in an outlying village." Alternatively, other Spanish origins may include a topographic name from Catalan *pagà* meaning "heath," from Latin *pagus* meaning "district," "outlying village."

Raised in Río Piedras, Puerto Rico, baseball helped Angel Pagan avoid the dangers of his neighborhood; he recalls, "It was tough to come out of that place a good person. Selling drugs or something. It was a bad neighborhood. A lot of my friends couldn't survive that world. But [my mother] made me strong enough to forget about that path and go to the positive one."

Pagan was a 4th-round pick out of high school by the Mets in the 1999 amateur draft. When the two parties failed to come to terms on a contract, Pagan played in community college at Indian River State College for a year, then signed with the Mets a day before they would have lost rights to him. He debuted with the 2000 Rookie league Kingsport Mets and hit .361/.410/.458 with six steals in seven tries in 19 games. In 2001, Angel hit .298/.365/.351 in 15 outings with the Single-A Capital City Bombers but spent most of the year with the Brooklyn Cyclones, slashing .315/.388/.374 and going 30-for-48 in stolen bases. He tied for the league stolen base lead. Pagan made the New York-Penn League All-Star team in the outfield and *Baseball America* rated him the league's #14 prospect.

In 2002, Pagan had a .279/.325/.338 line for the Bombers and stole 52 bases in 73 tries. With the St. Lucie Mets, he hit .343/.405/.448 in 16 games and stole 10 of 12. He was fifth in the minor leagues in steals overall. The next season, the 21-year-old struggled in St. Lucie, only hitting .249/.307/.313.

The 2004 season brought Angel to AA, where he had a good year for the Binghamton Mets (.288/.346/.406, 29 SB). In 2005, the outfielder was a stop shy of the majors, batting .271/.333/.395 for the AAA Norfolk Tides. He fanned 111 times and was caught 15 times in 42 tries to steal but did leg out 10 triples.

The Cubs purchased Pagan's contract from New York that winter. He played seven games in the minors but spent most of 2006 in the majors for Chicago as a backup corner outfielder and pinch-hitter, batting .247/.306/.394. Pagan hit .250/.310/.414 in 33 games for the Iowa Cubs in 2007 with six steals in seven tries then was called up to Chicago when Félix Pie was sent down. He hit .264/.306/.439 in 71 games for the Cubs.

Angel returned to the Mets that off-season in a deal for Corey Coles and Ryan Meyers. On May 7, 2008, Pagán made a spectacular catch in foul territory, falling into the stands, in Los Angeles against the Dodgers while playing left field. Although he originally stayed in the game, Pagán was later removed with left shoulder pain. The injury eventually caused Pagán to be placed on the disabled list. Pagán was undergoing rehabilitation in the Gulf Coast League and was expected to be on the active roster after the All-Star break. However, he left a rehab start with the Brooklyn Cyclones feeling pain when batting from the right side. Pagán had season-ending surgery on his shoulder at the end of July. He was limited to 31 games by the injury in 2008 and batted .275/.346/.374.

For the Mets in 2009, Angel had his best season up to that point, batting .306/.350/.487 with 11 triples as a back-up who played in 88 games, filling in at center field for Carlos Beltran when he was injured. Despite his part-time role, he was fourth in the National League in three-baggers.

Pagan became a starter in center in 2010. He hit .290/.340/.425 in 151 games that season, with 31 doubles, seven triples and 11 homers, scoring 80 runs and driving in 69, with an OPS+ of 108. All facets of Pagán's game improved in 2010, most notably his ability to make smart decisions while running the bases. For the year, he tied for eighth in the National League in triples, was second in steals and tied for third in outfield assists.

His 2011 season was less productive however, as he fell to .262/.322/.372 in 123 games, with 24 doubles and seven homers and an OPS+ of 94. He was second in the NL in outfield errors (10). Angel was traded to the San Francisco Giants in return for Ramon Ramirez and Andres Torres before the 2012 season.

On Jan. 16, 2012, Pagán signed a one-year deal with the Giants worth $4.85 million to avoid his final year of arbitration. His deal included incentives of an additional $50,000 for 550, 600 and 650 plate appearances. With 659 plate appearances in 2012, Pagán earned a salary of $5 million that year, and had a great year as the Giants' center fielder. He led the NL with 15 triples, to go along with 38 doubles and eight homers, hit .288 in 154 games, scored 95 runs and drove in 56 as the team's lead-off hitter. His speed was still excellent as he entered his age-30 season, as he stole 29 bases after swiping 37 and 32 in his last two seasons as a Met. In addition to triples, he was among the league leaders in runs (tied for seventh), doubles (tenth) and outfield putouts (second).

That year he got to play in the postseason for the first time, going 3-for-20 in the NLDS against the Reds, adding a homer, three runs and four RBIs. He went 8-for-33 with another homer in the NLCS against the Cardinals. He had a key hit in Game 1 of the 2012 World Series against the Tigers: With two outs in the third and the Giants leading 1-0, he hit a soft liner against Justin Verlander that took a lucky bounce off the third base bag and turned into a double; he then scored on Marco Scutaro's single and Pablo Sandoval followed with his second homer of the game, giving the Giants a quick 4-0 lead on their way to an 8-3 win.

After that season, he re-signed with the Giants for four years and $40 million. Pagán was the leadoff hitter and center fielder for the Puerto Rican national team that surprisingly finished second in the 2013 World Baseball Classic. He finished second in the Classic in hits and made the Classic All-Star team. In late May of 2013, Pagan injured his hamstring, eventually going on the disabled list.

He then re-injured the hamstring while playing a rehabilitation game with the Class-A Stockton Ports on June 20, and this time had to undergo surgery, putting the remainder of his season in doubt. However, he did come back in the last days of August and played regularly in September, finishing at .282 with five homers and 30 RBIs in 71 games.

2014 was another injury-plagued season for Pagan as he was again limited to fewer than 100 games due to a bad back which required late-season surgery to repair a bulging disk. As a result, he played his last game on Sep. 19 and was not available for the home stretch with the Giants battling for a postseason slot. In 96 games, he hit an even .300 with three homers and 27 RBIs and was successful in 16 of 22 stolen base attempts. It was his third straight year with an OPS+ of 110 or better. The Giants won another World Series title, but he was unavailable to play.

In 2015, he was healthy again and regained his starting job in centerfield, although his hitting was well down from his career norms. On Aug. 11, he was placed on the disabled list with patella tendinitis in his right knee, the result of his all-out style of play and not due to any particular incident. He finished the year at .262 in 133 games, with 55 runs, three homers and 37 RBIs.

He returned for a final season in 2016. After three injury-riddled seasons and advanced metrics that suggested worsening defense, the Giants moved Pagán to left field to make way for Denard Span. Pagán had not played left field since 2010, but accepted the transition and bounced back to hit .277 with 12 homers and 55 RBIs in 129 games. His OPS+ was 102, after having fallen all the way to 75 the previous year. The Giants made it back to the postseason, and Pagan went 1-for-4 in the Wild Card Game against the Mets, and 2-for-6 in their loss to the Cubs in the Division Series. These were his final appearances as a pro, as he became a free agent after the season and retired when no team expressed interest in bringing him back on a contract he would accept.

BEST DAY (BY WPA OR OTHER MEASURE): Pagan had many days that were very, very good and would have merited discussion here. We're going to go with a day in which he didn't pile up a bunch of "counting stats" but came through in the clutch with one of the most exciting plays in baseball. On May 25, 2013, the Giants trailed the Rockies 5-4 in the bottom of the tenth at what was then known as AT&T Park in San Francisco. If you've ever been to that particular stadium, you know that there is a huge expanse in right-center field where extra-base hits are plentiful. The natives call it Triples Alley, for good reason. It takes a skilled and speedy center fielder and right fielder to cover the ground and navigate the juts of the outfield wall out there. Well, with one out and Brandon Crawford on second carrying the tying run, Pagan stepped to the plate against Rockies closer Rafael Betancourt. Betancourt was a perfect 10-for-10 in save opportunities to that point in the season. On an 0-1 pitch, Pagan connected on a long drive to Triples Alley. The ball caromed hard off the bottom lower fence portion of the wall in right-center, bouncing away from right fielder Michael Cuddyer and center fielder Dexter Fowler. By the time Fowler retrieved the ball and got it back into the relay man, Pagan had rounded the bases (on what would turn out to be a bad hamstring that would put him on the disabled list right after the game). He became the first player in nine years to end a game with an inside-the-park walk-off homer, the first in 24 years to do so when his team was trailing, and the first in Giants history to do so.

THE WONDER OF HIS NAME: He was angelic when healthy and a devil when he wasn't, wasn't he? There aren't too many other people out there with given names and surnames that could be considered antonyms of each other.

NOT TO BE CONFUSED WITH: David Pagan (Former MLB pitcher. He played all or part of five seasons from 1973 until 1977 and was a member of the Seattle Mariners' 1977 inaugural season roster), Angel Faith (Known by the stage name Angel. Former American pop/R&B singer and songwriter. Before pursuing a solo career, she was originally from the American-British girl group No Secrets), *Heaven and Hell* (Ninth studio album by English rock band Black Sabbath and the first to feature vocalist Ronnie James Dio, who replaced original vocalist Ozzy Osbourne in 1979).

FUN ANAGRAMS: "Angel Manuel Pagan" anagrams to "Engage an anal lump."

EPHEMERA: 1) His mother, Gloria, was a fan of baseball and played in a men's fast-pitch softball league. 2) In May of 2019, Pagan was reportedly one of three people rescued off the coast of Puerto Rico after a boat capsized in a 15-foot wave. 2) He was the first person in major league history to hit his first two career home runs on his birthday. 3) On May 19 of 2010, he hit an inside-the-park homer and started a triple play in the same game. It had been 55 years since anyone had accomplished both feats in the same contest. Pagán started the triple play from center field in the fifth inning against the Washington Nationals on a ball hit by Cristian Guzmán. After catching the flare in short center, his momentum carried him right into the infield and he threw the ball in. Since the baserunners had already each advanced a base, if Pagan opted to run the ball in himself, he could have possibly recorded an unassisted triple play and would have been the first outfielder to ever do so. 4) He holds the Giants franchise record for a home hitting streak at 28 games. He also holds the San Francisco Giants team record for most triples in a season, with 15 in 2012. 5) He and his wife, Windy, have two daughters: Briana and Suil Angelina.

LIP PIKE
One of baseball's first "professional" players
(and its first Jewish pro player)

BIRTH NAME: Lipman Emanuel Pike
PRONUNCIATION OF DIFFICULT PARTS: None

LIPMAN PIKE,

NICKNAME: None
HEIGHT/WEIGHT: 5'8" 158 lbs.
BORN: May 25, 1845, in New York, New York
DIED: Oct. 10, 1893, in Brooklyn, New York
POSITIONS: Centerfielder, Second Baseman, Shortstop
YEARS ACTIVE IN THE MAJORS: 1871-1878, 1881, 1887
NAME ETYMOLOGY/DEFINITIONS: "Lipman" has Dutch origins, patronymic from a short form of the personal name "Philip." There are also Jewish (Ashkenazic) origins, from the Yiddish personal name "Lipman," derived from Middle High German words *liep* meaning "dear" or "beloved" and *man* "man." Its possibly a respelling of German "Lippmann." "Emanuel" is from the Hebrew personal name "Imanuel" meaning "God is with us." "Pike" has many possible origins. It has English roots, as the topographic name for someone who lived by a hill with a sharp point, from Old English *pic* meaning "point" or "hill," which was a relatively common place name element. Also, it could be a metonymic occupational name for a pike fisherman or nickname for a predatory individual, from Middle English *pike*, or a metonymic occupational name for a user of a pointed tool for breaking up the earth, from Middle English *pike*.

Lip Pike was the first great Jewish professional baseball player, playing from 1866 to 1881. No reliable statistical records exist for his career through 1870, but from 1871 through 1881 Pike hit .322 with a slugging average of .468. Pike was among the premier sluggers of his time, despite his small stature.

From a book titled *The Biographical History of Baseball* is the assertion that Pike was one of the first players for hire: "While others had certainly been paid before 1866, Pike, along with two teammates on the ostensibly amateur Philadelphia Athletics, was ordered to appear before the judiciary committee of the governing National Association of Base Ball Players to answer charges that he had accepted $20 for his services ... The incident exposed for the first time the widespread practice of paying supposedly amateur players." This was, perhaps, the first step in legitimizing the practice of play for pay.

Meanwhile, Pike had a fine 1866 season for the 23-2 Philadelphia Athletic club, playing the outfield as well as second and third base. In 1867, Pike split his time between the Irvingtons of New Jersey (playing third base) and the Mutuals of New York (in the outfield, first, second, and third base). He appeared exclusively for the New York Mutuals in 1868, hitting a gaudy .497, with a .661 slugging average for a Mutuals team that went 31-10. Pike returned to his native Brooklyn in 1869 and suited up for one of the nation's leading teams, the Brooklyn Atlantics. For the first time the National Association of Base Ball Players recognized the professional class of player and team. The Atlantics went 40-6-2 that year (ties were common in those days, with darkness cutting short some knotted-up games). Pike's first season as a full-time player yielded a .610 batting average with a slugging average of .883.[26] Pike stayed with the Atlantics as their second baseman through the 1870 season, in which the team went 41-17.

When the first system of government for professional baseball teams was organized for the 1871 season, The National Association of Professional Base Ball Players, Pike joined the Troy Haymakers of New York as their de facto player-manager. Pike's first year in the newly formed league was outstanding. Playing outfield, first base and second base (mind you, he threw left-handed), he tied for the league lead in home runs (with four), placed second in slugging average (.654), third in total bases, fourth in RBI, and sixth in batting average (.377).

Pike joined the Baltimore team for the 1872 season. The team owners had recruited outstanding players during the off-season, and the assembled squad finished in second place in the 11-team league. Overall, Pike led the league in home runs (with seven), and RBIs, finishing second in total bases, while hitting a respectable .298.

Continuing with Baltimore in 1873, Pike hit a fine .316 while again leading the league in home runs with four. Prior to the 1874 season, Pike, released from his

---

[26] In considering these stats, it should be noted that in 1869 the batter called for his pitch, telling the pitcher his preference for either a high or low ball, and foul balls did not count as strikes. In addition, the pitcher tossed the ball up to the batter in an underhand motion without snapping his wrist. Basically, the batter did not have to contend with either fastballs or curve balls.

contract with the bankrupt Baltimore organization, signed on with the Hartford Blue Stockings. He enjoyed another excellent season, finishing third in hitting at .355, second in on-base percentage and first in slugging (.504).

For the 1875 season, Pike signed on with the St. Louis club. In 1876, the National League replaced the National Association as the premier organization for professional teams. Virtually all the old Association teams simply registered with the new league. Pike remained with the new St. Louis NL squad and batted a solid .323, finished third in slugging (.472), and fifth in total bases.

Prior to the 1877 season, Pike changed teams yet again, this time signing on with the lackluster Cincinnati Reds. Despite leading his league in home runs again, hitting .298, and playing an excellent center field, Cincinnati finished last in the league for the second consecutive year.

Pike re-signed with Cincinnati for the 1878 season then moved back down to the minor leagues in 1879 and played for teams in Springfield and Albany. As player-manager and center fielder for the Springfield club, he appeared in a total of 53 games and hit .356.

Beginning the 1880 season with Albany, Pike played for the Albany team until it disbanded in July. He opened the 1881 season playing second base for his old Atlantic team in a minor league and working in the haberdashery business. In late August he was called up by the National League Worcester Ruby Legs. He joined Worcester on Aug. 27, played center field and batted second, and in six games went 3-for-25.

Pike's miserable play for the Worcester club led to controversy. On Sep. 3, he made three errors in the ninth inning to give Boston two runs and a 3-2 victory over Worcester. Worcester immediately accused Pike of throwing the game and suspended him. On Sep. 29, at a National League meeting, the league adopted a blacklist of players who were barred from playing for or against any NL team until they are removed from the list by the unanimous vote of the league clubs. Pike was one of the nine men on the list.

After the expiration of his year's ban, Pike continued an interest in the game, playing center field for an amateur club on Long Island. Finally, in July 1887, the now 42-year-old Pike made one final attempt to play at the major league level. He played center field and batted sixth for the New York Metropolitans, an American Association team. He was supposed to pitch but switched to the outfield at the last moment. The newspapers reported that his fielding was good, but the bat was quite weak.

BEST DAY (BY WPA OR OTHER MEASURE): In 1878, after playing 31 games and hitting .324 in the lead-off position, Lip Pike was released by the Cincinnati team to make room for Louis "Buttercup" Dickerson. Pike was signed by the Providence team and debuted with them on July 31. He got some measure of revenge on his old team that very first game, as he went 4-for-5 with three runs batted in, as Providence beat Cincinnati 9-3.

THE WONDER OF HIS NAME: The short abrupt pronunciation of "Lip Pike" is pleasing to the ear, and the first name hearkens back generations.

NOT TO BE CONFUSED WITH: Leo "The Lip" Durocher (Former MLB player, manager and coach. Upon his retirement, he ranked fifth all-time among managers with 2,009 career victories), Lipman "Lipa" Bers (American mathematician born in Riga), Christopher Pike (Captain in the *Star Trek* science fiction franchise), Liz Pike (Republican in the Washington House of Representatives).

FUN ANAGRAMS: "Lipman Emanuel Pike" turns into "I'm a plump, keen alien."

EPHEMERA: 1) According to *The Big Book of Jewish Baseball*, "The Pike family were Jews of Dutch origin. Lip had an older brother, Boaz, two younger brothers, Israel and Jacob, and a sister, Julia. The Pike family moved to Brooklyn when Lipman was very young. Boaz was the first of the Pike brothers to play baseball. Just one week after his bar mitzvah, Lip appeared in his first recorded game, along with Boaz. This was an amateur game." 2) On Aug. 16, 1873, at Baltimore's Newington Park racetrack, he raced a fast trotting horse named Clarence in a 100-yard sprint and won by four yards with a time of ten seconds flat, earning $250. 3) The publisher of Philadelphia's prestigious *Sporting Life*, Francis Richter, constructed hypothetical All-Star teams in 1911. Richter selected Pike as one of his three outfielders for the 1870-1880 time period. 4) His baseball career essentially over at the end of the 1881 season, Pike became a haberdasher in Brooklyn. 5) Pike died of heart disease in 1893. His funeral was a notable event, attended by much of the Jewish and baseball communities of Brooklyn. 6) *The Sporting News* published a series of tributes to Pike, indicating his stature as one of the greats of his time. 7) The Base Ball Writers of America held the inaugural election for the Baseball Hall of Fame in Cooperstown in 1936. Even though Pike had been dead for more than 43 years and his playing career had ended years before most, if not all, of the electors were born, he still received one vote. 8) *The Big Book of Jewish Baseball* also noted that Pike was elected to the Jewish Sports Hall of Fame in Netanya, Israel, in 1985. 9) Pike was inducted into the New York State Baseball Hall of Fame, Class of 2016. 10) As of 2018, Pike was one of seven Jewish managers in MLB history. The others have been Gabe Kapler, Bob Melvin, Brad Ausmus, Jeff Newman, Norm Sherry, and Lou Boudreau.

BOOTS POFFENBERGER
As colorful in person as was his name

BIRTH NAME: Cletus Elwood Poffenberger
PRONUNCIATION OF DIFFICULT PARTS: None
NICKNAME: Boots
HEIGHT/WEIGHT: 5'10" 178 lbs.
BORN: July 1, 1915, in Williamsport, Maryland
DIED: Sep. 1, 1999, in Williamsport, Maryland

POSITION: Pitcher
YEARS ACTIVE IN THE MAJORS: 1937-1939
NAME ETYMOLOGY/DEFINITIONS: "Cletus" is the shortened form of "Anacletus." The name "Cletus" in Ancient Greek means "one who has been called," and "Anacletus" means "one who has been called back." "Elwood" is a habitational name from a place in Gloucestershire, which is probably named from Old English *ellern* ("elder tree") and *wudu* ("wood"). "Poffenberger" is an Americanized form of German "Pfaffenberger," a habitational name for someone from any of several places in southern Germany called Pfaffenberg. Cletus "Boots" Poffenberger was reportedly named after his grandfather, Cletus Frame Zimmerman.

Boots Poffenberger was the proverbial "million-dollar arm and 10-cent head." As an example, he allegedly missed one game because he had been out late in a Chicago nightclub, having appointed himself conductor of the house orchestra.

He made his major league debut in June of 1937 with the Tigers. Upon his arrival he declared to his teammates, "Just call me 'Boots' and on time for meals. I'm here to stay. I am just a young punk from a small town and I don't know what the hell it is all about, but boy I can blow that apple in there and when I get smartened up a bit, I'll give those batters plenty to worry about."

Regardless of what the Tiger veterans might have thought of the brash rookie, they must have been impressed when, in his first major league appearance, Boots defeated future Hall of Famer Lefty Grove. The Detroit press loved Boots' boyish nature, and almost immediately the scribes began calling him "The Baron," because "Cletus Elwood Poffenberger" sounded like a royal moniker.

Bud Shaver, a writer with the *Detroit Times*, wrote a column that listed all of Boots' peculiar habits, which included "talks in his sleep, carries good luck charms all over his person, won't go near telephones, sleeps through team meetings, talks with bleacher fans and goes on buying sprees."

At one point Wheaties paid Boots for a live promo. The Wheaties man paid him the night before and when he came down the next morning, he was to say he was going to have Wheaties for breakfast. But when they asked him what he was going to have for breakfast he told them "A beer and a steak!"

After compiling a 10-5 record in 1937, his eccentricities and drinking got the best of Boots. By the end of May in 1938, manager Mickey Cochrane imposed a curfew primarily because of him, and Boots was the first to break it. Finally, Boots was sent down to Toledo on Aug. 2, where he went 8-3 and stayed out of trouble under manager Fred Haney. Recalled in September, Boots finished the 1938 season with a 6-7 mark.

He reported late and overweight to spring training in 1939. The Tigers had enough, and one day after farming out Boots to Toledo they sold him to the Brooklyn Dodgers. The Dodgers were managed by Leo Durocher, who proclaimed that he could handle the notorious Poffenberger.

However, Boots got into trouble on Brooklyn's very first road trip of the season, a three-game set in Philadelphia over the weekend of Apr. 21-23. The Dodgers were staying at the Bellevue-Stratford Hotel. According to Durocher, Boots arrived back at the hotel 30 minutes past the midnight curfew on Friday night, walking right past Brooklyn's skipper who was seated in the lobby. When Boots jumped the team in Cincinnati on May 23 after totaling only five innings of work on the season, the Dodgers suspended him for one month, then sent him out to their top farm club in Montreal. Boots set out for Montreal, never made it there, announced his retirement, and was ultimately placed on Commissioner Landis's list of banned players at Brooklyn's request.

That was the end of his major league career. He toiled in the minors and semi-pro leagues from 1940-1942, then went off to serve overseas. After the war ended, he pitched (ineffectively) a few more years in the semi-pros, ending his ballplaying days in 1948.

BEST DAY (BY WPA OR OTHER MEASURE): On May 29, 1938, Poffenberger hurled a complete-game four-hitter versus the White Sox. Though he walked five and struck out only one, he yielded only four singles and an unearned run in a 2-1 win.

THE WONDER OF HIS NAME: Not too many fellows named Cletus born in the state of Maryland. Heck, not too many fellows named Cletus, period. Poffenberger is just a cool name to say. It does sound a bit "hoity-toity" though.

NOT TO BE CONFUSED WITH: H.R. Pufnstuf (Children's television series produced by Sid and Marty Krofft as a live-action, life-sized-puppet program, originally shown in 1969), Puss in Boots (European literary fairy tale about a cat who uses trickery and deceit to gain power, wealth, and the hand of a princess in marriage for his penniless and low-born master), Boots Randolph (American musician best known for his 1963 saxophone hit *Yakety Sax*).

FUN ANAGRAMS: "Cletus Elwood Poffenberger" becomes (appropriately) ... "Blow off genteel procedures."

EPHEMERA: 1) At one point during his tenure with Detroit, the Tigers hired a detective to follow him. 2) In 1941 he was suspended for 90 days for throwing a ball at an umpire. During a game in Nashville, Poffenberger reportedly consumed "a few shots of gin" before taking the mound. He became angry at the umpire's calls and threw the ball at the umpire, resulting in the suspension. 3) He joined the Marines and served in the South Pacific during WWII. His photograph was used on Marine recruiting posters. However, he never completed boot camp, being assigned almost immediately to the Parris Island baseball team, one of the top service teams in the country. Reassigned to the Fleet Marine Force team in Hawaii in early 1945, Boots finished out the war pitching in paradise. 4) After his playing days were over, he worked sporadically at the Fairchild Aircraft plant in Hagerstown. He then went to work in the new Mack Truck plant in Hagerstown in 1960 as a heat treater. 5) He lived to the age of 84, succumbing to prostate cancer. 6) Perhaps as a nod to Boots, in 2003, actor Christopher Lloyd portrayed a character named Dr. Cletus Poffenberger on the television series *Tremors*.

ARQUIMEDEZ POZO
A "Quad-A" bat with shaky defense to boot

BIRTH NAME: Arquimedez Pozo
PRONUNCIATION OF DIFFICULT PARTS: None
NICKNAME: None
HEIGHT/WEIGHT: 5'10" 160 lbs.
BORN: Aug. 24, 1973, in Santo Domingo, Dominican Republic
POSITIONS: Third Baseman, Second Baseman
YEARS ACTIVE IN THE MAJORS: 1995-1997
NAME ETYMOLOGY/DEFINITIONS: "Arquimedez" is a Spanish variant of "Archimedes," the Greek mathematician, physicist, engineer, inventor, and astronomer. "Archimedes" is regarded as one of the leading scientists in classical antiquity. "Pozo" is the Spanish word for "(water) well."

Arquimedez Pozo was signed as an undrafted free agent in 1990 by the Mariners, and moved up the minors thanks to a more-than-competent bat. He slashed .322/.407/.544 for the Bellingham Mariners in the Northwest League (Short season A-Ball) as an 18-year-old in 1992.

In 1993, he put together a .342/.405/.526 line for the Riverside Pilots in the California League (Advanced A-Ball). 1994 saw him in AA at Jacksonville, and he continued to hit well (.289/.341/.456 in 119 games). He made it to AAA in 1995, and batted .300/.340/.436 for the Tacoma Rainiers in the PCL before he was brought up. He made his major league debut on Sep. 12, 1995, pinch-hitting for Joey Cora and popping out to second base.

After starting the 1996 season back with the Rainiers, he was traded in July to the Red Sox for Jeff Manto. At the time of the trade, Red Sox general manager Dan Duquette stated, in separate interviews: 1) "We'll try him as a (backup) second baseman. He has decent hands and he can hit." 2) "Arquimedez is a young infielder who has shown steady and significant improvement during the course of his career. He has excellent ability in the field, drives the ball extremely well and overall displays good offensive potential."

In the harsh reality of the majors however, Pozo's defense then sprung a leak. He made four errors in 66 chances over 20 games for the Red Sox in 1996. At the same time, his bat revealed itself to be more "Quad-A" than major league, as he slashed a woeful .172/.210/.310 in 58 at-bats with ten strikeouts and only two walks.

He spent most of 1997 in Pawtucket with the Red Sox AAA squad, hitting a robust .284/.358/.512 with 22 homers in 377 at-bats. But the parent club only got him into four games in the majors that season, where he went 4-for-15 with no walks and five strikeouts. He also made another error amidst his 19 chances.

After spending the entire 1998 season with the Pawtucket Red Sox (batting .305/.352/.494), he signed with the Yokohama BayStars of the Japanese Central League for 1999. In 2000, he played for the KBO's Haitai Tigers and the Tigres del México in the Mexican League, and that was the end of his playing career.

BEST DAY (BY WPA OR OTHER MEASURE): On July 28, 1996, in only his third game with the Red Sox, he hit a grand slam off Twins relief pitcher "Everyday Eddie" Guardado. It was the only home run of Pozo's career. (The Red Sox still lost that game, 9-8).

THE WONDER OF HIS NAME: It's another "double unique" name, and how could one not love a name like his, especially given his birthplace and how he was named after a famous Greek mathematician.

NOT TO BE CONFUSED WITH: Arquimedes Caminero (Professional baseball pitcher in the New York Mets organization as of March 2019), Pozzo (a character from Samuel Beckett's play *Waiting for Godot*. His name is Italian for "well" (as in "oil well").

FUN ANAGRAMS: "Arquimedez Pozo" turns into "Queer pizza mood."

EPHEMERA: 1) In 1994, *Baseball America*'s top ten Mariners prospects listed Pozo at number five, behind Alex Rodriguez, Mac Suzuki, Marc Newfield and Derek Lowe. 2) At the time of his homerun, Pozo became only the seventh Red Sox player to have his first major league homer be a grand slam, joining John Valentin (1992), Chuck Schilling (1961), Faye Throneberry (1952), Ellis Kinder (1950), Billy Goodman (1948) and Jim Tabor (1938). 3) He played for the Dominican national team that won Bronze in the 1990 Central American and Caribbean Games. 4) In 2016, he was coaching a youth baseball team back home in the Dominican Republic.

DORSEY RIDDLEMOSER
One very bad "cup of coffee"

BIRTH NAME: Dorsey Lee Riddlemoser
PRONUNCIATION OF DIFFICULT PARTS: None
NICKNAME: None
HEIGHT/WEIGHT: NA
BORN: Mar. 25, 1875, in Frederick, Maryland
DIED: May 11, 1954, in Frederick, Maryland
POSITION: Pitcher
YEARS ACTIVE IN THE MAJORS: 1899
NAME ETYMOLOGY/DEFINITIONS: "Dorsey" is more often a surname. As a surname, it has Norman origins as a habitational name, with the preposition *de*, from

Orsay in Seine-et-Orne, France, recorded in the 13th century as "Orceiacum," from the Latin personal name "Orcius" and the locative suffix *-acum*. "Lee" is derived from the English surname Lee (which is ultimately from a placename derived from Old English *leah* meaning "clearing" or "meadow"). Origin information on "Riddlemoser" is hard to come by, but a perusal of an Ancestry.com's message board for "Riddlemoser" revealed this possibility: "The Riddlemosers came from Bavaria, near the Austrian border. I got this info from a Bavarian woman who stated that the names are very specific to where they come from. In this case the family name is the merging of two family names, Riddle and Moser (Moser is Austrian). A common practice back in those times was to join names when a marriage occurred."

D orsey Riddlemoser pitched for the wonderfully-named Williamsport Demorest Bicycle Boys of the Central Pennsylvania League in 1897 and moved to York, Pennsylvania in 1898. Acquired by the National League's Washington Senators the following summer, he was blasted in his introduction to the majors. Relieving Dan McFarlan in the fifth inning of a game on Aug. 22, Riddlemoser pitched two innings, faced 15 batters, yielded seven hits and walked two more, and allowed four runs in what would turn out to be a 15-5 loss to Baltimore. He wouldn't set foot on a major league diamond again.

In 1900 minor league player-manager John Ray recruited Riddlemoser and several other players for the Newport News team on the supposition that he would manage them that season in the Virginia League. After stocking the team, Ray was then double-crossed by Newport News. His experience led him to lament in *The Sporting News* how a manager like himself who was not a great player would often hire a player who would usurp his job, as most clubs in the lower minor leagues didn't have the luxury in Ray's era of having a skipper who was a bench manager only. Riddlemoser, meanwhile, stiffed Newport News and left pro ball after stints with Allentown of the Class D Pennsylvania League in 1901 and Meriden of the Class D Connecticut League in 1903.

BEST DAY (BY WPA OR OTHER MEASURE): Best day? It was his only day in the majors!

THE WONDER OF HIS NAME: He might have gotten picked on as a kid for his name, but we celebrate it here. It may sound stuffy and pretentious, but in a certain light, it's pretty cool. Then you have his one-game major league career, and you have a memorable player.

NOT TO BE CONFUSED WITH: Michael Riddlemoser (In 1820, he was the first settler in a community originally named Moserburg, and he laid out the street plan in 1829. The community was later renamed New Baltimore, after Riddlemoser's hometown), Tommy Dorsey (American jazz trombonist, composer, conductor and bandleader of the big band era), Nelson Riddle (American arranger, composer, bandleader and orchestrator whose career stretched from the late 1940s to the mid-1980s).

FUN ANAGRAMS: Dorsey Lee Riddlemoser anagrams to "Rosier yodeler meddles."
EPHEMERA: 1) Riddlemoser gave up those four earned runs in two innings in his only game for the Senators in 1899. Later that same year, "Shady" Bill Leith also pitched in only one game for the same team (and similarly, that would be his only game in the majors), also giving up four earned runs in two innings. Not a single pitcher on the Senators had a winning record that season, but Riddlemoser and Leith ended up with the highest ERAs. 2) After baseball, he returned to Frederick and worked as a janitor at the local city hall. 3) A song titled *I am Happy with the Man I Love* was written by Riddlemoser in 1907. 4) Riddlemoser married a woman named Ruth Talmadge Biggs and they had two children, a son and a daughter. The son, also named Dorsey, was killed at the age of 19 while serving his country in the military during WWII. 5) One other major league player had the first name Dorsey and the middle name Lee. That player was Dorsey Lee Carroll, known as Dixie Carroll.

OSSEE SCHRECONGOST
Apparently no one could spell or pronounce his name

BIRTH NAME: Freeman Osee Schrecongost[27]
PRONUNCIATION OF DIFFICULT PARTS: Oh-see
NICKNAME: "Schreck" (as a shorthand for his last name) or "Rocking Horse" (which began when Williamsport teammate Humphries had called him that, in mispronouncing his name)
HEIGHT/WEIGHT: 5'10" 180 lbs.
BORN: Apr. 11, 1875, in New Bethlehem, Pennsylvania
DIED: July 9, 1914, in Philadelphia, Pennsylvania
POSITIONS: Catcher, first baseman
YEARS ACTIVE IN THE MAJORS: 1897-1899, 1901-1908
NAME ETYMOLOGY/DEFINITIONS: "Osee" is a form of "Hoshea" or "Hosea," meaning "salvation," with Hebrew origins. "Freeman" is primarily a surname, as a translation of German "Freimann" or "Freiman." "Freiman" is made up of the German *frei* meaning "free" and *mann* meaning "man," as the status name in

---

[27] There have been numerous spellings of his name, both first and last, and the spellings differ on some records of the day. His baptismal records list Osie Freeman Schreckengost. On his gravestone, the marker – not infallible itself – presents his name as Osee F. Schrecongost. An SABR member interviewed Ossee's grandson Charles Dundas and family genealogist Christine Crawford-Oppenheimer and concluded that the correct rendition of his name is F. Osee Schrecongost, that his father's name was spelled Naaman and that mother Sarah was born Sarah Caroline Protzman.

the feudal system for a free man as opposed to a bondman or serf. "Schrecongost" is a variant spelling of German "Schreckengost," which itself is an altered form of German "Schreckengast," a nickname from Middle High German *schreck* (imperative of *schrecken* "to frighten") and *den gast* meaning "the guest," presumably a nickname for an unfriendly innkeeper.

Osee Schrecongost was a standout with the town teams of 1893-1894. A newspaper at the time spelled his name Ossee Schreckengost. In 1895 Osee moved to Williamsport to play semipro ball for a team sponsored by the Domestic Sewing Machine Company. He wound up playing for the superbly-named Williamsport Demorest Bicycle Boys. The *Philadelphia Inquirer* carried him in box scores as "Schrecongost," though more often in the lineups as "Schr'st" and "Sch'st," and the like.

Schrecongost had an active year in 1897 and it's a little difficult to track just where he played and when, but the name variations continued. Late in the season the *Boston Herald* presented him as "Sch't" in the box score. That was the day Schrecongost first played in the major leagues, debuting with the National League's Louisville Colonels on Sep. 8, 1897. Pitcher Rube Waddell made his big-league debut in the same game, with Baltimore beating Louisville, 5–1. Around that time a Chicago paper had sent a telegram to Louisville's president Harvey Pulliam asking, "Is that catcher's name on the level?"

That first meeting between Schrecongost and Waddell ultimately led to a lifelong relationship. As noted in the newspapers, neither of them knew of the other before that day, and hardly anyone else had known who they were either. As the *Washington Evening Star* recounted: "'Who will be in the points today,' was asked of Manager Clarke before the game by the *Sun* reporter. 'This man will pitch,' he replied, pointing to the name 'Weddel' in the score card, and that tall fellow over there will catch. I don't know what his name is.' But he called to Schrecongost and got that young man to spell his name out for the newspaper man, regardless of how long it delayed the game. "When asked if 'Weddel' was the correct name, Manager Clarke replied, 'Don't know; you will have to ask him.'"

Schreck ended up playing for three teams in 1898. He began the season with Cedar Rapids (Iowa) in the Western Association, but that team disbanded on June 9 and the whole league followed suit on the 26th. Between the two June dates, Schrecongost caught for the team in Ottumwa, Iowa. After the league folded, he played the rest of the time with the last place but also outstandingly named Youngstown Puddlers in the Inter-State League.

Stanley Robison, owner of the National League's Cleveland Spiders, came to look over both he and pitcher Charlie Knepper. Ossee was sold to the Spiders for $300 in a deal announced on Sep. 27, getting into ten games for them and hitting .314 with ten RBI. In 1899, Schreck shuttled back and forth from Cleveland to St. Louis during the year. Early on (Mar. 28) the entire Cleveland ballclub was transferred to

St. Louis after the league expelled the earlier St. Louis owners and installed a new group in its place. Schrecongost was one of 16 Spiders – including manager Patsy Tebeau – so assigned.[28]

It turned out that brothers Frank DeHaas Robison and Stanley Robison each owned shares in both ballclubs in 1899. Frank had founded the Cleveland club, and he and Stanley were part of a group that purchased the bankrupt St. Louis Browns, and then moved most of the better players to St. Louis, loading up the team they dubbed the Perfectos but leaving Cleveland with a team that finished with a record of 20-134 (the worst in major league history).

The Cleveland club was sometimes given the nickname the Exiles in the national press. Schreck even beat St. Louis, winning one of those 20 games for the Exiles, with three hits – including a triple – in a 3–1 win over the Perfectos on June 25 in St. Louis. But then, on July 31, Osee was "re-acquired" by St. Louis. Schrecongost played the rest of the 1899 season for St. Louis and is listed as hitting .313 in his time with Cleveland and .286 for St. Louis, with two homers. He played a mixture of first base and catcher.

In 1900 Schrecongost was farmed out by St. Louis to the Buffalo Bisons (considered a minor league team), for whom he played in 125 games, batting .282, catching more than 75 percent of the games and playing first base the rest of the time.

Schreck joined that new American League in 1901, signing on early with the Boston Americans but destined from the start to be backup catcher behind Lou Criger. He appeared in 86 games – ten more than Criger – and hit .304. Criger was surer on defense, however, and – no small consideration – was Cy Young's favorite catcher.

Before the 1902 season, Boston traded Schreck to the American League's Cleveland franchise, who that year were called the "Bronchos." Though he was hitting .338 for Cleveland after 18 games in 1902, playing first base exclusively, Schreck was released in May.

Nine days later he signed as a free agent with Connie Mack's Philadelphia Athletics and that year appeared in 79 games for them (71 as catcher), batting .324. (Newspapers had generally dropped "Schrecongost" a year or two earlier and adopted "Schreck" or a mangled "Schreckengost" in their stories. Baseball researchers need to hunt for all three names.)

---

[28] In 1899, Chris Von der Ahe, the owner of the NL St. Louis Browns lost his club to a sheriff's sale. Frank Robison became the new owner. In a clever business deal, the club ownership passed through several hands before Robison finally landed it for $40,000. Then, Robison and one of the club's creditors formed a new corporation, the American Baseball and Athletic Exhibition Company. By creating the new entity, Robison avoided responsibility for the old club's outstanding debts. As the new owner and president of the St. Louis club, Robison placed his brother Stanley in charge of the Cleveland franchise. Fed up with poor attendance at the Spiders games despite their fine performance, Robison brought most of the Cleveland players to St. Louis, and saddled the Spiders with the dismal group of former Browns. Wanting to launch a new era of baseball in the Mound City, as St. Louis was called, he changed the color of the team's stockings from brown to cardinal red and called the club the Perfectos.

A few weeks after he started with Philadelphia, Schreck was reunited with Rube Waddell, who joined the Athletics in June. The two became roommates as well as batterymates. Philadelphia won the 1902 pennant and Waddell went 24-7, with a 2.05 ERA, both being the best marks on the club – all those victories coming in two-thirds of a season.

In 1903, the Athletics finished second, 14½ games behind Boston. Schreck fell off sharply in his batting, dropping from .324 to .255. He played in 13 more games than in 1902 but drove in only 30 runs and scored a mere 42 (down from 43 and 45 respectively).

In 1904, he played in 95 games and saw his production drop even further: hitting just .186, driving in 21 and scoring 23. He improved his defensive work behind home plate, however, climbing in fielding percentage from .960 to .975 and .979.

Schreck had an unusual style of catching one-handed, and somehow managed to deal quite well with Waddell's unpredictable pitches. (The eccentric pitcher didn't always throw the ball as signaled.) Schreck was also noted for his success in throwing out would-be basestealers.

Both Waddell and Schreck were eccentric, though, and the most widely circulated story regarding them as roommates (sharing a double bed, as baseball roommates often did in those days) is that Waddell refused to sign an Athletics contract one year unless manager Mack agreed to prohibit Schreck from eating animal crackers in bed. Another version had Schreck voicing that complaint about the Rube.

There's another tale that had Schreck getting a very tough steak at a hotel restaurant in Cleveland. He sent it back, and the same steak came back again, presented differently. After the third visit of the steak proved equally difficult to cut, he asked the waiter, "Say, can you get me a hammer and some nails?" He then took the steak, and the hammer and nails, into the hotel lobby and nailed the steak to the wall.

In 1905, Schreck missed most of spring training, due to the death of his father and then, not long after he returned to camp, his sister, Annie, died and he went back home once more. That season, Schreck hit .271, drove in 45 runs, improved his fielding percentage to .984 in 123 games, helped roommate Waddell post a 27-10 record with an ERA of 1.48 (leading the league in wins and ERA), and helped boost the Athletics from 1904's fifth place to the pennant. Schreck caught the first three games of the 1905 World Series against the New York Giants, hitting .222. (The Giants won in five games.)

Waddell had missed the last month of the season and the Series, with alcohol playing a factor in things falling apart. Connie Mack was reported to have felt compelled to hire a bodyguard for Waddell "to keep the Rube straight as possible, and now the latter's catcher, Ossie Schreckengost, has also fallen from grace." He had been "breaking the temperance clause in his contract."

The Athletics finished fourth in 1906, 12 games out of first place. Schreck had hit for a better average, .284, and been more productive in the games he played, but he appeared in 98 games, down 25 from 1905. And there were some suggestions that he hurt the team significantly. Sportswriter Francis C. Richter, writing from Philadelphia, told *Sporting Life*: "Mack sent catcher Schreck home from St. Louis because he remained out all night on Sep. 21 without the knowledge or consent of the manager. The latter made no bones of saying that Schreck had misconducted himself frequently during the second half of the season; that his conduct was one of the chief causes of the breakdown, and that Schreck stood suspended for balance of season."

In 71 games in 1908, Schreck hit .222 for the Athletics, with only 16 RBIs. Near the end of the season, he was ready to leave Philadelphia "and had outlived his welcome with the fans of that city," so Mr. Mack placed him on waivers. There were indeed recurring notes in his last few years that made it clear Schreck had a problem with alcohol. Only one team claimed him off waivers – the White Sox. He played in six games for them at the tail end of 1908 and had three singles in 16 at-bats, suffering a broken finger in the bottom of the eighth inning on Oct. 2. It proved to be his last game in the major leagues.

After his playing days were over, he did some scouting for Connie Mack – and, along with scout Al Maul, is credited with signing Shoeless Joe Jackson to the Athletics in 1908. According to the story, Schreck started traveling north with Jackson to bring him to Philadelphia, but when they got as far north as Charlotte, Jackson was getting homesick and jumped off the train, hiding from Schreck.

BEST DAY (BY WPA OR OTHER MEASURE): This might not have been his "best day," but it's the most notable in terms of sheer stamina. On July 4, 1905, he set a major league record which still stands, catching 29 innings in one day in Boston. (The team played a double-header that day, and one of the games went a then-record 20 innings).

THE WONDER OF HIS NAME: In baseball's history, there have been memorable names with impossible to remember spellings ... Yastrzemski, Mientkiewicz and the like. But seemingly no full name has been offered to the general public with the myriad of spellings as Ossee Schrecongost.

NOT TO BE CONFUSED WITH: Viktor Schreckengost (American industrial designer as well as a teacher, sculptor, and artist. His wide-ranging work included noted pottery designs, industrial design, bicycle design and seminal research on radar feedback), Shrek (Fictional ogre character created by American author William Steig. Shrek is the protagonist of the book of the same name and of eponymous films by DreamWorks Animation).

FUN ANAGRAMS: "Freeman Osee Schrecongost" becomes "Not scaremonger of cheeses." or "Ace references smooth song."

EPHEMERA: 1) His parents were listed as Naman (or Naaman) Shrecongost, a miner, and his wife, Sarah C. Shrecongost (Protzman). Their three children were Harry H., Osee F., and Annie I. 2) He took part in the first triple play in Boston Americans franchise history, on Aug. 7, 1901, at Baltimore, a 1-5-2-6-1 affair. 3) Schreck sold cigars during the winter after the 1902 and 1903 seasons. His application for a liquor license was rejected in April 1904. And the cigar business was said to be why his last name became truncated: "Owing to the limits of the building in which he does a cigar business, the Athletic backstop sawed his sign name down to O. Schreck." 4) His T206 tobacco card from the early 20th century lists him as "O. Schreck." 5) For a catcher, who presumably had a good eye for the strike zone, he didn't walk that much, just 102 times in 3,501 career plate appearances. His career batting average was .271 and his on-base percentage .297. 6).Rube Waddell died of tuberculosis in San Antonio on Apr. 1, 1914. When he learned of the pitcher's death, Schreck is reported to have said, "The Rube is gone, and I am all in. I might as well join him." One hundred days later, Schreck died "of a complication of diseases" at Northwestern General Hospital in Philadelphia. He was 39. His death certificate indicated heart disease and Bright's disease, a kidney disease. Uremia (kidney failure) was noted in newspaper accounts at the time.

URBAN SHOCKER
Changed name due to penchant of press to misspell his given name

BIRTH NAME: Urban Jacques Shockcor. Some books and similar reference sources list Shocker's original first name as "Urbain."
PRONUNCIATION OF DIFFICULT PARTS: None
HEIGHT/WEIGHT: 5'10" 170 lbs.
BORN: Sep. 22, 1890, in Cleveland, Ohio
DIED: Sep. 9, 1928, in Denver, Colorado
POSITION: Pitcher
YEARS ACTIVE IN THE MAJORS: 1916-1928
NAME ETYMOLOGY/DEFINITIONS: "Urban" has multi-ethnic origins from a medieval personal name (Latin *urbanus* meaning "city dweller," a derivative of *urbs* meaning "town," "city"). "Urbain" is the French variant of "Urban." "Jacques" is the French form of "James" or "Jacob." "Shockcor" is a bit of a mystery, as it is not listed in any surname reference books. It is likely of French origin.

One day in 1913 while catching for Windsor, a Class D Independent team, Urban Shockcor stopped a baseball with the tip of the third finger on his pitching (right) hand, breaking the finger in the process. When the broken finger healed, it had a hook at the last joint.

"That broken finger may not be pretty to look at," said Shockcor, "but it has been very useful to me. It hooks over a baseball just right so that I can get a break on my slow ball and that's one of the best balls I throw. If the finger was perfectly straight, I couldn't do this. As it is, I can get a slow ball to drop just like a spitter. Perhaps if I broke one of my other fingers, I could get the ball to roll over sideways or maybe jump in the air, but I am too easy-going to make the experiment."

Shockcor posted a 6-7 record with a 4.54 ERA for Windsor in 1913. He moved on to Ottawa of the Class B Canadian League, where he put up two terrific seasons. In 1914 Shockcor won 20 games and followed that up with a 19-win season the following year. Shockcor struck out 158 in 1914 while walking 60. He was even better in 1915, racking up 186 K's while opposing batters walked only 40 times. At the conclusion of the 1915 season, Shockcor was drafted by the big-league New York Yankees in the Rule 5 Draft. It is presumed that Urban Jacques Shockcor changed his name to Urban James Shocker around this time, as a result of writers continually misspelling his name.

He made his major league debut on Apr. 24, 1916, pitching three innings of relief in an 8-2 loss to Walter Johnson and the Washington Senators at Griffith Stadium. He was then optioned back to Toronto of the International League. On July 8, Shocker started a string of four straight shutouts covering 36 scoreless innings. On July 22, Shocker tossed an 11-inning no-hitter at Rochester. His string was eventually snapped at 54⅓ scoreless innings. For the year, Shocker was 15-3 with a 1.31 ERA and 152 strikeouts in 185 innings. He was recalled to New York and started nine games, going 4-2.

Shocker was used sparingly by New York manager Bill Donovan in 1917. He made 13 starts, going 8-5 with seven complete games for the Yanks. Donovan was replaced by Miller Huggins for the 1918 season. Huggins was looking for stability at second base, and no internal options provided the offense that Huggins desired. He set his sights on Del Pratt of the St. Louis Browns.

On Jan. 22, 1918, Pratt and pitcher Eddie Plank were sent east for five players, one of them being Shocker. Urban posted a 6-5 record with a 1.81 ERA before he got drafted by the army at the end of June. Shocker returned from France and rejoined the Browns the following year. He made his first appearance on May 11, 1919, losing to Detroit, but rebounded to win his next six of seven starts.

Shocker shocked even his heartiest admirers when he won 20 games in 1920. On July 13, 1920, he fanned a career-high 14 batters, whiffing Babe Ruth three times in the 6-4 Browns victory.

Shocker was one of 17 pitchers allowed to continue to throw a spitball when that pitch was banned. The 1920 season was to be a year of transition so that the spitball pitchers could wean themselves from throwing it. However, the players who relied on the spitball as their "money" pitch lobbied to be able to continue to use the pitch. The 17 pitchers were allowed to throw it until their careers ended.

In 1921, Shocker led the league in wins with 27. In 1922, he led the Browns with a 24-17 record and a 2.97 ERA. He also led the league in strikeouts with 149, while finishing second in the league in innings pitched with 348. The Browns finished 1922 in second place by one game, with a record of 93-61. They had dominated the rest of the league but were 8-14 against the Yankees. Shocker accounted for half those wins and losses, going 4-7 against New York.

Over the next two seasons, the Browns slipped back to the middle of the pack in the American League. George Sisler, the club's heavy-hitting First Baseman, assumed

271

command of the team in 1924, but that change made little difference in the club's fortunes.

Shocker ran afoul of management when he showed up late one day. Sisler fined his ace pitcher, who by some accounts made showing up late a habit. He was considered somewhat of a loner. Shocker often chose to either go off by himself, or more likely stay in his room when the team was on the road. He loved newspapers, subscribing to out-of-town papers. "I used the time reading the papers from the next city on our schedule," Shocker explained, "and that way I could keep book on the streaky hitters. Gave me a little edge."

Shocker's record slipped to 16-13 in 1924, and his ERA ballooned to 4.20. His age (34) and recent disagreements with management made him expendable. Miller Huggins coveted Shocker and jumped at the chance to snatch him up that December.

In 1925, for the Yankees, Shocker was an even 12-12. Babe Ruth was hospitalized in spring training and did not break into the lineup until June 1. Lou Gehrig was in his first full season, and except for Bob Meusel, who led the league in homers and RBIs, the team was barely treading water. They sank to seventh place.

Fortunes changed for the Yankees in 1926. Tony Lazzeri and Mark Koenig took over at second base and shortstop, respectively. The Babe rebounded to have one of the finest seasons in his career. Shocker would finish the year at 19-11, and the Yankees won the American League pennant by three games. In the World Series against the St. Louis Cardinals, Shocker got the starting assignment in Game 2, with the Yankees leading the series 1-0. The game was tied at two, when he surrendered a three-run homer to Cardinal right fielder Billy Southworth. The Cards went on to win the game, 6-2. Shocker's only other appearance was in Game 6, as he pitched ⅔ of an inning of relief as St. Louis battered New York, 10-2. The Cardinals eventually won the series in seven games.

By 1927 Shocker was fighting heart disease, although few people knew it. There was no drama in that year's American League race. New York outpaced second place Philadelphia by 19 games. Shocker posted a record of 18-6 with a 2.84 ERA. In the World Series, the Yankees swept Pittsburgh in four straight, but Shocker did not appear.

In Feb. 1928, Shocker announced that he was retiring. Huggins felt that Shocker was bluffing all along, and it turns out that Urban did change his mind and came to terms with the Yankees on a $15,000 deal just before the start of the regular season.

Shocker was battling a wrist injury, not to mention a dramatic loss of weight. When he was healthy, he weighed 190, but it dropped significantly to 115. He was also waiting to be reinstated by the Commissioner's office as he was still on the voluntarily retirement list until he got into shape.

Shocker made his only appearance of the year in a Memorial Day matchup with the Senators. He pitched two innings of scoreless relief. Not long after, Shocker was pitching batting practice at Comiskey Park when he collapsed. He was given his release on July 6, 1928, citing poor health as the reason. His career record in the major leagues was 187-117 with a 3.17 ERA. He registered 983 strikeouts and 657 walks. He would pass away two months later.

BEST DAY (BY WPA OR OTHER MEASURE): Shocker tossed 28 complete-game shutouts in his career. The most dominant of those might have been the one he hurled on Aug. 5, 1924 against the Washington Senators. Despite 1924 being a mediocre year for him on the mound, in that contest he allowed only two singles and one double, with one walk and four strikeouts.

THE WONDER OF HIS NAME: "Urban Shocker" sounds like a headline in a tabloid newspaper ... perhaps some crime wave in the inner city. The fact that Urban Shockcor changed his name to that adds to the legendary status of the name.

NOT TO BE CONFUSED WITH: Tupac Shakur (American rapper and actor. He is considered by many to be one of the greatest hip hop artists of all time), Urban Outfitters (American multinational lifestyle retail corporation headquartered in Philadelphia), Urban Meyer (American college football coach. He was the head coach of the Ohio State Buckeyes from 2011 until his retirement after the 2019 Rose Bowl).

FUN ANAGRAMS: "Urban James Shocker" becomes "Rambo searches junk."

EPHEMERA: 1) As the fifth of nine children, Urban was the only member of the Shockcor family to change his name. 2) Urban's father William was born in Philadelphia but may have had French ancestry, given his last name, while his mother Anna's lineage traces back to Germany. 4) In 1923 Shocker got suspended for the last month of the season, as he took a stand against the club rule prohibiting wives from accompanying the team on road trips. Shocker refused to join the Browns on a trip to Philadelphia without his wife, Irene. When Shocker was threatened with fines and suspension, he held his ground. He was suspended after his start on Sep. 7th. Shocker brought his case to Commissioner Landis, making a plea that he be declared a "free agent." A settlement was finally reached between Shocker and the Browns. Shocker got a pay raise that more than offset the fine, dropped his "free agency" request, but still couldn't bring his wife on trips. 5) Shocker's heart condition was so severe some books say he had to sleep either sitting or standing up. After his release from the Yankees in 1928, Shocker entered an exhibition tournament in Denver. He pitched in one game on Aug. 6, 1928, against a team from Cheyenne, Wyoming and fared poorly in that outing. Around this time, he contracted pneumonia, was hospitalized, and died as the result of heart failure.

HOSEA SINER
Part of the Indiana-born contingent on the 1909 Boston Doves

BIRTH NAME: Hosea John Siner
PRONUNCIATION OF DIFFICULT PARTS: Hoe-SHAY-ya or Hoe-ZAY-ya
NICKNAME: None
HEIGHT/WEIGHT: 5'10" 185 lbs.
BORN: Mar. 20, 1885, in Sullivan, Indiana

DIED: June 10, 1948, in Sullivan, Indiana

POSITIONS: Third Baseman, Pinch Hitter, Shortstop

YEARS ACTIVE IN THE MAJORS: 1909

NAME ETYMOLOGY/DEFINITIONS: "Hosea," son of Beeri, is one of the 12 Prophets of the Hebrew Bible. "John" is originally of Semitic origin. The name is derived from the Latin "Ioannes" and "Iohannes." The origin of "Siner" isn't totally clear. One theory is that it is a name for a person who was a person with lordly bearing, or the older of two people with the same name. The first is by analogy with the French *seigneur*, meaning "lord."

I n 1906, Hosea Siner broke in as a slick-fielding shortstop with Albany in the Georgia State League. In 1909 he was one of five Indiana-born members of the National League's Boston Doves. After stops at Calumet (Michigan), South Bend (Indiana) and Monmouth (Illinois), he joined Boston that summer. Pitchers Cecil Ferguson, Forrest More and Tom McCarthy, and catcher Bill Rariden – all native Hoosiers – also played for Boston that year. "Siner has the natural ability to play ball," observed the South Bend Tribune, "but he does not hit the ball hard enough." In the ten games he ended up playing in for Boston in 1909, he amassed only three singles in 23 at-bats (.130).

Siner went to Spring Training with Boston in 1910, but they sold his contract to Monmouth in the Central League. There he hit .250 and slugged .339 for the season. In 1911 he enjoyed his finest year, playing for Danville in the "Three I" League, batting .276 and making the all-star team as a second baseman. Siner liked to wrestle during the off-season, and after the 1911 season he suffered a wrestling injury that limited him to just 52 games and a .230 batting average in 1912. He retired after helping Great Falls (Montana) of the Union Association to a first-place finish in 1913. In that year, he batted .269 and slugged a respectable (for its time) .379.

BEST DAY (BY WPA OR OTHER MEASURE): His major league career consisted of those 10 games in 1909. He totaled three hits in his career. "Best day" might be hard to pick given this. On Aug. 9 of that year, in the next-to-last game Siner would play in for the Doves, he managed to reach base twice in four plate appearances. He singled and walked against a pitcher named Nick Maddox. Boston still lost the game 10-1.

THE WONDER OF HIS NAME: Well, for one thing, he's NOT Jewish despite the first name. Then you add in the difficulty in pronouncing his first name upon first glancing at it.

NOT TO BE CONFUSED WITH: *Hosea* (A genus of flowering plant in the *Lamiaceae* family, first described in 1908. It contains only one known species, Hosea lobbii. It is endemic to the Island of Borneo), Guy Siner (an American-born English actor best known for his role as Oberleutnant Hubert Gruber in the British television series "'Allo 'Allo!").

FUN ANAGRAMS: "Hosea John Siner" turns into "Oh ... in hero's jeans!"

EPHEMERA: 1) The Doves went 45-108 during the 1909 season when Siner played for them. Boston was winless in the five games Siner started, and 0-10 overall in games in which he appeared. 2) Hosea was one of seven children born to John Lawson Siner and Cynthia Jane Beecher. His sisters included Leota Lena, Cleo Antha Eugene and Sara Anarpy. 3) After he retired from the game, he returned to Indiana and organized an independent team named the Shelburn Maroons. 4) He married Sallie Springer in 1914 and had two children, John and Cozette. 5) He owned a farm near Sullivan county in Indiana and operated a service station there. He was also a county councilman and was on the local hospital board.

HOMER SMOOT
Five full seasons, then gone from the majors

BIRTH NAME: Homer Vernon Smoot
PRONUNCIATION OF DIFFICULT PARTS: None
NICKNAME: Doc, origin unknown
HEIGHT/WEIGHT: 5'10" 180 lbs.
BORN: Mar. 23, 1878, in Galestown, Maryland
DIED: Mar. 25, 1928, in Salisbury, Maryland
POSITION: Centerfielder
YEARS ACTIVE IN THE MAJORS: 1902-1906
NAME ETYMOLOGY/DEFINITIONS: "Homer" has English (West Midlands) origins as the occupational name for a maker of helmets, from the adopted Old French term *he(a)umier*, from *he(a)ume* meaning "helmet," of Germanic origin. Other English origins list it as a variant of "Holmer." Americanized form of the Greek family name "Homiros" or one of its patronymic derivatives. ("Homirou," "Homiridis," etc.). This was not only the name of the ancient Greek epic poet (classical Greek Homeros) but was also borne by a martyr venerated in the Greek Orthodox Church. There are also Slovenian origins as the topographic name for someone who lived on a hill, from hom (dialect form of *holm* meaning "hill," "height") and the German suffix *-er* denoting an inhabitant. "Vernon" has English (of Norman origin) roots as a habitational name from Vernon in Eure, France, named from the Gaulish element *ver(n)* meaning "alder" and the Gallo-Roman locative suffix *-o* (genitive *-onis*). "Smoot" is the Americanized spelling of Dutch "Smout," a metonymic occupational name for someone who sold fat or lard, Dutch *smout*, or a nickname for someone who had a taste for, and could afford, rich foods.

H omer Smoot spent his childhood in the small town of Galestown, on Maryland's Eastern Shore. He attended Washington College in Chestertown, Maryland, where he played baseball and football. In these same years, Smoot was also playing semipro baseball for Cambridge and Salisbury in his native state, and for Purcell and Laurel in Delaware.

He signed his first professional contract with the Allentown Peanuts of the Atlantic League in 1900. When the Atlantic League folded that June, Smoot caught on with the Worcester Farmers of the Eastern League. He returned to Worcester in 1901 and led the league with a .356 batting average.

The National League's St. Louis Cardinals signed Smoot to fill one of the gaping holes in their 1902 lineup after the team was raided by the cross-town and cross-league Browns. Smoot earned the club's starting center field position. On Apr. 25, Homer lived up to his name by socking two home runs, the second one in the tenth inning, to lift St. Louis to a dramatic 9-8 win. Smoot's heroics were all the more surprising considering that the Cardinals managed only ten round-trippers that entire season (three by Smoot). Smoot's .311 batting average and 20 swiped bags and good defense in center would help keep the young team respectable. All three members of the Cardinals' outfield batted .300. However, a dreadful pitching staff left the club with a sixth-place finish.

The 1903 season was a disaster for the Cardinals, who crashed to last place. Rookie pitcher Mordecai "Miner" Brown (better known today as "Three Finger" Brown) tied for the lead with a mere nine wins. Brown was shipped to Chicago at season's end in what turned out to be one of the worst trades in franchise history. Smoot hit .296, and his four homers were half of the club's total for the year.

The Cardinals rebounded to a fifth-place finish in 1904. Smoot batted .281, with a career-best 66 RBIs.

The 1905 campaign saw the Cardinals fighting to stay out of the cellar again, but Smoot put together his best season. He slashed .311/.359/.433 and posted a career-best totals for runs (73).

Smoot has a transition year in 1906. He was hitting a disappointing .248 in July, when he was traded to Cincinnati for journeyman Shad Barry. The change of scenery didn't do him much good, and he finished the season with a .252 average. Smoot's contract was sold to Toledo of the American Association at the season's end, and he would never again appear in a major league game.

Several explanations have been offered for the abrupt end to Smoot's major league career. One source claims that Smoot's diminishing eyesight caused his demotion. His obituary, however, specifically claims that Smoot's batting eye remained "undimmed," but that he was slowed by muscular rheumatism. In addition, his daughter claimed that Smoot never had eye problems, but that his rheumatism was so bad by his career's end that he sometimes had to stay in bed until noon to have the strength to play ball that afternoon. Finally, it is possible that Smoot was still good enough to play in the majors but never was given the chance.

Smoot spent three seasons with Toledo, batting .312 in 1907, .301 in 1908, and .270 in 1909. He split the 1910 season between Louisville and Kansas City, but hit a lackluster .236. He started the 1911 season with Kansas City and seemed to have regained his old form. In July he was hitting .379 when his contract was sold to Wilkes-Barre of the New York State League, where he played on the only pennant-winner of his professional career. He began the 1912 season as an assistant manager and a weekend player for Wilkes-Barre, but by June his rheumatism, which he had been dealing with for some time, had become too severe and his playing days came to an end.

BEST DAY (BY WPA OR OTHER MEASURE): Individual game logs are not available for that era. However, one of Smoot's 15 career home runs was particularly memorable: on July 22 of 1903, he hit a three-run home run on a two-strike pitch with two out in the bottom of the ninth to lift the Cardinals to an 8-7 victory over the Cincinnati Reds.

THE WONDER OF HIS NAME: You have to love kids bestowed the first name of Homer who happen to grow up to be baseball players. Through 2019, there have been fewer than 15 such-named players (a few others have it as a nickname or middle name). When you add in the mellifluous word "smoot" (c'mon ... it really is fun to say ... try it!), you've got a winning combo.

NOT TO BE CONFUSED WITH: The smoot (A nonstandard, humorous unit of length created as part of an MIT fraternity prank. It is named after Oliver R. Smoot, a fraternity pledge to Lambda Chi Alpha, who in October 1958 lay down repeatedly on the Harvard Bridge (between Boston and Cambridge, Massachusetts) so that his fraternity brothers could use his height to measure the length of the bridge), Fred Smoot (Former NFL cornerback who played in the league for nine seasons for the Washington Redskins and Minnesota Vikings).

FUN ANAGRAMS: Homer Vernon Smoot becomes "Never smooth ... moron."

EPHEMERA: 1) Homer Smoot was the first of three children born to Luke Smoot and the former Rebecca Wheatley. 2) In each of Smoot's five major league seasons, he collected at least 500 at-bats. The list of players who had at least one 500 at-bat season without a season with fewer than 500 at-bats: Smoot (1902-06), Joe Cassidy (1904-05), Irv Waldron (1901), Scotty Ingerton (1911), Al Boucher (1914), Dutch Schliebner (1923), Art Mahan (1940), and Johnny Sturm (1941). 3) A retrospective SABR project designated Smoot as the National League's best rookie in 1902. 4) One of his elementary school classmates was Geneva Gordy, who would become his wife in 1901. 5) After his playing days were over, Smoot was offered the opportunity to manage in organized baseball. However, he and his wife had started a family that would include two boys and three girls, and they preferred to see them grow up near where they had spent their own childhoods. Accordingly, he became head baseball coach at his alma mater of Washington College. After one season, he decided to leave baseball and spent the next ten years farming, raising chickens and operating a feed business in nearby Salisbury. 6) In 1927, Smoot's oldest son Roger signed with the Cardinals' farm system. 7) Smoot was elected to Washington College's Athletic Hall of Fame in 1992.

LOUIS SOCKALEXIS
Baseball's first recognized "minority" player

BIRTH NAME: Louis Francis Sockalexis
PRONUNCIATION OF DIFFICULT PARTS: None
NICKNAME: Chief
HEIGHT/WEIGHT: 5'11" 185 lbs.
BORN: Oct. 24, 1871, in Indian Island, Maine
DIED: Dec. 24, 1913, in Burlington, Maine
POSITION: Rightfielder
YEARS ACTIVE IN THE MAJORS: 1897-1899

NAME ETYMOLOGY/DEFINITIONS: Louis is the French form of the Old Frankish given name "Chlodowig" and one of two English forms, the other being "Lewis." The Frankish name is composed of the words for "fame" (*hlōd*) and "warrior" (*wīg*) which may be translated to famous warrior or "famous in battle." "Francis" is the English equivalent of the Italian Francesco personal name. This was originally an ethnic name meaning "Frank" and hence "Frenchman." As an American family name this has absorbed linguistic derivations from several other European languages. As for the origin/meaning of "Sockalexis," I wrote to Ed Rice, author of *Baseball's First Indian: Louis Sockalexis: Penobscot Legend, Cleveland Indian.* He stated, "I've read, in a couple of places, that it is French....Socque-Lexis...and that the intermarriage between Québecois, coming down into Maine as part of the boom period for the lumbering industry in Maine in the mid-1800s, and Penobscot/Passamaquoddy indigenous peoples also earning a living this way, led to a bastardization of spellings of the time. On the Penobscot reserve, you'll see spellings like 'Soccalexis' and others on old wooden crosses.' 'Socque' is a Québecois surname. Socque means 'clog' in French. 'Lexis' means 'defender' of the people."

Louis Sockalexis, a member of the Penobscot Indian tribe of Maine, played in only 94 major league games, but is remembered today as the first Native American, and first recognized minority, to play in the National League. Sockalexis was a multi-talented athlete who appeared destined for stardom, but alcoholism won out over physical talent.

In December 1896, Sockalexis enrolled at Notre Dame, but stayed there only a few months. In March of the following year, he was expelled from the college after a drunken row at a local tavern. He then signed a contract with the Cleveland Spiders and reported to spring practice in March of 1897. The local sportswriters were so taken with the newcomer that a headline in the *Cleveland Plain Dealer* on Mar. 20 referred to the team as (manager Patsy) "Tebeau's Indians." By the end of the month, the Spiders' original moniker was virtually forgotten, and the Cleveland club became the Indians.

Sockalexis started out the 1897 regular season on a tear. After twenty games, his average stood at .372, and he was a draw both at home in Cleveland's League Park and on the road. He was a sensation, though many fans bought tickets to jeer at the first Native American ballplayer in major-league history.

On May 13, Sockalexis belted a double and a triple off Boston's best pitcher, 30-game winner Kid Nichols, but the Indians lost the game by a 4-1 score. At the Polo Grounds on June 16, facing New York's strikeout champion Amos Rusie in front of more than 5,200 fans (most hooting and making Indian war cries at the Cleveland rookie), Sockalexis walloped a curveball from Rusie over right fielder Mike Tiernan's head. By the time Tiernan could retrieve the ball, Sockalexis had sped around the bases for a home run.

On July 3, his drinking caught up to him. He went out on the town in Cleveland that Saturday evening, and drank what onlookers recalled as a prodigious amount of alcohol. Sometime during the wee hours, Sockalexis either jumped or fell out of a second-story window, severely spraining his ankle. When he showed up at the ballpark in Pittsburgh for a game on Monday, July 5, he was limping noticeably. Tebeau pulled him from the lineup and sent him back to Cleveland to have his injury treated. A physician put his ankle in a cast and ordered him to bed, but Sockalexis reportedly spent the next several evenings in the local bars while his teammates carried on in Pittsburgh.

During a game a week later, Sockalexis appeared to be "FWI" (fielding while intoxicated), and his alcohol problem was now public knowledge, in Cleveland and around the league. In late July, the team suspended him without pay. When he was let back on the team, he played little in August and September, however, and ended his season with a .338 average and 16 stolen bases in 66 games.

Although Sockalexis appeared to stay sober in 1898, he lost his starting position in right field. He spent most of the season on the bench, appearing in only 21 games and batting .224. He relapsed and became so unreliable that he could not even play for what became the worst team in the game in 1899. After a game of May 13, in which he fell twice in the outfield, the club released him from his contract.

Despite a career batting average of .313, he never played again in the major leagues. He hooked up with some minor league teams haphazardly over the next four years. A series of news reports during those years detailed several arrests for public drunkenness and disturbances, and it appears he was reduced to homelessness and vagrancy. He spent several short terms in jail during this period. A short stint with Bangor in the Maine League in 1903 was his last connection with organized baseball.

BEST DAY (BY WPA OR OTHER MEASURE): As mentioned above, on June 16, 1897, Sockalexis and the Indians played the New York Giants at the Polo Grounds in New York. The starting pitcher for the Giants was their hard-throwing ace Amos Rusie. Fans were anxious to get their first look at Sockalexis, the Indian phenom, and they greeted him with war whoops and yells. As the third hitter in the Cleveland lineup, he stepped to the plate to face Rusie with two outs and the bases empty in the top of the first inning. Sockalexis swung hard and missed Rusie's first pitch, and while Sockalexis was out of position, Rusie quick-pitched his second offering. Sockalexis stabbed at it and sent a line drive to deep right field, beyond the reach of Mike Tiernan, the Giants right fielder. While Tiernan chased the ball, the speedy Sockalexis circled the bases for a home run. It was Sockalexis's third career home run and only the second home run allowed by Rusie during the 1897 season. It wasn't a perfect day for Sockalexis though. Later in the game, Tiernan drilled a liner at Sockalexis in right field, which Sockalexis misplayed. Tiernan reached third base on the error.

THE WONDER OF HIS NAME: It was 1869 when we first encountered (Cincinnati) Red Stockings. It wasn't until 1904 that baseball had White Sox and 1908 brought us Red Sox. "Louis Sockalexis" makes us smile because of the possible intermarriage angle and the "sock" portion of the surname having a baseball connotation of its own. "Sockalexis" is just fun to pronounce, and it doesn't hurt that his life story is so compelling.

NOT TO BE CONFUSED WITH: Socks Seibold (Pitcher from 1916-1933), Socks Seybold (Outfielder from 1899-1908), sockpuppet (Online identity used for purposes of deception. The term originally referred to a false identity assumed by a member of an Internet community who spoke to, or about, themselves while pretending to be another person).

FUN ANAGRAMS: "Louis Francis Sockalexis" rearranges to "'Scarface' is noxious, kills."

EPHEMERA: 1) He was born on the Penobscot reservation in Old Town, Maine, to Francis Sockalexis, a logger who later served as governor (formerly called "chief") of the Penobscot, and the former Frances Sockbeson. 2) After his playing days were over, he wound up back on the Penobscot reservation in Maine, playing for local town teams and teaching the game to young tribesmen. He piloted a ferryboat between Indian Island, home of the reservation, and the mainland. 3) Although he had apparently stopped drinking to excess, he caught colds and fevers easily, and dealt with a bout of tuberculosis. He also suffered from attacks of rheumatism and developed heart trouble in his later years. 4) When sports journalists attributed his rapid decline to alcoholism, they identified the disease as the inherent "Indian weakness." 5) In the fall of 1913, Sockalexis joined a logging crew that harvested trees deep in the Maine woods. While cutting down a massive pine tree on Dec. 24, 1913, he suffered a heart attack and died at the age of 42. He was buried in the cemetery on the Penobscot reservation. 6) Cleveland's American League team had for a time been called the Naps in honor of playing manager Napoleon Lajoie, but when Lajoie left the team after the 1914 season, a new nickname was in order. When they changed their name to the Indians in 1915, the franchise reportedly did so to honor Sockalexis. The Indians' official media guide says that the owners solicited sportswriters to ask fans for their favorite nickname, and the name "Indians" was chosen by a young girl who wrote to one of the sportswriters whose column requested suggestions. She specifically mentioned Sockalexis and his heritage. A brief story in the Feb. 28, 1915, issue of the *Plain Dealer* states that the Cleveland Indians would wear the depiction of an Indian head on the left sleeves of their uniforms to "keep the Indians reminded of what the Braves did last year." Some Native American and civil rights groups suspected that this explanation was a fabrication designed to sanitize a name – and the team's grinning, ruby-skinned mascot, Chief Wahoo – that they viewed as racist. The team finally eliminated the use of Chief Wahoo after the end of the 2018 season. 7) In 1956, Louis Sockalexis was inducted into the Holy Cross Athletic Hall of Fame, and in 1969 was a charter member of the Maine Baseball Hall of Fame. In 1985, he was named to the Maine Sports Hall of Fame, there joining his cousin Andrew Sockalexis, a U.S. marathon medal winner in the 1912 Olympics.

OAD SWIGART
One of the first major leaguers to serve in WWII

BIRTH NAME: Oadis Vaughn Swigart
PRONUNCIATION OF DIFFICULT PARTS: None
NICKNAME: None
HEIGHT/WEIGHT: 6'0" 175 lbs.
BORN: Feb. 13, 1915, in Archie, Missouri
DIED: Aug. 8, 1997, in St. Joseph, Missouri
POSITION: Pitcher
YEARS ACTIVE IN THE MAJORS: 1939-1940
NAME ETYMOLOGY/DEFINITIONS: "Oadis" may be a variation of "Otis." The 1940 United States Census lists his name as "Otis," but his draft card shows "Oadis." There are numerous instances of people with the given name of "Oadis" having a nickname of "Otis." "Otis" as a surname is derived from the Old French personal names "Odes," "Otes," "Odon," and "Otton." These are all derived from the Old German names "Odo" and "Otto," which literally mean "riches." "Vaughn" is a variation of "Vaughan" and those are better known as surnames, originally Welsh, though also used as a form of the Irish surname "McMahon." "Vaughan" derives from the Welsh word *bychan*, meaning "small," and so corresponds to the English name "Little" and the Breton cognate "Bihan." The word mutates to *fychan*, which literally means "small," but also "junior" or "younger." "Swigart" is perhaps an Americanized

spelling of German "Schweighardt" or "Zweigert." "Swigert" is an occupational name for a gardener or tender of fruit trees or vines, from an agent derivative of Middle High German *zwigen* meaning "to graft" or "to plant."

O ad Swigart signed his first professional contract in 1935 when he joined Jackson, Mississippi. He threw 151 innings of 3.46 ERA ball for Jackson and Oklahoma City (Class A Texas League) that year.

He hurled for Oklahoma City in 1936 and Davenport (Class A Western League) in 1937. With Davenport he went 14-12 in 28 games with a 2.67 ERA. Swigart was purchased by the Pirates in 1938 and joined their farm team at Montreal. He pitched for Knoxville of the Southern Association in 1939 and was called up by the Pirates in September.

His first major league game was against the Dodgers on Sep. 14 when he was defeated 8-4. But a week later, on Sep. 21, Swigart won his first, and subsequently his only, major league game, scattering eight hits as he shut out the Boston Bees at Forbes Field. He ended up appearing in three games that year and went 1-1 with a 4.44 ERA.

Swigart spent most of 1940 with Syracuse in the International League and posted an 8-9 record. Oad would get another chance with the Pirates in 1940, again late in the season, appearing in seven games, going 0-2 with a 4.43 ERA.

The 26-year-old was with the Pirates for spring training in 1941 but was inducted by the Army on May 1 – one of only four major league players who lost the entire 1941 season to military service. Swigart would serve at Fort Leavenworth, Kansas. By August 1941, Swigart was pitching for the Stearman Trainers, the semi-pro team of the Stearman Aircraft Corporation in Wichita, Kansas, who were state champions and reached the regionals of the National Semi-Pro Baseball Tournament. In 1942, Swigart served as the player/manager of the Fort Leavenworth Reception baseball team.

Swigart remained in military service until late 1945. He was 31 years old when he reported to the Pirates spring training camp at San Bernardino, California. Despite some good performances in intra-squad games, Swigart failed to make the Pirates' roster. It was the end of a brief major league career for the Missouri native who served nearly five years in the Army.

He finished up his baseball career, after his military service, with the Birmingham Barons in 1946, with an 0-2 record in five appearances. This gave him a minor league career record of 56-59 and a 3.79 ERA in 206 games. His major league record: 1-3 with a 4.44 ERA in 10 games. He pitched 46 innings, allowing 54 hits and 16 walks with 17 strikeouts.

BEST DAY (BY WPA OR OTHER MEASURE): If you win only one game in your major league career, that's going to be your best day. Swigart's start in the second game of a double-header against the Bees on Sep. 21, 1939, was not the most beautiful of shutouts. He allowed eight hits and walked two but got bailed out by his defense, as they turned four double plays behind him. The Pirates got a homer from Chuck Klein and the team pounded out ten hits in the 7-0 win.

THE WONDER OF HIS NAME: Whether you call him Oadis or Oad, it's a cool and unusual name, regardless of the era. He's also a "double unique."

NOT TO BE CONFUSED WITH: Jimmy Swaggart (American Pentecostal evangelist), Oddibe McDowell (Former center fielder who played from 1985-1994 for the Texas Rangers, Cleveland Indians and Atlanta Braves (see page 116), Odysseus (Legendary Greek king of Ithaca and the hero of Homer's epic poem the "Odyssey").

FUN ANAGRAMS: Oadis Vaughn Swigart becomes "His outward savaging."

EPHEMERA: 1) According to Swigart, his favorite player growing up was Carl Hubbell, and his nicest teammate was Arky Vaughan. 2) After baseball and his military service, Swigart worked for the Missouri Department of Conservation for 32 years. He was instrumental in developing the Honey Creek Wildlife Area in St. Joseph.

JIM TOY
This "Toy Story" was more of a mystery

BIRTH NAME: James Madison Toy
PRONUNCIATION OF DIFFICULT PARTS: None
NICKNAME: None
HEIGHT/WEIGHT: 5'6" 160 lbs.
BORN: Feb. 20, 1858, in Beaver Falls, Pennsylvania
DIED: Mar. 13, 1919, in Cresson, Pennsylvania
POSITIONS: First Baseman, Catcher, Outfielder
YEARS ACTIVE IN THE MAJORS: 1887, 1890
NAME ETYMOLOGY/DEFINITIONS: "James" has English origins from a personal name that has the same origin as "Jacob." However, among English speakers, it is now felt to be a separate name in its own right. This is largely because in the Authorized Version of the Bible (1611) the form James is used in the New Testament as the name of two of Christ's apostles (James the brother of John and James the brother of Andrew), whereas in the Old Testament the brother of Esau is called Jacob. The form James comes from Latin "Jacobus" via Late Latin "Jac(o)mus," which also gave rise to "Jaime," the regular form of the name in Spanish (as opposed to the learned Jacobo). "Madison" has English origins. Its commonly spelled "Maddison" in Northeastern England, and is a variant of "Mathieson," meaning "son of Matthew," although possibly occasionally standing for son of "Maddy," where "Maddy" is a pet form of "Maud." "Toy" has English origins as a nickname for a light-hearted or frivolous person, from Middle English *toy* meaning "play" or "sport," or from an occasional medieval personal name, "Toye." It also has French origins as the

metonymic occupational name for a sheath maker, from Old French *toie* meaning "sheath" (Latin theca).

Was Jim Toy the first Native American in the majors?[29] He would certainly have been among the first if his father was indeed a Sioux, but in any case Tom Oran (whom baseball historian Peter Morris states was the first Native American to play major league baseball), preceded him by almost a dozen years. One thing that couldn't be disputed was that at five feet six inches tall, Toy was amongst the smallest men ever to serve as a regular First Baseman.

Toy's professional baseball career began in 1884 with New Brighton in the short-lived Iron and Oil Association, a minor league that included teams from Western Pennsylvania and Ohio. His team disbanded before the season ended, and the league went under a few days after. Over the next two seasons, Toy played for three minor league teams in New York and one in Georgia. In 1887, he got lucky and got invited to join the newly created Cleveland Blues in the American Association, then a major league.

In announcing the signing, *Sporting Life* curiously described Toy as "tall." They also did mention that he was "a splendid back-stop and very fine thrower." He batted .222 in 109 games (82 of them at first) and slugged one of the team's 14 home runs.

The Blues were awful. They went 39-92 and finished last in the American Association. After the season, owners let go of 16 of the team's 25 players, including Toy. He spent the next two years toiling in the minor leagues for the Rochester Jingoes. He hit just .207 in 1888 and .171 in 1889 for Rochester, which cut him when the club was accepted into the American Association in 1890.

---

[29] In 1963, Lee Allen sought to obtain biographical information about every major leaguer who played. Allen, the National Baseball Hall of Fame and Museum's chief historian, sent a questionnaire to Hannah Toy of Beaver Falls. James M. Toy, Hannah Toy's son, filled out the questionnaire. On a line asking for the player's nationality, Toy typed: "SIOUX INDIAN." Allen replied immediately, writing: "I think he must have been the first Indian in major-league history …" Allen went public with the claim in his *Sporting News* column, "Cooperstown Corner." It's unknown what, if any, independent research he did to try to confirm the claim. Allen died in 1969. Journalist and author Ed Rice spent decades disputing the claim, starting in the 1980s as he began researching for a biography of Louis Sockalexis (see page 278). Rice, who formerly lived in Maine where the Penobscot Nation is based, contends that Toy didn't deserve the distinction – even if he was Native American – because he was not listed in a Census as an Indian or registered with a tribe. Furthermore, there are no accounts identifying Toy as being an American Indian or being identified by others as such. Toy never claimed to be Native American during his lifetime. Rice was so determined to prove Toy wasn't Native American that, in 2006, he said he lied to Cambria County officials in an attempt to obtain a copy of Toy's death certificate. He told them over the phone that he was a family member, and they mailed it. The certificate listed Toy's race as white. While numerous accounts suggest that the ballplayer's father was a Sioux Indian, records stored at the Beaver County Genealogy and History Center list the ballplayer's parents as James and Caroline (Caler) Toy. Toy's father was the son of Henry and Mary Toy, both of whom were born in Ireland. And results of a DNA test added recently to Toy's file in Cooperstown show that the ancestral composition of another one of Toy's relatives, James Woods, amounted to 0.0% Native American. On the other hand, there are some who state that Toy was attempting to "pass" for white so as to minimize discrimination against him.

Toy returned to the majors in 1890 with the American Association's Brooklyn Gladiators. They were even worse than the 1887 Blues, going 26-73 and folding before the season ended. Toy batted .181 and was cut by the team before they left the AA and he appears to have given up pro ball at that point.

BEST DAY (BY WPA OR OTHER MEASURE): Detailed game logs for the era in which Toy played are not available. He did go 2-4 in his major league finale, which brought his average up to its final mark of .181.

THE WONDER OF HIS NAME: This particular "Toy Story" really does go "to infinity and beyond" regarding the player's roots/ethnicity. But beyond that, for our purposes here, we just appreciate him for the fun surname, and hope that everyone played nice with the Toys.

NOT TO BE CONFUSED WITH: James W. Toy (Long-time LGBT activist, considered a pioneer among LGBT activists in Michigan), Jimmy Wynn (Nicknamed "The Toy Cannon," he had a 15-year baseball career with the Houston Colt .45s/Astros and four other teams, primarily as a center fielder. Nicknamed "The Toy Cannon" because his bat had a lot of "pop" for his small size [5'10" 160 lbs.]).

FUN ANAGRAMS: "James Madison Toy" becomes "I'm a majesty on sod." or "A mad joy moistens."

EPHEMERA: 1) Toy suffered a career-ending injury when a baseball struck him in the groin. The injury pained Toy for the rest of his life, according to his great-great-nephew. 2) After his baseball career had ended, Toy returned to Beaver County and took up work as a stove molder for the Howard Stove Co. 3) The 1900 Census showed him living in Beaver Falls with his wife of 14 years, Ida, and their three children: Pearl, Gertrude, and George. 4) The Beaver County Sports Hall of Fame inducted Toy in 1998, stating that he was the first Native American to play in the majors.

GENE VADEBONCOEUR
First Québecker in the Majors, and a bit of a mystery man

BIRTH NAME: Onésime Eugene Vadeboncoeur
PRONUNCIATION OF DIFFICULT PARTS: aw-neh-seem/va-deh-BON-cur
NICKNAME: None
HEIGHT/WEIGHT: 5'6" 150 lbs.
BORN: Sep. 5, 1859, in Louiseville, Québec, Canada
DIED: Apr. 16, 1893, in Sacramento, California
POSITION: Catcher
YEARS ACTIVE IN THE MAJORS: 1884
NAME ETYMOLOGY/DEFINITIONS: "Onésime" is the French form of "Onesimus," who was a bishop of Byzantium, as well as a runaway slave and early Christian convert mentioned in the New Testament of the Christian Bible. "Eugene" comes from the

Greek *eugenēs* meaning "noble," literally "well-born," from *eu* meaning "well" and *genos* referring to "race, stock, kin." "Vadeboncoeur" became a surname in France in the 17th century when the French Army began requiring soldiers to have distinct names in order to avoid confusion.[30]

Eugene Vadeboncoeur was born in the town of Rivière-du-Loup – renamed Louiseville in 1879 – in Québec's Mauricie region. According to SABR member Alexandre Pratt, baseball was not introduced to the Mauricie region until 1884, when an American student taught the game to his classmates, so it can be assumed that if the family had remained in Québec, the game would never have played a significant role in Eugene's life. However, the family moved to Syracuse while Eugene was a young lad, and he soon became a baseball enthusiast.

When the 1880 census was taken, the 20-year-old was living in the town of Otsego in western Michigan, where he was one of several young men who boarded with a host family and worked at a local chair factory. Exactly what brought Eugene to Otsego is unknown, but he may well have been pursuing a career in baseball. A Grand Rapids reporter wrote in 1911 that "a catcher named Vandeboncoeur [sic] and a pitcher and outfielder ... Blackburn, both from Otsego, were probably the first of the army of mercenaries which has in the interval of thirty years accepted Grand Rapids money for diamond feats. They were given soft jobs in the furniture factory on days when there were no games, to keep them in training, doubtless."

Vadeboncoeur moved on from Otsego to Grand Rapids and then to Port Huron in 1883, where he was part of a team dubbed the "little Michigan champions" for its dominance of the midwestern baseball scene.

From Port Huron, Vadeboncoeur moved to a professional career during which he spent time in such strong minor leagues as the Northwestern League, the Eastern League, the New England League, the Eastern New England League, and the Central League, in addition to what would be a very brief time in the National League.

He became the first native of Québec to play major league baseball when he took the field for Harry Wright's Philadelphia Quakers team in a game at the Polo Grounds on July 11, 1884. His National League career lasted all of four games, in which he

---

[30] Soldiers with common surnames were obliged to adopt noms de guerres or dit names and one of the most popular choices was Vadeboncoeur, which literally translates as "go with a good heart" but whose idiomatic sense corresponds more closely to "proceed with great courage." A select number of soldiers became so attached to that bold moniker that they retained it in civilian life. With regard to this player in particular, there is some confusion about his birth name, beginning with the order of his given names, which were either Onésime Eugène or Eugène Onésime. Additionally, his family sometimes dropped the first "e" from the last name, leaving it as "Vadboncoeur." When Eugene was about eight, his parents, Joseph Onésime Vadboncoeur and the former Angele Arsenault, moved the family to Syracuse, New York, where their name was a source of enough puzzlement that more modifications were made. Most family members seemed to have restored the Vadeboncoeur spelling, while some began colloquially using an abbreviated version: "Vady." With the name "Onésime" also unfamiliar to Americans, Eugene dropped it entirely and always gave his name as Eugene F. Vadeboncoeur.

amassed three hits in 14 at-bats, with three runs driven in and one run scored. He made four errors and committed nine passed balls behind the plate, but such was the state of catching back in that era.

He seemed to have been a popular, well-regarded figure, as there were regular notes about him in the sporting press. But by 1890, his playing days were winding down, and even a note that "Catcher E.F. Vadeboncoeur is disengaged, residing in Pascoag, Rhode Island," failed to result in an offer. Thus, his ballplaying career was over.

BEST DAY (BY WPA OR OTHER MEASURE): With only a four-game career to pick from, and no individual game logs to reference, we'll have to assume his debut at the Polo Grounds would have been his best day.

THE WONDER OF HIS NAME: If you read the bio footnote, you already know so much about his (varying) name. It was tied for the longest last name to play in the majors until Gene DeMontreville came along in 1894. Its French ... and who doesn't love French?

NOT TO BE CONFUSED WITH: Onésime (Comic strip drawn by Albert Chartier for "Bulletin des Agriculteurs," recounting the misadventures of a middle-aged Québecois), Alain Vadeboncoeur (Canadian emergency physician and science communicator. In addition to leading the Montreal Heart Institute's emergency department, he is active in the research community and is a frequent speaker in French-language media, dispelling myths about health issues).

FUN ANAGRAMS: "Onésime Eugene Vadeboncoeur" turns into "Revenue on media bounces ego."

EPHEMERA: Late in 1890, *The Sporting News* reported that Eugene had recently visited his parents and that he was now living in Denver. SABR baseball historian Tim Copeland was able to find two articles from February of 1891 that placed him in Denver, one of which stated that her was opening a barbershop in that city, while the other detailed a medical treatment provided to a man named "Vadeboncouer." In conjunction with the 1890 Sporting News article, this made a convincing case that Vadeboncoeur was out of baseball and living in Denver in 1891. Since nineteenth-century doctors often recommended the mountain air of Denver as a cure from a wide range of maladies, it also appeared that his health was failing. Copeland's research found a "E.F. Vadebuncaen" as a signer of a September 1892 petition published in a Sacramento newspaper, and then three months later a "Mr. Vadebonconor" was one of the performers in a Christmas play staged at Sacramento's First Baptist Church on Ninth Street. Four months later, on Apr. 19, 1893, there was a funeral of a young man named Eugene F. Vadeboncoeur, who had died of stomach cancer. According to a brief obituary published in the *Sacramento Record-Union* that day, Vadeboncoeur had passed away in that city three days earlier at the age of 26. The ballplayer would have then been 33, but other details pointed strongly to the conclusion that this was indeed the man who had been a major leaguer less than nine years earlier. In addition to spelling his name correctly and providing the middle initial that the ballplayer had adopted, both the obituary and a burial record at Sacramento City Cemetery indicated that he had been born in Canada, with the obituary more specifically giving his birthplace as Québec. The obituary also included a note requested that it be reprinted by newspapers in Syracuse, New York, and Blackstone, Massachusetts – the former city being the ballplayer's adopted hometown, while the latter town being just outside of Providence, one of the cities with which his career had been most closely associated. Kudos to Mr. Copeland for his detective work!

BILL WAMBSGANSS
An unassisted triple play in a World Series, but so much more

BIRTH NAME: William Adolph Wambsganss
PRONUNCIATION OF DIFFICULT PARTS: WHAMS-gans

NICKNAME: None that stuck, though reporters referred to him as "Wamby"
HEIGHT/WEIGHT: 5'11" 175 lbs.
BORN: Mar. 19, 1894, in Cleveland, Ohio
DIED: Dec. 8, 1985, in Lakewood, Ohio
POSITIONS: Second Baseman, Shortstop
YEARS ACTIVE IN THE MAJORS: 1914-1926
NAME ETYMOLOGY/DEFINITIONS: "William" is a popular given name of an old Germanic origin and a derivative of "Wilhelm." It became very popular in the English language after the Norman conquest of England in 1066 and remained so throughout the Middle Ages and into the modern era. It is derived from the Germanic *wil* (meaning "will" or "desire") and *helm* (meaning "helmet" or "protection"). "Adolph" is the usual (hypercorrected) spelling of the German "Adolf," which was first introduced by the Normans, displacing the Old English equivalent "Aethelwulf" (meaning "noble" and "wolf"). It did not become at all common, however, until it was reintroduced by the Hanoverians in the 18th century. The Wambsganss name was German in origin, with the family roots possibly from the Alsace-Lorraine region. There has been some speculation that the name seemed to combine components of the word for overcoat, or at least a word that might have been used as overcoat in early 20th century German usage.

Wamby studied for a while at a seminary in St. Louis. He graduated in 1913 but had enjoyed playing second base on the school's varsity baseball team. His idol growing up was Indians second baseball Nap Lajoie. As Bill's father was a baseball fan himself, he gave his blessing for his son to pursue the calling to play ball.

Bill spent his first year in the pros, 1913, with the Cedar Rapid Rabbits of the class D Central Association, playing shortstop and batting .244 in 67 games. He improved to .317 the next year, playing in 84 games.

The Cleveland Naps and their owner, Charles Somers, coveted the hometown hitter, and bought him in August 1914 for a reported $1,250. His major league debut came when Manager Joe Birmingham put him in a game against the Washington Nationals, replacing Ray Chapman at shortstop late in the game. Batting in the bottom of the ninth, Wambsganss grounded a ball to Wally Smith, the second baseman, and a run scored when Smith misplayed it. During that first year, as Chapman's sub, he appeared in 43 games, batting .217 and driving in 12 runs. He also filled in during four games for his childhood hero Lajoie. The Naps finished dead last.

In January 1915, Lajoie was sold to the Philadelphia Athletics, and Wamby took over at second base. The Cleveland team, renamed the Indians, climbed one notch in the standings, to seventh place, but were 44½ games behind the first-place Red Sox.

Wambsganss had an even more anemic bat (he hit .195 for the season, driving in 21 runs) but was valued for his slick fielding. He appeared in 121 games, 35 of them at third.

The day before the 1916 season began, the Red Sox traded one of their biggest stars, Tris Speaker, to the Indians for Sad Sam Jones, $55,000 in cash, and Boston's choice of either Wambsganss or infield prospect Fred Thomas. Indians manager Lee Fohl wanted to keep Wamby, so he benched him in favor of Joe Evans in order that the Red Sox scouts couldn't get a good look at him. The ploy paid off, and after the Sox selected Thomas, Wamby was in the lineup and off to a hot start.

Chapman suffered several injuries that season, so Fohl put Wamby at shortstop. He appeared there in 106 of his 136 games, and boosted his batting average to .246, with 45 RBIs.

Wamby's defense was highly regarded. A *Washington Post* look ahead to1917 wrote of manager Fohl, "He looks for Wambsganss to be even more of a sensation than he was during the last campaign."

Wamby bumped his average up a bit to .255 in 1917. Everything else stayed very much the same, except that Chapman reclaimed shortstop and Wamby played almost the whole season (137 games) as the second baseman. They were considered by some to be the best double-play combination in the league.

In July 1918, with the United States now in the World War, Wambsganss received his orders to report to Camp Taylor in Louisville, Kentucky. He left behind a .295 season average with 40 RBIs in just 87 games. In 1919, with the war over, Lt. Wambsganss was back with Cleveland in time to put in a full 139-game season.

The 1919 season ended with Wamby hitting .278 and driving in a career-high 60 runs. For the second time in his career, Wambsganss led the league's second sackers in errors, with 30, but this was more a testament to his terrific range than his lack of skill.

The 1920 season was the year in which "Wambsganss" eventually became, if not a household name, at least well-known in the world of people who've learned unusual facts about baseball. During the regular season he batted a pedestrian .244, and again he led all second basemen in errors with 36. The team however, made it to the World Series.

Wamby was 0-for-3 in Game 1, 0-for-3 in Game 2, and 0-for-3 in Game 3. It was a best-of-nine Series; Cleveland won the first game, but Brooklyn beat them in the next two. Some Indians fans were starting to get down on Wambsganss. He apparently confided in F.C. Lane, the editor of *Baseball Magazine*, that he was still really struggling with the loss of his double-play man Chapman, who had died a day after being felled by a pitched ball from Carl Mays in August (the only player fatality related to an in-game event in MLB history). In Game 4, Wamby got going with a first inning walk and scored the first run of the game in a 5-1 Indians win. He led off with a single in the third and scored again, and singled again, driving in the Indians' fifth run of the game, in the sixth.

In summarizing Game 5, there could have been any number of headlines. Wambsganss was one of four runners to score on right-fielder Elmer Smith's grand slam. (It was the first grand slam in World Series history). Then pitcher Jim Bagby homered, a three-run shot in the fourth inning. (It was the first home run by a pitcher in a World Series). The score was 7-0 Tribe after four innings.

But Bagby got himself in trouble in the top of the fifth, though, allowing back-to-back singles to second baseman Pete Kilduff and the catcher, Otto Miller. Kilduff held up at second. Two on, nobody out, and Mitchell was up—Clarence Mitchell, the left-handed reliever who had taken over for Brooklyn starter Burleigh Grimes. Mitchell was a decent hitter and Robinson had used him occasionally to pinch-hit. Wambsganss deliberately played back on the outfield grass, as Mitchell often hit to right and Wamby wanted to keep the ball from getting through and perhaps scoring a run. When the count reached 1-1, Brooklyn put on a hit-and-run play, which had everything to do with the execution of the play that followed.

Mitchell hit the ball hard, and it was heading toward center field several feet to the right of second base. Wambsganss had broken toward the bag, or he wouldn't have been able to make the play. He caught the ball in mid-flight with his outstretched glove. Kilduff was almost to third base and Miller rapidly approaching second. Momentum carried Wamby in the direction he was going, and two or three strides took him to second base. The minute his foot hit the bag, Kilduff was out. And Miller's own momentum brought him right to Wamby. He pulled up short and didn't have time to turn back and try to retreat. He was just five feet away.

"He stopped running and stood there, so I just tagged him. That was all there was to it," Wambsganss explained. "Just before I tagged him, he said, 'Where'd you get that ball?' I said, 'Well, I've got it and you're out number three.'"

It was all over in a flash. Three outs. (In modern baseball history, there have only been 15 unassisted triple plays, making them rarer than perfect games.) There was dead silence in the park as everyone took in what they'd witnessed, and then an explosion of celebration. The Indians won the game in the end, 8-1, and took the next two as well. They were the world champions. Wamby hit just .154 in the Series, but had a perfect fielding percentage of 1.000, with 21 putouts. The three all made on the same play ensured that his name would go down in history.

In 1921, Bill overcame a broken arm suffered early in the season and improved at the plate, hitting .285, driving in nearly as many runs as he had the previous year, and scoring only three fewer despite being in just two-thirds as many games. Wambsganss was a particularly good bunter, often bunting for hits: In both 1921 and 1922, led the league in sacrifice hits (43 and 42, respectively). He hit .262 in 1922. He drove in 47 runs each of the two years.

A broken finger on July 1 cut a couple of weeks out of the middle of the 1923 season, but he still appeared in 101 games and hit for an average of .290, driving in 59 runs. He cut back dramatically on his strikeouts, whiffing only 15 times in 419 plate appearances while drawing 43 walks.

Wamby was unexpectedly traded to Boston in January 1924. The trade reunited him with manager Lee Fohl, now skipper of the Red Sox. Wamby expressed disappointment about not playing for his home team any longer, but happiness to be play for Fohl again.

Wamby played well, appearing in 156 games and participating in an even 100 double plays. He hit .275, and *The Sporting News* noted his "steadying, stabilizing influence in the infield is invaluable in measuring team values." The Red Sox did rise out of eighth place and finished only a half-game behind the sixth-place Indians.

In early May of the following season, a 4-for-4 game on May 9 pushed Wamby's average to .380. It was all downhill from there, though, with an 0-for-6 game on May 18 plunging him from .310 to .289. He never reached .300 again and tailed off to .231 by the end of the year.

Even with a team as bad as the Red Sox were, they thought they could do better. He was placed on waivers and no one initially claimed him, but the Red Sox still held rights to his contract. The Athletics then picked him up in December for the $4,000 waiver wire price.

But 1926 was Wamby's last year as a major leaguer. He appeared in only 54 games, with only 25 coming as a fielder. He batted .352, scored 11 times and drove in but a single run. Wambsganss still had a lot of baseball in him and played seven more seasons of minor-league ball. In addition, after coaching New Orleans of the Southern League in 1930, he returned to the Kansas City club as manager in 1931.

Decades later. Wambsganss was still irked about the "one event" focus of his career. When interviewed in the 1960s by Lawrence Ritter for the classic oral history *The Glory of Their Times,* he recalled: "Funny thing, I played in the big leagues for 13 years, 1914 through 1926, and the only thing that anybody seems to remember is that once I made an unassisted triple play in a World Series. Many don't even remember the team I was on, or the position I played, or anything. Just Wambsganss-unassisted triple play! You'd think I was born on the day before and died on the day after."

BEST DAY (BY WPA OR OTHER MEASURE): "Wamby" didn't do much with the bat, with a career OPS+ of a mere 78. His best day at the plate took place on June 15, 1925, as a member of the Red Sox. He went 4-5, the only four-hit game in his career, with two doubles, an RBI and a run scored in Boston's 13-5 win.

THE WONDER OF HIS NAME: To paraphrase that old expression … "Whams-gans …. Thank you, man!" "Wamby" possesses a unique assortment and string of letters, and there is the mystique of just what his last name actually means.

NOT TO BE CONFUSED WITH: Namby-pamby (meaning lacking in character or substance)

FUN ANAGRAMS: "William Adolph Wambsganss" gives us "Now shag ball as dismal wimp."

EPHEMERA: 1) Baseball Reference lists his middle name as "Adolf" while most other sources go with "Adolph." 2) In 1917, he married Cleveland-born Effie Mulholland. They set up house in Lakewood, Ohio, near Cleveland, and raised their children Mary, Bill Jr., and Lois. 3) The gymnasium at Concordia Theological Seminary is named in his honor. 4) He managed for four seasons in the All-American Girls Professional Baseball League (AAGPBL) for the Fort Wayne Daisies (1945-1946) and the Muskegon Lassies (1947-1948). Other teams in the AAGPBL included the Rockford Peaches, Milwaukee Chicks, Minneapolis Millerettes, Grand Rapids Chicks, Peoria Redwings, Chicago Colleens, Springfield Sallies, Kalamazoo Lassies, Battle Creek Belles and the Muskegon Belles. 5) "Wambsganss" didn't fit into newspaper box scores. Invariably it would show up as W'ganss, Wam'g'ss, Wambs's, W'bsg'ss, and any number of other renditions. According to *The Sporting News*, when the scorecard printing company at League Park asked him if they could shorten his name to "Wamby," he replied "(I was asked if) it would be OK if they shortened me to Wamby, so the name would fit better on scorecards. I told him I thought it sounded pretty good." 6) Of his last name, Wambsganss once remarked, "I don't know whether it fits me or not, but I have worn it all my life and will probably carry it with me to the end." Not everyone in the family wore it as well. Bill's wife had it listed as "Wamby" in the telephone directory. William Adolph Wambsganss Jr., took on the last name of Wamby, as did Bill Wamby III. Another grandson named Robert preferred the most historic last name, while a grandson named Michael uses the surname Wamby.

JOHNNY WEEKLY
One of the original "Colt .45s"

BIRTH NAME: John Weekly
PRONUNCIATION OF DIFFICULT PARTS: None
NICKNAME: None
HEIGHT/WEIGHT: 6'0" 200 lbs.

BORN: June 14, 1937, in Waterproof, Louisiana[31]
DIED: Nov. 24, 1974, in Walnut Creek, California
POSITIONS: Outfielder, Pinch Hitter
YEARS ACTIVE IN THE MAJORS: 1962-1964
NAME ETYMOLOGY/DEFINITIONS: "John" is originally of Semitic origin. The name is derived from the Latin "Ioannes" and "Iohannes." "Weekly" has English origins as a variant of "Weekley." "Weekley" has English origins as the habitational name from a place in Northamptonshire called Weekley, from Old English *wic* meaning "settlement," perhaps in this case a Roman settlement, Latin *vicus* and *leah* meaning "wood" or "clearing."

Johnny Weekly was born in Louisiana, but graduated from high school in Pittsburg, California, and attended Diablo Valley College in Pleasant Hill, California. His career began in the New York Giants' organization in 1956 as a 19-year-old, but he wasn't called up by them while they were in New York.

He never made the Giants after they moved to Weekly's home San Francisco Bay Area in 1958. Instead, Weekly was selected in the 1961 Rule 5 draft by expansion team Houston, set to enter the majors in 1962. Weekly's big-league debut came in the Colt .45s fourth-ever game, on Apr. 13. He grounded out to the second baseman as a pinch-hitter off Jack Hamilton of the Phillies in the ninth inning of a 3–2 defeat at Connie Mack Stadium. Six days later, he collected his first major league hit: a solo home run off the Cubs' Don Cardwell in a 6-0 Houston triumph at Wrigley Field.

Weekly was returned to the Giants' system in mid-May after starting five games in the outfield and 13 total appearances; his five hits included three extra-base blows, among them his second big-league homer (off Pete Richert of the Los Angeles Dodgers). After finishing 1962 with the AAA Tacoma Giants, he was reacquired by Houston and assigned to the AAA Oklahoma City 89ers, where he had his finest minor league season in 1963, batting .363 with 86 hits in 67 games.

That earned him a promotion to the Colt .45s in midseason for a 34-game stint. Weekly batted .225 with three home runs and 18 hits. Weekly was an outfielder, and while his batting stats look bad, they have to be considered in the context. In 1963, when he got two-thirds of his lifetime major league at-bats, he hit .225 on a team that hit .220. Teammate Rusty Staub hit .224, second baseman Ernie Fazio hit .184,

---

[31] Back in the 1830s, one of the most popular spots for covered wagons crossing the Mississippi River was just north of present-day Natchez. As many as 50 wagons a day would cross, carrying settlers bound for Texas. Many of them tired of the journey, and simply stopped on the Louisiana side and made that spot home. Often this area was under water, and on one such occasion, Abner Smalley, one of the early settlers, stood high and dry on a small strip of land waiting for a steamboat to make its usual landing for a refill of cordwood. The captain cried out to Mr. Smalley, "Well Abner, I see you're waterproof," and that's how the name of this town was born. Present-day Waterproof is two and a half miles from its original location, having moved three times to escape flood waters. This led to the construction of a huge levee which snakes around the town, upon which you can walk and drive for a close view of the river.

and shortstop Bob Lillis hit .198. (The 1964 Colt .45's were full of youngsters such as 17-year-old Larry Dierker, 20-year-old Joe Morgan and the 20-year-old Staub.)

Weekly made the Houston roster coming out of spring training in 1964 but had only two hits in 15 at-bats and returned to Oklahoma City. Weekly was 25 years old in 1962, and so was a youngster on an old team that year, but by 1964, he was 27 and much older than the youngsters that Houston would end up using in the long run. On June 15, he was traded to the Orioles, but logged only nine games for the Orioles' AAA affiliate before returning to the Houston organization and being assigned to the minors. After one more full year with the 89ers, in 1965, Weekly left professional baseball.

BEST DAY (BY WPA OR OTHER MEASURE): Weekly set some personal career bests at Crosley Field on Sep. 18, 1963 as his Colt .45's visited Cincinnati. A sparse crowd of 2,950 turned on a Wednesday evening in the next to last week of the season. Houston was in their second season of existence, and just trying to avoid 100 losses. It was going to be a tall order besting the Reds' Jim Maloney, who came into the game sporting a 22-6 record. Maloney struck out Weekly in top of the first. Trailing 3-0 in the fourth, Weekly lifted a flyball to center for the first out of the inning. With the score 4-0 in the fifth, the Colt .45's finally got to Maloney for three runs on three hits and two walks. Weekly capped that rally with a two-RBI single. Houston still trailed 4-3 in the top of the eighth when Weekly doubled leading off with Maloney still on the hill. Two more doubles (the first scoring Weekly with the tying run) and a two-RBI single followed and finally chased Maloney from the game. Moving to the ninth, Houston tacked on insurance runs to what was a 6-4 lead. Weekly provided that insurance with a two-run homer off Dom Zanni. It was the fifth and last homer of his career. The Colt .45's ended up winning 8-4. In the game, Weekly tied a career high for runs scored (2) and set career highs for RBIs (4) and hits (3).

THE WONDER OF HIS NAME: You have to love names that reference time units. Why, I can talk about them for hours ... days even. "John Weekly" could refer to someone with extreme constipation issues? Maybe? Kinda?

NOT TO BE CONFUSED WITH: Bill Daily (American actor and comedian known for his sitcom work as Roger Healey on *I Dream of Jeannie* and Howard Borden on *The Bob Newhart Show*), Hugh Daily (Born Harry Criss and nicknamed "One Arm" Daily. He was a right-handed pitcher who played for seven different teams from 1882-1887. His nickname is a reference to his left arm; he had lost his left hand to a gun accident earlier in his life. To compensate for this injury, he fixed a special pad over the affected area and caught the baseball by trapping it between the pad and his right hand), Entertainment Weekly (American magazine, published by Meredith Corporation, that covers film, television, music, Broadway theatre, books and popular culture).

FUN ANAGRAMS: "Johnny Weekly" becomes "Lenny ... why joke?"

EPHEMERA: 1) On Sep. 27, 1963, the Colt .45's made news by fielding an all-rookie team. In that game, Weekly was the first non-rookie to appear in the game, when he came in as a pinch-hitter. 2) On Apr. 23, 1964, Houston's Ken Johnson pitched a brilliant nine-inning no-hitter against his former team, the pennant-contending Reds – and lost, 1-0. No major-league pitcher had ever met such a frustrating fate. Down 1-0 in the ninth, the Colts' Pete Runnels reached on Deron Johnson's error at first base with two outs. First base umpire Stan Landes called Runnels out but home-plate umpire Augie Donatelli overruled Landes, saying Johnson did not have control of the ball when he stepped on the first-base bag. The Reds played the game under protest. Bob Lillis came in to run for Runnels, but Weekly was called on to pinch-hit and then called out on strikes to end the game.

ZELOUS WHEELER
The first name … doesn't mean anything

BIRTH NAME: Zelous Lamar Wheeler
PRONUNCIATION OF DIFFICULT PARTS: None
NICKNAME: None
HEIGHT/WEIGHT: 5'10" 220 lbs.
BORN: Jan. 16, 1987 in Childersburg, Alabama
POSITIONS: Third Baseman, Rightfielder
YEARS ACTIVE IN THE MAJORS: 2014
NAME ETYMOLOGY/DEFINITIONS: "Zelous" is a totally made up name. As Wheeler himself states, "Everybody wants to know about the name. It's just something my mom came up with, and the rest is history. There's no real story behind it – it's not a family name or anything. She just liked the sound of it, I guess. My dad's a Sam, and my younger brother's a Brian." (While with the Milwaukee Brewers, his teammates called him "Z." Wheeler once stated, "Growing up, everybody just called me 'dude' … hardly anybody calls me Zelous.") "Lamar" is possibly a variant spelling of French "Lamarre." Possibly also Spanish origins as a habitational name for someone from either of the two places called Mar in Asturias, probably named with *mar* meaning "sea" and the article *la*. "Wheeler" has English origins as the occupational name for a maker of wheels (for vehicles or for use in spinning or various other manufacturing processes), from an agent derivative of Middle English *whele* meaning "wheel."

Think of Kirby Puckett attempting to play shortstop. That's what the 5'10" 220 pound, barrel-chested, stout lower-bodied Zelous Wheeler sometimes did coming up through the minors. Before that though, Wheeler played baseball and (not surprisingly) football at Childersburg H.S.. A linebacker on the football team, Wheeler was named among the best players of the state of Alabama. He received offers to play college football from several Division II schools, including Jacksonville State University, Miles College, and Livingston College. He chose instead to play baseball at Wallace State Community College. In 2006, Wallace State won the Alabama Community College Conference championship, and finished third in the

National Junior College Athletic Association World Series. In 2007, Wheeler shifted from third base to shortstop for the Lions. The Milwaukee Brewers selected him as a third baseman in the 19th round of the 2007 Major League Baseball Draft. He signed and played for the Helena Brewers of the Rookie-level Pioneer League. He played for the West Virginia Power of the Class A South Atlantic League in 2008, and the Brevard County Manatees of the Class A-Advanced Florida State League in 2009, being named an All-Star in both seasons.

In 2010, Wheeler played shortstop for the Huntsville Stars of the Class AA Southern League. The Brewers moved him between third, short and second during his journey through the minors, and there were growing pains. He made 32 errors in 93 games at short in 2010. That off-season, Wheeler remarked, "Everyone always says I don't look like a middle infielder ... but I'm pretty quick on my feet." He proved his footspeed by swiping 34 bases and legging out 75 doubles from 2008 to 2010. Given that body type, it was a bit surprising he didn't show much home run power, logging only 77 longballs in nearly 3,500 career minor league plate appearances.

In 2011, Wheeler began the season with the Nashville Sounds in the AAA PCL but missed two months due to an injured posterior cruciate ligament. He played for both Nashville and Huntsville in 2011.

After the 2011 season, Wheeler was assigned to the Arizona Fall League. The Brewers also added him to their 40-man roster to protect him from being selected in the Rule 5 draft. However, the Brewers signed Aramis Ramírez to a three-year contract to become their full-time third basemen, blocking Wheeler.

In spring training in 2012, Wheeler competed with Taylor Green and Brooks Conrad for a reserve role as an infielder. He began to work out at catcher to increase his versatility. At the end of spring training, the Brewers waived Wheeler, and he was claimed by the Orioles, who assigned him to the Norfolk Tides of the International League.

While playing for the Bowie Baysox of the Class AA Eastern League in May 2012, the Orioles designated Wheeler for assignment, removing him from their 40-man roster. He cleared waivers and was assigned to Bowie. In the offseason, Wheeler played for the Algodoneros de Guasave in the Mexican Pacific League. He finished the MPL season tied for second in home runs and third in RBIs.

He split the 2013 season between Norwalk and Bowie, then after the season ended signed a minor league contract with the Yankees, receiving an invitation to spring training in 2014. In camp, Wheeler competed with Eduardo Núñez, Yangervis Solarte, Dean Anna, and Scott Sizemore for a reserve infielder role. The Yankees promoted Anna and assigned Wheeler to the Scranton/Wilkes-Barre RailRiders of the International League to start the 2014 season.

After missing the first 18 days with a back injury, he returned to bat .299 with seven home runs in 66 games. On July 2, 2014, the Yankees promoted Wheeler to the major leagues. The next day, Wheeler got his first major league hit, a home run, in his second at-bat. Wheeler batted 8-for-30 (.267) with two home runs and three

RBIs in 16 games for the Yankees, before he was optioned to Scranton/Wilkes-Barre in August following the Yankees acquisitions of Martín Prado and Stephen Drew.

He was recalled three weeks later, when Carlos Beltrán went on the DL with an elbow injury. He finished the season batting .193/.230/.298 with two homers, two walks and 12 strikeouts. After spending eight seasons in the minors and with his Yankees future unknown, the Bombers sold Wheeler to the Tohoku Rakuten Golden Eagles of Nippon Professional Baseball's Pacific League.

After spending two years over in Japan, Wheeler signed a two-year contract with Rakuten worth approximately $3.5 million in October 2017, including incentives and a club option for the 2020 season. Rakuten gave Wheeler a chance to play every day, and he took advantage of it, slugging 89 homers between 2015-2018.

BEST DAY (BY WPA OR OTHER MEASURE): For many players, their first game in "The Show" is their best day. For Wheeler, whose major league career lasted only 29 games, his debut was in fact his best day. On July 3, 2014, he batted eighth and played third base on a cloudy evening in Minnesota, as the Twins hosted the Yankees. On the hill for Minnesota happened to be former Yankee Phil Hughes. Hughes had been an 18-game winner for the Bronx Bombers in 2010 and won 16 more in 2012, but injuries and ineffectiveness led to a 4-14 campaign in 2013 and the end of his tenure in pinstripes. He signed a free agent contract with Minnesota in December of 2013. Four weeks prior to this July 3 start, Hughes had stifled the Yanks on three hits over eight innings in New York. Wheeler's first at-bat came with the Yankees down 1-0 with a runner on first and no out in the top of the third. Wheeler popped out in foul territory to first baseman Chris Parmelee. Down 2-0 in the fifth, New York got to Hughes. Consecutive singles by Mark Teixeira and Brian McCann were instantly brought home on a Carlos Beltran homer to deep right-center. After Ichiro Suzuki grounded out, Wheeler worked the count to 3-1, then whacked the next pitch over the left-center wall to give the Yanks a 4-2 lead. With the Yankees' lead down to 4-3 in the seventh with one out, Suzuki walked against Hughes, and Wheeler singled to center. Brendan Ryan doubled in a run, chasing Hughes from the game. Brett Gardner greeted reliever Brian Duensing with a run-scoring single to center, plating Wheeler. Derek Jeter finished the scoring with an RBI groundout. The Yanks held on for a 7-4 win. Wheeler finished 2-4 with two runs scored and one driven in, and he started a nifty 5-4-3 double play in the field.

THE WONDER OF HIS NAME: Reasonably common last name. Reasonably common middle name. Totally unique, parent-generated first name. Pardon me if I'm ... overzealous in my adoration for the Z-man. Gotta love the monogram on his luggage "ZLW."

NOT TO BE CONFUSED WITH: Zelus (Greek, literally "zeal;" the daimon that personifies dedication, emulation, eager rivalry, envy, jealousy, and zeal. The English word "zeal" is derived from his name), Todd Zeile (Former MLB third baseman, catcher, and First Baseman. He played sixteen seasons, from 1989-2004), Zack Wheeler (Pitcher for the Philadelphia Phillies).

FUN ANAGRAMS: "Zelous Lamar Wheeler" anagrams to "Hello! We amaze rulers!"

EPHEMERA: 1) While at Wallace State, his teammates were future major leaguers Derek Holland, Craig Kimbrel, and Jake Elmore. 2) Wheeler's brother Brian was taken in the 44th round of the 2008 draft by the Tigers. 3) He has two uncles who were in the NFL: Dameian Jeffries, who played defensive end for a few games with the Saints in 1995 and Marcus Knight, who was a receiver with the Raiders in 2001-2002 and the Arena league. 4) Yankees radio announcer John Sterling's homerun call for Wheeler was: "Wheels up for Zelous!" (not his best one by a long shot) 5) On July 25, 2015, Zelous and his wife, Ashley had a son, whom they named ... Zethan (yes, Zethan).

IVEY WINGO
Record-setting catcher during the 1910s and 1920s

BIRTH NAME: Ivey Brown Wingo (a few sources list his first name, erroneously, as "Ivy")

PRONUNCIATION OF DIFFICULT PARTS: None

NICKNAME: None

HEIGHT/WEIGHT: 5'10" 160 lbs.

WINGO-ST.LOUIS-NAT.

BORN: July 8, 1890, in Gainesville, Georgia (Other accounts state he was born in Norcross, Georgia)

DIED: Mar. 1, 1941, in Norcross, Georgia

POSITION: Catcher

YEARS ACTIVE IN THE MAJORS: 1911-1926, 1929

NAME ETYMOLOGY/DEFINITIONS: "Ivey" has English roots (of Norman origin) as the habitational name from Ivoy in Cher, northern France. "Brown" has various origins. For example, within English, Scottish, and Irish heritages, "Brown" is generally a nickname referring to the color of the hair or complexion, from the Middle English *br(o)un*, from Old English *brun* or Old French *brun*. This word is occasionally found in Old English and Old Norse as a personal name or byname. *Brun-* was also a Germanic name-forming element. Some instances of Old English Brun as a personal name may therefore be short forms of compound names such as "Brungar," "Brunwine," etc. As an American family name, it has absorbed numerous surnames from other languages with the same meaning. "Wingo" is probably an Anglicized form of the French Huguenot name Vigneau.

vey Wingo entered professional baseball in 1909 with the Greenville club of the Carolina Association, a Class D level ball club. He earned a salary of $50 per month. Roger Bresnahan and the St. Louis Cardinals purchased Wingo's contract late in the 1910 season. He was used to warm up pitchers at the tail end of the season with the Cardinals.

On Apr. 20, 1911, Wingo made his major league debut. He went on to appear in only 25 games that season. In 1912 he became a regular catcher for the Cardinals, hitting .265 in 100 games. A left-handed hitter, Wingo was known more as an offensive catcher. Still, he was a good handler of pitchers with a strong arm. Wingo held records for most errors by a catcher both in a season and career post-1900, but for his career he caught 46% of all base-stealers (which was about league average in those days).

He continued as a Cardinal in 1913. Wingo played the 1914 season in St. Louis, hitting .300 for the only time in his career. *Baseball Magazine* named him to its all-league team. In October 1914 it was announced that he had signed a contract with Buffalo of the Federal League. He did not play there as he was traded from St. Louis to Cincinnati and signed – according to the Feb. 10, 1916, issue of *The Sporting News* – a large "war time" contract to stay in the National League.

Bidding wars between the new Federal League and the established National and American leagues raised many players' salaries. Wingo's salary bumped up to $6,500 a season, an increase of $2,000.

In 1915, following the demise of the Federal League, the Reds attempted to trade Wingo to remove his large contract from their budget. Fans in Cincinnati signed a petition requesting the Reds to not trade him; Reds management gave in and kept him.

In 1919 Wingo helped lead the Reds to their first world championship. He platooned with Bill Rariden throughout the season; Rariden generally played against lefthanded starters, and lefty-swinging Wingo played against the righthanders. Wingo hit .571 in the World Series as the Reds defeated the notorious "Black Sox" of Chicago. Ivey remained with the Reds as a player through the 1926 season, serving mainly as a coach that final season.

Wingo turned down an assistant manager's job with Cincinnati in 1927, instead looking for a manager's position. He received his release from the Reds in order to take the helm for Columbus of the American Association. Columbus was a club Reds owner and president Garry Herrmann had purchased to serve as a farm club for Cincinnati. Wingo was not successful there as the team finished in last place with a record of 60 wins and 108 losses.

Ivey returned to the Reds as a coach in 1928 and 1929. The following year saw him ending his professional playing career with his release from the Atlanta club of the Southern Association, where he served as a coach for manager John Dobbs and played a few games as a catcher. He served the Reds one last time as a coach in 1936.

Ivey Wingo retired with the National League record for games caught in a career, 1,233. In his career he caught nearly 10,000 innings. He batted .260/.307/.355 for his career, which was better than average for a catcher during that era.

BEST DAY (BY WPA OR OTHER MEASURE): On Oct. 1, 1919, in Game 1 of the World Series with the Chicago White Sox took place in Cincinnati. Wingo stepped to the plate with two out in the bottom of the fourth inning and runners on first and second in a 1-1 game against starter Eddie Cicotte. Wingo singled to right field to score Larry Kopf from second base. It was the second of five consecutive hits against Cicotte, which would drive him from the game. Wingo also threw out two of three would-be base-stealers in the game, and the Reds coasted to a 9-1 win. Wingo would end up appearing in three games in the World Series, going 4-for-7 with three walks.

THE WONDER OF HIS NAME: Another "double unique," and "Wingo" is a cool-sounding word that rolls off the tongue.

NOT TO BE CONFUSED WITH: Ivey Merwin Shiver (An American football and baseball player. He was an end for the Georgia Bulldogs football team in college, and later an outfielder for the Detroit Tigers and Cincinnati Reds), Harthorne Wingo (A retired American professional basketball player).

FUN ANAGRAMS: "Ivey Brown Wingo" turns into "Groove ... win by win." or "Virgin by now? Woe!"

EPHEMERA: 1) Ivey's dad had a memorable name also ... Absalom Holbrook Wingo. 2) Ivey's brother, Absalom Holbrook "Red" Wingo, also played major league baseball. Red Wingo followed Ivey into professional ball and played in the major leagues with the Philadelphia Athletics and Detroit Tigers. 3) After the 1913 season Wingo was selected to participate in a world tour led by John McGraw and Charles Comiskey. The tour began in the states immediately after the season was over. They played 33 games in small towns as they headed west from Chicago. Eventually ending up in Vancouver, they sailed from there to Japan. Games were played in Japan, China, Australia, the Philippines, Egypt and Europe. Returning from Liverpool, England, they were delivered to the U.S. shore by the ocean liner Lusitania. A year later the Lusitania was to be sunk by a German U-boat during WWI. 4) As a member of the Reds, Wingo was involved in one of the few protested games to ever been successfully upheld. In the contest against the Pirates on May 28, 1921, after an unagreeable call at home plate, Reds pitcher Dolph Luque threw the ball into the Reds' dugout where someone then threw it out to center field where Wingo was playing (he made a handful of appearances in the outfield during his career). Wingo was able to run down a Pirates baserunner for an out. Needless to say, the Pirates protested the game (originally won by the Reds by a 3-2 score) and it was restarted June 30, 1921. The Pirates eventually won 4-3. The *New York Times* story on the game played the next day by the same two teams notes another interesting fate of a ball: "The ninth inning was featured by a freak home run when Barnhart's hit into right field went under a roll of canvass. The ball was recovered by a small boy, who fled with it, and the hit went for a homer." Apparently, there was no protest about this. 5) Ivey's competitive nature was shown in an incident during his minor league managing career. One umpire twice removed Wingo from the same game. He was first ejected for arguing and was later chased again when he was found to be hiding in the bullpen. 6) Wingo returned to his hometown of Norcross and his wife, Mattie May Jones (whom he had married in 1916), after his baseball career. He was retired for only a short time, passing away on Mar. 1, 1941. His wife and a son, William Jones (Hamilton) Wingo, survived him. William would eventually have a son of his own, whom he named "Ivey Brown Wingo." 7) In 1993, Wingo was selected to the Georgia Sports Hall of Fame.

MELLIE WOLFGANG
Small in stature, big in relief

BIRTH NAME: Meldon John Wolfgang
PRONUNCIATION OF DIFFICULT PARTS: None
NICKNAME: Red
HEIGHT/WEIGHT: 5'9" 160 lbs. (though many newspaper accounts had him at 5'6" and 150 lbs.)
BORN: Mar. 20, 1890, in Albany, New York
DIED: June 30, 1947, in Albany, New York
POSITION: Pitcher
YEARS ACTIVE IN THE MAJORS: 1914-1918
NAME ETYMOLOGY/DEFINITIONS: "Meldon" is of English origin and means "from the hillside mill." Meldon is also the name of a hamlet in West Devon, on the edge of Dartmoor in Devon, England. The hamlet's main features are the Meldon Quarry, the Meldon Reservoir and the nearby Meldon Viaduct. The name "John" is the English form of "Iohannes", the Latin form of the Greek name ("Ioannes"), itself derived from the Hebrew "Yochanan" meaning "YAHWEH is gracious," from the roots (yo) referring to the Hebrew God and (chanan) meaning "to be gracious." "Wolfgang" is of German origin from the Germanic personal name Wolfgang, composed of *wolf* (wolf) and *ganc* (going; on a path or journey). From the late 10th century it became popular in Bavaria and the south as the name of a saint, Bishop Wolfgang of Regensburg.

Mellie Wolfgang was a diminutive spitballer for the Chicago White Sox of the mid-1910s. Prior to his time in the majors, he played for his hometown Albany Senators for two seasons. He then moved on to Lowell of the New

England League, where he put together three consecutive 20-win seasons, including a 27-5 log in 1912.

These achievements drew the attention of big-league teams – first the St. Louis Browns in 1911 and 1912, and the White Sox in the seasons after that. However, his short stature dissuaded many major league franchises at first. Said Wolfgang in March of 1913: "I've been turned down so many times I'm really used to it ... I got my first taste of the harpoon in 1911, when the Boston Nationals, managed by Fred Lake, turned me back. The same thing happened the spring of 1912 when Bobby Wallace, then leader of the St. Louis Browns, told me I was too small. I hope Manager Callahan (White Sox manager Jimmy Callahan) don't hand me the same story."

Callahan indeed had reservations and sent him to Denver for one final year in the minors. When he finally made the White Sox big league team in 1914, he proceeded to have three straight seasons of a sub-2.00 earned run average as a spot starter/swingman. Over his five years with the Sox, he appeared in 77 games, 27 of them starts, and he completed 15 of those.

However, his pitching acumen was often overshadowed by the likes of Eddie Cicotte, Lefty Williams and Red Faber. He pitched just 26 innings across 1917 and 1918 due to poor health and that was the end of his career. He was not a part of the infamous 1919 "Black Sox."

BEST DAY (BY WPA OR OTHER MEASURE): On Aug. 29, 1914, Wolfgang outdueled the great Walter Johnson by a 2-1 score for his first complete game. He only struck out one batter, and he did yield seven hits (only five through eight innings of shutout ball), but he also made an amazing ten assists on balls put in play.[32]

THE WONDER OF HIS NAME: It's another "double unique" ballplayer name. His first name isn't Mel or Melvin, but Meldon (Mellie). And ... how often do you come across "Wolfgang" ... as a last name?!

NOT TO BE CONFUSED WITH: Wolfgang Van Halen (Son of guitarist Eddie Van Halen and member of the band "Van Halen"), Wolfgang Amadeus Mozart (Composer)

FUN ANAGRAMS: "Mellie Wolfgang" anagrams to "Well! Flaming ego."

EPHEMERA: 1) During the 1912 season in Lowell, he made league history by throwing ten perfect innings against Lynn. It didn't count as a no-hitter because it was broken up with a leadoff single in the 11th. 2) According to the *Greenville News* newspaper of Jan. 9, 1927, after the 1918 season, with his big-league career over, Wolfgang suited up as a left-handed third baseman for the Charleston Pals of the South Atlantic league. 3) He returned to Albany after his career, and apparently spent the rest of his life there, making a living out of being a professional gambler.

---

[32] Baseball Reference lists Wolfgang with 10 assists. However, the 2018 edition of *The Elias Book of Baseball Records* and various newspaper accounts list him with 11 assists that day, tying him for the record by a pitcher in a nine-inning game.

RALPH WORKS
Not only was he the "Judge," but apparently also the jury and executioner

BIRTH NAME: Ralph Talmadge Works
PRONUNCIATION OF DIFFICULT PARTS: None
NICKNAME: Judge, supposedly because of his scholarly countenance
HEIGHT/WEIGHT: 6'2" 185 lbs.
BORN: Mar. 16, 1888, in Payson, Illinois
DIED: Aug. 8, 1941, in Pasadena, California
POSITION: Pitcher
YEARS ACTIVE IN THE MAJORS: 1909-1913
NAME ETYMOLOGY/DEFINITIONS: "Ralph" is derived from the Old Norse "Raðulfr" (with *rað* meaning "counsel" and *ulfr* meaning "wolf") through Old English "Rædwulf" and the longer form "Radulf." "Talmadge" has English origins as the metonymic occupational name for an itinerant merchant, from Old French *talemasche* meaning "knapsack" (a word of uncertain origin). "Works" is a variant of the surname "Work" which has English origins from Old English *(ge)weorc* meaning "work," "fortification," hence probably a topographic name or an occupational name for someone who worked on fortifications or at a fort.

At the beginning of his playing career, while still living in Payson, Illinois, Ralph Works was pitching for a semi-pro team in nearby Quincy that was managed by a man named Harry Hofer. Works was sent from Quincy to Peoria of the "Three-I League" and as the story goes, did something to peeve the Peoria manager. That manager decided to farm him out as far away from Peoria as possible. Getting out a map he found that Medicine Hat, Canada, was just about the spot and Ralph was sent there for the 1907 season. Apparently, it was just what Works needed, for he won 26 games and lost only two games, all the while batting .341.

In August of 1908, he was purchased by the Detroit Tigers and he made his major league debut the next Spring. Works played all or part of five seasons in the majors with the Tigers (1909–12) and Cincinnati Reds (1912–13). Throughout his career, he split his workload between starting and relieving. He had a career record of 24-24 with a 3.79 ERA. He appeared in the 1909 World Series, allowing two earned runs on four hits and got two strikeouts in two innings of relief. His best season was 1911 when he went 11-5 in 30 games for the Tigers. He ranked fifth in the American League in winning percentage (.688) in 1911, seventh in shutouts with three and eighth in games finished with ten. This was despite making only 15 starts that season.

BEST DAY (BY WPA OR OTHER MEASURE): On Saturday, Oct. 7, 1911, the Tigers were coming to the close of a successful season. They wouldn't be winning the AL pennant, that would be going to the Philadelphia A's (who would finish with a gaudy

101-50 record). But the Tigers were sitting 88-63 with three games left in the season and had clinched second place. Works took the mound that day against the worst team in the American League, the 43-106 St. Louis Browns, who were sending out Ed Hawk. For Hawk, this would be the fifth and final game of his big-league career, and he nearly matched Works on the day. Hawk pitched a complete game, allowing one run on seven hits, walking one while striking out seven. That run was scored in the fifth inning by George Francis "Squanto" Wilson. Works bested him by allowing only three hits, all singles, and one walk with six strikeouts across nine innings. Additionally, while not known for his batting, he went 2-4 at the plate that day. His 1-0 win would end his season at 11-5.

THE WONDER OF HIS NAME: This guy makes our "All Verb" team (or he could be on the "All Noun" team I suppose). He could have been part of the Abbott and Costello "Who's on First" routine ...

    Costello: Your pitcher?
    Abbott: Works.
    Costello: Your pitcher works?
    Abbott: Yes, Works.
    Costello: Yes, I know he works, but who works as your pitcher?
    Abbott: No, who's on first.
    Costello: I'm not asking about first. I'm asking about the pitcher.
    Abbott: I told you. Works.
    Costello: I *know* he works, but I'm asking what his name is!
    Abbott: What's on second.
    Costello: I guess he works too?
    Abbott: No, he's the pitcher.
    Costello: Who?

NOT TO BE CONFUSED WITH: "Caddy" Works (American basketball and baseball coach. He was the head basketball coach at UCLA from 1921-1939, compiling a record of 173–159), Ralph Wilson (American businessman and sports executive. He was best known as the founder and owner of the NFL Buffalo Bills), Jimmy Work (American country musician and songwriter best known for the country standard *Making Believe*).

FUN ANAGRAMS: Ralph Talmadge Works becomes "Parked, small warthog." or "What sparkled glamor!"

EPHEMERA: 1) Works was the last of four children born to Perry Works and Lavina Olive Cunningham. 2) Works served in the military during WWI. By that time, he was already married (to a woman named Nellie Barnes, which would be the first of his two marriages) and had the first of two children. 3) After his playing career ended, he managed minor league ball for a couple of seasons and then worked as a sales representative for Rand McNally, selling schoolbooks. 4) On Aug. 26, 1941, the Associated Press published this account of the end of Works' life: "Captain of Detectives Stanley Decker said tonight Ralph T. Works, 52, former pitcher for the Detroit Tigers, evidently shot and killed his wife, Linda (Eloise Weatherford), 46, and then committed suicide after a domestic quarrel. The bodies were found in their bungalow. Newspapers left untouched on the front porch indicated they had been dead since that date. 'The house was in disorder,' Capt. Decker said. 'Furniture had been broken, the lights were still on, an electric fan was running, and the radio apparently had been on until it burned itself out. The place was littered with beer and whisky bottles, some of them partly filled.'"

JOE ZDEB

"Mr. Gorman, if I cut my hair, will I become a better ballplayer?"

BIRTH NAME: Joseph Edmund Zdeb
PRONUNCIATION OF DIFFICULT PARTS: Zeb
NICKNAME: None
HEIGHT/WEIGHT: 5'11" 185 lbs.
BORN: June 27, 1953, in Compton, Illinois
POSITIONS: Leftfielder, Pinch Hitter
YEARS ACTIVE IN THE MAJORS: 1977-1979
NAME ETYMOLOGY/DEFINITIONS: "Joseph" has English, German, French, and Jewish origins, from the personal name, Hebrew "Yosef" meaning "may He (God) add (another son)." In medieval Europe this name was borne frequently but not exclusively by Jews; the usual medieval English vernacular form is represented by "Jessup." In the Book of Genesis, Joseph is the favorite son of Jacob, who is sold into slavery by his brothers but rises to become a leading minister in Egypt (Genesis 37–50). In the New Testament Joseph is the husband of the Virgin Mary, which accounts for the popularity of the given name among Christians. "Edmund" is derived from the Old English elements ēad, meaning "prosperity" or "riches," and mund, meaning "protector." "Zdeb" is from the Polish zdeb meaning "wildcat," a nickname for a disagreeable, idle person.

J oe Zdeb attended Maine South H.S. in Park Ridge, Illinois, where he played both baseball and football. A fullback, he signed a letter of intent to play football at the University of Missouri, with a promise that he would also be allowed to play baseball. However, when he was made the 4th round pick of the Kansas City Royals in the 1971 amateur draft, he chose to join the Royals organization instead.[33]

In his first season of professional baseball, Zdeb was assigned to the rookie league Billings Mustangs, where he batted .184. He also spent 1972 in rookie ball with the

---

[33] In 1977, Zdeb made what would now be considered a rather racist statement regarding his choice of football over baseball. He said "I was confident I could play football in college, but I never thought I could play professionally. I was a running back and you gotta be black to do that. But I thought I had a chance to play pro baseball."

Kingsport Royals, where he improved to a .319 batting average with 12 home runs. In 1973, he began the year at Waterloo in the Midwest League, where he hit .355, earning him a promotion to the High-A San Jose Bees, where he struggled, hitting .195.

In 1974, Zdeb returned to San Jose. In his first full season there, he batted .295. Over the next two seasons, he continued to move up the ladder, playing at AA Jacksonville in 1975 and AAA Omaha in 1976. He compiled a .298/.376/.392 line in 117 games at Omaha.

At some point during minor league spring training, he showed up to camp with long hair, which was against team policy. Manager Joe Gordon refused to give him a uniform, so he approached general manager Lou Gorman, asking "Mr. Gorman, if I cut my hair, will I become a better ballplayer?" Gorman said he needed to cut it to properly represent the organization, and after initially refusing, he did so a couple days later.

After the 1976 season, the Royals traded their primary backup outfielder, Jim Wohlford, to the Brewers, opening a spot for Zdeb. With the left-handed Dave Roberts on the mound for the Tigers on Opening Day, the right-handed hitting Zdeb wound up starting in left field, going 1-for-4 with a run scored in his major league debut.

Zdeb platooned over the rest of the season, and the rookie finished with what turned out to be a career high .297 batting average in 105 games. He also had what would turn out to be career bests with two home runs and 23 RBIs. His first homer in the majors would be of the pinch-hit variety on June 25th, driving in Pete LaCock.

In the 1977 American League Championship Series against the Yankees, Zdeb appeared in four of the five games, failing to get a hit in nine at-bats, although he did steal a base. In 1978, Zdeb saw his playing time reduced with the arrival of Willie Wilson, and even wound up back in the minors briefly. When he got sent down, one of his Royals teammates had this to say (anonymously): "This organization tells its young players if they work hard, they'll be rewarded. well, here's a guy who busted his hump for them all last year and this year. He did everything they asked of him ... then they dump on him like this. It's not fair."

With three players sharing left field, Zdeb wound up appearing in just 60 games. His batting average fell to .252, with no homers and just 11 RBIs. With Wilson named the full-time starter in left field for the 1979 season, Zdeb found himself in strictly a reserve role to start the season. After 15 games in which he batted just .174, Zdeb was sent down to the minor leagues. However, he also struggled in Omaha, batting just .224, and was not given a September call-up.

In January 1980, Zdeb was traded to the White Sox for pitcher Eddie Bane. He finished his professional career that year, splitting the season between the White Sox Iowa Oaks affiliate and the Tidewater Tides in the Mets organization. His struggles at the plate continued, as he hit a combined .194, and after the season he was out of professional baseball.

306

BEST DAY (BY WPA OR OTHER MEASURE): Joe Zdeb's best day in the majors would undoubtedly be the game of July 1, 1977 at Cleveland Stadium. With the Royals trailing 2-1 with one out in the top of the second, Zdeb singled to left off starter Rick Waits but was left stranded. He singled to right field off Waits in the fourth. After the Royals took the lead 4-2 and knocked Waits out of the box, Zdeb capped Kansas City's five-run fifth inning outburst with a three-run blast off reliever Al Fitzmorris. The Royals continued the onslaught in the sixth, padding the lead to 10-2 before Zdeb doubled in the final run of the inning off Don Hood. He capped his day off with a ninth inning double off Sid Monge. Final tally: a career-high five hits in five at-bats, two doubles, a homer, one run scored and a career-high four driven in.

THE WONDER OF HIS NAME: That pesky "d" in the middle of his last name! You think its "z-deb" but it's not! Who throws in random consonants in their last name like that? (The Polish do, that's who and I love them for that ... and also for giving us kielbasa.) He's the only "Zd-" to ever make the majors, and the closest we've come to such a player since then is one "Zachary Zdanowicz" who played Indy ball in 2014-5.

NOT TO BE CONFUSED WITH: "Zeb" (Zebulon) Terry (Infielder for the Boston Braves, Chicago Cubs, Chicago White Sox, and Pittsburgh Pirates from 1916-1922).

FUN ANAGRAMS: "Joseph Edmund Zdeb" becomes "He'd jump dozen beds."

EPHEMERA: 1) While in Waterloo in 1973, he lived in a rented trailer with a mattress that cost $5. 2) In 1997, when he was asked about his last name, Zdeb replied "Aw, it's a little bit Irish and some Polish ... who knows?" (He lists his ancestry as German.) 3) Zdeb was the first Royal to make his major league debut as a starter on Opening Day. 4) After retiring from baseball, Zdeb has been a financial advisor in Overland Park, Kansas. 5) Maine South H.S. has received mention in national media as the alma mater of Hillary Clinton, a member of the school's first graduating class in 1965. No word on whether Zdeb has ever had any email/server issues. 6) Maine South was also the high school of former major leaguer Dave Bergman. 7) Zdeb and his wife, Diane, have three children: Rachael, Joey and Josh. Rachael Zdeb attended Mississippi State University, where she was an outfielder for the school's softball team.

ACKNOWLEDGMENTS

More than 20 years ago, I wrote a humorous skit for a talent show at a Scrabble tournament. Yes, there are such things as Scrabble tournaments, and this particular one had its own after-hours tourney participant talent show, complete with parody songs, poems and other acts having to do with Scrabble. After my skit (a take-off on the local news, laced with made-up stories about notable personalities in the Scrabble tournament universe) was over, and my performance was voted the best of the show, a woman named Sheree Bykofsky walked up to me. She said, "you're very funny ... you should write a book."

Sheree was a literary agent.

Well, it only took two-plus decades, but here's the book. It's most likely *not* the one Sheree envisioned me writing, and my choice to self-publish should in no way be taken as a slight towards her. The world of self-publishing has been an eye-opener for me, but also quite liberating. Of course, going it alone can lead to all sorts of problems that a literary agent could otherwise solve. However, I originally pitched the idea for this book to a few small, niche publishers back in 2012, and was basically told, "Privately, we love the concept ... but it just won't sell enough to be worth our while." Let's see if this proves otherwise.

Beyond Sheree, first and foremost, I'd like to thank SABR and its Baseball Bio Project. As I mentioned in the Introduction, their work made much of this book possible. (A portion of the proceeds of this book will be donated to SABR as an additional "thank you.") Beyond the bios on the SABR website, the 19th century biographical reference books of baseball historian David Nemec were a tremendous resource. I also want to give a shout-out to SABR's Bruce Brown, keeper of a canonical list of "double uniques."

Big thanks to Justin Leites and Chris Patrick Morgan for editing/proofing assistance.

I'd like to thank SABR's John Thorn, the Official Historian of Major League Baseball, for always answering every question I posed to him, no matter how trivial, with regard to various players, rules, leagues and the like.

Thorn, Cecilia Tan and Jacob Pomrenke of SABR were extremely helpful in my navigating the tricky waters of photo acquisition. John Horne of the National Baseball Hall of Fame and Museum and Andrew Aronstein of TCMA were terrific in helping me acquire some of the images you see in the book.

I'd like to thank the following people for being inspirational/helpful in my writing pursuits, whether on this specific project or past ventures: Christina Kahrl, David Schoenfield, Alex Belth, Cliff Corcoran, Jay Jaffe, Emma Span, Barbara Mantegani and Dave Raglin, D. Bruce Brown, Lyn and Steve Elsberry, Jayson Stark, Brian Kenny, Dorothy Seymour Mills, John Robertson, Andy Saunders, Gregg Gaylord.

Throughout the writing process, I posted updates on the book's progress on Facebook and Twitter. If you "liked," "shared," "loved" or "retweeted" such an update, I thank you for the feedback and encouragement.

Closer to home, hugs and smiles go out to the following folks (and if I somehow missed you in this list, my deepest apologies): The Ponzo family, Natalie McDermott, Chris Economos and Ed Hepner, Judy and Milt Kass, Lynn Cushman, Jessie Klein (and Susan and Lev), Debbie Stegman, Shirley Feinstein, Eve Hoffman, Sal Piro, Jeremy Hall, Paul Avrin, Mark and Verna Berg, Joel and Larry Sherman, Jeremy Frank and Jacky Grossman, Ira Rubin, Bryan Richgruber, Janine Silver and Wendy Milazzo.

ABOUT THE CONTRIBUTORS

By day, **D.B. Firstman** (author) is a Data Analyst for the City of New York, crunching large datasets using SPSS and Excel. D.B. has been a member of SABR off and on since the late 1980s. Besides the baseball blog, *Value Over Replacement Grit*, D.B.'s work has appeared at ESPN.com, *Bronx Banter*, *Baseball Prospectus*, *The Hardball Times*, and in *The Village Voice*. D.B.'s research on the origins of the "Three True Outcomes" in baseball (home runs, strikeouts, and bases on balls) was included in the Spring 2018 edition of the *SABR Baseball Research Journal*, with an accompanying poster presentation on the subject winning an award at that year's national convention. D.B. lives in Queens, New York.

Jayson Stark[34] (foreword) is the 2019 winner of the J.G. Taylor Spink Award for "meritorious contributions to baseball writing" and was presented with the award in Cooperstown during the Hall of Fame's annual induction weekend. In addition to his work at MLB Network, he is also a senior baseball writer at *The Athletic* and the host of *Baseball Stories* on Stadium TV. In his profile on the Hall of Fame's website following the Spink Award announcement, Stark was described as "a curator for all things weird, wacky, unique, statistically inclined and historically rare in the game." His popular *Useless Information* column at *The Athletic* is a regular collection of notes, quotes, numbers, oddities and laughs. And in his previous stops at ESPN.com and the *Philadelphia Inquirer*, he was the creator and author of the nationally syndicated *Baseball Week in Review* column, which looked at the sport in a similar irreverent vein.

Stark spent 17 years covering baseball for ESPN and ESPN.com. Besides writing columns for the website, he made numerous television appearances on *Baseball Tonight, SportsCenter* and *Outside the Lines*, and won an Emmy for his work on *Baseball Tonight*. He was also a regular guest on *Mike and Mike*, where he contributed his famous weekly trivia question. Stark previously spent 21 years covering baseball for the *Philadelphia Inquirer*, where he was twice named Pennsylvania Sportswriter of the Year.

He appears regularly on radio stations around the country and formerly hosted *The Jayson Stark Show* on 97.5 The Fanatic in Philadelphia.

He is the author of three books, *Wild Pitches: Rumblings, Grumblings and Reflections on the Game I Love* (Triumph Books, 2014), *The Stark Truth: The Most Overrated and Underrated Players in Baseball History* (Triumph Books, 2006) and *Worth The Wait: Tales of the 2008 Phillies* (Triumph Books, 2009).

In May of 2017, he was inducted into the Philadelphia Jewish Sports Hall of Fame. He is a finalist for the 2019 National Sports Media Association's national-sportswriter-of-the-year award. He also appeared in the 2014 film, *Million Dollar Arm*, starring Jon Hamm. And in 2018, Topps issued an actual Jayson Stark baseball card.

---

[34] Anagrams to "Joy sank rats."